Praise for *Let Your Hearts and Minds Expand*

"This compilation of essays by Tom Rogers, a Mormon intellectual in the best sense, displays the evolution of his thinking over a lifetime of service as a creative writer, teacher, and leader. His critical but appreciative discussion of diverse ideas—from those of Pushkin to Sartre to Mother Teresa—in the light of the restored gospel offers a valuable perspective on the unfolding of a keen, believing mind."

—John L. Sorenson
Author of *Mormon's Codex: An Ancient American Book*

"This insightful, vital, eminently readable book dwells in a place where artistic expression, spiritual inquiry, and passionate espousal of timeless truths are a natural part of discourse. Tom Rogers's honesty, bravery, and erudition shine through on every page. There are essays here challenging church culture—and challenging the challengers; letters to those struggling in their faith—and claiming kinship with them; talks delivered to large audiences—and intimate chats with just a few, or one; muscular poetry; travel accounts as a patriarch to the whole of Russia; and explications of Tom's most celebrated, brilliant plays. If you want to know why and how a truly thoughtful and generous human being believes in the gospel of Christ, read this beautiful book."

—Tim Slover
Professor of Theatre
University of Utah

"Is there a place in our literary canon for a thoughtful discussion of discipleship? Thomas Rogers provides here a resounding 'Yes.' Essay after essay offers rich rewards for the exploring reader who wants to probe substantial ideas in a personal, affective, and intellectually broadening manner. These essays and commentaries add new dimensions to Tom's literary and ministerial careers. As in his dramas, the writer's voice invites dialogue on the most sensitive and significant issues. Like the pastel paintings he has created in recent years, Tom's literary palette is somber, but rays of light illuminate the shadows, suggesting hope and purpose."

—Cherry B. Silver
Past president of the
Association for Mormon Letters

"I love this collection because it reveals what a rare modern disciple Thomas Rogers is—a man who is as rigorous in his pursuit of the life of the mind as in his devotion to the riches and wonders of the spirit, and a disciple who is as comfortable with his liberal politics as he is with his conservative community. Like Joseph Smith, Tom has sought truth by being willing to prove contraries. He reads widely and deeply, which is also how he thinks—and believes. This collection is an education in the humanities, a discipline so easily denigrated in contemporary culture but essential to civilization's survival because it encourages responsible critical and speculative inquiry. Just as the humanities are often coupled with the arts, so are they in Tom's life. As a creative artist—a playwright, poet, and painter—Tom shows that it is possible to celebrate the imagination as well as the mind—beauty and meaning as complements to faith and reason."

—Robert A. Rees
Visiting professor of Mormon Studies
Graduate Theological Union

"These writings offer the wisdom of an eighty-three-year-old scholar whom I've known as a friend for over seventy years. I have been blessed by that lifelong association with Tom as we've explored challenges in the perennial contest between faith and reason. I am gratified to know his words, profound and still pertinent, will reach a wider audience."

—Douglas Alder
President emeritus
Dixie College

"Tom Rogers has written an inspiring book for those of us who, like himself, 'ascribe equal status to Faith and Reason.' Although Jack Welch affirms that we Mormons 'don't have to check our brains at the door' when we get to church, the Mormon intellectual can arouse suspicion. Admitting to doubts about any gospel subject is even more hazardous. So it is uplifting to read someone as faithful and as incredibly well-read as Tom candidly sharing his questions, explaining how he deals with them and how using his divinely given intelligence has kept him close to the 'glory of God.' This work is not only a marvelous window on a well-stocked creative mind and a burning testimony, it is a treasure trove of insightful quotations."

—Donald Jarvis
Professor emeritus of Russian
Brigham Young University

"I found these essays nearly impossible to get through. I kept stopping on insightful passages and contemplating not just the implications but with whom I wanted to share them. Had I the power, I would personally urge everyone over age fifty to read this book, and would require it of everyone else."

—Margaret Blair Young
Coauthor of *Standing on the Promises*

"Tom Rogers has lived his faith all over the world—in China, India, Ukraine, Bulgaria, Russia, and elsewhere. The experiences he relates from these far-flung places—mingled with thirty-one years as a BYU professor of Russian—give remarkable insight into the hard work always involved when we practice charity, 'the pure love of Christ.' In these essays Rogers is a defender of the faith, but his words move us well beyond typical apologetics. His Mormonism serves as the bedrock for discussions on the life of the mind, the value of literature, and the challenges of religious orthodoxy. A common thread is the journey of those who've become disenchanted with their faith. Having asked all the right questions, they've somehow found themselves on the outside, uncertain if they want to come back. Rogers speaks to them—and to that part in each of us—calling for reasonable, faithful, even joyful, reunion."

—Jack Harrell
Author of *A Sense of Order and Other Stories*

"Many have heard of Tom Rogers and some even feel they 'know' him, but as you complete a reading of this excellent collection of his finest essays, epistles, and poetry, you will marvel at the range and depth of his intellectual and creative accomplishments. Throughout, he lays bare shallowness and hypocrisy and enshrines integrity, courage, charity, and belief. Tom is a genuine Mormon intellectual—with the faith of a saint!"

—Gary Browning
Professor emeritus of Russian
Brigham Young University

"This volume represents the definitive life work of the renowned Mormon intellectual Tom Rogers, whom I have known and associated with for over thirty-five years. His essays, plays, letters, and poetry span a fascinating spectrum of history, literature, and philosophy—always informed by academic rigor, yet invariably infused with a vision of the divine. For all those he encounters, whatever their creed, orientation, or station in life, Tom recognizes, affirms, and learns from the divine in each of them. In doing so, he takes us on a literary tour that can be heart-wrenching at times but is always erudite and edifying. At its core, this book offers a vista of the spiritual growth and sublime joy that can be ours through the atonement and the gospel of Jesus Christ."

—Daniel Austin
Associate professor
Northeastern University School of Law

"What strikes one on reading these essays is the deep humility with which Tom Rogers approaches his faith, his doubts, and the lives of those who struggle to find a way forward. One feels that his vast reading has been sanctified by his service to his fellow man and his deep love of Jesus Christ."

—Sterling Van Wagenen
Filmmaker

"In the course of his career, Tom Rogers has been a student, a teacher, a professor of Russian literature, a playwright, a missionary (Berlin), a mission president (St. Petersburg), a bishop, a patriarch (Eastern Europe and Russia), a husband and father, and, in all circumstances, a man of faith. However, not for him the unexamined life or unexamined faith. In this collection of essays, talks, and letters, he addresses four wellsprings of his life: faith, reason, charity, and beauty. He has read widely and thought deeply about all of them and how they run together. In these essays you will find remarkable insights, a pervasive wisdom, and an exceptional affirmation of faith."

—Thomas Wood
President emeritus
Mount Royal University

"Who reads this compelling collection will commune with one of Mormonism's great minds, one nourished by other great minds, both past and present, in and out of the Latter-day Saint church. Tom Rogers is a modern Renaissance man—a consummate scholar, teacher, and Christian philosopher equally at home in the works of Euripides and Freud. He is also Mormonism's best-known playwright, a poet, and a humble, prayerful servant who built his mind and heart on a 'bedrock of experience'—a lifetime of service to his church, his community, and his family."

—Mary Bradford
Author of *Lowell L. Bennion: Teacher, Counselor, Humanitarian*

Let Your Hearts and Minds Expand

A
Living Faith
Book

LIVING FAITH books are for readers who cherish the life of the mind and the things of the Spirit. Each title is a unique example of faith in search of understanding, the voice of a scholar who has cultivated a believing heart while engaged in the disciplines of the Academy.

Other LIVING FAITH books include:

Adam S. Miller, *Letters to a Young Mormon*

Samuel M. Brown, *First Principles and Ordinances: The Fourth Article of Faith in Light of the Temple*

Steven L. Peck, *Evolving Faith: Wanderings of a Mormon Biologist*

Patrick Q. Mason, *Planted: Belief and Belonging in an Age of Doubt*

Let Your Hearts and Minds Expand

Reflections on Faith, Reason, Charity, and Beauty

Thomas F. Rogers

Edited by Jonathan Langford and Linda Hunter Adams

Foreword by Terryl L. Givens

Brigham Young University
Provo, Utah

A Living Faith book
Neal A. Maxwell Institute, Provo 84602 | maxwellinstitute.byu.edu

Printed in the United States of America.

Cover design: Sarah Skriloff
Cover image: Thomas F. Rogers, *Turtle Bay, Oahu*, pastel
Book design: Andrew Heiss

Library of Congress Cataloging-in-Publication Data

Names: Rogers, Thomas F., author. | Langford, Jonathan, editor. | Adams, Linda Hunter, editor.
Title: Let your hearts and minds expand : reflections on faith, reason, charity, and beauty / Thomas F. Rogers ; edited by Jonathan Langford and Linda Hunter Adams.
Description: Provo, Utah : Neal A. Maxwell Institute, Brigham Young University, [2016] | ?2016
Identifiers: LCCN 2016002352 (print) | LCCN 2016003087 (ebook) | ISBN 9780842529761 (print : alk. paper) | ISBN 9780842529785 (ePub) | ISBN 9780842529778 (Kindle)
Subjects: LCSH: Christian life—Mormon authors. | Church of Jesus Christ of Latter-day Saints—Doctrines. | Mormon Church—Doctrines. | LCGFT: Essays.
Classification: LCC BX8656 .R646 2016 (print) | LCC BX8656 (ebook) | DDC 248.4/89332—dc23
LC record available at http://lccn.loc.gov/2016002352

♾ This paper meets the requirements of ANSI/NISO Z39.48-1992 (Permanence of Paper).

ISBN 978-0-8425-2976-1

As you increase in innocence and virtue, as you increase in goodness, let your hearts expand—let them be enlarged towards others—you must be longsuff'ring and bear with the faults and errors of mankind. How precious are the souls of men!

—From a discourse given by Joseph Smith on
April 28, 1842, in Nauvoo, Illinois;
reported by Eliza R. Snow in the
Relief Society Minutes

Thy mind, O Man, if thou wilt lead a soul unto salvation, must stretch as high as the utmost Heavens, and search into and contemplate the lowest considerations of the darkest abyss, and expand upon the broad considerations of eternal expanse; he must commune with God.

—From a letter by Joseph Smith
written in Liberty Jail on March 20, 1839;
parts later included in Doctrine and Covenants,
sections 121, 122, and 123

Cover image and paintings by the author

Scripts of Thomas F. Rogers's plays and contact information for production rights are available from the Maxwell Institute website at publications.mi.byu.edu/rogerscollectedplays.

Contents

Foreword

Tom Rogers is one of modern Mormonism's treasures. I have never felt before such a need to get out of the way and let you the reader get on with the joy and challenge of reading what lies before you. But I will briefly explain why you should.

The first thing I would say about the man behind the writings is that he sees things from a skewed perspective—which is, incidentally, what we all need in times such as these. He sees dangers where others don't, and doesn't where others do. That is his gift to the open-minded and his Cassandra-like curse to the comfortable. For example, he insists that "learning is not the dangerous if necessary enterprise"; staying too close to shore is. He reminds us, without saying so explicitly, that Latter-day Saints too often forget our legacy that sets us apart: we are supposed to believe the adventure loomed *outside* the Garden. This does not mean for him that we should take gospel principles and standards less seriously, but more seriously. His is an adventuresome mind and spirit, and he is as well traveled in his moral imagination as he is in geographical reality. He exemplifies as well as any person I know the mandate to "stretch as high as the utmost heavens, and search into and contemplate the considerations of the darkest abyss, and expand upon the broad considerations of eternal expanse."[1]

We often require "too comfortable a margin of safety," he urges provocatively, reminding us of historian Jacob Burckhardt's truism that "the essence of tyranny is the denial of complexity." Rogers is drawn to complexity—moral complexity in particular. Not for its own sake, I sense, but rather because he understands that the primal human tragedy in the Garden sets the pattern for all subsequent human striving: painful tensions, wrenching collisions of conscience, competing loyalties, and anguished trade-offs. That is why he finds such themes inexhaustibly rich both aesthetically and ethically.

Most readers will know Tom's work through his dramatic treatments of the most morally ambiguous dilemmas that have faced the tragic characters of our Mormon past. In his most celebrated works, *Huebener* and *Fire in the Bones*, he transposes the Hegelian dilemmas first limned by Sophocles into an LDS setting. He is, as Mormon essayist Gene England wrote, "the best Mormon playwright, on the evidence of cumulative, consistent achievement."[2] This present collection is invaluable for giving us access to a wide-ranging corpus of letters, essays, talks, and reminiscences, wherein he expands and elaborates the investigations of conscience plumbed in those and other works for the stage.

To study Tom's essays, as readers will find, is to have one's discipleship vigorously contested. His insights are no cheap palliative to the weary road warriors on the path to Zion. As he reminds us (borrowing from philosopher Paul Tillich), simple "religiosity" (and here, as always, he looks searchingly inward, not cynically outward) "does not mean much more than the religious consecration of a state of things in which the religious dimension has been lost." It is that genuinely religious dimension that Tom so beautifully endeavors to recapture, bringing together, as in Orson Pratt's crude adobe structure, the temple and the observatory. He is astoundingly well-read and harvests a rich bounty of insights and wisdom from the vast library of Western—and Eastern—literary and religious texts. To read his essays is to be both moved by his erudition and embarrassed by one's own limited repertoire. More importantly, perhaps, one will be inspired by his capacity to question himself, his presuppositions, and his own judgment—all in an effort to refine and preserve that which is most essential, most indispensable, in the life and belief of a disciple of Christ.

What sets Tom apart, in my mind, from a plethora of gifted LDS writers and cultural critics is the love and generosity that underlie his contributions to the discussion. This note is sounded immediately in his explanation of his dislike of "Why I Stay" as a symposium panel title: "I'd have preferred a more affirmative and celebratory heading." That impulse is to be felt throughout his work, and I applaud him for it at a time when steadfastness in the faith is too often portrayed as a position of last resort rather than a joyous offering, a defensive posture rather than full-hearted quest.

Finally, a word about one of my favorite truths Tom recuperates for a culture as ours, so threatened as it is by the perils of conformity and the tragic confusion of unity with sameness and obedience with corporate loyalty. What I mean is that Tom pursues the redemptive task he associates with literary critic Richard Ellman: "to save what is eccentric and singular from being sanitized and standardized." Historically, Mormons have never found an easy peace, collectively or individually, with our position at the margins. We hunger for acceptance, have become adept at assimilation, and eagerly respond to praise from a world and culture and establishment whose institutions and values we once shunned. Tom invites us to reconsider the beauty—and the view—from "the edge of the herd." "Away with stereotyped Mormons!" Brigham thundered, and Tom demonstrates why Mormonism at its richest defies pat labels and categories. "How glorious we all are in our imperfection!" he says. "Good can be radical," he writes, quoting philosopher Hannah Arendt. "Evil can never be radical, it can only be extreme." "Only he who is capable of attention" can be truly empathic, he insists, quoting essayist Simone Weil.

The writings herein will be of invaluable benefit to those capable of such attention, such introspection, such willingness to "turn the question around," as Tom often proposes; be more tentative in our conclusions, as he urges; be more voraciously curious about the perspectives and wisdom of the Other.

Professor Edmund Morgan once said to a Yale class what I say to those about to read this volume: "If you learn anything, it ought to change your minds. . . . It will be a sign that we have both wasted [our time] if you leave here thinking pretty much the same way that you do now."[3]

—Terryl L. Givens
University of Richmond

Notes

1. Joseph Smith, *Personal Writings of Joseph Smith*, ed. Dean C. Jessee (Salt Lake City: Deseret Book, 1984), 396; spelling modernized.

2. Eugene England, review of "God's Fools: Plays of Mitigated Conscience," by Thomas F. Rogers, *BYU Studies* 26/3 (1986): 114–18.

3. Quoted by Tom Rogers in "Remarks to Members of the BYU Honors Program," in this volume.

Author's Preface

Several important triads have widely captivated human thought. Though individually distinct, each component of a particular triad is, I sense, intended to operate in tandem with the other two. One of the earliest is Plato's idealistic concept of the True, the Good, and the Beautiful. Then there are Faith, Hope, and Charity—the virtues Paul ascribes to the followers of Christ. Closer to the present, Russia's most celebrated philosopher, Vladimir Solovyov, identifies Faith, Reason, and Beauty (as manifested in the various arts) as three important avenues for comprehending transcendent truth.

For daring to ascribe equal status to Faith and Reason, Solovyov's scheme—though echoing the views of Catholicism's celebrated theologian Thomas Aquinas—will doubtless seem naive and a contradiction in terms to some. For me, however, this apparent disparity accurately reflects the experience of people like me who find ourselves drawn to believe while also exercising our intellect in order to understand more fully *what* we in fact believe. That tension is evident in a favorite expression of a late dear friend, Marden Clark, that was for a while my working title for this collection: "Yes, but . . . " As a professor of literature who has devoted much of my life to writing plays and to dramatic performance, I am also innately drawn to Solovyov's insistence on Beauty as a means for drawing close to an understanding both of the human condition and of timeless verities. To Solovyov's three, I have added that "greatest" of Pauline virtues, Charity or Christlike love, as one of the organizing categories of this collection.

The essays that follow came about in a variety of ways. Some were first delivered in front of an audience as part of an organized event. Others are more personal. They include expressions stretching over some forty years related to my teaching responsibilities, church callings, playwriting endeavors, scholarly discussions related to Russian literature, and more. Each reflects both the impulse to write as a way of thinking through issues and concerns and also the central importance of the gospel in my life, both as a motivating force and as intrinsic to my way of seeing the world. Taken together, they reveal mutating trends in my thought as well as my sometimes-vacillating critical stance and shifts in mood. I trust that more than a few readers will identify with my previous self's wavering states of heart and mind. It is, if we are totally honest, also an aspect of *la condition humaine*.

In reviewing, updating as necessary, and in some cases substantially revising the pieces that follow, I've come to further appreciate the many ways that each of my predominant categories—Faith, Reason, Charity, and Beauty (and its aesthetic perception)—is often tempered or even modified by one or more of the others. Many of this volume's entries could have been placed in a different section. The discussion of Charity readily blends with what strike me as reasonable social concerns. The witness to and urging toward greater Faith is not without an appeal to what strikes me as, again, most reasonable, while I view nonaugmented Reason as limited and largely suspect. Instead, I choose to utilize reasoning in behalf of faith and gospel principles. Similarly, even as I argue for the efficacy and essential role of aesthetic experience and literary expression, I do so in terms of what they can realistically teach us about our nobler selves and about one another.

To the extent that I'm capable of judging such matters, I've also come to sense that what these selections offer is less theological exegesis than meditations on the gospel's proper application in our relationship with others—an ever-present challenge. As such, they are the highly personal product of my thoughts, beliefs, and individual experiences, including my interactions with other people. They are also rooted in the profound blessings that have periodically come my way in the form of ecclesiastical or church-related callings for which I was in each instance far from prepared or deserving. These have included the following:

- During my senior year at the University of Utah, 1954–1955, service as the interchapter president of what was then an LDS men and women's fraternity, Lambda Delta Sigma

- After graduation, a two-and-a-half-year mission involving memorable interaction with East German Latter-day Saints (prior to the erection of the Berlin Wall), including the calling of second counselor to two successive mission presidents
- Elders quorum callings during graduate studies in New Haven, Connecticut, and Washington, DC
- Thirty-one years as a professor of Russian at BYU, from 1969 until my retirement in 2000
- Two years as director of the BYU Honors Program in the 1970s
- Service as a campus branch president at BYU and later as a branch president at the Provo Missionary Training Center
- Service as a mission president in Russia shortly after the fall of its communist regime
- Teaching at Peking University with my wife, Merriam, under the auspices of the BYU China Teachers Program
- Once more serving our Russian fellow members at the Stockholm Sweden Temple and sealing a number of their unions and family ties
- Similar service at the Bountiful Utah Temple
- From 2007 to 2014, my calling as an itinerant Russian-speaking patriarch to seven Russian missions as well as to missions in nine former Soviet satellite countries attached to the LDS Church's Europe East Area

Each of these opportunities to serve was a tender mercy that has further shaped me, pulled me upward and outward, and significantly blessed our now extensive family. They further attest, I believe, to the way in which the restored church of Jesus Christ blesses so many with its manifold opportunities for service.

Several former colleagues and student acquaintances who once shared a similar commitment have since repudiated the importance of the gospel and the church in their lives. I do not judge them. Why, I ask, was I so repeatedly—and needfully—blessed *not* to follow their example? Why me and not them? I have no definite answers.

A project such as this one involves the work of many hands. Jonathan Langford, a former student of mine whom I'd also mentored as a missionary at the Provo Missionary Training Center, was the first to suggest such a collection. Linda Hunter Adams, who with the help of her students for many years supported the publication of a variety of books and journals at BYU, offered additional encouragement and put me in touch with the Neal A. Maxwell Institute for Religious Scholarship. Together, Jonathan, Linda, and I pored over almost 150 items filling four boxes, paring down again and again before arriving at a final selection. These two then meticulously scoured each entry, offering numerous suggestions for more precise and felicitous expression.

I am equally indebted to a third gifted and "street smart" editor, the Maxwell Institute's Blair Hodges, who provided valuable input, and to his associate Shirley Ricks, who undertook the book's final production. Thanks as well to Douglas Meredith, who scanned a number of documents from typewritten hard copies; Jeanette Anderson, who assisted with text entry; Marny Parkin, who helped to track down and convert several electronic files; and Andrew Hall and Nathan Langford for exceptional source sleuthing. Thanks as well to Terryl Givens, who graciously agreed to write the foreword to this collection, and to my literary agent C. Michael Perry, who made available for reading purposes the scripts of all of my plays, which are posted on the Maxwell Institute website.

Perhaps the greatest debt is owed to all of those who in one way or another helped to shape the thoughts and experiences that eventually found expression in these essays. These include Lowell Bennion and Jae Ballif, my most influential philosophical and religious mentors, and Marden Clark, who—though he probably did not know it—became for me toward his life's end and during the final stages of my own teaching career a cherished father figure. Another influential figure has been the late Arthur C. Wiscombe, who not only was committed to the life of the mind and to humane causes, but also despite formidable challenges remained a faithful and engaged Latter-day Saint.

My appreciation for the restored gospel's distinctive nuances and its singular comprehensiveness has since the time of Truman Madsen, Neal A. Maxwell, and Hugh Nibley been further stoked and fortified by Philip Barlow, David Bednar, Samuel Brown, Richard Bushman, Terryl and Fiona Givens, Grant Hardy, Jeffrey Holland, Adam Miller, Boyd Petersen, Robert Rees, and Dieter Uchtdorf. I am deeply indebted to and feel a strong affinity toward each of them. I am personally best acquainted with Bob Rees, who in myriad ways is, as a committed disciple, a role model to us all. I owe as much to my deeply cherished and highly respected department colleagues at BYU—particularly Gary Browning, the late Don Gubler, David Hart, Don Jarvis, Alan Keele, Michael Kelly, and Raisa Solovyova—as well as a number of others with whom I team taught in the honors program or otherwise closely interacted, particularly the late Ivan Crosland, who championed and directed both BYU productions of the play *Huebener*. Nor must I overlook my wife Merriam, our children, and theirs—each of whom has profoundly contributed to the person I am still in the process of becoming.

To each of these persons I gratefully dedicate this book.

About the Author

PERHAPS BEST KNOWN FOR HIS 1976 HISTORICAL PLAY *HUEBENER* about a Mormon youth who defied the Nazis, Thomas F. Rogers—professor of Russian at Brigham Young University from 1969 until his retirement in 2000—has written extensively on topics related to faith, literature, and the challenges and rewards of religious life. He has also written about his experiences living in and learning about the languages and cultures of various parts of the world, including Germany, Russia, China, and India. This collection represents a selection of his writings, including some previously published and some unpublished, from the 1970s through the present.

A noted playwright, essayist, teacher, and scholar, Dr. Rogers served as director of the BYU Honors Program for two years in the 1970s, as a BYU campus branch president, and as a branch president at the Provo Missionary Training Center. From 1993 to 1996, he was president of the LDS Church's Russia St. Petersburg Mission; a memoir of his experiences and observations was published in 1999 as *A Call to Russia: Glimpses of*

Missionary Life (Provo, UT: BYU Studies). Subsequently, he and his wife Merriam served in the Stockholm Sweden Temple. From 2007 until his release in 2014, Rogers was a traveling LDS patriarch assigned to the church's Europe East Area.

Described in a 1988 Distinguished Service citation from the Mormon Festival of the Arts as "undoubtedly the father of modern Mormon drama," Rogers is the author of almost thirty plays, many on Mormon subjects. In addition to *Huebener*, these include *Fire in the Bones*, the first literary treatment of the 1857 Mountain Meadows Massacre. A collection of four of Rogers's plays received a 1983 award for drama from the Association for Mormon Letters, and in 2001 the organization awarded him with an honorary lifetime membership.

Rogers is the author of numerous professional articles, reviews, essays, and stories, including two book-length studies on Soviet writers: *"Superfluous Men" and the Post-Stalin "Thaw"* (The Hague: Mouton, 1972) *and Myth and Symbol in Soviet Fiction* (San Francisco: Edwin Mellen Press, 1992).

Since retiring, Rogers has largely focused his creative efforts on painting—mostly portraits and landscapes. For over a decade, he has been associated with the Lamplight Art Gallery in Bountiful, Utah. His preferred medium is pastel.

Tom and Merriam Rogers currently live in Bountiful, where he spends time painting and visiting their seven children and forty grandchildren.

Part 1

The Just Shall Live by Faith

It's humbling and perhaps needful to be reminded of both the finiteness of our physical condition and the limitations of our mortal understanding. There is no proof to the contrary and much to be existentially gained by continuing to trust in Christ's teachings and promises. The equal need of our very loved ones—spouses and children—for spiritual nourishment and an eternal perspective is a key to the endurance required of us in the face of trials.

—From "It Satisfies My Restless Mind"

It is very hard to live for and maintain [the Lord's Spirit], but so worth it that anyone who has once experienced it is either stupid or insane not to do everything necessary to have it with him or her at all times. One must therefore conclude that we are all to some extent stupid or insane.

—From "The Miracle of Conversion"

Following page: Thomas F. Rogers, *Thorvaldsen's Christus*, watercolor

It Satisfies My Restless Mind

An earlier version of this personal statement was originally delivered as part of the Sunstone Symposium's traditional "Why We Stay" panel. As I hope what follows will suggest, I'd have preferred a more affirmative and celebratory heading. Like my entry at the Mormon Scholars Testify website (mormonscholarstestify.org), it represents my expression of gratitude that although born in the faith, I finally "found" the church, as must all genuine converts—and that the church "found" me. Despite its title, this also largely represents an affirmation of faith—hence its placement in this section.[1]

I HAVE NEVER SERIOUSLY CONTEMPLATED leaving the LDS Church, although I have imaginatively identified with those who have, among them a few lifelong friends. I have written plays about two excommunicants, Helmuth Huebener and John D. Lee,[2] who, although they did not choose to be disenfranchised, were, at the end of their lives, equally alienated. I may at times resonate to Yeats's profound lines: "The best lack all conviction, while the worst are full of passionate intensity."[3] It is a temptation to sometimes simplistically apply such labels to fellow Latter-day Saints, many of whom are nevertheless devoted friends and neighbors.

I have been spared the test of faith and humility that ecclesiastical censure in whatever form involves. This may be due to my essentially deferential (perhaps cowardly and obsequious) personality. Along with my respect for the sanity and moderation that I heard advocated by former Jordanian ambassador Muhammad Kamal[4] and the cardinal Christian virtues of charity and humility stressed by Protestant theologian Reinhold Niebuhr,[5] I strongly sense the practical need to defer, to accommodate, to fit in—for which the closest equivalent I can find in scripture is *temperance.*

I am a product of the "know nothing, do nothing" generation that came of age after World War II. In the church, this coincided with the ecclesiastical helmsmanship of the ever-so-compassionate and genteel David O. McKay. President McKay was amicably disposed to the life of the mind and was, in hindsight, legendary in his tolerance. Sterling McMurrin, a professor of philosophy at the University of Utah, once recounted to me the cases of various LDS Institute of Religion teachers and others who had come under fire and for whom he intervened with President McKay. That McMurrin had such entrée with the president speaks volumes about that leader's large-souled openness. On more than one occasion, I have been the less-than-perfect recipient of such acceptance and goodwill from church leaders.

In this regard, I think of the four BYU Russian professors who have served as mission presidents in the former Soviet Union. Each of my former colleagues had remarkable administrative skills, but these were less evident in Salt Lake City at the time of their calls than those of the professional executives who are more routinely called to such positions. For instance, Gary Browning's role in the early days of the LDS Church in Russia was truly groundbreaking and highly effective. Even so, no one was more surprised by his call than he was. He had earlier headed up the small BYU chapter of scholars opposed to the nuclear arms race and had, he felt, incurred considerable displeasure from various ultraorthodox conservatives in Salt Lake. There is no question that we four were seen as especially useful because of our language background and that this helped prompt the extension of such a privileged trust, but I like to think that despite our less-than-already-proven reputations and in some cases our dubious political correctness, surprisingly fruitful outcomes resulted from that wider sharing of such a weighty stewardship.

Seven reasons

Allow me now to suggest the following seven reasons for my active engagement in church life:

1. I am locked in by extensive ancestral and familial ties. As a father of seven and grandfather of forty, I sufficiently appreciate the church's blessing to my progeny that I do not want to discourage their attachment to it. I realize that by itself, this is a strictly pragmatic, subjective, and ultimately inadequate criterion, but I offer it here for the sake of candor. Further, I find that the faith and faithfulness of so many of our children, grandchildren, and their partners profoundly reinforces my own testimony of the value of the church in their lives and my own.

2. There is nothing better out there, in my opinion. Few religions are nearly so comprehensive in addressing the individual and group needs of their adherents. A nonbelieving friend and former member tells me he still considers the church to have the "most comprehensive social benefit program" he has ever encountered. I agree. For instance, what contribution the Word of Wisdom alone has made to my personal well-being! What broadening and refining have come from my association with church members with whom I may disagree on many points and with whom I otherwise have very little in common! It has stretched me, made me less elitist—and doubtless done the same for them. Would my saintly wife have settled for me without the church's nudging me to be more other-directed and well-rounded? Would our children have turned out to be such decent, caring people? This may still not be a good enough reason to stay, but it is a factor.

3. I have a testimony of the inspiration behind the church. A testimony is a gift—though in the Mormon view, an earned one. It is a choice too, and not a bad one. As Mother Teresa said, "If you pray, you will have faith. And if you have faith, you will love. And if you love, you will serve. And if you serve, you will have peace."[6] A great-great-grandfather's sacrifices doubly charged me and his now vast progeny. After barely surviving the march of the Mormon Battalion, Thomas Karren was called to leave his family and serve a mission to the Sandwich Islands. Hawaii wasn't a tourist mecca then, and a number of those first missionaries did not hold out. One sentence leaps at me from his missionary journal, dated February 17, 1854: "There is nothing but a realizing sense of the duty I owe to my priesthood and calling as a minister of Christ that would induce me for one moment to stop here and live in the manner that I have."[7]

4. The restored gospel's explanation of life and human destiny satisfies my restless and contemplative mind. It appeals to me much like Joseph Smith described certain truths as "tasting good,"[8] and many of its practical emphases strike me as truly remarkable. I briefly mention four:

- *The concept of family continuity and eternal lives.* Certain critics deride this concept and its corollary of divine heirship as non-Christian, but I find them substantiated even in the New Testament, existentially right, and highly edifying.
- *The balance between faith and reason, obedience and personal revelation.* I respond with a resounding *Yes!* to the image of a faith-traveler's holding onto an iron rod while also responding to the less tangible illumination of an individual Liahona (see 1 Nephi 8:24; Alma 37:38–40). While studying a range of belief systems and interacting in Russia with people from many denominations, I've been made aware of how rare such balance really is. In many religious traditions, one worships, trancelike, by completely turning off one's critical faculties and hypnotically chanting, fingering beads, or repeating set prayers. At the other end of the spectrum are those who relish speculation at the expense of doctrine and structure so that anything goes. I value how, at least in theory, Mormonism moderates both approaches.
- *The way the LDS Church keeps pace with life's constant fluctuations, fully taking into account the mutual interdependence of individuals at all stages of the life cycle.* In its daily operations and wide focus, the church manages to respond not only to our constantly mutating individual lives but also—through its great attention to those of a younger age—to the inevitable displacement and succession of one generation by the next. While many other traditions focus more narrowly on the single relationship between the individual and his or her god or priest, Latter-day Saints worship together as families and in many ways interact with members of all ages and at various stages of spiritual development.

- *Mormonism's claims about the reality of actual historical events as the source of our church's legitimacy and our gospel understanding.* We share this valuing of history with pristine Christianity and perhaps the inception of Islam, quite in contrast to other Christian groups. This attestation is extremely concrete and earthbound—even audacious. It invites incredulity but can also forcefully persuade. It poses for everyone a hard but simple challenge: Did it really happen or didn't it?

5. While Joseph Smith's radical initiatives emerged at the time of a larger movement to restore Christ's church in the pristine form described in the New Testament, it is my sense that none of his contemporaries so fully approximated its significant features as did the organization that came forth under his direction in 1830 and continued to evolve thereafter. Those features include the following:

- Universal lay leadership
- Designated offices of a nonprofessional and not academically trained priesthood
- A distinct understanding of the gospel's first principles, including the purpose of its essential ordinances—baptism and communion—and the importance of both agency and personal accountability in formally covenanting to Christian discipleship
- The operation and application of the gifts of the Spirit
- Continuous revelation and adaptation to new and changing circumstances
- The thrust of its several recently reaffirmed missions involving member welfare, extensive missionary endeavor, salvific work for the dead, and service to others as central aspects of Mormonism's dynamic religious enterprise

6. In Paul's words from his letter to the Ephesians, we are, in our congregations, "fellow citizens" in the "household of God," within which our mutual edification derives from a lay priesthood and complete involvement by all members (Ephesians 2:19; 4:12). This edification

takes place each Sunday through exhortation and partaking the sacrament, which reinforce our common commitment to Christ and his purposes. We often participate largely from a sense of duty, while perhaps begrudging the frequent redundancy and long-windedness of our meetings, but it instills interest in, toleration toward, and concern for others—and does us good.

7. My final reason takes precedence over all the others and is tied again to what we call a testimony. In all religions, the principle of obedience to God is fundamental. If we are potentially glorious, as the restored gospel tells us we are, it is also true that we are infinitesimal in the scheme of our Creator's grand universe. This paradox requires that should we sufficiently believe it, we no longer have a choice about our commitment. As Muslims so devoutly and sometimes recklessly say, "*in sha' allah*!"—"if God wills!" In language the Latter-day Saints are more familiar with, he invites, "Be still, and know that I am God" (Psalm 46:10; see also D&C 101:16).

Hooks

There are, moreover, a number of what I call promptings or *hooks* that, as I now look back on them, seem to have steered my life in ways I could never have foreseen. These often arose as invitations or opportunities that required a choice between two alternative courses of action—one leading to greater personal fulfillment, the other to stagnation. I view such encouragement toward greater activity as a tender mercy, delivered through the whisperings of his Spirit. I believe this is most often how God operates in our lives.

As a church patriarch, I was privy to that process in the lives of over 2,600 Latter-day Saints to whom I was privileged to give blessings throughout the vast territory of Eastern Europe. Each time I traveled abroad on this assignment, I witnessed the transformation in the lives of those I interviewed—which, as they frequently testified, took place when they acquired a testimony and through the Spirit's transcendent power and their determination to exercise the discipline necessary to change, often dramatically.

Like our convert ancestors, new church members are spiritually quickened. Paradoxically, their vital, whole-souled response to the missionaries' message fortifies not only their own lives but those of the missionaries too. Meanwhile, those in succeeding generations have as much need of that same quickening in order to overcome the complacent drag that comes if we assume the whole thing is a mere consequence of family heritage. This applies to all who have mostly just "gone along" with the church's teachings and programs.

The human condition spares neither us nor our loved ones trials, discouragement, and sorrow. For those who lack faith in immortality and salvation, the prospect can be utterly grim. There seems to be an innate craving in us for the assurance of Christ's atoning mission. We are therefore truly blessed when, with faith (and despite whatever skeptical arguments occur to us), we respond to the gospel's assurances and begin to cultivate belief. We have each experienced both spiritual nurture and its opposite. I find that living by faith is an immense blessing. I could never allow the sum total of inequities, people's shortsightedness, or the idiosyncrasies of equally human ecclesiastical leaders to rob me of the gift of being fully open to what Christ offers us.

Paul, again, asserted that we peer "through a glass, darkly" (1 Corinthians 13:12). Even so, I have at times felt the mind of God that Paul knew contrasts with the mind of man (see 1 Corinthians 2:11–14). I like to call this the epistemology of the gospel. Our faith easily wanes from one moment to the next and from day to day. For me, it has been reassuring to know I can still entertain doubt after the witness I received as a young missionary.

It's humbling and perhaps needful to be reminded of both the finiteness of our physical condition and the limitations of our mortal understanding. There is no proof to the contrary and much to be existentially gained by continuing to trust in Christ's teachings and promises. The equal need of our very loved ones—spouses and children—for spiritual nourishment and an eternal perspective is a key to the endurance required of us in the face of trials.

Conclusion

I consider the restored gospel to be distinctively comprehensive and efficacious in meeting our individual and social needs. It is so reasonable in its explication of Judeo-Christianity and so grand in its perspective of our ultimate eternal possibilities that I see it as the essence of humanism and a literal fulfillment of the grand ideal of the fraternity and sisterhood of humankind. Meanwhile, I remain pensive and deeply stirred by writer Simone Weil's observation that "instead of talking about love of truth, it would be better to talk about the spirit of truth in love."[9] I sense such love in many of my fellow Latter-day Saints and would like to do better at emulating them in that regard—or, more specifically, in emulating the example of Jesus, which for me will always involve active participation in his church.

Notes

1. Together with statements from other "Why We Stay" respondents over the years, an earlier version of this essay appeared in *Why I Stay*, ed. Robert A. Rees (Salt Lake City: Signature Books , 2011), 1–10; reprinted by permission.

2. *Huebener* premiered in the fall of 1976 at BYU's Margetts Theater, but church authorities, fearing repercussions in the German Democratic Republic, requested that we not schedule additional runs of the play. Some considered my compliance with this request to be heroic while others saw it as the opposite. In my mind, my quiet acquiescence reflected nothing so much as a strong preservationist instinct. For more details related to this, see "Why I Wrote *Huebener*," in this collection. *Fire in the Bones* premiered in the spring of 1978 at the Green-Briar Theatre in Sandy, Utah. It was, to my knowledge, the first literary treatment of the Mountain Meadows Massacre, just as *Huebener* was the first such treatment of the tortured response to Nazism among native German Mormons. The text of both plays is available from the Maxwell Institute website at publications.mi.byu.edu/rogerscollectedplays.

3. William Butler Yeats, "The Second Coming." During the two and a half years of my first mission, now almost sixty years past, I began to discern the rationalizations people sometimes give for putting off what they know in their hearts is right. I sometimes detect that kind of hollow defensiveness in statements by associates when they tell me why they no longer support the church.

4. In a discussion at the David Kennedy Center at BYU, Mr. Kamal commented, "What this world most needs is moderation and humility, and there is plenty little of that anywhere in the Middle East." At the suggestion of Mr. Kamal, the LDS Church cooperated with the country of Jordan in establishing a Center for Cultural and Educational Affairs in Amman. The center dispenses humanitarian aid to displaced Palestinians and others and arranges student and cultural exchanges between Jordan and the LDS Church, specifically Brigham Young University (see "Global Mormonism Project" online at Brigham Young University, globalmormonism.byu.edu).

5. "Nothing that is worth doing can be achieved in our lifetime; therefore we must be saved by hope. Nothing which is true or beautiful or good makes complete

sense in any immediate context of history; therefore we must be saved by faith. Nothing we do, however virtuous, can be accomplished alone; therefore we are saved by love." Reinhold Niebuhr, *The Irony of American History* (New York: Charles Scribner's Sons, 1952), 63.

6. Inscribed on the pedestal of a statue of Mother Teresa in a New Orleans cemetery. These ideas were stimulated through a wonderful conversation with another former student, Sterling Van Wagenen.

7. Typescript available in the LDS Church History Library, Salt Lake City; original manuscript, MSS 4065 Thomas Karren mission journals, L. Tom Perry Special Collections, Harold B. Lee Library, Brigham Young University, Provo, Utah. Capitalization modernized.

8. Joseph Smith, *Teachings of the Prophet Joseph Smith*, comp. Joseph Fielding Smith (Salt Lake City: Deseret Book, 1976), 355.

9. Simone Weil, *The Need for Roots: Prelude to a Declaration of Duties toward Mankind*, trans. Arthur Wills (Boston: Beacon Press, 1952), 253.

Limbs

Unlike my other two poems in this collection, "Limbs" is both allusive and elusive. Its juxtapositions of Old Testament figures (exclusively women) with ourselves, diverse forms of obeisance, deviousness with directness, evoke the atonement in ways that may seem incongruous or even irreverent but that nonetheless haunt and move me.[1]

For Christ plays in ten thousand places,
Lovely in limbs, and lovely in eyes not his
To the Father through the features of men's faces.
—Gerard Manley Hopkins
"As Kingfishers Catch Fire"

With her weak left hand,
Rachel measured the mandrakes
For Jacob's tea.

But we must pass over,
From point of pain to point of pain,
From frail left to mighty right wing.

Each with her deception:
Mother Sarah loosed Ishmael,
Mother Rebekah Esau,
Mother Rachel her sister's sons.

But for us there is no loosening.
The pain must penetrate, enter the palm,
Break through to open sky.
No dalliance. No half measures.

Later the Children
Went a whoring after strange gods
And kings.

For us no such carefree ostentation.
We raise the hand in greeting,
But no one sees the hidden scar.

The schoolmaster instructed them
How to walk and where to turn
And on what days.

But for us no prodding, no penalty prescribed,
Only the double sureness
As, welding arms at points of pain,
We bring each other forward

Till, standing in the mist,
Wrestling, like Jacob his angel,
With cut, disjointed knee,
We fall and . . .

By the ram's horn
The walls of Jericho were leveled
And never again the same.

. . . face the One
And, brought to embrace,
Find the words and calmly smile

Because we did not please that world too
much with us
But in our constant reaching, our strangeness
and solitude,
Took his path . . .

A crooked path made straight.

. . . and bore his pain.

Now, linked together, sealed,
A seamless garment,
Clasped by those who love us,
No longer strangers,

We bear his many names—
Counselor, Prince of Peace,
Brother, Son, Omniscient Father,
Author of fathomless Light and Love—

And Ruth said, Entreat me not to leave thee,
Or to return from following after thee:
For whither thou goest I will go.

And find both him and them
Our natural Home.

Note

1. Originally published in *Dialogue: A Journal of Mormon Thought* 14/2 (1981): 132–33.

On "Fate" and Circumstance

This essay is a meditation about, among others, two men with whom I served my earliest mission, now long dead. Many of the acquaintances mentioned here died before their "allotted time," due in some cases to the consequences of their lifestyle and its associated behavior. I am saddened by their loss but, since they left us, less inclined to dwell on what took them so prematurely than to revere the good in them and everything about them that was so endearing. I believe that in his merciful, omniscient judgment, the Lord will be at least as kindly disposed to all of us.[1]

In Varanasi, holiest of India's cities, women beggars, traditionally cast out by their children when widowed, spend their remaining years waiting for death and a more blissful new life. Some were widowed at a very young age, even as child brides, but most are content to blame their past karma and make the best of what strikes a Westerner as an intolerable and unjust circumstance. How naive can these women be, one asks. Why do they allow it?

Lives cut short

Two of my acquaintances now lie forever still, so far as this life is concerned. Neither was any older than I; one was several years younger. He was physically more vigorous than I—played basketball, skied—an ectomorph, not a spare ounce of fat on his tall, thin frame. At the time his heart stopped, he was a faculty peer, a city councilman, and the bishop of a student congregation. He'd recently announced his intent not to run again for office in order to spend more time with his wife and children. He was, in every way I know, a model disciple and citizen. He also tended to be extremely conscientious in serving others and kept within himself the pressures that came with his several stewardships. This may have intensified the strain (if strain it was) that brought on his cardiac arrest.

Even that might not have been so consequential if he'd not been alone, found who knows how many minutes later on a Saturday morning by a student custodian in a university men's room. Had the event occurred on a weekday, there would have been many to take immediate notice and call for help. Ironically, what brought him there that Saturday morning at the outset of another school year was a planning session on behalf of the students he'd been called to shepherd ecclesiastically. His counselors had apparently just left when, feeling unwell, he made his way to the lavatory and there collapsed.

He lay in bed some thirteen months before succumbing, never regaining consciousness. Given his otherwise excellent physical condition, he, like some others, might well have remained alive, though brain-dead, for additional years or decades. As it was, his and his family's ordeal seemed an eternity.

The other was a man with whom I last associated as a fellow missionary some thirty years ago. I had known him even earlier as an undergraduate and fraternity brother in a student organization then sponsored by the LDS Church. When I arrived, he was just leaving the field, having completed his service as mission secretary. Years later, I learned that while serving as a full-fledged bishop and a father of four, he had, during a TV talk show in his community, "come out of the closet"—which was apparently how he announced his newly declared status to his family and congregation. (He always had a flair for the dramatic.) I mention him because just recently I learned that he is now dead, one of more than half a million US victims of AIDS.

Thinking of this friend and recalling our common missionary experience, I was reminded of the boy who succeeded him as mission secretary. (We were all really just "boys" back then, if we aren't still.) Already an expert accountant, he spent whole nights without sleep, often weeping with discouragement, to bring the mission financial and statistical records—accumulated since before World War II—into expert order. After his mission, he completed his CPA degree. Several years later, I happened on a brief notice in the newspaper that he had just been sentenced to seven years in prison for attempting to embezzle several million dollars from the firm that employed him.

I can think of at least three other exemplary missionaries from that period whose later lives failed to conform to our expectations of each other back then. Each served for a time as a counselor to the mission president. Two also became professors. The third, who first took me tracting and helped ease my initial adjustment to the missionary routine with the greatest understanding and sensitivity, was a fine pianist and aimed at becoming a surgeon. I will never forget what a difference he made for me and my mission. He was truly an "angel" to me at a critical juncture in my life and church membership, though I doubt he ever knew it. He is dead now too. Some twenty years after we served together as missionaries, I learned from two of his nephews—students of mine—that he had not become a doctor. In fact, he never married and was no longer active in the church. He had involved himself to some extent in restauranteering in San Francisco. In his midforties, he returned to the remote Utah town of his birth on the Green River, where he was nursed by an older sister until his death from cancer. It's possible, in retrospect, that he too was infected with AIDS, one of its earliest victims.

I visited with one of the others just a month ago. He is now the academic vice president at a liberal arts college in his community. We had not seen each other for at least sixteen years. Along with his genuine goodwill, he indicated to me his extreme mistrust of the sentimentality we generally associate with both religion and infatuation. The two seemed to him to fit the same description. I found his detachment impressive but disturbing. I do not judge him for that. In fact, we agreed about a great many things, theoretically. It's just that I can't conceive of being that totally cerebral, that fully in control of one's feelings. Nor does it seem to me desirable or healthy, even if possible.

I don't judge any of these men. Each strikes me as having had the need in his later life to achieve that "individuation" Jungians speak of. At nineteen or twenty-one, none of us had truly reached that stage of development, even though at the time we mostly considered ourselves as having "arrived"—perhaps more so than ever before or since. In our naiveté, we thought we had escaped the ravages that come to the less blessed and less committed. Obviously, we still had much to discover and confront about life and about ourselves.

Promise unfulfilled?

With my students, I have recently reexamined that last provocative play by Euripides, *The Bacchae*, which features a reversal as stark as any in the plays of Sophocles. First the Theban King Pentheus, the symbol and enforcer of convention and civic order, taunts an unfamiliar upstart, the young exponent of a new ritual and divinity. Later in the play, this mysterious stranger, though imprisoned by Pentheus, induces the latter to climb the hills and witness the rites of his new order, the Bacchantes. The stranger is their divinity, Dionysus, in whose name the very tradition of tragedy and of theatre as we know it today first arose in Athens. When Pentheus is drawn to the revels of Dionysus's worshippers, he is destroyed, dismembered by his own mother, one of Dionysus's principal devotees.

Euripides's implied celebration of the primordial creative energies Dionysus represents has been seen as his final testament—his affirmation of the need in each of us to give our essential self, the *id* as Freud called it, its necessary development and expression. But the play is also cautionary. Because he fails to recognize and properly deal with the elemental chaos Dionysus stands for, Pentheus is literally destroyed. Perhaps Pentheus and Dionysus are two aspects of the soul or *psyche* in each of us. If so, *The Bacchae* tells us that the seeming irreconcilables in us must inevitably confront each other at great, even tragic personal risk. We should then view this struggle—in others, as in ourselves—with humility and compassion.

Where are those missionary peers we once so admired, even hero-worshipped—those now dead and those still living? How are they faring? Are they no longer growing and progressing? Have any made irretrievable choices of eternal consequence? If so, what provoked them? Were some of them victims of forces over which they had no control? I've seen the beauty and goodwill, the light in each of their souls. Are some at this point irredeemably, qualitatively different from others whose lives seem, on the surface, far more fortunate? Or is the reverse possibly as true? Does it even matter? How can I be sure or ever presume to know, at least in this life? The gospel, as I understand it, cautions against that kind of presumption.

And what of the two I first mentioned? What did either do that he might have avoided (or vice versa)? Would prior knowledge of certain freak circumstances and their consequences—of the need to cancel a meeting during a state of precarious fatigue and go golfing instead, or to avoid at all costs contact with a deadly virus—have made some difference? Or, going farther back, might an earlier knowledge of a perhaps genetic predisposition to certain diseases or behavior have helped them to recognize what might be done to resist those predispositions or offset their effects? In each case, a life was cut abnormally short.

On the surface, the two cases are vastly different. The first individual apparently did nothing deliberate to jeopardize his life or complicate the lives of his immediate kin. In contrast, the second seems to have done just the opposite, although unaware of where it would lead him. But their ignorance—and ours—about what may have driven and finally thwarted them must also lead us to pity both—though pity may only assuage us, the living, in our confusion. It is presumably far less needful where they now are.

Meanwhile, both *lived*. Both *were*. At various times, both served others in a variety of meaningful ways. As professors in the humanities, each entertained a rich variety of reflections about our common life and doubtless acquired insight from matching his own life and sensitivities, however vicariously, against those of the world's most comprehensive minds. Both knew the love of significant others. Both gave love—as, to some extent, all bishops, all fathers, and all of us as individuals do. I do not doubt that both expressed their love as best they knew how. Which of them was least wise? More unfortunate? What can we say about mistakes, blame, guilt, divine punishment, or even accident that fits one case better than the other? Charitably, even realistically, we can only conclude that both their abruptly terminated lives served their own and God's broad purposes and had positive worth. As with every other life, they diminish us by their departure until we can be with them again.

Embracing life

This essay was also occasioned by the funeral we recently attended of a boy we knew (or think we did). He was eighteen when he died, Pentheus-like, on a residential street, speeding his motorcycle to elude a policeman. From earliest childhood, he'd been what is called "hyperactive" and probably couldn't help himself. The funeral sermons took this into account but admonished the rest of us with his negative example. We were challenged to consider long-term values and the folly of instant gratification, to avoid compulsiveness and emotional agitation, to prefer and live instead for spiritual serenity, a quiet conscience, and a concomitant exalted, eternal life.

The sermons and the event itself sobered us, as religious services are meant to do. We were made more conscious of our mortality and the seeming futility of a life that bears no postmortal promise or, equally depressing, a life whose conduct would not assure its fullest realization in the hereafter.

Love was also mentioned in this context—the self-denying, commiserative *agape*, the sense of others' value and sacredness that separation by death most powerfully brings to mind. I was reminded of the Schopenhauerian notions that are metaphorically summed up in both the title and emotive power of "Der Liebestod" ("love in death"), Wagner's climactic duet from *Tristan and Isolde*. But I was also, at least for the moment, powerfully swayed by the old utilitarian argument that no amount of austerity, suppression of urges, or self-denial is too much for the rewards held out to those whose lives are sufficiently compliant and enduring.

One of those in attendance was heard a day later to pronounce in prayer at the table of his hostess: "We thank Thee that we are friends and neighbors, but more that we are Christians, and even more that we are good Mormons." It is wonderful, I suppose, for those who can reduce life's ultimate purpose and challenge to a distinct label, a particular affiliation, and strictly undeviating conformity to its prescribed norms. But I wonder if this alone affords sufficient common ground for authentic fellowship. Too often, it may come across like a flat and less-than-inspired story or poem lacking fresh and concrete imagery, bloodless and only proximate to the life within us.

I also wonder, as I view those who so contentedly settle for abstract, stereotypical, conventionally proper notions and the language that attends them, if they are necessarily any more compassionate, giving, or self-perfecting than others. With their accretion of days and years, are they growing any more than others, maintaining a sense of awe and wonder before the Mysteriously Inexplicable that keeps life so zestful, remaining truly open and flexible? Are they becoming any more "as little children" in their humility before what they must increasingly recognize they do not comprehend?

And I wonder if our civilization's long-standing, pharisaical consignment of so much in life that is innately pleasurable, temporal, and unregulated to the category of reckless evil doesn't deny a creaturely side in us which is there anyway—and which we *will* wind up accommodating or sublimating in one or another disguised "worldly" way, even if we are too ashamed to celebrate it. Any sense of moral superiority from our rejection of this side of ourselves is petty, judgmental, mostly illusory, and ultimately evil. It seems likely that refusing to make choices through inner conviction because of social pressure simply delays the moment when, in distraught frustration, the soul must, to assert its very integrity and volition, reject what was heretofore so suffocatingly and untrustingly thrust upon it—at least until it can freely choose the object of its loyalty and commitment for its own personal, divinely inspired reasons. What can we ever genuinely achieve if our principal motivation is, however subtly, rooted in fear?

Finally, I wonder if our tendency to define *Good* mostly in terms of avoiding *Evil* doesn't tend to miss much of the broad reach of human experience. Most of life *is* good and fulfilling and sufficient unto itself, and most of us aspire to it without special prompting. To what extent do we too much ignore and deny ourselves that broad neutral ground—the goodness of life as such—which is essentially free of valences? It simply *is*, and, as the God of Genesis himself describes his creation, is "good." Such interim good (with a lowercase *g*) affords even that portion of eternity we call the present its very piquancy and richness, its immediate moment-by-moment significance.

To what extent, for example, is what has long been traditionally viewed as "carnal" or "lustful" in the human psyche simply innate and, albeit without imposing on others' privacy and freedom of choice, necessary for total health, contentment, and wholeness? Should or even *can* our love for some others divorce itself from the physical yearning that so spontaneously accompanies our awareness of them? Does the suppression of some urges frustrate the sense of submission to something overpowering that sacredly foreshadows both the *Liebestod* in human fate (i.e., our sense that we value a person's life, once departed, despite how that person may have once beset us) and communion with the Divine? How needful we may be of this kind of "making love" rather than (when its impulse is too thoroughly repressed) making war.

Embracing each other

The restless, agitated youth, greedy for sensation, who seemed to flit from one novelty to the next and in his self-absorption so weakly perceived that others too have feelings and largely unfulfilled desires now, in his perfect stillness, acquires a dignity he did not have before. No longer there to aggravate and worry us, he is sorely missed. He provokes us to question in ourselves the imprudence that, like his, might bring disaster—if not to us directly, then to those we love. Does death then somehow unavoidably define us so that all we live for here and now must seem vain and ephemeral—so that only the desperate hope of *something* afterward, however stringent its terms, makes any sense or bespeaks true wisdom? Perhaps death is compensated for by the depth of our love for others, knowing that, in terms of this existence, they are mortal—just as on other occasions (and perhaps for the same reason) we so desperately cling to nature, friends, and our intensely passionate moods, fearing we will never have enough of them.

These are vital questions that those who are so certain about what is right and wrong, particularly where others are concerned, are not inclined to ask. The urge to take an extreme position in either direction for the sake of the certainty we would all naturally prefer may be the greatest failing of our race. A greater wisdom, as certain pagan Greeks urged, may be found in that difficult middle ground from which we are all so inclined to stray.

Recently, I attended a memorial service for the man who, with his wife, had some years ago founded a foreign-language theater in a nearby city—one of the few such outside their native land. The service was restricted to immediate family members and those who had acted in the man's theater. Seated on the theater's stage, relatives reminisced about but did not particularly eulogize the deceased. They acknowledged his unusually forceful, domineering personality, along with his remarkable gifts and accomplishments. In the aftermath, those negative traits somehow no longer interfered with our fully accepting him as he had been, or missing and loving him for what he was. We required nothing more or less of him.

Surely, if we are capable of sentiments as positive and magnanimous as these, then the Creator is at least as positively disposed toward each of us—whatever awaits us in that grappling with experience (both bitter and sweet, both our doing and not our doing) that is the primary reason for our mortal sojourn. Meanwhile, that persons *are*, or even *were*, itself suffices—for as spiritual and physical kin, we are (though we too seldom recognize it) literally one, *in* each other. And that is wonderfully sacred. It is everything. Praise to the Maker for one another and for this our existence. Life and the people in it are too wondrous, too fine, too precious for us ever to think or feel otherwise.

In Varanasi, holiest of India's cities, women beggars, traditionally cast out by their children when widowed, spend their remaining years waiting for death and a more blissful new life. Some were widowed at a very young age, even as child brides, but most are content to blame their past karma and make the best of what strikes a Westerner as an intolerable and unjust circumstance. How naive can these women be, one once asked. Why do they allow it? Now one marvels at their stoic wisdom and wishes the same for oneself.

Note

1. A slightly different version of this essay was originally published in *Sunstone*, February 1989, 8–10.

Letter to a Doubting Former Student

What follows is the reply I sent to the young man whose prior letter to me is quoted in "Riding the Edge of the Herd" (elsewhere in this collection)—let us call him Mark—following a personal conversation with him in the 1970s. I never found out if my response was at all helpful.

Dear Mark,

I AM DEEPLY TOUCHED by your very thoughtful expression of such sensitive concerns and the courage even their formulation must represent, as well as by your trust in sharing them with me.

I feel inadequate in my response. I hope that nothing I said to you made you feel more despondent or less committed than otherwise. I had to endorse your sentiments, however, because fundamentally I so much share them. Still, like everyone else, we are both looking "through a glass, darkly" (1 Corinthians 13:12) and may in some respects be mistaken. And so I want to say whatever else I can that might reassure and reconcile you to what we have both experienced.

You asked why I still seem, under the circumstances, to be so much "with" the church. I fear I did not give you as full an explanation as I might have. For complete honesty, it is probably necessary to note first that even more than you, I am deeply locked into the system. I am beholden to it for my financial security and must remain with it to maintain ideological harmony with my family, including my wife and children. I am therefore less inclined to question or dismiss it than even you.

Still there are benefits, without which I do not believe I could live nearly so happy, contented, or successful a life. Let me enumerate them:

1. The *sense of selflessness and high personal moral standards*, in which, I feel certain, I would have defaulted (more than I have) if I were not conditioned by influences in the church to believe that they are critical (uncompromisable) and that I am capable of applying them ever more consistently, and therefore successfully, in my life. I *know* they make me a better, more other-directed, and happier person—and that their violation only complicates one's life and seriously undermines one's permanent relationships with others, particularly one's spouse and family members.

In our own day especially, secular "specialists"—doctors, psychologists, etc.—will tell you that what we deem immoral behavior is not only arbitrary but normal and even necessary for emotional health. If I didn't know better due to my own personal experience in "overcoming," I would readily believe that argument, even *want* to believe it, and act accordingly—not immoderately, I imagine, but occasionally, with (as I see it) nevertheless dire consequences. Without the searing influence of conscience, I am that weak, as I suspect most of us are. The doctrine of personal sanctification, so clearly and forcefully expounded in latter-day scripture, particularly thrills me and motivates my daily behavior.

2. The *special emphasis the church places on the importance of family*—on working and sacrificing for it, making it one's first priority and keeping it, as much as possible, inviolate. The longer I am married and the older my children become, the more I realize that they, my wife, our parents, and other family members—ultimately of course the entire human family, but with varying degrees of affinity and concern—are my greatest possession: particularly the bonds of love, harmony, and unity between us, and my contribution to their personal success.

This is still too much a theoretical concept with me. I don't think about it consistently enough, but when I do, I know it is true, and my emotional response to it is unequivocal. I sense how empty and tarnished eternity would be if one could not realize that ideal. And yet that ideal would *not* be my highest priority if the church had not made me so aware that it should be. I would have neglected my family (more than I do) and assumed until it might be too late that things would work out satisfactorily enough without my expending any special concern or effort in their behalf.

3. The *eternal and potentially exalted self-image* (intimately tied to both of the foregoing), that—again thanks to the church—my understanding of the gospel and my faith give me. I am consequently motivated, thanks to this glorious eternal perspective, to try harder than I otherwise would. And I truly believe that the revelations to Joseph Smith provide a vision in this respect that no other faith can equal. I am grateful that I am still idealistic enough that I can respond to that vision, and that I am somehow so blessed that as I do so, I genuinely believe it.

4. Truman Madsen's notion that Mormonism renders (or *can* render) all earthly things spiritual[1] and Ernst Benz's that it has *preeminently sacrilized history*[2]—insights from a Mormon and non-Mormon scholar, respectively. These ideas deeply thrill me and satisfy my yearning for a sense of wholeness and total eternal relevance in all I experience and must undergo.

5. The concept that we are all *literally children of deity*, so sublime even if so unrealized in our everyday relationships with deity and with one another.

6. The *serenity, the "peace that passeth understanding,"* that descends upon us when we (too infrequently) open ourselves in the proper way to the influence of the Comforter, the Holy Spirit—and that the church, more than any other agent or institution, has made me aware of and urged me to seek and cultivate.

Even as I write these words, I feel the Spirit and cannot deny its existence or its importance. And it is again the church (though indirectly) that I must credit. Perhaps this suggests that despite the many disappointments that seem to attend our involvement with the church, it is still very much worth it.

It is also helpful, I believe, to keep reminding ourselves that those disappointments are mostly (if not entirely) attributable to the default, weakness, and shortsightedness of other people—that what they do or don't do that so displeases us is, in the long run, a manifestation of human nature (whatever that is) and can be expected anywhere in any social context. There is wisdom, I believe, in the Taoist doctrine and in the so-called logotherapy of psychiatrist Victor Frankl,[3] both of which suggest it is possible to lower one's level of expectation, if necessary, so that one cannot possibly be disappointed with whatever happens. I am also very fond of the following statement by philosopher George Santayana (from *The Sense of Beauty*), which I do not view as necessarily relativistic:

> Familiarity breeds contempt only when it breeds inattention. When the mind is absorbed and dominated by its perceptions, it incorporates into them more and more of its own functional values, and makes them ultimately beautiful and expressive. Thus no language can be ugly to those who speak it well, no religion unseemly to those who have learned to pour their life into its moulds.
>
> Of course these forms vary in intrinsic excellence; they are by their specific character more or less fit and facile for the average mind. But the man and the age are rare who can choose their own path; we have generally only a choice between going ahead in the direction already chosen, or halting and blocking the path for others. The only kind of reform usually possible is reform from within; a more intimate study and more intelligent use of the traditional forms.[4]

I also recall how in so many instances I have seen the gospel become viable in the social setting of the church: here on campus in the branch where I served, and earlier in the instance of various converts during my mission. I know you have had similar experiences. Even if we are not having them now, we must maintain the hope that if we remain faithful, we still can and will have such experiences again in the future, probably when we least expect it—and that we will then again realize how unexpendable both the gospel and its vehicle, the church, are in the scheme of our eternal destiny.

Those are my feelings at this moment. It has done me good to express them to you. I fully expect to have other feelings and other moods again in the future, but do not believe that they—or those you and I have both experienced thus far—necessarily contradict what I have said here.

Please feel free to continue to share with me your honest feelings, as you see things. I love and admire you for it.

Sincerely your brother,
Thomas F. Rogers
Director, BYU Honors Program

Notes

1. Truman Madsen, *Eternal Man* (Salt Lake City: Deseret Book, 1970).
2. Ernst Benz, "Mormonism and the Secularization of Religions in the Modern World," forum address delivered at Brigham Young University, March 30, 1976; published in *BYU Studies* 16/4 (1976): 627–39.
3. Victor Frankl, *Man's Search for Meaning*, trans. Ilse Lasch (Boston: Beacon Press, 1963).
4. George Santayana, *The Sense of Beauty* (New York: Dover, 1955), 166–67.

Letter to My Son

This letter, dated 1990, was occasioned by the unexpected declaration one Sunday by one of our sons, age sixteen, that he could no longer abide being in the church. I was then serving in our ward bishopric. It was during one of those rare sacrament meetings when the bishopric members join the congregation to take in the annual Primary children's program. I have to admit that on that occasion the program was particularly inane: each sweet young child coming to the rostrum and speedily reciting a phrase or two that he or she did not appear to comprehend. All at once, our son, who was sitting next to me, gave me to understand that there was something he urgently needed to tell me. Together, we exited the chapel and entered the bishop's office, where he made his declaration. Now, a quarter century later, Merriam and I are still waiting for the fuller explanation and exchange requested in this letter.

My dear son,

I don't know if you learned the word *Gestalt* while you were studying German. My sense of the word is that it means a complex or network of associations—an all-inclusive concept. In many respects, that is equally true of any culture into which we may have been born, however arbitrarily—including family, an ethnic group, a nationality, or a religion, particularly one so all-encompassing as Mormonism. To propose a rupture or disassociation at any one level is to some degree to affect a number of others. That is something to consider, along with the proposition that something either is or isn't "true" (or, more accurately, what at a given time in one's life may or may not seem to be "true").

You probably know that the most sophisticated philosophers in our own day are fairly skeptical about what anyone can or cannot know. So when, even as scientists or scholars, we talk about Truth (with a capital *T*), we end up, in our very fallible human state of limited understanding, having to settle for certain other values that are more accessible to our experience and that we can with greater surety call "Truth." Foremost of these is Love. I wonder therefore if we—and I in particular—have not failed to manifest enough love toward you, which on an emotional level (after all, the most powerful level of all) would have bonded you more closely to us—the family, its religion, its culture—and made you more comfortable in and accepting of it. More than wonder, I even feel certain this is so. Whether that could be made up for—which I believe it still can—would of course depend on the desire and goodwill of all parties. However, it would require a reciprocal effort. Please let me know how you feel about that sometime.

I still stand in awe of your declaration last Sunday—the courage and forthrightness you displayed, the obvious longstanding pain and suffering behind it, together with your concern about how we would "take it" (though you had already said as much to us in a number of unspoken ways) and your what I take to have been sincere and unusual and to some extent very reassuring and gratifying compliment about my parenting. You were almost like a Joseph Smith in reverse—and little more than his same age at the time he first began to make such bold assertions.

You are still very young, however precocious (which you also certainly and impressively are)—particularly in terms of personal life experience. This leads us to question whether you understand the gospel as much as you might and on a fully adult level. Do you recognize what are some of its truly distinctive and utterly profound characteristics—not only doctrinally but in terms of the communal welfare mechanism and the personal spiritual development (that of, say, missionaries and lay leaders over a lifetime, mundane and unimpressive as they may come across in other ways) that few if any other religious denominations even come near approximating?

You were never really specific about what must be a number of grievances. Your mother and I would like you to spell them out to us and let us discuss them with you sometime.

Another concept that is too often lost sight of on the part of those who opt to reject or pick and choose a religion is that if there is a God—which you concede you believe there is—and if he at all cares to be concerned with his offspring and creations, then it is—to do him any justice whatsoever—not for us to decide what we do or do not like but to seek his will for us, however difficult and constraining that may appear to us. That and that alone is true faith (the subject of your talk not many weeks ago). The witness that makes sense out of all this—makes it purposeful, even exciting—also does not come without our paying a certain long-term price. Though when it does come, it does so unexpectedly, as a free gift, and mostly undeserved. That's at least my sense (and experience) of it.

We'd be glad to talk with you further about these or other matters—any time. There are things I've written and would like to share with you—but not unless you are sufficiently interested. Let me know.

All my love,
Dad

P.S. Perhaps another good indicator of how much that elusive "Spirit" is or is not with us is the extent to which we are detached, serene, and generous—inclined to inconvenience ourselves in extending ourselves to others. Surely that is something we all need to work on, but it starts, I believe, with the impulse that comes from without as much as from within us, is at least fostered and encouraged by traditions and institutions, and may come as close as anything we can ever experience in mortality to what is both True and Good. It brings its own great reward—the return, generally, of all that has been given. We've been told this in a variety of ways. And, though it's easy to accept theoretically and when put into practice ever so rewarding, it is also harder to apply.

An Insider's View of the Missionary Training Center, 1993–1996

This essay evolved from my response to a paper whose presenter, though himself a returned missionary, was highly critical of the Missionary Training Center (MTC) in Provo. He was a graduate student whose critique mirrored a hypothetical model in his chosen field, sociology. This was in the early 1980s when I was serving as a branch president at the MTC, and my own experience there—my sense, despite its regimentation, of the esprit of the missionaries I closely interacted with—was just the opposite. My defense of the institution was, I believe, at least as long as the paper to which I was responding. My paper was eventually shared by the MTC president with other branch presidents there. Although a good three decades have come and gone since then along with various organizational protocols and procedures, I seriously doubt that the individual missionary's transformative odyssey is today very different from what I here describe. It fosters a perennial conversion experience for each succeeding generation—whether for missionaries or for those they teach.

The three years I served as a spiritual mentor to approximately fifteen hundred young missionaries proved as meaningful as my later service for about the same length of time as a mission president in St. Petersburg, interacting there with about the same number of missionaries. In both instances, I was among their most enthusiastic and admiring "converts."[1]

For the last three years, I have been privileged to serve as one of some thirty branch presidents to those who, during the first weeks of their missions, intensively prepare themselves in the basics of a language, review of doctrine, teaching skills, and the standard missionary discussions at the Missionary Training Center in Provo. With each new wave of incoming elders and sisters, I am reminded of the understandable fear and outright suspicion with which some are inclined to view the experience that awaits them. Such apprehension is often prompted by the offhand remarks of recently returned missionaries who fail, I contend, to remember what, for all the MTC had required of them, also afforded the most profound spiritual growth they had so far known.

Mistaken impressions

Before receiving my call to serve at the MTC, I had more or less pitied my BYU colleagues who had already been recruited as branch presidents there. I assumed they were essentially "processing bodies" and had little close or meaningful acquaintance with those they were charged to look after. How tedious and superficial, I'd thought, must be their experience.

My first contact with the MTC as an outsider was rather misleading. Having noted that two elders who were then having a difficult adjustment were former BYU honors students, Paul Felt, then a counselor in the MTC mission presidency, invited some of us who had been their teachers to come to their aid. I distinctly remember how at the time the two I spoke with made me feel: their eyes were lusterless; they felt oppressed; one had been scolded when, failing to invite his companion to accompany him, he had momentarily left the classroom for a drink of water in an adjacent hallway. Both missionaries were on the verge of going home, but they held out. One went to Argentina, the other to Taiwan. I have spoken with both since the completion of their missions and even attended the marriage of one of them. As so often happens, both have considerably mellowed. I now recognize, as I believe they do, that as precocious, highly self-confident honors students, they had not been very teachable and were too easily offended. I later discovered that they were also atypical. Of those I have since worked with—a fair sample—I am aware of only at most three (one-fifth of one percent) who were deeply distressed or whose attitude as much distressed me when they entered the field.

To my immense and pleasant surprise, I have found my interaction with each missionary to be close and personal. Though the time we spend together is fairly brief—about two months with those learning a foreign language—our contact is intense: I am instantly their surrogate parent and they my surrogate sons and daughters. To witness their earnestness and, with but few exceptions, their spiritual growth and the strengthening of their testimonies has been enthralling.

Personal challenge and growth

The MTC experience discloses each missionary's personal quirks and emotional/spiritual disorders. But despite the occasional incident and ensuing friction with a companion, teacher, or even branch president, most recognize that no one is making them do anything and that their free will is as inviolate as ever. (No real learning ever took place when forced, and this principle is fully understood at the MTC.) On the whole, the missionaries also readily sense the goodwill of those on the staff and in the ecclesiastical arm who are there to serve them.

Mission rules are explicitly spelled out, it is true. They are issued by the General Authorities and posit essentially the same standards to which missionaries are traditionally expected to adhere in the field. Whereas their violation or neglect is not and should not be condoned, the individual is nevertheless allowed full freedom to choose how conscientiously he or she will obey. Sensing this, missionaries generally try even harder to live up to the trust placed in them. As Joe J. Christensen, one of the MTC mission presidents with whom I have served, routinely assured them: "We respect you. We have confidence in you. We trust you. And we love you."

The same basic trust extends to the branch presidents, the content of whose weekly gospel discussions with branch members is left to their own inspiration and personal discernment of members' needs. Administrative styles vary with the branch presidents' particular training and temperament—a high proportion of whom also serve on the BYU faculty. There is also a keen sense among the MTC's administrators of the need to innovate, improve already existing procedures, keep pace with change, and be ever responsive to the missionaries' special needs and personal requests. It need not be that way, but it is. The open and outward-reaching spirit that stems from such leadership is a joy to work with.

There is always, of course, the possibility of discouragement and "guilt trips"—especially on the part of an extremely conscientious missionary. Rather than intensify their emotional burden, the thrust of my and my colleagues' counseling has been to recommend patience and reassure such missionaries that, whatever the state of their progress, they should, if they are doing their best, feel good about their efforts. Many fail to realize, especially at first, that languages are not learned nor discussions mastered in a day. If an occasional missionary leader or returned missionary instructor becomes in the least dictatorial, he or she is in turn lovingly urged to respect his or her charges' agency.

Some express understandable anxiety with respect to the state of their testimonies and their ability to witness to others. Here again, missionaries are encouraged not only to detect those signs of the Spirit that may have eluded them but also to exercise patience along with faith as they await the moments up ahead when confirming impressions will come. By far the greater number readily experience such feelings while still at the MTC. In the process, they spontaneously recapitulate what every convert undergoes and what their own future investigators will too. The process is ongoing. Some missionaries have already dramatically experienced it, especially those who are themselves recent converts. Some, especially from the Wasatch Front, encounter it for the first time while at the MTC, at least consciously.

I have tried to explain the testimony-strengthening process to myself and others as follows: finding himself or herself in a temporarily discomforting situation and unable to cope, the missionary turns to Jesus Christ. In sensing the difference that doing so has made, the missionary comes to recognize just how real both the Savior's intervention and hence the Savior's person really are. More specifically, I have observed five stages in the spiritual development of missionaries at the MTC:

1. In one respect or another, the new missionary is brought to recognize his or her weaknesses and limitations. These challenges are invariably intrinsic to the missionary—and, while exposed at the MTC, are not directly caused by his or her circumstances there. These challenges may include learning a new foreign language; memorizing the

discussions; observing mission rules; overcoming discouragement; coping with a highly regimented routine that allows little privacy or leisure; dealing with homesickness; developing a witness of one's calling as a missionary; adjusting to a companion who is arbitrarily assigned and equally frustrated; withstanding personal temptation in relation to former transgressions; and remaining patient and content, even finding fulfillment, if and when the foregoing obstacles no longer offer a sufficient challenge. In one or another ingenious way, every missionary seems to encounter this type of personal brick wall. As one elder expressed it, "There is nothing like the MTC for stripping away every pretense and revealing the true self."

2. In desperate response to these shortcomings, the missionary falls to his or her knees and appeals to the Lord more earnestly than perhaps ever before. The missionary acknowledges his or her dependence on the Lord and petitions for the intervention of higher powers, ultimately bringing closer contact with the Lord's Spirit. The missionary is thus humbled, becomes teachable, grows in testimony, and is miraculously assisted to overcome personal limitations. The missionary eventually experiences a breakthrough. Sensing the Lord's impact in his or her life, the missionary now has both a greatly strengthened testimony that the Lord lives and a more profound love for him.

3. The missionary next perceives that further progress can be made only by removing the focus from self—however much he or she may still feel the need for further time and attention—and focusing instead on those who, in one way or another, are struggling even more. Many missionaries have testified that in thus assisting others, they surmount their own problems and learn all the more thoroughly and effortlessly. "You have to learn," attests the same elder, "to take the work seriously, but not yourself." In the process, each missionary becomes a disciple of the Savior—which is the most essential qualification to represent the Lord, beyond knowledge of a foreign language, doctrinal understanding, principles of teaching, or anything else he or she may meanwhile have acquired at the MTC.

4. At this point, a group of missionaries coalesces and becomes a harmonious working unit. They mutually experience a depth of love, rapport, and spiritual ecstasy that, for most, is totally unprecedented. The general response is one of heightened awe, appreciation, serenity,

discernment, conviction, and spiritual strength. The gifts of the Spirit come to the fore. One is at times reminded of how the original apostles must have felt on the Day of Pentecost. Each missionary is further amazed that, despite all they now share in common—a thing so universally absolute it is almost impersonal—they remain such distinct individuals. Their diverse personalities assert themselves all the more distinctly—but with maturity, with dignity and stature. The expression "charismatic" seems to fit them in a twofold sense. (What they have achieved for themselves, others would pay for dearly but still would not attain because they lack the proper motivation, which is both selfless and spiritual.)

5. With inevitable disappointment, the missionary soon learns that to maintain such a spiritual "high" requires great diligence. But the feelings the missionary has come to know are so powerful, so real, that he or she is doubly resolved to make that effort. The trade-off with other, more self-indulgent feelings is—despite the hold they may have earlier had on the missionary—simply not worth it. This struggle is something each individual will have to work at throughout the mission and particularly thereafter—for the rest of his or her days, and maybe forever.

What the missionary has learned are laws of life: great spiritual principles of universal significance. The MTC is truly a rite of passage that, if routinely entered into with the same sincerity and good intent by those in their late teens and early twenties across the Earth, would surely transform humankind—without the unpredictable and often less than ideal consequences of group training/therapy programs like est.[2]

Celebrating the MTC experience

I suppose this is what so disappointed me in a recent *Newsweek* exposé of the MTC by the journalist Kenneth L. Woodward.[3] It seemed to me that despite all he mentions while visiting the facility in Provo, there is no indication he ever allowed himself to hear out the very missionaries then undergoing training. The day after I read his article, I received from the thirty or so missionaries in my immediate ecclesiastical charge the following typical and unsolicited expressions about their experience there:

- "I really am grateful for this opportunity to be a missionary. I have never felt better about anything I've done in my entire life."
- "I've found myself change a lot since being here. I've found feelings inside of me . . . and a closeness to the Lord that I've never felt before. It's great!"
- "I have been here a week now. It is really great to be here. I have learned a lot. Not just the language, but how to be a friend and share my time with others."
- "I am so happy that I made the decision to come on a mission, and I'm working hard because I realize it's not my time anymore, but my time belongs to the Lord."
- "I have found this to be a very growth-promoting place."
- "I've tried to exercise more patience and tolerance with myself and others. I've also been more outgoing and open with my fellow elders. I've learned to accept and return their love, and it feels really good."
- "I want to tell you how I love you. . . . You know, I can't recall a time in my life where I've been able to tell that to anyone, and now, I must say, the Spirit constantly tells me to do so, and moreover to my family and the elders and sisters here. You know the Spirit is a very unifying thing. . . . I've been experiencing the Spirit here time and time again."
- "You learn a lot here. You learn to tell people how much you really love them."

The very subheadings in Woodward's article—"Transgressions," "Deception," "Strain"—belie the meaningful personal growth, spontaneous fellowship, and attendant satisfaction reflected in the foregoing statements.

I find it difficult to understand how the MTC can other than overwhelm those who come near it when its clients—at least those I have come to know so intimately, excluding perhaps the three previously mentioned—so unitedly concur with the view also expressed by one of them: "I honestly wouldn't want to be anywhere else right now." Or when a significant number substantiate the words of yet another: "I never had a real spiritual witness until I came here and had problems."

Much of the program's success clearly derives from the encouragement and example to new arrivals of slightly older peers and the profound fellowship that, despite personality clashes, all endeavor to cultivate and that generally abounds among them. It is not uncommon for missionaries to observe just days after arrival that they have never had closer friends. Contrary to what so many presuppose, the spirit of rivalry and competition has no place at the MTC. Instead, the missionary learns to be supportive of and root for others as much as self and not to mind if he or she performs less well than some. Priesthood self-government is indeed an important ingredient in the effectiveness of the various MTC branches.

As I have commented in a handout to my own branch's new members—not so much to propagandize them as because it happens to be the case:

> We want you to know how much we have all come to love the MTC, for it is one of the most sacred places on earth. It is a place of miracles—foremost of which are the astounding personal transformations we behold here every day. President Christensen has truly said this is the mission with the least baptisms but the most conversions. Everyone's testimony is greatly strengthened for having spent some time here, and all of us are challenged to push beyond our former complacent limits as we strive as never before to become more mature and whole, to perfect our lives. No one forces us to do so either. No one could. We innately want to. But—as with missionary work in the field, for which, though different, the MTC provides a reasonable foretaste—the effort required is not easy. In fact, this will probably be one of the hardest things you have ever done. That's why people grow here. But the joy you will come to know is proportionate to the difficulty and the effort you expend.

My own euphoria derives from what, by their unwitting example, so many of these spiritual giants less than half my age have done for me and my own outlook on life and whom I now count among my most precious, eternal friends. It has impelled me to exclaim more than once while in their presence that, yes, the church is true: I see it each week in so many transformed lives. The missionaries' allegiance and dedication to such a noble and glorious cause, so much more profound than any single mortal's petty personal ambitions, gives them a perspective on life that brings true peace and a fullness of joy. It also unites them in such sublime bonds of unity, fraternity, and love that all they can do, and I with them, is be grateful that somehow our eyes have been opened and our hearts so softened.

And we naturally wish the same for all others. One of the fairly predictable effects of the personal growth realized at the MTC is the way in which the hearts of those, particularly males, who were until so recently to some degree rebellious teenagers, now literally turn to their fathers. The recognition of all that they owe their parents and of all their families mean to them is one of the training's most impressive and sacred consequences.

What a beautiful thing that, working through us, the Lord enables us to enjoy relationships and experience feelings that we are otherwise generally inclined to repress or replace with envy, resentment, or indifference. A colleague at BYU who preceded me as a branch president once confessed to me that for months after receiving his call, he was haunted by the disparity between the feelings he so intensely enjoyed at the MTC and the quite normal tensions he experienced when returning to his immediate family. The contrast made him all the more conscious of his default as an all-too-typical Mormon husband and father.

Conclusion

We need to dispel the myths that circulate about this phenomenal institution, the MTC. The way of life our sons and daughters so diligently pursue there and the spirit it engenders have much to teach the church at large. It is for the entire church a great model and a distilled glimpse of celestial society. It fortifies the missionaries, heightening their personal expectations for future companionships, both in the field and in a more eternal sense. It is a powerful witness to the viability of the church in action and of the gospel when fully applied. The families of those who have spent time there have some intimation of it from the letters that are sent them attesting to the amazing change and maturation in their offspring, which in many cases induce similar change, increased devotion, and outright conversion in the missionaries' parents. If there are those who don't know this already—and many do not—they should either go on a mission or support someone in doing so and in that way partially participate in the spirit of the MTC, a spirit that is essentially the spirit of loving one's neighbor. I would challenge each of us and call the church membership at large to make the discovery of, wherever it may now be lacking, that which we all so hunger for—a much less intimidated expression of genuine religious devotion. The MTC changes everyone's life for the better—hopefully with some permanent consequence. It has mine, and I'm eternally grateful.

Notes

1. This essay is adapted from a presentation given at the Sunstone Symposium in Salt Lake City in the early 1980s.
2. Est (Erhard Seminars Training) was a series of training seminars presented by Werner Erhard, popular in the late 1970s and early 1980s, aimed at "transforming" the lives of those who took part in the seminars.
3. Kenneth L. Woodward, "Onward, Mormon Soldiers," *Newsweek*, April 27, 1981, 87–88.

The Miracle of Conversion

One December in the late 1970s, I was invited to address our residential ward in a sacrament meeting. Perhaps it was the cumulative impact of the rich spiritual interaction I'd enjoyed for nearly a decade with students and other members of the BYU faculty (including my service as a branch president first on the BYU campus and later at the Missionary Training Center), the significant plays I'd begun to author, and/or the evolving dynamic in the life of our family as our last children came "on board" (twins). In any event, this is how I was made to feel just then—a truly memorable epiphany. I now view that experience as one of those periodic spiritual "highs" that sustain us by the memory of how good things have been and the promise of how excellent they can be again.

THE SEASON IS FAST UPON US when, by convention, we express gratitude for the birth of Christ and, by implication, everything consequent to it. In doing so, we generally think of all he has done for us—but in the past tense. Should we not also be grateful for the Lord's very presence—for that Spirit we are promised in partaking of the sacrament and that we should strive at all times to have with us?

When we are so blessed, it is often unexpectedly and out of a special sense of deep personal need. (Perhaps we therefore ought to constantly seek those challenges in life that create such a need.) On such occasions we recognize how *real* it all is, much as did Alma when he asked, "My brethren of the church, have ye spiritually been born of God? Have ye received his image in your countenances? Have ye experienced this mighty change in your hearts?" (Alma 5:14).

I do not believe, however, that many of us often feel the Lord's Spirit very deeply. And far fewer of us do so constantly. It is very hard to live for and maintain, but so worth it that anyone who has once experienced it is either stupid or insane not to do everything necessary to have it with him or her at all times. One must therefore conclude that we are all to some extent stupid or insane.

In his *Confession*, Tolstoy wrote, "One can only live while one is intoxicated with life."[1] I have a theory that all humans crave the Lord's power and influence in their lives and in fact seek it—in one form or another. However, the ways by which we seek that divine "intoxication" or communion are most often counterfeit: drugs, promiscuity, materialism, public recognition, intellectual titillation, aesthetic titillation, even "spiritual" titillation. Each of these has a selfish or elitist overtone. None truly satisfies, and all are dangerous, even lethal, to the spirit.

Only the real thing can afford us a profound and lasting emotional "high." It is also far more sublime. It is still and steady. It abides with us (or can). It includes the peace that "passeth all understanding" (Philippians 4:7). What it feels like is perhaps best described in those choice metaphors from Lehi's dream and Alma's discourse on faith, which almost literally induce us to "taste" what it is like:

> I beheld that it was most sweet, above all that I ever before tasted. Yea, and I beheld that the fruit thereof was white, to exceed all the whiteness that I had ever seen. And as I partook of the fruit thereof it filled my soul with exceedingly great joy; wherefore, I began to be desirous that my family should partake of it also; for I knew that it was desirable above all other fruit. (1 Nephi 8:11–12)

> And because of your diligence and your faith and your patience with the word in nourishing it, that it may take root in you, behold, by and by ye shall pluck the fruit thereof, which is most precious, which is sweet above all that is sweet, and which is white above all that is white, yea, and pure above all that is pure; and ye shall feast upon this fruit even until ye are filled, that ye hunger not, neither shall ye thirst. (Alma 32:42)

Nephi's explanation of his father's dream (particularly in 1 Nephi 11:13 and 21–22) leaves no doubt that the feelings described in these passages are to be associated with the Savior's nativity and "the love of God," which, in consequence, "sheddeth itself abroad in the hearts of the children of men" (1 Nephi 11:22).

The Lord has clearly told us why he does not come to us more often:

> And the whole world lieth in sin, and groaneth under darkness and under the bondage of sin. And by this you may know they are under the bondage of sin, because they come not unto me. (D&C 84:49–50)

In other words, he does not come to us because, under the prescribed conditions, *we* fail to come to *him*. We turn and face in the opposite direction. We do so because the price we must pay to be sanctified is so all-inclusive: it is that we completely forsake this world and totally consecrate our lives to him:

> And if ye shall deny yourselves of all ungodliness, and love God with all your might, mind and strength, then is his grace sufficient for you, that by his grace ye may be perfect in Christ. . . . And again, if ye by the grace of God are perfect in Christ, and deny not his power, then are ye sanctified in Christ by the grace of God. (Moroni 10:32–33)

How we need to feel in paying that price is best described in the verse that reads, "Ye shall offer for a sacrifice unto me a broken heart and a contrite spirit" (3 Nephi 9:20). That is why, of all the so-called mysteries, the Spirit of the Lord is for many the most mysterious. For all who so compulsively cling to their self-indulgent vices or to any of the surrogate forms of inspiration—for those who in other words are not "pure in heart" and do not seek to learn the Lord's will for them and make it their own—the expression of genuine spiritual ecstasy is uncomfortable and provokes a defensive and obstinate skepticism, for they cannot comprehend it (though they may at least subconsciously begin to desire it).

But if the Spirit of the Lord and the Holy Ghost are, in this restricted sense, "mysterious," they are also truly miraculous in their capacity to radically transform lives. When they are fully in force:

- We are serene and not unduly worried, whatever our circumstances.
- We are grateful and less disposed to find fault. We sense that doing so would repel the Spirit.
- We are more honest. On a far more finely calibrated scale than previously, our conscience makes us so miserable when we even begin to violate our integrity that we quickly desist. Again, we sense that not to do so would be to lose the Spirit, and that is simply too high a price.
- We are in control of our carnal appetites. This becomes both exhilarating and easy.
- We are more disposed to love others. Our minds are less on ourselves.
- We yearn for the fellowship of those whose faith is similarly quickened and through whom the Lord in turn testifies to us.
- The scriptures become wellsprings of insight that leap out at us with added significance.
- We readily and spontaneously fall to our knees—deeply and meaningfully communing with the Lord because we crave his abiding presence, thirst for it, and feel naked without it.
- Everything that has otherwise seemed difficult or impossible is potentially resolved, including concerns we have about our own duplicity or that of others.
- We fear neither death nor any other man—only God (but in the most positive sense).

This is the miracle of conversion. One who has experienced these things, though materially invisible, knows how real they are—and how visibly manifest, both in oneself and in others. Such a person cannot contain his or her desire to testify of them to others.

That is my testimony to you this day. I sense the reality of it more fully than ever before in my life. I do not altogether know why. I realize of course that I am currently under the profound spell of the missionary spirit, as that spirit so forcefully emanates from the Missionary Training Center northeast of the BYU campus. But I do not fully understand why I deserve to feel this way—why I have become so sensitized. It may simply be a grace by reason of some particular need at this time. Why now and not earlier? Why now at all? I only know that I need not have waited this long—because I have seen a few others, less than half my age, who were so penetrated by the Spirit that I and everyone else in their proximity were deeply affected. In their presence the Lord was also clearly present, and the rest of us could only wish to be more like them.

I have more cause to be grateful this holiday than ever before. And I can only wish the same blessing—and as fully—for each of you.

Note

1. Leo Tolstoy, "A Confession," in *The Portable Tolstoy*, ed. John Bayley, trans. Aylmer Maude (New York: Viking Penguin, 1978), 679.

On the Importance of Doing Certain Mundane Things

This essay, presented shortly after my wife Merriam's and my return from presiding over the Russia St. Petersburg Mission (1993–1996), appeared in the December 1998 issue of Sunstone *magazine. Drawing upon journal entries from that mission experience, it represents perhaps my most assertive insistence on our need to harmoniously serve in the Lord's church, deal patiently and tolerantly with one another, and avoid egotistically dogmatic extremes in the positions we take vis-à-vis the gospel and toward those who may perceive it differently. This has continued to be an almost obsessive theme about which I have expressed myself, both before and since—its violation my unshakable bête noire. It already prominently figures in my 1979 play* Reunion.[1]

I PREFACE MY REMARKS WITH A CONFESSION. For some, I am about to commit one of two heresies. And while these heresies are, I know, among the least of my sins, some will find them displeasing. If I alienate you, I apologize. What are these heresies? For some, it is that I am at a Sunstone forum. For others, it is that I will be politically incorrect as I attempt to defend or apologize for certain aspects of our church life that have in times past, if we are honest, set the teeth of all of us on edge.

Concerning honesty or forthrightness, I take my cue from a frail old man with a flowing white mane not unlike that of the prophet David O. McKay, who in other uncanny ways further resembled President McKay. This was Ammon Hennacy, a member of the Catholic Worker Movement, the anarchist and proprietor of Salt Lake's first and at the time only shelter for the homeless, the Joe Hill House of Hospitality. Ever since our meeting in the late 1960s, I've carried Hennacy's card in my wallet, largely for the arresting credo on its reverse side:

> Love without Courage and Wisdom is sentimentality, as with the ordinary church member; Courage without Love and Wisdom is foolhardiness, as with the ordinary soldier; Wisdom without Love and Courage is cowardice, as with the ordinary intellectual. Therefore one with Love, Courage and Wisdom is one in a million, who changes the world, as with Jesus, Buddha and Gandhi.[2]

I shared that card with fierce atheists in Moscow who already knew of my religious background, and it did much to break the ice—simply because of its oblique reference to the infamous labor leader Joe Hill, who was hanged for murder in Utah in 1915 after a controversial trial where his defenders asserted that he had been framed by anti-union forces. It was only then that I learned Hill had a revered niche in the communist pantheon of socialist martyrs.

One could hardly fault Ammon Hennacy for lack of courage. For his unwillingness to respond to the draft in World War I, he had served a prison sentence. And in the coldest weather, though sickly, he would lead demonstrations in Salt Lake City for civil rights and against nuclear testing.

Not wishing in any way to disparage Hennacy or the great good he accomplished among us, I note with a certain irony that on his calling card, along with the advertisement "Free Meals . . . Transients Bedded on the Floor Anytime," is the then-innocent, now-ominous specification just below his address: "2 blocks South of Vitro Smokestack." (The site later proved to be highly radioactive.)

How relevant is any of this to my topic—"On the Importance of Doing Certain Mundane Things"? Wait and see. I'm aware that the root meaning of the word *mundane* is "worldly," meaning that it normally lacks any "otherworldly" or spiritual connotations. I use *mundane* in its more common, colloquial sense, implying deeds or acts that are menial, routine, even tedious. However, I expressly focus on those deeds or acts that serve a divine or sacred purpose—which, when you think of it, is particularly appropriate for Mormons, for whom all things are, or should be, spiritual.

Enduring the mundane

We variously respond to a number of expectations

To illustrate, during the two Saturday general sessions of a recent LDS general conference, my students and I dutifully stopped a play rehearsal to listen. During one of the talks, my teaching assistant—an honors student and returned missionary and one of the most spiritually sensitive people I know—suddenly grabbed his coat and bolted. Speaking at the time was one of the General Authorities whose close acquaintance I had made during my recent mission and whose personal graciousness and dedication to his calling had inspired both my wife Merriam and me and put us at considerable ease. Like many other conference speakers, and with an almost studied plainness and simplicity, he addressed certain gospel fundamentals. There was no obfuscation, no possible confusion or misunderstanding—the words were familiar and at a level any Primary child could readily comprehend.

I think I know what so distressed my assistant on this occasion, because I felt, I suspect, the same way, though I didn't let on. As a listener, I generally hunger for new insight or a slightly different angle on the subject, or at least some fresh personal or anecdotal underpinning—none of which were evident. The expected fervor was there, and the speaker's immense sincerity, and so was what we are from time to time reminded is truly as important as any words—the Spirit. Still, listening to that talk was a trial to the intellect, mine no less than that of my assistant.

I have acquaintances, LDS members of record, who affiliate themselves with the Unitarians on Sunday afternoons. Some attend our sacrament meetings quite regularly, but never Sunday School or priesthood. Others we never see at church. I'm sure they engage with the Unitarians in lively and stimulating discussions that touch on many of the social and ethical issues in which I have an avid interest. Deep down, I envy their opportunity to be involved in such discussions with other thoughtful and questing minds, and doubtless with a more liberal spin than they encounter with fellow Saints in their resident wards. But that type of discussion is really not why the Lord founded his church.

As we all well know, one of the mundane things Latter-day Saints are expected to do is listen, rather indiscriminately, to others' lessons and sermons—sermons and lessons that markedly vary in their appeal and effectiveness. (In this regard, Apostle Jeffrey R. Holland's strong expression of concern in the April 1998 general conference about the quality of teaching in the church sends an encouraging message.[3])

Other mundane expectations that variously pose a "trial" for many include home teaching (both doing it and graciously, enthusiastically receiving visits), temple work, and welfare or service assignments. For many of us, the last, whose consequences are more visible and immediate, are perhaps the least difficult to engage in. I suspect that most others, like me, invariably come away from a four-hour stint at the local LDS cannery with an unexpected good feeling. I am still rather amazed at the deep satisfaction expressed by those who are set apart to serve in temples. For some of us, because the resulting benefit is less evident and thus requires even greater faith, the ordinances performed there may require greater initiative and enthusiasm. (Since serving as a temple worker myself, subsequent to the initial publication of this essay, I have thankfully come to experience this same satisfaction.) Still, if there is anything to heavenly transcendence and the eternal value of individual lives—which all religions more or less affirm—then such vicarious labor in behalf of deceased persons, one on one, becomes both an entirely fitting and a needful endeavor. Through this ultimate expression of regard for total strangers as well as for one's immediate kin, the two, in fact, profoundly merge.

Doing the mundane

Laboring with Russian saints underscores the dynamic of building Zion

Allow me to return to our mundane efforts to preach and teach, whether from the pulpit, in the classroom, or as we visit in one another's living rooms. Though such activity often seems terribly perfunctory, that may be because we fail to understand what it is meant to accomplish. I acquired some insight about this as, for a recent period of three years, my wife and I attempted to encourage and hold together some of our newest members among those wonderfully soulful and strong-tempered Russians. Rereading the journal I kept at the time, I find that I believe just as much in the validity of those same impressions as I did then. Perhaps they can be instructive for some in conveying the perspective and concerns of those at the institutional helm.

One day, I made the following entry:

> After every sacrament meeting talk and every Sunday School lesson, we should have gotten to know each other a little better—so that we can care more about each other. The purpose of our constant and recurring meetings must be to that end as well as to "pump us up," as some of our missionaries put it—to help maintain our desire to live otherwise and remind ourselves that we do so not for ourselves alone but for a number of particular others.

To get to know each other better, I still believe, should be a most important by-product of all our comings together, but it meaningfully occurs only when, in our gospel conversation, we speak from the heart, as freely and self-disclosingly as possible.

While in Russia, I had another realization, one that saved me from much needless worry and, hopefully, from exerting too much stifling control over others. In the Lord's work, whatever our assignment, it is important to conscientiously "be there," if only to witness. Only when we have this understanding is the Lord in a position to function through us.

Again from the journal, this corollary:

> There's a remarkable principle that operates extensively in the church, even when we are so mortally inclined to question it. It has to do with the chain of trust that the operation of the Lord's church requires of everyone involved, both up and down. Absolutely no one is equal to a new calling. No one is sufficiently qualified, and, in many respects, all are undeserving. But when trust is extended to those with a sincere desire to learn and do their best, people do qualify and together they help accomplish what is seemingly impossible.

More than once in St. Petersburg, incidentally, the Relief Society sisters would tell my wife how the gospel and their association with the church had given them, as women, a sense of individual worth they had never experienced before.

Time and again, I found myself recording sentiments like the following:

> Elaine Pagels contends that early Christianity became extremely diverse at an early point in time,[4] which only substantiates what we have all along understood about the great apostasy (or departure from a single pristine tradition). In my own experience here, as I monitor our now nearly thirty branches and groups, such a departure can happen in not just a century or year or month, but in a single week. Invariably, it starts when we bypass the established priesthood line of authority in arriving at policies or decisions affecting the entire group; on the other hand, some individuals exacerbate the problem by asserting that very authority for all they're worth. The safe countermode to both tendencies is, as we've been advised, to always "govern by councils." For the first time, we are encountering rare but assertive efforts on the part of certain members, formerly leaders themselves, to draw away other members and disparage the existing church (a further parallel to the restored church in the mid-nineteenth century).

On yet another occasion, I wrote:

> I think I understand much better now—because I've experienced it myself on a certain level—how totally crippling dissension can be to the major purposes of the church, to the unity that needs to be there among the members. I'm talking about *intellectual dissidence*, particularly when it goes public. I don't like to hear members talk about "*our* church." I wish they would get rid of that expression, because we don't own it. It's *his* church. We really need to remember, in this collective effort, that when we're called to do certain things, it's not according to *our* light and understanding. Otherwise, the Spirit does not direct us. We need to be willing to be submissive and recognize our own inadequacy in the process. That

> lesson has been renewed for me here on an almost daily basis. It's an important lesson that many of us need to understand better than we do.

Again, looking back at our mission experience, I made this further entry:

> I'd like to do one more thing when I return home. I hope I've learned this lesson from having had to run interference with so many people who have their own private agendas. They come at you constantly, and their motives are often impure. They come to you because you're a figurehead in the church, and they want something out of you for their own personal gain, or they want to "make the church over" according to their own particular preconceptions—which is not how the church works or what it is there for. They are takers and not givers. Or they are dictators, the church's secret rivals. They don't understand that although we are a privileged part of Christ's church, we do not own or control it. It is his church, not ours, and, as Elder Max Caldwell pointed out to the mission presidencies once in Frankfurt, there is no one with a calling in the church who is not accountable to someone else. One of the lessons I have learned is that I would never want to create that kind of interference or complicate the lives of my leaders in any way, beginning with my bishop. I don't want to ask for special privileges, or to tell him how to run his show (even if I'd do things some other way). I'll try instead to be there, to fit in and support his efforts and those of our other leaders at every level.

Those of sufficient age will recall J. Reuben Clark Jr.'s frequent plea to the members regarding the need for unity—a theme as fervently stressed in the April 1998 general conference by Apostle Henry B. Eyring. During a visit to St. Petersburg and while serving as an education and humanitarian service representative in the church's Baltic Mission, Bob Rees, the remarkable former editor of *Dialogue: A Journal of Mormon Thought,* put it this way:

> When you're working in a primary way with the basic issues of the gospel with people who are learning them for the first time and applying them to their lives, there is no room or luxury for

> criticism or negativity. People who leave the church have lost their memory of that primary witness from the Holy Ghost. It is nevertheless the genius of the church that it provides so many ways to reinforce it. People who take extreme positions at either end of the critical spectrum also tend to lack charity.[5]

For a community to be free of criticism is far from easy. This should come as no surprise to anyone who has read the epistles of Paul, which are filled with diatribes against the gossip and backbiting that were standard fare in the early church, whose equivalent we claim to be. Why then would we not be as divisive and contentious and in as much need of the long-suffering invoked by both Paul and Peter, as well as by King Benjamin, Alma, and Moroni to another early church of Jesus Christ? (See Philippians 2:14–15; 1 Thessalonians 5:14–15; 1 Peter 3:8–12; Mosiah 2:32–33; 18:21; Moroni 7:3–4, 45.)

Where there is discord or perceived injustice, silence may often be the best response. A friend once suggested as a precedent the way Noah's two righteous sons averted their gaze upon finding him drunk and naked. Perhaps this is why I am, in terms of my or others' critical expression, disposed to more oblique, essentially aesthetic, and consequently often more affective modes of commentary.

But there is also a concomitant need and obligation to value those who, because of their disposition, temperament, or immaturity, tend to impose and importune. In this regard, I share yet another, slightly longer excerpt from that St. Petersburg journal:

> While conducting a conference, the district counselor Brother L. suddenly cast aspersions on an absent branch president (not by name—although since this was the only branch president *not* there, it was easy enough to figure out whom he had in mind), suggesting that by his non-attendance the branch president was a sinner. It was clearly an unfortunate remark. I tried to put the awkward incident out of my mind, hoping that others would, too. In the second hour, the mission's young men's leader passed a note my way, asking if he could bear testimony—an irregular request for any church conference. But, for some reason, I gave in and invited him to come forward after the next speaker—which he then did. His testimony

proved as unusual as his request. What he did, calmly and courteously, was chastise Brother L. for maligning another in a public meeting and tell him that we should not treat one another that way. He said what I would have wanted to say—"Hear! Hear!"—or would have liked his district president to say to Brother L. later, in private. Brother L. seemed to take it in his stride, and nothing more was said. I was as intrigued by it all as I was slightly dismayed. I was more dismayed when, during the next several weeks, we buried both L and the young men's leader, both still quite young men. L had succumbed to a belatedly diagnosed tumor of the brain, while the young men's leader had fallen from a rooftop while viewing a fireworks display during a national holiday. Who could have foreseen, that day, that neither would much longer be with us? Death called to our attention not only these brethren's personal idiosyncrasies but their remarkable devotion and, despite all else, our love for them and the realization that we now truly missed them. How, in the mission field, does one more fully perceive both one's self and one's fellow members? Much, I suspect, like our Creator views us—as both flawed and precious. How, at home, do we more often tend to view one another—and often ourselves? As less flawed and also less precious.

Self and society

The need for balance, for skepticism but not cynicism

I am something of a disciple of Carl Jung, whose hypothetical opposition of Society and Self is not unlike the division his mentor, Sigmund Freud, draws between Superego and Id. With specific reference to the Isis-Osiris legend, Jung disciple Erich Neumann has, in his arresting exploration of mythical archetypes, suggested that the Self's autonomy is, to some degree, subject to external suppression, both sexual and intellectual, and that castration and beheading in such legends are violent metaphors for that process in real life.[6] Social forces can, indeed, too much suppress an individual, but to assume that individuals need not bridle any expression of certain cherished idiosyncratic notions or sometimes almost uncontainable chthonic urges is to ignore what the daily news tells us about those who must have thought themselves exceptions—the tyrants, major or petty, the violent mobs that do their bidding, or wife abusers and child molesters, whose name is and perhaps always was "Legion."

What particularly appeals to me in Jungian theory is the notion that each opposing force that makes up and pulls at the human creature nevertheless has its own validity—and that the process of individuation, the task we each must take upon ourselves to realize our full potential, involves the respectful accommodation of those same forces. This is perhaps our most difficult challenge: to juggle competing goods in a world where the True, the Good, and the Beautiful have yet to be circumscribed into a compatible whole. This outlook accords with the wisdom of Aristotle's golden mean as well as with the New Testament's recurring admonition to be temperate in all we do. (See 1 Corinthians 9:25; Galatians 5:23; Philippians 4:5; and 2 Peter 1:6.)

Besides our prophets, there are others who have taught me the need for—and fueled my own fitful aspiration toward— humility, self-discipline, altruism, and spiritual transcendence. The list includes Dietrich Bonhoeffer, Thomas Merton, Simone Weil, Reinhold Niebuhr, and the Orthodox priest Aleksandr Yelchaninov.[7] More recently, the list has come to include the small corpus of films by Andrey Tarkovsky—truly the most spiritually profound creations I have ever encountered in that medium. Consider the following marvelous prayer from Tarkovsky's *Sacrifice*. It is spoken by an atheist-turned-Christ figure who, at the likely outset of a third world conflagration, petitions for God's deliverance: "Our Father, who art in Heaven . . . Deliver us in this terrible time. . . . all those who love Thee and believe in Thee, all those who do not believe in Thee because they are blind, those who haven't given Thee a thought simply because they haven't yet been truly miserable, all those who in this hour have lost their hope, their future, their lives and the opportunity to surrender to Thy will."[8]

And listen now to Niebuhr's vintage elucidation of the triune Christian virtues: "Nothing that is worth doing can be achieved in our lifetime; therefore we must be saved by hope. Nothing which is true or beautiful or good makes complete sense in any immediate context of history; therefore we must be saved by faith. Nothing we do, however virtuous, can be accomplished alone, therefore we are saved by love."[9]

There is another list I cherish just as much. It contains the names of those who have mentored me in the skepticism I think we need to teach along with faith. No, the two lists do not blend, but they balance each other. Like contrasting tiles in a mosaic, they produce, in their tension, a more coherent, vivid, and ultimately more reliable perspective and image. As a text for this proposition, I offer Jesus's admonition to be both "wise as serpents" and "harmless as doves" (Matthew 10:16). If the concept is ironic, dissonant, and dialectic (or, like so many of the Savior's utterances, logically paradoxical), our failure to apply its dual admonition results in polarized extremism.

Here are two examples. First, a common liberal assumption all too blithely lumps together, then dismisses, to cite a recent commentator, "discrimination, venality, religious orthodoxy, wrong-headedness, perversity, and snobbery."[10] Second, a statement posted on a Mormon discussion website lists, among its snide paraphrases, the following self-righteous parody of liberals: "We believe in the same organization that exists in the late twentieth-century Liberal Church, namely, scholars, intellectuals, feminists, homosexuals, journalists, and so forth."[11] Failing, among other things, to recognize our existential need for tenuousness—in musical terms, for sustaining unresolved chords—the second statement betrays the Christlike spirit it professes to defend, while the first position also defaults in the fundamental toleration of difference it nevertheless espouses and upon which a truly democratic society depends.

During my lifetime of church membership, I have never experienced such polarization within the church so generally and to such an extreme as now. It seems to parallel or partake of our late century's zeitgeist—the primitive, vengeful demonization and, where possible, dismissal or nullification of one ethnic or interest group by another, in turn provoking that almost inevitable Newtonian equal and opposite reaction. Many in the church are, I fear, presently closer to fulfilling the haunting pre-World War I prophecy William Butler Yeats made in his poem "The Second Coming" than ever before: "The best lack all conviction, while the worst are full of passionate intensity."

My list of cherished skeptics, which if anything gets longer as I continue to read and ponder, includes, besides Montaigne and Voltaire, advocates of *saguna* (as opposed to *nirguna*) Hinduism (the existential principle *tat tvam asi*—"that thou art"—over, say, the elephant-headed

Ganesh); Aristotle (as opposed to Plato); Euripides (instead of Sophocles); Ben Jonson's comedy (over Shakespeare's); Racine (over Corneille); possibly Goethe (more than Schiller, though the latter is a far better dramatist); Keats (rather than Shelley or Wordsworth); Flaubert, Zola, and Proust (over Balzac, Dumas, and Hugo); Dostoevsky (more than Tolstoy, although which of the two was more questioning is not a simple issue); Tagore (more than Gandhi); Camus (over Sartre); Sakharov (more than Solzhenitsyn); Aleksandr Herzen, Isaiah Berlin, Learned Hand, Richard Rorty, John Ralston Saul, and many a contemporary investigative reporter.

Perhaps I need to clarify what I mean by "skepticism." It does not involve cynicism; it does involve honest, candid critical examination. There is a tremendous difference. These words of Learned Hand nicely make that distinction:

> The spirit of liberty is the spirit which is not too sure that it is right . . . seeks to understand the minds of other men and women . . . weighs their interests alongside its own without bias . . . remembers that not even a sparrow falls to earth unheeded . . . is the spirit of Him who, near two thousand years ago, taught mankind that lesson it has never learned, but has never quite forgotten; that there may be a kingdom where the least shall be heard and considered side by side with the greatest.[12]

And elsewhere,

> We do not seek to teach truth; but how to think; that is the chief difference between ourselves and all totalitarians. . . . Almost any experiment is in the end less dangerous than its suppression. . . . Life is complex and universals slippery and perilous. . . . The temper of detachment and scrutiny is not beguiling; men find it more often a cool jet than a stimulus . . . [but it is] anything but cold or neutral, for the last acquisition of civilized man is forbearance in judgment and to it is necessary one of the highest efforts of the will. . . . I adhere to the notion . . . stated by Holmes, that in politics—and for that matter in ethics—we are always faced with the insoluble

> problem of striking a balance between incommensurables, and that for the solution there are no standards or tests, save what will prove the most nearly acceptable compromise; what will most accord with existing conventions.[13]

How reminiscent of the Prophet Joseph's assertion: "'By proving contraries,' truth is made manifest."[14] Skepticism is, in Hand's words, knowing "how to think"; it is critical thinking, not criticism; "forbearance in judgment" rather than the forcing of nice resolutions and all-too-neat conclusions. There is in disjointedness a certain reality and corresponding wisdom. If we try too much to codify or contain it, we violate a veritable life principle, rendering that principle all too predictable and monotonous, lifeless, static, and, according to Lehi, dead (see 2 Nephi 2:10–11).

Neither abandoning nor overly criticizing the church enables one to maintain that essential life-giving balance. Instead, in my experience, surrendering to the mundane things the church prescribes noticeably stretches one in the direction of becoming less self-referential and both more aware of and more genuinely caring toward others. This process involves our putting up with those with whom we would otherwise not choose to associate; to do any less would surely be to default against the Lord's ultimate imperative that, without exception, we love all others. It may involve curbing our own precocious babblings or anything we might say that could be misunderstood or give offense. It also entails our joining the chorus of optimistic, faith-filled affirmation vis-à-vis the church's mission and everything else that would strengthen others' fundamental testimonies and respect for the institution and the gospel it calls us to live.

It may be easier for me to speak this way and to advocate mundane things because of my age. With time we become, it is said, creatures of habit and more ritualistic. (I've also heard that we become less dogmatic, which may help balance the first tendency.) From a distance, many of us tend to admire the asceticism of more ancient and esoteric traditions—for example, the austerity of celibate monks with their rosaries and prayer wheels. Perhaps Mormons achieve a similar beatific state with our hymns and the increasingly formulaic rhetoric of our ecclesiastical discourse. A closer parallel might be Hasidic Jews and their self-insulated families. And maybe that isn't all bad. But in the sense I'm using the term, settling for the mundane involves a lot more. Its most challenging aspect is attitudinal—how we view both others and what, overtly or not, we are charged with in their behalf.

The humanities and the bedrock of experience

The choice between sympathy and intellectual distance

I have said little thus far of what is, for me, the important contribution of philosophically serious art and literature.

The late Isaiah Berlin perhaps best expressed the unique and vital function of truly humane letters. As he made clear, the humanities at their best (like nothing else I know of except the Holy Spirit, with which they have much in common) require discrimination and discernment regarding the nuances and complexities, the moral ambiguity of real life in a way that pious, self-assured pronouncements seldom do. They do something else, as I think the following statement suggests: human beings "demand sympathy, and a sympathy that is extended only to obedient or likeable characters is not worth having. Real sympathy is the benign sentence handed down to those who do not deserve it. . . . We know that ______ is the real home of this sympathy precisely because it routinely demands from us a sympathy that we could not possibly want to extend, in real life, to real people—to murderers, to bores."[15] To fill in that blank line, what expressions come most readily to mind? Perhaps "the Savior." Or "the gospel." Or "the Holy Spirit." In fact, the statement's context is a discussion of the German writer Thomas Mann, and the term I deliberately withheld was "the novel." However, the statement's author, a literary critic, also adds the following important precaution, which the aesthetically and intellectually disposed often fail to heed: "The very freedom of art—that it is not the same as life—can lull us into isolation."[16] Or, as I recall Tolstoy scholar R. P. Blackmur somewhere expressing it, "There is between sensualists and intellectuals an identity of ends. The one pursues a titillation of the flesh, the other a titillation of the mind."

My own disclaimer, again from the previously quoted missionary journal and reflecting impressions during a fuller than ordinary and far more intense immersion in church activity:

> I often think these days of that charge by higher critics of the church that we are all robots, all sheep. Then I look at what rugged individuals our outstanding members have to be in this environment, how self-denying and committed and discerning our leaders have to be—each at every step required to exercise initiative along with constant inspiration—how mature all must be to work together in team fashion (and by contrast how egotistical and self-centered those are who can or will not). And I have to smile at how, in fundamental ways, those higher critics are dead wrong. Of course, common agreement on and full acceptance of certain fundamental principles is presupposed by the church. But what's so wrong with that if they're also true principles, and the Lord's? That's reason enough to defer to those who are the stewards of the structure that allows the entire dynamic we call the church to work at all. This leads me to a keener sense of why intellectuals rarely join the church: in their versatile, resilient minds they can, under any circumstances, too readily distract themselves. Others, less verbally or conceptually disposed, are more vividly aware of our common existential deficiency—for which life's cruder, more obviously escapist distractions clearly do not compensate. The life of the mind and the aesthetic sense are, moreover, such powerful and comprehensive surrogates, such subtle spiritual imitations (and often as not religion's legitimate enhancements) that intellectuals can remain too easily distracted, too comfortable, too self-satisfied.

But back to Isaiah Berlin's particular insight about aesthetic and intuitive sensitization, in the characterization of yet another commentator:

> Berlin argues that below the regular phenomena of public life, which provide grist for the mills of social scientists, there exists a . . . level of reality which is apprehended best by novelists, historians, and statesmen. Those unlikely allies have one thing in common: an appreciation of the particular, the concrete, and the ineffable. At their best, they work with a sense of tact about unprecedented situations. They know how to capture the character of an event and to feel the texture of a culture. By a kind of intuition, which cannot be defined, they get at

> the bedrock of experience, which cannot be reduced to laws. They work aesthetically with the *je ne sais quoi* of life. . . . It is a kind of knowledge, but not the kind that lends itself to general propositions, because it exists at the "level of half-articulate habits, unexamined assumptions and ways of thought, semi-instinctive reactions, models of life so deeply embedded as not to be felt consciously at all."[17]

In my view, such art—and such literature—provides what, in his recent commencement address at BYU, Sir John Templeton, the recipient of an honorary doctorate, described as "a bracing dose of reality."[18]

Nowadays, psychologists and counselors generally recognize that what they call "denial" and the suppression of horrendous experience is self-destructive and far worse than its confrontation. Our mandate to so confront the less than ideal stems directly from the Savior, who, as cited in John, declared that to know the truth is to be made "free" (John 8:32). As the Prophet Joseph Smith memorably asserted: "Thy mind, O Man, if thou wilt lead a soul unto salvation, must stretch as high as the utmost Heavens, and search into and contemplate the lowest considerations of the darkest abyss, and expand upon the broad considerations of eternal expanse."[19]

That is also the enterprise in which particularly Mormon intellectuals thoughtfully and sensitively engage—again upon the enlightened premise that, as one essayist described Hannah Arendt's views,

> Good can be radical; evil can never be radical, it can only be extreme, for it possesses [no] depth . . . yet—and this is its horror!—it can spread like a fungus over the surface of the earth and lay waste the entire world. Evil comes from a failure to think. It defies thought for as soon as thought tries to engage itself with evil and examine the premises and principles from which it originates, it is frustrated because it finds nothing there. That is the banality of evil.[20]

I also believe that intellectuals mostly endeavor, in the words of Richard Ellman, "to save what is eccentric and singular from being sanitized and standardized, to replace a morality of severity by one of sympathy"[21] (again that secular term, which does not, I believe, seriously depart in either spirit or intent from the nonjudgmentalness and charity we are charged with in the scriptures). Thomas Cahill echoes the same sentiment in his claim that "in the Gospel story, the passionate, the outsized, the out-of-control"—the same kinds of oddball, off-center personalities that attracted Jesus—"have a better shot at seizing heaven than the contained, the calculating, and those of whom this world approves."[22] But even if Cahill is correct in his claim, it does not excuse us from trying to get along with others. As Mormon intellectuals, we too often naively assume we can—with our heady, unconventional insights—reach and appeal to the majority of our sisters and brethren, with whom ongoing fellowship and rapport are equally essential for at least our salvation, if not theirs. But what attracts us may repel them. That is our dilemma.

John Sorensen, the respected Mormon anthropologist, recently called to my and others' attention an insightful little book, *Systems of Survival*, that makes a useful distinction between two kinds of social organization: "commercial" and "guardian." Almost all religions unavoidably belong to the second category and expect their adherents to "be obedient and disciplined," "adhere to tradition," "be loyal," "show fortitude," and "treasure honor."[23] The author, Jane Jacobs, lists other features of the same syndrome that are, at least on the surface, less praiseworthy. Still, she asserts our need for both systems as a kind of counterbalance to each other and, I would add, because there are truly important values variously associated with both. If we are not careful, we can too easily dismiss and denigrate those values with contentiousness and excessive criticism—as serious and costly a problem as the imbalance in the opposite direction through gullibility, naiveté, or the failure to discriminate and discern. (Religion itself reminds us that we cannot successfully counteract such imbalance without the influence of the Spirit and a willingness, with its help, to perceive and respond in ways that often contradict our personal views or inclinations.) Surely one of the values stemming from the "guardian" or religious system is sacrifice, which, in a subtle but meaningful sense, may entail the personal forfeiture of our often strongly held notions—or at least of our insistence that others agree or even hear us out.

The church as a schoolmaster

As we do our mundane homework, we are trained and train others in the solidarity of becoming Christ's

As for that other often mundane assignment we so frequently honor in the breach or superficially—home and visiting teaching—I think I understand, as the leader of a high priests group, what an important difference it not only can but often does make, though we may not so readily sense it. It can be a real lifeline. Even the shortest, irregular visit reminds the "less active" that they are still affiliated with and remembered by the body of the church. Without home and visiting teaching, I believe we would, even among the active and in our neighborhoods, become as much strangers to one another—as limited in our sphere of acquaintances and as lonely—as is generally the case in the larger, secular society of which we are also, sometimes far too much, such an integral component.

Just this week, after another seemingly perfunctory series of personal priesthood interviews with home teachers, I recognized as never before how much so many of those with whom I associate willingly, almost invisibly, extend themselves beyond mere words in behalf of our ward's many widows and single mothers: repairing cars, taking the widows to restaurants, befriending and effectively counseling with young persons bent on self-defeating courses of action. In most such cases, I really see no one else but their home teachers standing by in behalf of these members. True, not everyone is that kind of a home teacher, though all should be. And not every home or visiting teacher is given the chance.

The three committees designated for doing the work of the church in each local priesthood group or quorum—focusing on preaching the gospel, redeeming the dead, and perfecting the saints—are a further case in point. In most wards where I have lived, these committees are either perfunctory or defunct—not appreciably relieving the bishop or addressing the needs of individual members. But where they do meaningfully function, what a difference! The men involved begin to sense the exhilaration of exercising their priesthood in a truly helpful way and become closer. This seems to bear out another inviolate principle: the more we expend ourselves in any worthwhile endeavor, the more purposeful and precious it and our attachment to it then become. (From what I have seen, recent initiatives involving young men and women ages 12–18 in more actively conducting their own meetings and teaching one another—even before they are old enough to serve missions—is having the same salutary effect in stimulating faith and strengthening testimony.)

In this mortal state, we do not, as far as we know, choose the families to which we end up belonging. Nor do we as parents choose those utterly unique and sometimes difficult personalities who come into our charge and then obligate us to claim and love them as forever our own. There also seems to be a providentially wise purpose in requiring us to fellowship and address as "brother" and "sister" those with whom we might otherwise have next to nothing in common and whom we must similarly make the effort to get to know, care about, and—however inconvenient or annoying—put up with. The Lord loves each of them as much as he loves you and me. As stewards for one another—they for us and we for them—we truly become his disciples and pastors as we could in no other way.

Bonhoeffer put it best:

> The Bible speaks with remarkable frequency of "bearing." It is capable of expressing the whole work of Jesus Christ in this one word. . . . It is the fellowship of the Cross to experience the burden of the other. If one does not experience it, the fellowship he belongs to is not Christian. . . . It is, first of all, the *freedom* of the other person . . . that is a burden to the Christian. . . . The freedom of the other person includes all that we mean by a person's nature, individuality, endowment. It also includes his weaknesses and oddities, which are such a trial to our patience, everything that produces frictions, conflicts, and collisions among us. . . . This will prove especially difficult where varying strength and weakness in faith are bound together in a fellowship. The weak must not judge the strong, the strong must not despise the weak. The weak must guard against pride, the strong against indifference. . . . If the strong person falls, the weak one must guard his heart against malicious joy at his downfall. If the weak one falls, the strong one

> must help him rise again in all kindness. The one needs as much patience as the other.[24]

Bonhoeffer might well have added that by almost everyone's (particularly almost every intellectual's) definition, "the strong" is oneself, while "the weak" represents those who oppose that self or disagree.

A final journal entry echoes this Old Testament passage: "And now, Israel, what doth the Lord thy God require of thee, but to fear the Lord thy God, to walk in all his ways, and to love him, and to serve the Lord thy God with all thy heart and with all thy soul, To keep the commandments of the Lord, and his statutes, which I command thee this day for thy good?" (Deuteronomy 10:12–13). The entry:

> What characterizes those who distinctively and positively contribute to the kingdom as opposed to those who just go along for the ride (recognizing that there is a little of both in each of us)?
>
> 1. Generosity and caring about others, with an inclination and a willingness to be inconvenienced and sacrifice in their behalf—to be more a giver than a taker;
> 2. Subordination of one's will and idiosyncratic preferences to the Lord's will, particularly in the context of his church (which also means complying with the expectations of those we consider his mouthpieces). This requires meekness and humility, which can be a further test of those who are already generous and caring but mostly in their own preferred way;
> 3. Common sense and moderation, avoiding the irrationality and fanaticism that too often beset us; and
> 4. Constancy and reliability in exercising the three foregoing qualities, without which we can readily undo what we may have already accomplished.

In the 1980s, the valiant Polish shipyard workers inspired us and gave all peoples a new communal slogan, *solidarność*. In "the household of the Saints," we can do no less than cultivate our own solidarity with one another—which solidarity no one, no faction, is absolved from fostering and promoting.

In Galatians, Paul argues that "the law was our schoolmaster to bring us unto Christ, that we might be justified by faith. But after that faith is come, we are no longer under a schoolmaster" (Galatians 3:24–25). Perhaps the process of spiritual growth and ongoing discipleship is similar to the historical movement from the Old to the New Covenant. "Process" is here an important notion, because the schooling Paul alludes to and our need for it seem never-ending. In any event, the church serves us individually as such a schoolmaster. Schoolmasters are not always charismatic, nor are their assignments particularly enticing. But the assumption is that as we do our homework, we are disciplined and trained to do what will in turn most meaningfully serve both our needs and those of others.

Yes, I increasingly believe in the importance of doing certain very mundane things. What things? My young bishop, who is also my son-in-law, keeps a list on his office wall, mostly as a self-reminder. On the list are three items: home teaching, temple attendance, and well-prepared family home evenings. He likens these to the exercises we need to put ourselves through in order to play the piano—the Wieck and Czerny that precede the Chopin and Scriabin. So what things do I believe it's important to be doing? All the prescribed things. And then the many other things. "These ought ye to have done, and not to leave the other undone" (Matthew 23:23).

Notes

1. An earlier version of this essay was presented at the 1998 Sunstone Symposium and published in *Sunstone*, December 1998, 48–58.

2. See also Patrick G. Coy, "The One-Person Revolution of Ammon Hennacy," in *A Revolution of the Heart: Essays on the Catholic Worker*, ed. Patrick G. Coy (Philadelphia: Temple University Press, 1988), 168.

3. Jeffrey R. Holland, "'A Teacher Come from God,'" *Ensign*, May 1998, 25–27.

4. Elaine Pagels, *The Origin of Satan* (New York: Random House, 1995).

5. Personal correspondence from Robert A. Rees.

6. Erich Neumann, *The Origins and History of Consciousness* (Princeton: Princeton University Press, 1954); see pages 66–101, 220–56.

7. A sample of the works I have in mind from each of these authors is Dietrich Bonhoeffer, *Life Together*, trans. John. W. Doberstein (New York: Harper, 1954); Thomas Merton, *Seeds of Contemplation* (Norfolk, CT: New Directions Books, 1949); Simone Weil, *Waiting for God*, trans. Emma Crauford (New York: Putnam, 1951);

Reinhold Niebuhr, *The Essential Reinhold Niebuhr: Selected Essays and Addresses*, ed. Robert McAfee Brown (New Haven, CT: Yale University Press, 1986); and Alexander Elchaninov, *The Diary of a Russian Priest*, trans. Helen Iswolsky (London: Faber and Faber, 1967).

8. Andrey Tarkovsky, *Sacrifice* (Sweden: Svenska Filminstitut [Beverly Hills, CA: Pacific Arts Video], 1986), motion picture.

9. Reinhold Niebuhr, *The Irony of American History* (New York: Charles Scribner's Sons, 1952), 63.

10. Alan Wolfe, "Groups and Happiness," review of Nancy L. Rosenblum's *Membership and Morals: The Personal Uses of Pluralism in America*, *New Republic,* June 1, 1998, 40.

11. "Articles of Faithlessness of the Church of Liberal-Dissenting Scholars," Scholarly & Historical Information Exchange for Latter-Day Saints (SHIELDS) website, accessed May 14, 2015, www.shields-research.org/Humor/AoFless.htm.

12. Gerald Gunther, *Learned Hand: The Man and the Judge* (New York: Alfred A. Knopf, 1994), 549.

13. Gunther, *Learned Hand*, 628–29, 387, 495.

14. Dean C. Jessee, ed., *The Papers of Joseph Smith, Volume 1: Autobiographical and Historical Writings* (Salt Lake City: Deseret Book, 1989), 447.

15. James Wood, "The Master of the Not Quite," *New Republic,* June 1, 1998, 32–33.

16. Wood, "The Master of the Not Quite," 36.

17. Robert Darnton, "Free Spirit," *New York Review of Books,* June 26, 1997, 11.

18. Sir John Templeton, BYU commencement address, April 23, 1998, not published.

19. Joseph Smith, in Dean C. Jessee and John W. Welch, "Revelations in Context: Joseph Smith's Letter from Liberty Jail, March 20, 1839," *BYU Studies* 39/3 (2000): 137; spelling and punctuation standardized.

20. Amos Elon, "Introduction: The Excommunication of Hannah Arendt," in Hannah Arendt, *Eichmann in Jerusalem: A Report on the Banality of Evil* (New York: Penguin, 2006), xiii–xiv.

21. Richard Ellman, *Oscar Wilde* (New York: Alfred A. Knopf, 1987), 589.

22. Thomas Cahill, *How the Irish Saved Civilization: The Untold Story of Ireland's Heroic Role from the Fall of Rome to the Rise of Medieval Europe* (New York: Doubleday, 1995), 123.

23. Jane Jacobs, *Systems of Survival: A Dialogue on the Moral Foundations of Commerce and Politics* (New York: Random House, 1992), 215.

24. Bonhoeffer, *Life Together,* 101–2.

Part 2

Now Come, Saith the Lord, and Let Us Reason

To those who in their turn selectively handle Mormon history and discourage our probing it in a number of areas, one needs to say (or at least to ask): Haven't we been, if anything, overly cautious, overly mistrustful, overly condescending to a membership and a public who are far more perceptive and discerning than we often give them credit for? Haven't we too much deprived individuals of needful occasions for personal growth and more in-depth life-probing experience?

—From "Thoughts about Joseph Smith: Upon Reading Donna Hill's *Joseph Smith: The First Mormon*"

I see the truly religious more readily presupposing that if there are wrongs, injustices, and misunderstandings, it is not so much for them to scapegoat and project blame as to look to themselves, change their own uncharitable viewpoint, and—irrespective of who is most culpable—still accept, forgive, and nonjudgmentally commit to resolving differences. In this mode, believers are, I submit—both emotionally and spiritually—far more flexible and open to change, to be worked upon and to work upon themselves, as well as more amenable to future contingency.

—From "'Bumping': On Reconciling Contemporary Views of Knowledge and Causation with the Restored Gospel"

Following page: Thomas F. Rogers, *Buddhist Monk*, Nanjing, China, pastel

Riding the Edge of the Herd

During my time as director of the BYU Honors Program, I was privileged to receive some frank communications from students touching on their feelings about BYU and the church. As much as possible, I did my best to address their concerns and encourage them in their faith. At the same time, I also tried, when and where I could, to be an advocate in appropriate ways for their concerns. The following represents one such attempt, in the form of a letter (edited here for clarity and length) to a longtime friend and fellow academic who was at the time directing the honors program at another university and simultaneously serving on the church's Correlation Committee. Although it's been almost forty years since I wrote the following letter, it seems to me that much of it still applies today. I never heard back from my friend in response, and I doubt that my letter was ever shared with other members of the committee. (My response to the student whose letter I quote here at length is included in this volume as "Letter to a Doubting Former Student.")

Dear Friend,

I AM IMPELLED TO WRITE IN HOPES you will share my comments with your colleagues on the Correlation Committee—not that any of you haven't already entertained, even espoused these same thoughts before now. My purpose is mostly to reinforce to what extent it is an ongoing concern in my mind and that of others.

The other day, I observed to you that at times, some of us here at BYU feel "muzzled." As I recall, your response was something along the lines that this should not surprise us: after all, what more can we expect? That, I suppose, is what I would like to speak to here. What, as an institution of higher learning, ought we at BYU to be able to expect, and why?

The truth is that not all of us are capable of the kind of self-restraint that would keep our muzzles consistently in place. So we give ourselves away from time to time, even when we don't intend to. And even if some busybody doesn't report us, we feel guilty—assuming that if such a thing were to happen, the leaders we serve and really want to please would automatically take the side of the person objecting to our opinions. But should we have to think so, and should we have to endure such paranoia? For the sake of the church, particularly its youth, I hope not.

Let me illustrate their poignant dilemma by sharing a desperate plea from a virtuous and sensitive former student of mine, now in his second year at the J. Reuben Clark School of Law. Here is his statement:

> I am frankly having a difficult time reconciling the way I currently perceive the world with a sustained commitment to the church as an institution. I'm going to try to lay out some of my concerns and would be interested in your response or in some opportunity to discuss them with you when you have time.
>
> . . . It seems to me that the church has gone to great lengths to institutionalize pseudo-events. For example, general conference is now a carefully staged performance where our deepest concerns and problems are hinted at only abstractly. . . . We seem primarily concerned with projecting an image that will impress the outsider and not offend the weakest of the saints. Honest I–Thou communication between speaker and hearer is therefore infrequent. . . .
>
> Our family has always been quite close. Yet, formal religious observances such as family home evening have tended to be destructive rather than conducive to family spirit. Perhaps my father is just too pious when he decides it is time to be officially religious. In any event, the spontaneous closeness that so often has characterized our relationships tends to disappear when an attempt is made to institutionalize it.
>
> Testimony bearing and interviews of course are intended as outlets for what is in the heart. For me they have generally been occasions only to try to meet the expectations of the hearer, and my pronouncements often have had less than a one-to-one correspondence with what was going on inside.

Home teachers of course are often the last persons many members of the church would ever confide in. Nonetheless an enormous amount of guilt production compels many of us to continually carry out routine and meaningless visits. . . .

Second, I think members of the church in their adherence to forms tend to escape from freedom and responsibility, thus limiting severely the possibility of their development as individuals. For example, the endless quest for strict guidelines regarding Sunday activities, movie viewing, and permissible educational and artistic pursuits, the willing deliverance to the church of nearly all free time, and the continual effort to identify the providential design behind every happening strike me largely as efforts to eliminate the burdens of being free agents. If the hand of God can be found behind all occurrences, it is easier to accept them and feel absolved of responsibility to shape events. If church leaders provide rules delimiting all behavior, the anxiety attending difficult choices is eliminated and the possibility of despairing what might have been disappears. Insofar as responsibilities for choices are eliminated, the capacity to make choices atrophies. People, I think, may become self-defeated rather than self-actualized.

Third, I think too rigid observance of forms leads us to view people primarily as filling roles rather than as being viable human beings who have human frailties and susceptibilities to biological needs. Consequently, we overburden ourselves with guilt when we respond in human fashion to stimuli in ways that are not consistent with perceived rules. When I was in high school, I thought I had to be an example. I carried around the weight of the world on my shoulders. I couldn't miss seminary to play on the freshman basketball team. I couldn't act like a kid. I responded emotionally to the gospel but felt it to be an enormous burden and felt then, and do now, that an enormous burden would be lifted from my shoulders if I could find out that it wasn't true. Still, that would be a horrifying discovery for I have always viewed the alternative to the gospel as chaos. . . . [My sister] has a friend who my parents suggested to her would make a great Mormon. Her reaction: "You wouldn't want to do that to her." . . .

This year as I have struggled along I have enjoyed church occasionally, been disturbed occasionally. My most profound

> religious moments have been when I was alone, a couple of them when I could not bear to attend priesthood meeting and simply read while enjoying the beauty of the outdoors. Emotionally I feel very deeply committed to my past spiritual experiences, and to my cultural heritage. To sever ties with these would be impossible. On the other hand, I cannot imagine how I am going to be able to commit large amounts of my time, energy, and efforts to the church when I see it . . . damaging people as a result of prejudices deeply rooted in the institution's image of itself.
>
> You obviously have had similar conflicts. How do you resolve them?

How does one answer such strong charges? Not, I submit, by denying or minimizing them. Note that one of this student's chief concerns is the thought control, the facile glossing over, and the outright dishonesty (however subtle) that he sees here and there in the church. Perhaps most others would never pick up on much of what he perceives. But even if he is in the intellectual minority among church members, it is an increasingly important minority, many of whom are as loyal as the most devout "iron rodders," or leastways wish to be. And they have much to offer us. We dare not lose them by selling them short or riding roughshod over their concerns. Not even, I believe, if there were only one of them. I think the Savior had something to say, for that matter, about paying particular attention and giving special care to exceptions, to "the one," the "lost sheep." And how often, when—angrily, disrespectfully—one of them lashes out at us, or at the church in general, do we fail to recognize the cry for help, for acceptance, for long-suffering love and fellowship such outbursts really entail? I am sure the Savior would see them in that benevolent light, even when we do not and when we consequently withhold what they most need and what would heal them, which is anything but our condemnation.

In the church, as in the world, there is presently too much apathy, indifference, intolerance, suspicion, mistrust, disdain, and judgmentalness. I see this depressing array of demeaning attitudes at work in several directions: between peers, from subordinates toward those in authority, and from those in authority toward subordinates. This state of affairs is, I believe, aggravated by our failure to respect, let alone appreciate, one another's individuality and that diversity in taste and outlook that render our individuality meaningful and sacred. We are intolerant of different views, even if sincerely subscribed to, even when they do us no real harm except to intimate that perhaps we, like others, ought not always be so sure of our opinions. For some reason, we are disposed to insist on certainty in all things, insecure and threatened when others aren't certain along with us and in the same way. This causes us alternately to fear and to resent one another, to erect barriers of mistrust and suspicion instead of reaching the bedrock of complete candor, mutual acceptance, and unimpeded soul-to-soul communion.

Such was always the social condition of humanity and such it will always be, with perhaps one or two notable or fortunate exceptions in the experience of some of us. But it is disappointing when such trust and rapport are not more in evidence in the society of the church. They are the foundation of any profound brotherly love. Their absence only impedes it. That is why, I believe, so many in the church, and, yes, on the BYU campus, are in fact so lonely. They are playing obsequious roles. They fear letting their true selves "hang out" and so never really make contact, except superficially.

This is probably less true, proportionately, of honors students. I have observed more than once, half but only half in jest, that what distinguishes them from other students is mostly their glibness and their self-confidence. But there is something else: they also tend to be more serious in pursuing the life of the mind. They therefore tend, to a greater degree, to question, to objectify, to be critical—and hence, right or wrong, to be frustrated and sometimes deeply disappointed with the answers at hand. In my view, this in no way diminishes their worth or their worthiness. Often just the opposite!

Toward these same students I have, in the last two years, though without any official mandate, acquired a deep sense of philosophical purpose and personal mission. I have felt an increasing need and urgency to insure that the BYU Honors Program would serve: (1) to "stretch" certain of our students in their attitudes, toleration of alien views, and breadth of insight, as well as to encourage an increased posture of tentativeness with respect to issues that are less simple and for which answers are less clear or definitive than is often assumed, and (2) to provide an atmosphere in which well-intended, essentially loyal but often impulsive and troubled young intellectuals can assert their opinions without fearing censorship or disapproval from either their peers or their mentors and can even err in their struggle to arrive at understanding and still feel they are accepted and fellowshipped by other Latter-day Saints. I've wanted potential dissidents to feel there is at least one place in the church and at BYU where the door is always open—where, if they so care, a place will gladly be made for them.

These students' dilemma is, I believe, not only concerned with but itself illustrative of the hard but sympathetic analysis Thomas O'Dea, a non-LDS sociologist of religion, has put to us:

> Has [the Mormon church] attempted to devise new programs to point the way to meaningful action that are in any way commensurate with the magnitude of the problems themselves? Or has it continued by and large its older, highly active and highly organized programs along conventional lines, programs that the critics of Mormonism a decade and a half ago saw as stereotyped routinization and fast becoming "activity for activity's sake"? . . . Does the Mormon church offer its converts a pathway to significant living amid the great transition of our age or does it offer them a defensive halfway house in which they can escape the confrontation that modernity presents to them? Does it offer them a context for growth and maturation in the face of the enormous challenges of the times or does it give them an anachronistic community, segregated in spirit, that makes life easier but avoids precisely those challenges that the modern religious man must face if he is to find ethical and religious authenticity? In short are the Mormon converts converted because they find in the Mormon church a deeper understanding of the divine–human encounter and consequently a more authentic religious life that enables them to live reasonably and ethically with the upsetting crisis of our day? Or are they converted because they find in the Mormon church a reinforcement of older values and attitudes that had been undermined and threatened by the conditions of our times?[1]

The same questions are reiterated by our church historian Leonard Arrington: "Whether a program-oriented approach to the ideological and social conflicts of today can continue to receive the full commitment of the Mormon people, and especially the young, remains to be seen." Although Brother Arrington reassures us that "as of the moment there is impressive external evidence that it is doing so,"[2] I am here of course suggesting that we look at the *internal* evidence as well—however more difficult it might be to measure, however less rosy its prognostications.

There is of course a fine and even treacherous line between the exercise of one's independence, integrity, and fortitude (all spiritual attributes) and their perversion in a wanton, insubordinate transgression of sacred standards. That may nevertheless be one of the risks we are expected to take in this life. And many of us who profess to "profess" to LDS youth draw that line, in my view, with far too comfortable a margin of safety. In so doing, we lose credibility and the very respect we would engender in behalf of the religious viewpoint we endeavor to represent to those we teach.

As for the questions alluded to by O'Dea and Arrington, *we* do not necessarily raise them. Our students raise them for us. In accommodating such questions—which, again, I think are symptomatic of the concerns of many youth outside the honors program and throughout the church (hence my reason for sharing this with you)—I do so on the following assumptions:

1. If our youth are not encouraged, at least while in college, to think for themselves, many will be found wanting and ill-equipped when finally tested or subjected to moral or spiritual crises at some later time in their lives. For some, that time is *not* in fact later, it is *now*, or even several years ago.

2. If we are confident enough that the gospel, as we understand it, embraces the truth, we need not fear the truth, whatever its context. Our ability always to discern truth is of course another matter; but there is nothing in the doctrine that, to my knowledge, suggests we should not confront all theories and all propositions and would not be able, if we are in tune with the Spirit, to so discern. For that same purpose we ought, I believe, to expose ourselves more than we do to antithetical viewpoints: for example, inviting those with diverse views to the BYU campus, if only in order to "know our enemy."

3. It follows from all that we say about the sacredness of agency that we should demonstrate a particularly high level of tolerance for one

another's right and need to think and act according to our individual light, respecting one another's integrity and good conscience. Sincerity is of course not integrity, nor is integrity objective truth. But what is so wrong with allowing someone else to be wrong (at least as we view him or her), meanwhile encouraging though never requiring that person to see things as we do?

4. Because so much in life is paradoxical and uncertain, the wisest posture to take toward its abundant mystery and complexity is one of tentativeness. Here the adage seems apt that we tend to be most certain of that about which we are most ignorant. BYU President Dallin Oaks (later called as an apostle) has himself said, "Some people . . . don't have tolerance for uncertainty. I think we need to mature in that area; as a people we need to be more mature in our ability to handle differences of opinion and uncertainties about the extent of our knowledge."[3] (Because the sources of religious knowledge are of another order and, in fact, to the religious mind, the one thing in this life we can completely rely on, we need of course to make a notable exception for what one can know by faith.)

5. The appropriate degree of reliance upon ecclesiastical authority also needs to be wisely discerned. For this purpose the landmark guidelines set down by J. Reuben Clark Jr., then a member of the First Presidency, serve as an inspired and weighty precedent. According to President Clark, the requirement for us to be moved upon by the Holy Ghost in order to know when church leaders are speaking by the power of the Holy Ghost "shifts the responsibility from [the speakers] to us to determine when they so speak."[4] In this connection, he quotes Brigham Young's statement about being "more afraid that this people have so much confidence in their leaders that they will not inquire for themselves of God whether they are led by Him."[5]

6. In dealing with one another, truth, interpersonal harmony, and individual spiritual growth are all best served by far-reaching perspective, circumspection, and appreciation for and demonstration of meekness, gentle persuasion, and respect for others' agency and intellectual independence. Trust breeds further trust—developing conscience, inspiring loyalty and goodwill—and needs to be risked and exercised with greater faith than we are generally inclined to do. Trust is also a

wise strategy when those who are trusted are themselves individuals of good faith, however limited their vision and understanding.

I would add that there has been a self-congratulatory facet to our celebration of the United States Bicentennial and an excessively patriotic identification of Mormon with American tradition (and mores), which, as an international church, we can ill afford. A more independent-minded and truly history-conscious membership would have a more far-reaching perspective. How ironic indeed that the vigilante mentality of our politically most vocal and most self-assured members so closely resembles how one historian characterizes the attitudes of the church's enemies in nineteenth-century Missouri and Illinois:

> The exposure of subversion was a means of promoting unity, but it also served to clarify national values and provide the individual ego with a sense of high moral sanction and imputed righteousness. Nativists identified themselves repeatedly with a strangely incoherent tradition in which images of Pilgrims, Minute Men, Founding Fathers, and true Christians appeared in a confusing montage. . . . As the nativist searched for participation in a noble cause, for unity in a group sanctioned by tradition and authority, he professed a belief in democracy and equal rights. Yet in his very zeal for freedom he curiously assumed many of the characteristics of the imagined enemy. By condemning the subversive's fanatical allegiance to an ideology, he affirmed a similarly uncritical acceptance of a different ideology; by attacking the subversive's intolerance of dissent, he worked to eliminate dissent and diversity of opinion; by censuring the subversive for alleged licentiousness, he engaged in sensual fantasies; by criticizing the subversive's loyalty to an organization, he sought to prove his unconditional loyalty to the established order. . . . In a rootless environment shaken by bewildering social change the nativist found unity and meaning by conspiring against imaginary conspiracies.[6]

Sound familiar?

Equally distressing is the "super-American" image we have so unreservedly assumed since the 1890s, leading us to confuse spiritual with rank materialistic and philistine values, venerating affluence and settling all too readily for the electronic media's synthetic pop culture. There is something sinful about the television habit, something terribly wasteful of life and spirit, just as there is about cultivating a false appetite for superfluous leisure goods such as our adult toys (boats, campers, motorcycles) and ultrafashionable clothing and inducing people to pay more for them than they are worth. This is not to deny the inspiration and genius behind the Mormon amalgam of the spiritual and material, the heavenly and earthly. But we are true to the spirit of this unity of the spiritual and temporal only when our motive is pure and when we handle material and temporal phenomena in a consecrated manner. While we as a people give lip service to that notion, the world is still too much with us—in all the wrong ways.

Much as I have always been leery of what Christian philosopher Paul Tillich could possibly have to say to Mormons, his critique of Norman Vincent Peale strikes me as uncomfortably apropos:

> He heals people with the purpose of making them fit again for the demands of the competitive and conformist society in which we are living. . . . In many cases the increase of church membership and interest in religious activities does not mean much more than the religious consecration of a state of things in which the religious dimension has been lost. It is the desire to participate in activities which are socially strongly approved and give internal and a certain amount of external security.[7]

Tillich astutely points out the incompatibility of a certain lifestyle with an essential facet of any deeply personalized religion:

> No one can experience depth without stopping and becoming aware of himself. Only if he has moments in which he does not care about what comes next can he experience the meaning of this moment here and now and ask himself about the meaning of his life. As long as the preliminary, transitory concerns are not silenced, no matter how interesting and valuable and important they may be, the voice of the ultimate concern cannot be heard. This is the deepest root of the loss

> of the dimension of depth in our period—the loss of religion in its basic and universal meaning.[8]

There is evil in banality and in shortsighted materialistic busyness, and we need to be told about and reprimanded for it along with our other, more blatant sins. Instead, we tend to pay high obeisance to the propertied and those among us whose business it is to promote that very commercialized, covetous, conformist lifestyle—those for example in a position to invest and speculate or who wield corporate power. One of our stake presidents, about the most Christlike man I have ever known, has, I know, long deplored the special attention we give our "successful" businessmen—naming buildings for them and the like—and the consequent identification this creates in many a student's mind between material success, prominence, and "making it" in the church. It is no coincidence that today the majority of our brighter students aim for the more lucrative professions—particularly business administration, law, and medicine—and often evidence, as they do so, an all-too-eager hardheadedness about completing their undergraduate requirements and getting on with their graduate preparation. The absence of the relaxed, contemplative spirit that Tillich argues is so important to a profound religious mood precludes much authentic learning-for-its-own sake on the BYU campus—thus mocking the ideal of liberal or general education. Meditation, not *pre*meditation, is an essential component of both the spiritual and the truly consecrated life. But how much do we encourage it?

My viewpoint coincides with that of Elder B. H. Roberts as expressed in an article from the March 1933 *Improvement Era*:

> Moral Government . . . rests upon teaching the truth, leaving it by its innate force to win its way into the convictions of men and produce in them a self-control which will lead to adherence to truth, and hence to the right conduct as set forth by truth. This "Moral Government" rests upon "persuasion, long-suffering, gentleness, and meekness, and by love unfeigned, by kindness, and pure knowledge which shall greatly enlarge the soul without hypocrisy, and without guile, reproving betimes with sharpness when moved upon by the Holy Ghost"; but "no power or influence can or ought to be

> used," except by the principles named above, "and then showing forth afterwards an increase of love towards him whom thou hast reproved, lest he esteem thee to be his enemy." These are the forces operating in "Moral" or God's government.
>
> "Effective Government" is man's government and ultimately rests upon force, compulsion, fines, imprisonment, death itself; it rests ultimately upon bayonets. . . . Whatever may be conceded as to the necessity of enforcement of "Effective Government" for the purpose of restraining men from injuring one another, or to secure good order in society, it should never be invoked for enforcing orthodox beliefs or Church discipline.
>
> When "Moral Government" forsakes its high functions of teaching truth and leaving that truth to win its way by its own force of reasonableness, beauty, and beneficent effects as applied to life and turns to the uses of "Effective Government," it abandons its field of religion, confesses its own weakness, and its lack of faith in the power of truth to stand upon its own merits and win its way.[9]

So in reply to the assumption that in professing our disciplines my colleagues and I must be subject to the personal whims of one or another highly placed ecclesiastical spokesperson, I can only aver that however politic such a tactic may seem to be, it is also morally impossible. We should not have to be on the defensive in such matters. In fact, if we are to be worthy of our hire and at all adequately fulfill our particular mission in behalf of the youth who come to us, thereby serving the Lord and his kingdom, we dare not do so.

In magnifying our positions with basic goodwill and the best intent, moreover, we would, I hope, be recipients not only of our leaders' indulgence and toleration but their trust and their approbation. Those of my colleagues who have come under some of their hardest censure are among the church's most competent, most thoughtful, and essentially most loyal teachers. They particularly have earned that consideration.

I would also hope that if from time to time we upset one or two lone cranks, that too would be seen in perspective and weighed against the greater good and the enlightened cause we aim to serve, and that at the very least due process would be invoked in behalf of the parties involved. (That has not always been the case.) I would hope finally that there could be more appreciation for the difficult but important role we play in occasionally "riding the edge of the herd," as LDS historian Juanita Brooks's father so profoundly put it to her:

> My father early recognized my tendency to question, to disagree, to refuse to take many of the Old Testament stories at face value. I could not admire Jacob's ethics in stealing his brother's birthright; I did not believe that the wind from tin horns would blow down the walls of Jericho, but insisted that they "fell" figuratively when the guards panicked and ran; if bears came out and devoured the children who called Elijah "old bald-pate," I didn't think God sent them, etc., etc.
>
> One day Dad said to me, "My girl, if you follow this tendency to criticize, I'm afraid you will talk yourself out of the Church. I'd hate to see you do that. I'm a cowboy, and I've learned that if I ride *in* the herd, I am lost—totally helpless. One who rides counter to it is trampled and killed. One who only trails behind means little, because he leaves all responsibility to others. It is the cowboy who rides the edge of the herd, who sings and calls and makes himself heard who helps direct the course. . . . So don't lose yourself, and don't ride away and desert the outfit. Ride the edge of the herd and be alert, but know your directions, and call out loud and clear. Chances are, you won't make any difference, but on the other hand, you just might."[10]

I hope it is clear that this is not a personal attack on the church's leaders and certainly not a disputation of doctrine or even a critique of the institution so much as a lament for certain fundamental values of which we have, as a people, too much lost sight—to the peril of our salvation and the total efficacy of our mission to the world. My concern here is solely for the improved quality of our common endeavor. If I have belabored the obvious, I apologize. If I am deluded or in error, I beg to be corrected. If my attitude is perceived as heretical, then I am truly sorry, but so be it.

Sincerely your brother,
Tom

Notes

1. Thomas F. O'Dea, "Sources of Strain in Mormon History Reconsidered," in *Mormonism and American Culture*, ed. Marvin S. Hill and James B. Allen (New York: Harper & Row, 1972), 153–55.

2. Leonard J. Arrington, "Crisis in Identity: Mormon Responses in the Nineteenth and Twentieth Centuries," in *Mormonism and American Culture*, 184.

3. Dallin H. Oaks, "A Conversation with Dallin H. Oaks, President of Brigham Young University," *Ensign*, October 1975, 21.

4. J. Reuben Clark Jr., "When Are Church Leaders' Words Entitled to Claim of Scripture?" *Church News* section of *Deseret News*, July 31, 1954, 9.

5. Brigham Young, *Journal of Discourses*, 9:150.

6. David Brion Davis, "Some Themes of Counter-Subversion . . . ," *Mississippi Valley Historical Review* 47 (September 1960): 205–24, reprinted in *Mormonism and American Culture*, 66, 72–73.

7. Paul Tillich, "The Lost Dimension in Religion," reprinted in *Adventures of the Mind from the* Saturday Evening Post, ed. Richard Thruelsen and John Kobler (New York: Alfred Knopf, 1959), 55.

8. Tillich, "Lost Dimension," 50–51.

9. B. H. Roberts, "What College Did to My Religion," *Improvement Era*, March 1933, 261.

10. Davis Bitton and Maureen Ursenbach, "Riding Herd: A Conversation with Juanita Brooks," *Dialogue: A Journal of Mormon Thought* 9/1 (1974): 12.

Gospel Continuities

Mathematicians contend that the most powerful axioms and equations are at once the most simple and the most comprehensive. One day while presiding over a BYU student branch, a calling in which I frequently discoursed about the gospel with its members, I was struck by a sense of the restored gospel's profound universality. The term that most readily came to mind was continuity. *I was pleased to share that insight with those present, and later with new missionaries at the Missionary Training Center.*

What is the nature of those great visions that, as recorded in the Pearl of Great Price, were given to Enoch, Abraham, and Moses? We cannot know their full import. But from the accounts of these visions and from other latter-day scriptures, we catch a rewarding glimpse of the gospel's sweep and magnitude that had not been revealed to humanity for nearly two millennia—that is, since the ministry of Christ and his early disciples. Hence our profound understanding of Adam's fall (see 2 Nephi 2:15–25; Moses 5:11) and of the atonement (for example, see 2 Nephi 9–10; Alma 7:12).

As we consider these and other glorious doctrines, we begin to sense the awesome scope of God's plan and our own limitless possibilities. Particularly striking is the breadth of vision which, at a number of intriguing levels, the restored gospel affords. These metaphysical vistas might, for want of a better term, be labeled *continuities*. Each forcibly argues the restored gospel's uniqueness.

Eternal continuity

No other religion entertains such a sweeping vision of eternity. The concept of our limitless existence as intelligences, coexisting with God himself (see D&C 93:29), can only shock traditional theologians. But this teaching avoids the problems of a creation *ex nihilo* and the otherwise logical assumption that God, if he indeed created us entirely, is ultimately responsible for all we are and do. It validates free will as no other view of creation can. The doctrines of a premortal existence and a prior spiritual creation are in no other religious tradition spelled out so definitely or completely.

Similarly, while our understanding of the afterlife is vague in many particulars, the promise of exaltation, divine inheritance, joint dominion of the universe, celestial glory, and a literal resurrection are nowhere so fully comprehended or so explicitly stated as in Doctrine and Covenants 132 and the Book of Mormon's several assurances of a universal resurrection of our physical bodies and the perpetuation of our distinct personalities after death. In view of this limitless and glorious vision of eternity, no people have ever had greater incentive to live the commandments and to pattern their lives on that of the Savior.

Temporal continuity

The tie between Old and New Testament traditions, the concept of distinct historical dispensations, and the revelation of priesthood, baptism, and gospel principles from Adam forward is a perspective fully embraced by few if any others in either Judaism or Christianity. The identification of Christ with the Old Testament Jehovah (see 3 Nephi 15:4–5) and the Book of Mormon's explanation of Adam's fall (see 2 Nephi 2:18–25; Moses 5:11) add further consistency and purposefulness to our understanding of human history.

Global continuity

It took a non-Mormon, a scholar in comparative religion, Professor Ernst-Wilhelm Benz of the University of Marburg, to point out that only Mormonism has accounted for the spiritual history and destiny of both the Eastern and Western Hemispheres.[1] The Book of Mormon is obviously the principal source of such insight, but the revelations that locate Adam-ondi-Ahman and the second Jerusalem in middle North America further emphasize the role of the Western Hemisphere in the Lord's scenario.

Physical–spiritual continuity

It is again Professor Benz who has so expressively reminded us that more than any other religion he has studied, Mormonism sacrilizes the secular. In this context, again unique among theologies, Mormon scriptures proclaim that "the spirit and the body are the soul of man" (D&C 88:15) and that "there is no such thing as immaterial matter. All spirit is matter, but it is more fine or pure" (D&C 131:7). Thus the Word of Wisdom is viewed as a *spiritual* commandment. And thus the emphasis on the literal glory and eternal continuance of our physical bodies, to acquire which was an essential purpose for our earthly probation. Thus also the teaching that the Earth itself will be the future celestial kingdom after its ultimate fiery purification, renewal, and paradisiacal glorification (see Articles of Faith 1:10).

Continuity of the human family

The oft-quoted scripture in Malachi regarding the coming of Elijah and the turning of "the heart of the fathers to the children, and the heart of the children to their fathers" (Malachi 4:6), we now more than ever realize, has a twofold application. One relates to the programs of family history and temple work for all the Earth's deceased inhabitants; the other, to the fostering of unity and bonds of love among the living, particularly within our immediate families. Together, these emphases extend the sense of kinship, the sacredness of family ties, and the importance of permanent, quality family relationships in both directions on the time continuum: back to Adam, the founder of the race, and forward to his and our future posterity. Nothing could more practically foster an appreciation of the literal brotherhood and sisterhood of humankind, our mutual dependency, the desirability of living together in peace and harmony, and the prospect of eternal reunion with those who have gone before.

Since my original writing of this short essay, a number of impressive Mormon scholars have recognized Joseph Smith's undeviating quest to unite the entire human family as mutually recognized kin.[2] This unflagging impulse accounts for, among other practices, the church's ongoing missionary endeavor, the gathering of converts, temple ordinances for deceased ancestors, eternal marriage, ritual adoption, plural marriage, and the recognition of humankind's literal kinship with deity and our divine potential. These extraordinary efforts to embody that vision in mortal relationships, despite opposition and numerous obstacles, challenge everyone to decide whether this project was only Joseph Smith's, or God's as well.

Continuity between humanity and God

The idea of universal human brotherhood and sisterhood is further enhanced by the concept of our literal divine parentage—so seemingly presumptuous, even heretical, to those with a more traditional understanding of our relationship to God. Its value in prompting us to speak with God in all trusting earnestness, like a child to our earthly father, and the motivation it affords to perfect our lives in his image are incalculable—and wholly admirable. Consider the Lord's ultimate promise to those who obtain and live worthy of his eternal priesthood—a promise embracing both men and women—and whom he addresses, as he did the first apostles, as his "friends" (see John 15:15; D&C 84:77): "He that receiveth my Father receiveth my Father's kingdom; therefore all that my Father hath shall be given unto him" (D&C 84:38).

We can barely conceive of the ultimate heritage of all who sufficiently prove themselves, which is to share with the Father his power and all that he possesses, including the entire universe. The human conception of ownership is exclusive; God's, inclusive. The human notion of power is self-serving; God's, to endow, to increase oneself by enhancing others.

Continuity with one's eternal self

Ultimately, the revelations about God and his purposes, whose principal source in our day was the Prophet Joseph Smith, enable us to recognize our true identity as God's spirit offspring and—in relation to him and one another—to comprehend our glorious eternal destiny.

This vision, this promise, with the admonition to perfect ourselves, including our minds—for "it is impossible for a man to be saved in ignorance" (D&C 131:6), and "whatever principle of intelligence we attain unto in this life, it will rise with us in the resurrection" (D&C 130:18)—offers the most satisfying explanation of life and the most gratifying personal challenge ever afforded humanity. It can only elate. It is only rejected because, thinking so poorly of themselves, many who consider it rationally can only assume it is too good to be true.

Conclusion

The gospel, properly understood through its latter-day restoration, is indeed unique—a "pearl of great price." May we always be grateful that we have been privileged to make its acquaintance and for the difference it has made and may yet make in our lives.

Notes

1. Ernst Benz, "Mormonism and the Secularization of Religions in the Modern World." Forum address delivered at Brigham Young University, March 30, 1976. Published in *BYU Studies* 16/4 (1976): 627–39.

2. See, for example, Terryl Givens's BYU forum address, "'Lightning Out of Heaven': Joseph Smith and the Forging of Community," November 29, 2005 (see speeches.byu.edu/talks/terryl-l-givens_joseph-smith-forging-community); Philip L. Barlow, "To Mend a Fractured Reality: Joseph Smith's Project," *Journal of Mormon History* 38/3 (2012): 28–50; Samuel M. Brown, "Believing Adoption," *BYU Studies* 52/2 (2013): 45–65; and Robert A. Rees, "Joseph Smith and the Face of God," unpublished MS based on a devotional of the same title presented on August 2 at the 2014 Sunstone Symposium in Salt Lake City.

Thoughts about Joseph Smith: Upon Reading Donna Hill's *Joseph Smith: The First Mormon*

Donna Hill's biography of Joseph Smith (1977) has been superseded by more in-depth accounts of the Prophet's life, notably Richard Bushman's excellent Rough Stone Rolling *(2005). However, Hill's book awakened me to the disparate views of those who knew Joseph both as a young neighbor and, later, as a religious figure. The facts about Joseph Smith were in some cases otherwise than I had previously known them—something I earnestly wrestled with, as I now believe we are all meant to do. It initially affected me much as others have been challenged by the more recent barrage of detraction (especially online) that has contributed to what some have called a "faith crisis," in which members of the church—especially young members—are shaken in their faith by encountering unfamiliar facts and criticisms. Hill's book forced me to review and more attentively reconsider my own reasons for believing in Joseph Smith's prophetic calling. The ultimate result was a reaffirmation. My discussion of Hill's book is thus less a review of its data than an account of my personal reaction. Perhaps those who are earnestly struggling with their testimonies today may identify with my experience. I am also pleased by the church's recent efforts to discuss frankly in official venues some of the more difficult aspects of Joseph Smith's experiences, as with the new "Gospel Topics" piece on the translation of the Book of Mormon. (See lds.org/topics/book-of-mormon-translation.)*[1]

> "*Toute vue des choses qui n'est pas étrange est fausse.*" (Any view of things which is not strange is false.)
>
> —Valéry[2]

DONNA HILL'S *JOSEPH SMITH: THE FIRST MORMON* (1977) strikes me as the man's first fully adequate biography[3]—comprehensive, detached, balanced, and fair. Or so it seems. Either what is therein claimed about the Prophet is true or it is not. So far, no one has come forth to dispute its assertions. And I am in a state of shock—or was for weeks after I read it. Nothing has so much forced me to reexamine my most cherished preconceptions. As a middle-aged professor who has for some time dealt with the literary expression of humankind's thorniest dilemmas, I have found the play of ideas a delightful stimulation. I have not found it particularly difficult to live with the ambiguity and paradox that seem to abound at life's every turn and that are even attested to in the scriptures—to remain tenuous about so much that seems to "throw" some aspiring believers. At the same time—thanks in part to a number of choice experiences afforded by callings in the church—my testimony regarding the restored gospel and the reality and divinity of the Savior has never been stronger, my faith never more profound.

Surprises in the life of Joseph Smith

If what has only so recently come to my attention about Joseph Smith—much of which I had earlier relegated to malicious rumor—can have startled me as it did, at least temporarily, I can well understand how in the past those who were aware of these facts may have been anxious to keep the Prophet's image so vaguely idealized. But I believe that doing so fails to recognize the nature of the revelatory process in almost every dispensation and why prophets have been so universally misunderstood, even detested.

In his King Follett Discourse, the Prophet insisted that no man knew his history.[4] Reading Hill's book confirms that statement. The more one ponders the available biographical detail, the more enigmatic the man emerges—and the more puzzling, at least on the surface, appear his motives. Like nothing else, the experience reminds me of that existential trauma we all underwent when first indoctrinated, whether by peers in the back woodshed or by parents, about the birds and the bees. Those who first dissected the human body must have been similarly amazed and, for a time at least, equally dismayed by what they beheld. The facts of life and the reality that is more than skin-deep do not generally accord with a child's uninformed suppositions. Why then should the truth about another human being, easily as taxed and torn as we know *ourselves* to be, prove any less complex? These are the thoughts that have occurred to me as I have pondered the man Joseph Smith after having read Hill.

Joseph Smith's syncretism

What has been perhaps most disconcerting is that practically everything Joseph Smith enunciated and brought forth was so syncretic—appears, that is, to have been suggested by the ideas and the experiences he randomly encountered in his particular social environment. The coincidences, if that is what they are, suggest a consistent pattern of impressionability and truly ingenious adaptation of both the most bizarre and seemingly most mundane sources of inspiration—often secular, even spurious in character. We can no longer deny, for instance, that prior to discovering the golden plates and the Urim and Thummim, Joseph was several times hired to seek buried treasure by means of a so-called peep stone, being sought after for his adeptness in its use. Moreover, although there is nothing substantively in common between the Reverend Ethan Smith's *View of the Hebrews* and the Book of Mormon, the earlier work, published in 1823 by a contemporary in a neighboring state, advances a similar thesis, claiming to trace the history of descendants of the lost ten tribes among the American Indians, and could well have been known to the Prophet. One of the Book of Mormon's most significant archetypes—Lehi's vision—bears striking parallels to a dream Joseph's own father had earlier shared with his family members (at least according to the 1845 account of Joseph's mother).[5] Moreover, consequent to a dramatic conversion late in life, Joseph's maternal grandfather had published a book of Christian exhortation and thereupon traveled about, peddling it in the capacity of an itinerant missionary—a striking parallel to the later active proselytizing of Joseph Smith and his followers.

Another puzzling "coincidence" occurs with the Book of Mormon's ostensible quotations from certain New Testament scriptures. The inclusion of passages from Isaiah in 2 Nephi is, given the plates of Laban, quite understandable. It also seems plausible that in visiting the Nephites, the Savior would reiterate, even verbatim, the wisdom of the Sermon on the Mount. But the almost word-for-word echoing in Mormon's teaching of the familiar utterances of both Paul on charity (compare Moroni 7:45 with 1 Corinthians 13:4–7) and John on divine sonship (compare Moroni 7:48 with 1 John 3:2–3) can only be reconciled by assuming that such statements are so profound and memorable, which these in fact tend to be, that Christ repeatedly enunciated them and that both in Jerusalem and among the Nephites they were subsequently passed from one generation of disciples to the next. (Another possibility, proposed by LDS author Roger Terry, is that the Book of Mormon's actual *translator* was Moroni himself and Joseph Smith his medium. There is no indication by Joseph or his transcribers that the Bible itself was ever consulted in restating the various biblical passages that appear in the Book of Mormon.[6])

Consistent with the statement in the New Testament that "there are also many other things which Jesus did, the which, if they should be written every one, I suppose that even the world itself could not contain the books that should be written" (John 21:25), Mormon asserts that "there cannot be written in this book even a hundredth part of the things which Jesus did truly teach unto the people" (3 Nephi 26:6). The foregoing seems a plausible explanation, but without it, credibility would—at least for those who recognize and ponder such matters—be considerably strained.

In addition, there is the convoluted history of the Egyptian sarcophagi that Joseph Smith acquired from the descendant of a sideshow entrepreneur that contained papyri which, when translated, produced a substantial portion of one of the LDS Church's four sacred scriptures. And there is Sidney Rigdon's prior experience with communal living among the Campbellites—who, after he rose to leadership in the new church, probably urged Joseph to consider instituting the law of consecration and stewardship and the United Order. Finally, the correspondences between the Masonic ritual, to which Joseph Smith was initiated, and both the apparel and symbolic gestures of the endowment ceremony in LDS temples are so striking that it is hard not to imagine that exposure to the one readily led to the genesis of the other.

Now that these circumstances have so fully come to light, it would ill serve the cause of the church to pretend they are not so. Those both within and without who know otherwise will expect their recognition and further explanation, while those who learn of them from non-Mormon sources will risk even greater disenchantment.

Joseph Smith's character

Let us, therefore, as we can best discern them, take a reading of the other aspects of Joseph Smith's personality and behavior to determine how well these corroborate the notion that he was or was not a charlatan *par excellence.*

First, a strong case can be made—though it does not substantiate his claims—that Joseph was basically innocent and deeply sincere. As a fourteen-year-old with, by present-day standards, an extremely limited education and knowledge of the world at large, he was, upon entering the sacred grove, ideally suited to become the transparent vessel for receiving and disseminating astoundingly pristine principles which those more knowledgeable or steeped in Western theology might have been far more prone to qualify and compromise. Such persons would also have been less inclined to seek answers from deity than to rely on both already-established tradition and their own intellectual assumptions.

By contrast, from the moment of his hearing of the passage in James that prompted his inquiry about the true church, the pattern emerges—so natural it seems profane—that no revelation, no inspiration, would ever come to Joseph without first being prompted by some immediate stimulus that in turn impelled him to inquire about it by petitioning deity. It is also worth noting that Joseph Smith did not always appear to have so fully understood the import of the answers he received as those who came after him. For example, while what Joseph expressly went to the grove to learn was fully communicated—no existing churches were authorized by Jesus Christ and God the Father—the overarching significance of their appearance as separate personages with glorified anthropomorphic bodies does not seem to have dawned on him, at least at the time, nearly so much as on subsequent Latter-day Saints. This may be another reason why the first vision was not recorded or even mentioned until some time later.

Nor did Joseph ever emphasize the fact that the nature of his experience in the grove, including his initial encounter with the powers of darkness, was in the archetypal manner of trial and initiation (always in some isolated natural setting) that the founders of previous dispensations appear to have undergone prior to their divine commission to embark on their respective missions. Both the endowment ceremony and the Pearl of Great Price recount comparable incidents in the case of ancient prophets such as Adam, Enoch, Noah, Abraham, and Moses. The Old Testament suggests something similar for Isaac, Jacob, and Joseph, as does the New Testament for Christ during his forty days in the wilderness. But Joseph Smith never made anything of the parallel in his own instance. It is likely that it did not even occur to him. All of this suggests that far from exploiting a number of circumstances that might have served his personal self-aggrandizement, the young Joseph was naively oblivious to their possible implications. It makes him seem far less a scheming manipulator of other's minds.

Another area in which Joseph Smith seems less than shrewd was in his uncompromising sense of urgency regarding the principles and practices that lost for him the support of so many associates and made him and his movement, in the minds of their non-Mormon neighbors in Missouri and Illinois, so much more suspicious and threatening. His undeviating persistence in such matters led in fact directly to his martyrdom. Chief among these was polygamy. As Hill points out, "Joseph seemed more and more determined that the Saints accept the doctrine of celestial marriage as holy and necessary." Citing Joseph F. Smith, she adds, "As the late President George A. Smith repeatedly said, to me and others, 'The Prophet seemed irresistibly moved by the power of God to establish that principle, not only in theory, in the hearts and minds of his brethren, but in practice also, he himself having led the way.'" Hill elsewhere asserts, "It never occurred to Joseph and his followers that their teachings had given gross offense."[7]

One of Joseph's most endearing qualities was his magnanimity and generosity—his deep, impulsive affection for others, particularly those of humble circumstances. LDS gospel scholar T. Edgar Lyon, for one, recounts a number of anecdotal instances from reminiscences by various members in the early days of the church.[8] Joseph's failure as a storekeeper in Kirtland because he could not withhold credit from needy church members is also well established. The account of his great distress at the loss of those who died of cholera in Zion's Camp speaks to his deep compassion. Similarly, his joyous weeping on the occasion of his own parents' baptisms attests not only to his deep feelings toward his family but also to his genuine belief in the enterprise he had helped initiate. It is surely meaningful that, knowing their son as only Joseph Senior and Lucy could, they and all his siblings were sufficiently convinced of Joseph's integrity, credibility, and claim to be a prophet. The great love and undeviating lifelong trust in Joseph of such practical and worldly wise men as Heber C. Kimball and Brigham Young are also a strong testimonial to his character, and Brigham's last dying words—"Joseph! Joseph!"—a poignant evocation. Hill's sensitive analysis further suggests to what extent the Prophet's insistence on extended kinship and polygamous marriage evinced an uncontainable Christlike love for all his fellowmen.[9] As Bushman later expresses it, Joseph "did not lust for women so much as he lusted for kin."[10]

Reading Hill's account of the Prophet's life further strengthens the impression that, upon leaving the grove and for the rest of his life, Joseph never again knew a moment's respite from persecution—or from misunderstanding on the part of his closest friends, even his wife Emma. One wonders how he or anyone could have borne it and still maintained all he did if he did not know with a surety that the cause he pursued was "well pleasing" in God's sight. The severe test of that saving knowledge—mentioned in the sixth lecture on faith—without which we must ultimately weary and fall short if we do not willingly sacrifice "all earthly things," including our very lives, is profoundly attested by the faithfulness and eventual martyrdom of the Prophet himself.[11] That he fully knew what he professed is nowhere so plainly and forcefully asserted as in Doctrine and Covenants 76:22–23: "And now, after the many testimonies which have been given of him, this is the testimony, last of all, which we give of him: That he lives! For we saw him, even on the right hand of God."

Despite his claims to be the Lord's vessel, Joseph was, in a number of instances, also remarkably self-effacing and far more willing than most latter-day Mormons to admit his own personal fallibility. On one occasion, according to a gentile journalist, "he remarked that he had been represented as pretending to be a Savior, a worker of miracles, etc. All this was false. . . . He was but a man, he said; a plain, untutored man; seeking what he should do to be saved. . . . There was no violence, no fury, no denunciation. His religion appears to be a religion of meekness."[12]

According to Hill:

> [Joseph Smith] said publicly that he had his failings, passions and temptations to struggle against, just as had the greatest stranger to God, and that no man was justified in submitting to his sinful nature. He did not want his followers to sanctify him. In a speech of May 21, 1843, he said, ". . . I do not want you to think I am very righteous for I am not very righteous." To keep his actions from being misconstrued, Joseph frequently pointed out the difference between his behavior as a man and as a prophet. On one occasion he told visitors to Nauvoo, "A prophet is only a prophet when he is acting as such."[13]

In addition, there are in the Prophet's teachings and public utterances a number of striking statements that further convey his truly sublime understanding and espousal of the greatest commandment:

> If you will throw a cloak of charity over my sins, I will over yours—for charity covereth a multitude of sins.[14]

> Nothing is so much calculated to lead people to forsake sin as to take them by the hand, and watch over them with tenderness. When persons manifest the least kindness and love to me, O what power it has over my mind, while the opposite course has a tendency to harrow up all the harsh feelings and depress the human mind.[15]

> You must enlarge your souls towards each other. . . . Let your hearts expand, let them be enlarged towards others.[16]

> The mind or the intelligence which man possesses is co-equal with God himself. . . . All the minds and spirits that God ever sent into the world are susceptible of enlargement . . . so that they might have one glory upon another.[17]

So what was Joseph Smith? A facile or not-so-facile plagiarist? Or someone so in touch with the spiritual essence in otherwise earthly phenomena that—somehow divinely directed to it in the form of seer stones, sarcophagi, and Masonry—he was also led to interpret and wrest from them a significance entirely alien to his culture and his times but of astoundingly universal import, further substantiating the notion that "all things denote there is a God; yea, even the earth, and all things that are upon the face of it" (Alma 30:44)? Was Joseph Smith unusually naive and impervious to the ways of men and to respectable, civilized religious tradition? A megalomaniac who would rework it all to suit himself, in his own fashion? Or was he, by virtue of his youth and cultural isolation, still sufficiently pliable and open to what for almost two thousand years God had waited to recall to humanity's attention when circumstances would once again allow such a cataclysmic intrusion in our settled affairs, our rationally ordered but strictly temporal and self-serving alignments of secular, economic, ecclesiastical, and domestic forces? Was Joseph Smith just unusually stubborn? Or was he faithful unto death, one of God's few true martyrs? Was he merely sentimental or filled, like few others, with Christlike love and a seer's vision of humankind's glorious potential as God's own offspring? For all Hill's sound, instructive investigation into his life—a life not yet 150 years past with roots and a social context not unlike that of many other English-speaking Americans—we seem no closer to a satisfying answer than previously.

False prophet or true?

The only adequate confirmation of Joseph Smith's prophetic calling must, it would seem, be a transcendent one. But how appropriate and how needful that, point for point, Joseph's authenticity as a prophet would elude and baffle those who seek to understand spiritual matters by strictly rational means. Was Joseph in this respect really so very different from the many other prophets, including Christ himself, who were so often rejected by those closest to them? To Jesus's contemporaries, his teachings were hardly more popular than those of Elijah to *his* contemporaries, who cried, "The children of Israel have forsaken thy covenant, thrown down thine altars, and slain thy prophets with the sword; and I, even I only, am left; and they seek my life, to take it away" (1 Kings 19:14), or of Jeremiah, who complained, "The word of the Lord was made a reproach unto me, and a derision, daily" (Jeremiah 20:8; see also Isaiah 6:5–11, which characterizes the austere, "unnatural" nature of a prophet). Christ seemed less than surprised that this was so (see John 6:64–65). Time and again he seems, almost deliberately, to provoke those who are inclined to take offense at his words: "I am the living bread" (John 6:51), he asserts, insisting that "except ye eat the flesh of the Son of man, and drink his blood, ye have no life in you" (John 6:53). "From that time," we are told, "many of his disciples went back, and walked no more with him" (John 6:66).

Whenever a prophet arises in any given generation, he is often least recognized by those who are most attached to the prophets who preceded him. When the Pharisees taunted Christ for blasphemy, he reminded them that in their cherished Torah their revered fathers had been told, "Ye are gods" (John 10:33–36; see also Psalm 82:6). Perhaps we too should make sure that whatever tends to violate our immediate sense of what is proper and appropriate does not preclude our better perception of as yet unapprehended, ultimate truth. By analogy with the way we first reacted to sex and the design of our bodies, we might well expect other realities to shock us. Cosmologist Carl Sagan vividly describes with what tenacity and courage Johannes Kepler finally came to recognize that the orbits of the planets were elliptical and not, as seemed to everyone till then, indisputably circular. Of himself, Kepler said, "The truth of nature which I had rejected and chased away, returned by stealth through the back door, disguising itself to be accepted. . . . Oh, what a foolish bird I have been."[18] Sagan adds: "The Thirty Years' War obliterated his grave. If a marker were to be erected today, it might read, in homage to his scientific courage: 'He preferred the hard truth to his dearest illusions.'"[19]

In this regard, one recalls the statement attributed to the renowned historian of Renaissance Italy, Jacob Burckhardt: "The essence of tyranny is the denial of complexity." One also notes the deep moral that underlies the otherwise seemingly frivolous poem "Delight in Disorder" by Shakespeare's contemporary Robert Herrick:

> A sweet disorder in the dress
> Kindles in clothes a wantonness:
> A lawn about the shoulders thrown
> Into a fine distraction:
> An erring lace, which here and there
> Enthralls the crimson stomacher:
> A cuff neglectful, and thereby
> Ribbands to flow confusedly:
> A winning wave (deserving note)
> In the tempestuous petticoat:
> A careless shoe-string, in whose tie
> I see a wild civility
> Do more bewitch me, than when art
> Is too precise in every part.

Life is doubtless so wonderful because it is so much more novel than our limited minds and imaginations would have it be. The claims made by and for Joseph Smith are themselves so novel, so distinctive, their implications so universally profound, that no one can afford to be indifferent or to avoid their serious, unbiased investigation.[20]

The larger question

As I, a humanist, address this body of, among others, historians—some, like myself, believers in Joseph Smith's prophetic claims, who sometimes doubt despite their desires; some, skeptics who perhaps at times are overwhelmed and wistful to believe "if it were only true"—what I would now like to say is simply to remind you and myself that matters of faith and religion are, by definition, fraught with logical uncertainty. We can never disprove or prove their claims of authenticity, however absurd or repulsive certain features may strike us on the one hand, or however consistent, comprehensive, and edifying they may seem to us on the other. So we should stop trying. If we are really professional, we will, when addressing such phenomena, dissociate ourselves from whatever may be the prejudices and presuppositions to which we are viscerally inclined. Or we will at least try.

It may also help to remind ourselves that, in whatever we ultimately place our credence, we have, as Catholic theologian Hans Küng would say, consciously chosen to do so, and also that choice is unavoidable: "Not to choose is itself a choice."[21] Therefore, meaningful conversion to any religious proposition—even its rejection—involves a freely and consciously willed personal choice and a commitment to a particular metaphysical worldview.

This is not to say that one's choice and commitment should not rest upon the very best, most conceivably rewarding and spiritually redeeming grounds. Indeed, those grounds seem to me highly redeeming in the case of Joseph Smith, despite some appearances to the contrary.[22] Nor ought we to deny the importance of transcendental witness and spiritual confirmation, or that they are possible. These are, after all, the essential epistemological component of all religion. The apostle Paul said, "The natural man receiveth not the things of the Spirit of God: for they are foolishness unto him: neither can he know them, because they are spiritually discerned" (1 Corinthians 2:14). The logical man, the scholar, *is* the natural man of whom Paul spoke. No scholar is objectively equipped either to dismiss or to verify the things of the spirit, at least not in this life. No scholar is objectively equipped to call Joseph Smith either "a conscious fraud" *or*, by implication, an unconscious one.

Moreover, when we too freely begin to prescribe what we think is best for a given religion, though it be in the light of what we consider most reasonable and just, we are no longer submitting *our* mind and will to that of the Lord but subjecting it to *our own* instead. And that, however enlightened, is no longer religion. As Anglican specialist Kenneth Cragg avers, "With religions comparative, one becomes comparatively religious. Decisive faith appears unnecessary or intolerant."[23]

But all we have considered so far has at least been couched in a comfortable Christian context. What about the other world religions in which Christ does not supremely figure—those "other guides than ours to life and meaning" which, as also in the case of too many a so-called Christian, "have not, for the most part, been options freely chosen . . . but rather denominators of birth and culture, of language and geography"?[24] How ought we to address them without feeling threatened, yet without condescension?

As Cragg asserts, "The art of loyalty and the art of relationship must be understood, and practiced, as complementary. . . . Here . . . we have to do with felt and lived religious meaning, rather than with its abstraction into -ism."[25] Cragg further pleads the case of

> reverence for reverence and the need to penetrate faiths as their insiders know them, if there is to be hope of reciprocal awareness. This does not mean a sentimentality oblivious of the compromises or the crimes of which religions have been guilty. But realism has its positive duties, too, and the first of these is a hospitable mind.[26]

No less should be expected of those who take it upon themselves to study the origins, its founding prophet, or any other aspect of Mormonism.

Accommodating uncomfortable truths

To those who in their turn selectively handle Mormon history and discourage our probing it in a number of areas, one needs to say (or at least to ask): Haven't we been, if anything, overly cautious, overly mistrustful, overly condescending to a membership and a public who are far more perceptive and discerning than we often give them credit for? Haven't we, in our care not to offend a soul or cause anyone the least misunderstanding, too much deprived such individuals of needful occasions for personal growth and more in-depth life-probing experience? In our neurotic cautiousness, our fear of venturing, haven't we often settled for an all-too-shallow and confining common denominator that insults the very Intelligence we presume to glorify and is also dishonest because, deep down, we all know better (to the extent that we do)? Isn't our intervention often too arbitrary, reflecting the hasty, uninformed reaction of only one or a couple of influential objectors? Don't we in the process too severely and needlessly test the loyalty and respect of and lose credibility with many more than we imagine? Isn't there a tendency among us, bred by the fear of displeasing, to avoid healthy self-disclosure—public or private—and to pretend about ourselves *to* ourselves and others? Doesn't this in turn breed loneliness and make us, more than it should, strangers to each other? And when we are too calculating, too self-conscious, too mistrustful, too prescriptive, and too regimental about our roots and about one another's aesthetic, intellectual, and spiritual life, aren't we self-defeating?

Ultimately, we come to understand the things of greatest worth only through Christlike love. The nature of truth lies not in knowledge, but in love. If we would constantly keep this in mind we would not fear exposure or what others could ever say about us. We would have more confidence in the redeeming light we've been given. We would fearlessly let it shine, and it would convince others—how *many more* others?—despite themselves and their own feeble logic. The rest would not matter if our own faith were only not so feeble, and if we were also that righteous. But forgetting this, we become wary and reticent to be fully disclosing, to the point that we are discouraged from alluding much to even so familiar and fundamental a feature of the Mormon past as polygamy. It may not be prudent to disseminate problematic historical facts or freely allude to every complex and difficult real-life circumstance. We justly resent the common imputation by so many elsewhere that present-day polygamous groups are part and parcel of the mainstream LDS Church. But it is equally ineffective to suppress the ostensible facts or to intimidate those who know of those facts and are attempting to be reconciled to them. Suspicion, mistrust, the leveling of intellectual expectations, the condescending slanting of available data will not do.

Credibility indeed suffers, and the unwarranted idolization of other human beings, even divinely appointed persons, prevents us from loving them as much as we might if we knew *them* better—as opposed to the traditions we associate with them. That is surely even more the case for those who do not particularly cherish such persons and traditions: in other words, those outsiders we would most like to interest in them. It also offers a field day to those who wish to disparage what we hold sacred, the implication being that the more we deny some things or appear to do so, the more we must ourselves harbor serious doubts and have something to hide. If we cannot afford to investigate and face up to possibly warranted claims made by critics of the church as these come to our attention and must instead be content with the most favorable, safe, and stereotypical generalizations, are we not, besides cheating ourselves of a more approximate and more real acquaintance with the persons and events in question, submitting to self-deception?

The dilemmas are not only historical. They abound, as they always have, in the context of our contemporary social and institutional life. What is needed is, in the first order, a willingness to be more open and honest, more self-disclosing about our doubts and fears. The consequence of doing so is not necessarily, as some suspect, the dissolution of faith. And here I fully agree with Professor Lawrence Foster that such openness need not "reduce the sense of awe, mystery, and power in Mormonism."[27] Indeed, all that the Prophet Joseph ever suggested regarding "unrighteous dominion" (e.g., D&C 121:37) seems most applicable here, particularly in terms of our need for, and right to, personal intellectual inquiry.

No, life and religion are not so simplistic. God's ways are not ours. Reality (with a capital "R") is indeed paradoxical and full of surprises. Our best attempts to make it seem respectable, predictable, and homogenized in fact avoid and even thwart the necessity to come to know and believe it alone through the witness that transcends and surpasses our natural capacity for comprehension—a very personal undertaking. Moreover, we cannot possibly force ourselves to agree with what we cannot confidently grasp or what disturbs our conscience. To pretend otherwise is to live a lie.

What—along with our faith—we are intellectually in need of is an essential *empiricism* that allows for, in fact prescribes, the prudent holding in balance of seemingly contradictory phenomena and the statements made about them. Admittedly, this is an approach few if any mainstream members of ethnic and religious groups are ever encouraged to consider. But for those confronted by the dilemmas others manage to ignore, it can make a critical difference. Here are the perceptive comments of a returned missionary and graduate student:

> My mission was a glorious experience: I may say, without boasting, that I did some amazing things, rare things, miraculous things, because I realized that no one but me could be the judge and director of my work; yet that realization made me sometimes feel alone, almost existentially "nauseated" with the freedom and ensuing responsibilities I had. When the sky is the limit (and not 60 hours proselyting time), then you realize, not without a great deal of fear and trembling, that you

> alone determine the success you will have, and not that success automatically follows cheerful, but unthinking, obedience. In light of all that, then, I think my question is: How do you, in the environment where obedience operates in a causal fashion, try to instill a sense of the awesome freedom and responsibility each individual missionary has? Or perhaps that is a sacred, and therefore ineffable, secret, that only those find out who need to. I suppose many of my companions never felt such an emotion, not to their loss, they are just different. . . . Did I go too far in the mission field to realize that obedience and visible results are not causally connected, that I was horrifically free? Do I go too far now when I realize that though I have the gospel, there are still . . . an awful lot of subtleties I must supply for myself? That I ask these questions suggests I do not think there is a simple answer.[28]

Note these further remarks by a recent convert and returned missionary:

> There is no question of *if* but only of *when* members of the church will be confronted and confused by paradox. . . . Is the confusion and insecurity caused by confronting paradox any greater than that caused by confronting family and friends (as a convert) and feeling all their negative social pressure? Is it any greater than the confusion and insecurity produced when the investigator with his shaky newfound faith has to confront his temptations and weaknesses and overcome them to live the commandments? And if paradox is avoided, can a meaningful conversion take place? Confidence and conversion occur after the trials of our faith, and if we avoid certain trials, what does that tell us about our confidence in the Lord and ourselves, as well as the . . . [depth] of our conversion?[29]

If we do not *now* feel called upon to walk such a razor's edge, we may later be called upon to do so—as certain information even inadvertently comes to our awareness. How likely is it, for those so exposed who lack sufficient training and sophistication, that coping will be at all easy, let alone successful? For those already exposed (an increasing number), how—without violating their innermost integrity—can such information be ignored and not somehow reconciled, even if it is largely secondary and, like all other earthly information, incomplete and subject to further qualification? Only weeks ago, I received a pamphlet from the "Ex-Mormons for Jesus" that was intended to disturb me with respect to the correspondences between Masonry and the endowment ceremony. How grateful I was that I had already read a transcript of the Masonic rite and was already reconciled to the strong possibility of syncretism in the founding of the church and of this being revelation nonetheless. But those who dare not entertain that possibility could easily be "thrown" by the surface truth in such assertions.

The need for mutual respect

The entire experience has reminded me of the importance of respecting the religious traditions of others, while expecting that they respect ours in turn. While all of us, of whatever tradition, believe in our particular faith's access to truth, we have no right to assume that those in other traditions do not have as valid and meaningful an access to transcendent virtue and inspiration. If we are encouraged to recognize and embrace whatever is "virtuous, lovely, or of good report or praiseworthy" (Articles of Faith 1:13)—hence sublimely true—in our own spiritual experience, we should also rejoice when others can so witness for theirs. This applies to both believer and critic. But Mormons and their critics rarely see things this way.

"Dogma," Cragg insists,

> often thought of as defensive, preservative, even clinical, ensuring truth, must be seen also as hospitable and inviting. Frontiers that need guards and guardians also enclose areas in which liberties are secured. Faith, as credally defined, is a territory to inhabit, a house to occupy, as well as a fence to maintain and a wall to build. What matters is that habitation should be open to prospectives as well as defensible to inhabitants. Doctrine means invitation to discovery as well as warning against deviation. . . . The deep sense the Christian must surely feel . . . that he is in trust with truth he has no mandate to barter but only to serve and to share, must always be paramount. The question about witness is not Whether? but How? There must be no evasion of issues. . . . But they must be

> appropriately joined. This means that they must be allowed to emerge *within*, rather than merely against, the intimate meanings and preoccupations of the other man's world. An alert sense of the relevance to us and to our witness, of what otherwise we might be minded to dismiss or to dispute, is truly consistent with the positive and inward loyalties of Christian doctrine. . . . In so far as religions are cultures . . . with legacies of pride and tradition, the lesson is clear. It is when they are allowed their cultural selves that they can best reach beyond themselves. It is when they are consciously under threat that they are suspiciously isolated in temper. It is only when we are allowed our own humanity that we seek an inclusive humanness. Reciprocal courtesy is, therefore, the wisest, as well as the truest, prescript for relationship. . . . Relevance *in* any religion is relevance *for* all. While they may be deliberately separate in their findings, they are common in their human habitation. Perhaps the largest test of their integrity is their integrity about each other.[30]

I believe any commitment of faith that fosters reverence for the source of life—that affirms life itself and the special significance of the life in every individual, sustains hope, and encourages decency and goodness—is sacred and deserves our respect.

Conclusion

The intent of this paper has simply been to point out those aspects of Joseph Smith's biography that argue in his favor as opposed to those that imply he was a charlatan and to reflect on the implications of historical messiness for one's faith. I suggest that the enigmas and controversies that invariably arise as, with Donna Hill, we view the Prophet's earthly record, nevertheless tend to suggest that few can be totally indifferent or dispassionate toward Joseph Smith and the claims of the restored church and that where, for whatever reason, people resist them, they also tend to draw their own often unwarranted conclusions—a kind of testimony by default.

"No man knows [his] history"—so why should any historian? We can view Joseph Smith with great confidence, but only when assisted by the Spirit and by thoughtfully weighing all he has given us. As we do so, may we, like Johannes Kepler, always prefer "the hard truth" to "our dearest illusions."

Notes

1. This paper is adapted from a presentation at the Mormon History Association meetings on May 7, 1982, in Ogden, Utah, later published in *By Study and Also by Faith: Essays in Honor of Hugh W. Nibley,* ed. John M. Lundquist and Stephen D. Ricks (Salt Lake City: Deseret Book, 1990), 2:585–618. The complete essay as previously published is available at the Maxwell Institute website, mi.byu.edu.

2. Cited in Brian Stimpson, "Counter-fiction," in *Reading Paul Valéry: Universe in Mind*, ed. Paul Gifford and Brian Stimpson (Cambridge: Cambridge University Press, 1998), 139.

3. Donna Hill, *Joseph Smith: The First Mormon* (Garden City, NY: Doubleday, 1977).

4. Joseph Smith Jr., *The Words of Joseph Smith: The Contemporary Accounts of the Nauvoo Discourses of the Prophet Joseph*, ed. Andrew E. Ehat and Lyndon W. Cook (Provo, UT: Religious Studies Center, Brigham Young University, 1980), 355.

5. Hill, *Joseph Smith*, 44.

6. Roger Terry, "Archaic Pronouns and Verbs in the Book of Mormon: What Inconsistent Usage Tells Us about Translation Theories," *Dialogue: A Journal of Mormon Thought* 47/3 (2014): 53–80.

7. Hill, *Joseph Smith*, 345, 114.

8. T. Edgar Lyon, "Recollections of 'Old Nauvooers': Memories from Oral History," *BYU Studies* 18/2 (1978): 143–50.

9. Hill, *Joseph Smith*, 342-43.

10. Richard Lyman Bushman, *Joseph Smith: Rough Stone Rolling* (New York: Alfred A. Knopf, 2005), 440.

11. Lecture 6:7, 12, in the 1835 edition of the *Doctrine and Covenants*, http://josephsmithpapers.org/paperSummary/doctrine-and-covenants-1835.

12. Hill, *Joseph Smith*, 273.

13. Hill, *Joseph Smith*, 343.

14. *History of the Church*, 4:445.

15. *History of the Church*, 5:23–24.

16. Joseph Smith, *Teachings of the Prophet Joseph Smith*, comp. Joseph Fielding Smith (Salt Lake City: Deseret Book, 1976), 228.

17. Joseph Smith, *Teachings*, 353–54.

18. Carl Sagan, *Cosmos* (New York: Random House, 1980), 62.

19. Sagan, *Cosmos*, 67.

20. The full essay expands on these points.

21. Hans Küng, *Does God Exist? An Answer for Today*, trans. Edward Quinn (Garden City, NY: Doubleday, 1980), 438.

22. The full essay elaborates further on these grounds for confidence in Joseph Smith.

23. Kenneth Cragg, *The Christian and Other Religion: The Measure of Christ* (London: Mowbray, 1977), 13.

24. Cragg, *Christian and Other Religion*, xi.

25. Cragg, *Christian and Other Religion*, xii–xiii.

26. Cragg, *Christian and Other Religion*, xiii.

27. Lawrence Foster, "New Perspectives on the Mormon Past," *Sunstone*, January–February 1982, 45.

28. Self-evaluation from a student in the BYU Honors Program.

29. Self-evaluation from a student in the BYU Honors Program.

30. Cragg, *Christian and Other Religion*, 25–28, 38.

Why the Book of Mormon Is One of the World's Best Books

The LDS Church's most prominent scripture has by now received immense exegesis and commentary. Although Grant Hardy's illuminating Understanding the Book of Mormon *more extensively explores the work's narrative structure,*[1] *I have yet to encounter any mention of the few noteworthy features that came to mind when I wrote this short essay—possibly in the early 1980s, though I no longer recall the occasion or with whom I may have shared it at the time. The Book of Mormon is clearly everyone's domain, with still more to plumb and consider.*

A CURSORY VIEW OF THE BOOK OF MORMON can be deceptive. It can leave the impression that the ancient Nephite record is simple-minded, drab, and repetitious, lacking in continuity and a purposeful organization. Mark Twain's proverbial dismissal of the book as "chloroform in print" is indicative.[2] But for those who take this book of scripture seriously and study it conscientiously, nothing could be further from the truth. Viewed at a deeper level, the Book of Mormon is a profoundly unified work, a challenge to the most sophisticated scholar. Its complexity and integration are manifest in a variety of subtle ways.

Structural complexity and untidiness

The work's multiple abridgments, editorial interjections, and apostrophes to the modern reader are anything but neatly arranged. How frequently one scribe's remarks intrude upon those attributed by the title of a particular section to some other—Jacob's upon those of Nephi, Helaman's upon Alma's, Moroni's upon the Jaredite record and that of his father Mormon. A noteworthy pattern in fact suggests the extent to which sons record their more experienced fathers' exploits and utterances: 1 Nephi is as much the account of Lehi's inspired leadership as Nephi's own; the book of Mosiah of his father Benjamin's powerful preaching; the books of Alma and Helaman of the exploits of illustrious fathers by their respective namesakes; the book of Moroni largely the repository of his father Mormon's teachings, including two epistles. The thematic implication of a highly deferential response by sons toward their fathers' words is mentioned below. (With the Book of Mormon as precedent, the concern sometimes voiced regarding the multiple authorship of Isaiah seems quite groundless. As with many another historical text, the Book of Mormon has passed through and been modified by a number of redactions, even before it got to Joseph Smith.)

The Book of Mormon spans a full millennium of history, but concentrates on selected moments of special spiritual significance. Not every leader or every generation receives equal time and attention. Thus a full half of the BC period, three out of six centuries, is passed over in seven out of more than 500 pages. By contrast, 262 pages, constituting the books of Mosiah, Alma, and Helaman, are devoted to the last 130 years before Christ's coming. Only certain events in the Old Testament are treated in such a sustained dramatic-narrative fashion: notably the lives of the patriarchs and the history of David. The compression that follows in 4 Nephi—nearly 300 years in four pages—is in turn as intense as that occurring earlier in Enos, Jarom, and particularly Omni. (A mere fabricator would, from a sense of neatness and symmetry, be inclined to divide his material into equal time periods, with each unit restricted to the words of its ostensible author—just his and no one else's. Not so Moroni and Joseph Smith.)

The plot proper is at times equally intricate. As pure military history, the concurrent campaigns of Moroni and Helaman, together with their opponent Amalickiah's successive stratagems, read like the most elaborate tale of adventure—which of course they are. (In Alma the Younger, the famed ancient Greek historian Thucydides finds a worthy successor.)

The Book of Mormon is "untidy" in still another respect. It takes many needless chances, which might easily confuse the superficial reader. The killing of Laban raises the issue of ends justifying means; the antipolygamy sentiments in Jacob appear to run counter to the very practice Joseph Smith was eventually to introduce to his people; the references to glass and elephants in Ether strike one as anachronistic and even inaccurate (or at least would have done so in Joseph Smith's day). Why invite scholarly skepticism by appearing to plagiarize other—in some instances later—scriptures: the Sermon on the Mount in 3 Nephi; 1 Corinthians 13 and 1 John 3:2 in Moroni; and lengthy sections of Isaiah in 1 and 2 Nephi, Mosiah, and 3 Nephi? There are also the interesting problems raised by the repetition of Jaredite names among the Nephites, such as Corihor (spelled as Korihor among the Nephites; see Ether 7 and Alma 30) and Coriantumr (see Ether 1, 8, 12–15; Helaman 1), and by the almost ritualized behavior of the daughter of a later Jared in Ether (see Ether 8:8–18), anticipating that of Salome in the New Testament.

Difficult as it would be to successfully fabricate even a single historical epoch, the Book of Mormon handles several series of events that, though parallel in their progress and their consequences, are, without seeming any the less credible, substantially different. This difficult variation on a theme is seen in the book's subtly nested accounts of three distinct immigrant peoples; the frequent oscillation of fortune over the Nephite generations due to their affluence, pride, and consequent godlessness; and the many poignant conflicts between concerned parents and their recalcitrant offspring. There are also the distinct personalities that emerge in the expression and point of view of each Book of Mormon prophet: Nephi's youthful devotion; King Benjamin's fearless preaching; Jacob's almost philosophical explication of doctrine, coupled with his compassion; the intimate spiritual yearnings of Enos and the brother of Jared; Alma's stress on "restoration" and compensatory reward, which interestingly contrasts with Mormon's stoic resignation to lead his people not because they deserve to win or because he thinks they will but out of pure principle. (How like Camus's Dr. Rieux, fighting the plague, is Mormon as he anticipates his people's annihilation.[3])

Thematic scope

The thematic scope of the Book of Mormon, ingeniously reflected in its typology—for example, the tree of life (and of faith), allusions to migration, and the "wilderness"—is in some respects more comprehensive than that of any other extant scripture. Its philosophical range is not easily grasped and cannot be adequately expressed in a commentator's words. The Book of Mormon poses a paradoxical formula that in turn accounts for the ultimate destiny of all humankind. This formula, nowhere more explicitly stated than in Alma 28:14—"and thus we see the great reason of sorrow, and also of rejoicing—sorrow because of death and destruction among men, and joy because of the light of Christ unto life"—opposes the two furthest reaches of human possibility. Its positive aspect is the work's fundamental doctrine: the atonement of Christ, seen as the central event in human history. (It is significant that all but 6 of the scripture's 239 chapters allude to the Savior.[4])

Moreover, the atonement is here treated with a remarkable ecumenical sweep. In addition to the recurring testimony of Christ by New World prophets from Nephi to Moroni, the Book of Mormon cites the testimony of Old World prophets even beyond those appearing in the Bible (Zenos, Zenock; see 1 Nephi 19:10). The message of the gospel is explicitly described as being "unto all nations, of their own nation and tongue" (Alma 29:8; see also 2 Nephi 26:13). The book's dramatic center is the appearance of Christ himself, providing not only a testimony of the risen Savior and reprise of his key teachings from the New Testament but also a climactic moment in the history of the Nephite and Lamanite peoples, ushering in a lengthy period of unequaled peace and prosperity for the survivors of earlier destruction.

The other side of the Book of Mormon equation is presented in two instances of the complete self-destruction of an entire people. Such a tragic fate has rarely been dealt with in any literature and nowhere so fully in other scripture. (The *Iliad*'s account of the fall of Troy comes most nearly to mind.) The fate of the Jaredites and Nephites is treated, interestingly, in consecutive sections of the Book of Mormon, thus reinforcing the tragic denouement that appropriately follows the history's high point in 3 Nephi. These peoples' tragedy is further compounded by the fact that they perish spiritually as well as in the body because of the "hardness of their hearts," which causes "the day of grace" to pass them by (Mormon 1:17; 2:15). (The notion of cultural evolution, so seriously advanced before the cataclysms of the twentieth century, is time and again belied by the capriciousness of humans so realistically chronicled in the Book of Mormon.) But the fulcrum, balancing Christ's atonement against everlasting spiritual death, is not a human collective, no illusory body politic, but the single individual—together with, more often than not, the family of which that individual is a member. Men and women do not win their eternal reward because they belong to the "right side." Time and again, the Book of Mormon shows the decline of the Lord's chosen people because of hubris—while some from the apostate tradition such as Samuel the Lamanite, the Ammonites and their stripling sons, and the Lamanites praised by Jacob for their faithfulness in marriage become exemplars of virtue and righteous behavior.

An individual's relationship to God is, moreover, constantly correlated with that person's allegiance to his earthly father and other family members. This may be another of the book's sublime motifs: filial piety reflecting the proper relationship between humanity and God. More specifically, the example of so many Book of Mormon scribes who deferentially recorded an account of their fathers' lives sets for us a pattern, equaled in no other scripture, of how our hearts can all the more fully turn to our fathers.

How many such readily identifiable role models and object lessons the Book of Mormon affords us. How relatively impoverished the Christian world is without them. The Book of Mormon profoundly sweeps between the extremes of life and death—but, as with Tolstoy's masterpiece *War and Peace*, its ultimate objective correlative is not so much public events as domesticity, that far more difficult and subtle battleground where every individual secures or forfeits his or her own soul and loved ones forever.

Conclusion

These profound thematic patterns are not so much stated as shown, not so much shown as implied. They are often only hinted at, mostly expressing themselves "between the lines." This is why the Book of Mormon requires and also rewards close and careful reading. It is such a powerful teacher because it does not so much explicate as entice the reader to discover its significance for himself or herself. Such discovery in turn produces strong conviction. The Book of Mormon should therefore be studied within a personal frame of reference. Just as Nephi "did liken all scriptures unto us, that it might be for our profit and learning" (1 Nephi 19:23), so should we. For the same reason, when it is taught, the Book of Mormon should be presented with respect for the student's unique background, intelligence, and ability, with faith, to discover its truth on his or her own terms and in his or her own individual way.

Notes

1. Grant Hardy, *Understanding the Book of Mormon: A Reader's Guide* (New York: Oxford University Press, 2010).
2. Mark Twain, *Roughing It* (New York: Harper and Brothers, 1899), 1:132.
3. Albert Camus, *The Plague*.
4. For the reference to the number of chapters that refer to Jesus, see Robert J. Matthews, "What the Book of Mormon Tells Us about Jesus Christ," in *The Book of Mormon: The Keystone Scripture*, ed. Paul R. Cheesman (Provo, UT: Religious Studies Center, Brigham Young University, 1988), 21–43, citing Monte S. Nyman.

Remarks to Members of the BYU Honors Program, Fall 1976

This was my charge to our students in my second year as honors program director. My remarks were honed by what my associates and I had learned from the students we'd worked with the year before—a most valuable and exhilarating education, for me anyway. We should have paid tuition along with our students.

We are fond of citing Brigham Young's admonition to Karl G. Maeser when founding this institution that nothing should be taught here without the spirit of God: appropriate advice for the Lord's university.[1] I fear, however, that our interpretation of that prophetic counsel and the underlying concern it reflects may often be too restrictive. As a people, I think we too often view learning as a dangerous if necessary enterprise, a treacherous current studded with sirens, Scylla and Charybdis, beneath which protrude deadly sea monsters and jagged coral shoals—all too ready, should we profoundly immerse ourselves, to destroy and "dismember" us. My double entendre is intentional.

At times, unfortunately, the image fits. A heady but deceptive sense of power and omniscience has often deluded those who style themselves intellectuals and make learning their profession, if not also their religion. Their prideful assumptions, not their learning itself, as surely corrupt them as the love of money, not money itself, perverts the rich and covetous. Even very competent scholars are not, as a whole, necessarily wiser, less vain, or more mature than other people. Professors are not always as emotionally stable as their students.

Spiritual benefits of learning

Having conceded this much, it is nevertheless important to consider the Lord's expectation that we study diligently, "teach one another" history, languages, science, and also read "out of the best books" (D&C 88:118). If any people ought ever to have felt impelled to pursue learning as their religious duty, it should be the Latter-day Saints. But to what extent are learning and spirituality in fact mutually supportive, if not inseparable?

Allow me to confirm what I personally consider to be the spiritual benefits of our scholarly and intellectual endeavor. Like those of "pure research," they are mostly intangible and must be taken on faith—but make a profound difference. For me, they explain why we cannot be "saved in ignorance" and why "the glory of God is intelligence" (D&C 131:6; 93:36).

Learning ought to

- Broaden our awareness of reality.
- Enable us to cope better with our environment and deal more effectively with others.
- Discipline us, enabling us to think more precisely and more discerningly.
- Teach us humility and integrity (through tentativeness), as well as sensitivity and toleration—*if* learning is pursued to God's glory and not our own.
- Assist us to enjoy and appreciate experience for its own sake, even under adverse circumstances. This is because learning is so highly vicarious. Learning, in other words, can lead to the personal satisfaction and joy that a righteously lived life also promises us.

Do we take our learning seriously?

With such potential benefits in mind, those of us at this institution and in this program ought to be particularly concerned about our scholarship. We should be sensitive to whether we are truly learning or simply playing at it. Fortunately, there are certain clues to help us assess whether we have arrived or are at least moving in that direction.

One of these, I suggest, is simply the extent to which we like to read. Reading is surely a fair indicator of the degree to which we are engaged in others' ideas and, in general, with the life of the mind. Nor do we read unless we are willing to sacrifice for it a variety of other diversions: television, movies, season tickets to our favorite sport, travel, even sleep. Another important indicator is that we not confuse excellence with or find too much satisfaction in statistical criteria for success, avoiding the kind of facile comparison associated with the words "more than" or "better than," as well as the complacency implied by the terms "normal," "average," and "common denominator."

Having by now interviewed hundreds of applicants for presidential scholarships, Danforth fellowships, and highest honors designations, I sense certain attitudes that our most impressive scholars have in common. Interestingly, those attitudes have little to do with what we normally think of in terms of IQ or pure intelligence.

First, they reflect an intense curiosity and excitement about ideas. Even in spite of themselves, they are broadly informed. They have not relied on their classes or on authoritative spoon feeding for what they know. They think imaginatively and on their own. To have one's own thought, to think for oneself, involves, I believe, a subtle moral dimension: one must first of all have certain convictions, be committed to particular values, and hold to a set of ethical standards. Solzhenitsyn has characterized his former persecutors by their lack of just such a commitment: in *The Gulag Archipelago*, he says, "They forced themselves *not to think* (and this in itself means the ruin of a human being). . . . They had no *individual* position."[2]

There are, I believe, at least two applications of this disposition to think independently. A student so disposed "shops" not only for the institution he or she hopes to attend but also for teachers, facilities, programs, and courses. Such a student also finds ways to cope with and meaningfully assimilate the great volume of data that confronts us in today's world: he or she learns to *conceptualize*.

Perhaps hardest but most needful is the capacity and inclination to think not just imaginatively but also responsibly. Acquisition of this skill requires that we push ourselves. We must seek the kind of discipline that entails habits and patterns of response of which all are capable but that few achieve. We must tenaciously commit ourselves to any contracted routine and rank our priorities so we have adequate time for what we intend to accomplish. (To do so is an indication of just how realistic we can be, as well as how honest.) We must also motivate ourselves to overlearn, reinforcing partial learning through self-initiated, systematic, frequent review of the material we intend to master. In a similar vein, we should, when we write, perfect what we put on paper. Anticipating the need for multiple drafts, we should start early enough to allow for more than one revision. We should strive for cogency and clarity, be self-critical, and invite criticism of our work by others along the way.

In thinking responsibly, we must be moderate and patient, avoiding rash and impulsive conclusions. We must listen to and try to understand alien viewpoints without misrepresenting them, learn to disagree without becoming hostile or fearing disapproval, and discern and remain tenuous about all in our experience that is arbitrary or uncertain. And always we need to be aware of the price we must pay in order to become to some degree experts—the trade-offs involved, especially social and recreational. Never forget the main reason you are here at BYU; try to make study itself a social and recreational outlet. The honors program provides an atmosphere and the mechanism for doing so.

Finally, none of us can afford to ignore the counsel from Brigham Young that I previously mentioned—to seek the guidance of the Holy Spirit as we teach and also as we learn. There is something healthy about sensing our dependence and fallibility. We must be humble and prayerful, not only to avoid worldly evil but also as a necessary corrective to the dangers of overconfidence and self-delusion.

Knowing oneself

When, if ever, does one cross the line and become an authentic honors student, scholar, intellectual? One clue, I suggest, is a certain lack of self-consciousness, which is ultimately a matter of personal confidence—but not overconfidence.

I am reminded of a former honors student, now on a mission, who wrote, incidentally, the best short story I have yet seen by a Mormon student. While interacting earlier with his peers in our seminars, this brother—for whom I have a high personal regard—seemed in some ways stifled and unable to express a very original idea. His problem, as

I finally came to perceive it, was simply that feeling inferior to others, he attempted never to say anything that would meet with their disapproval. As intellectuals, *they* had already arrived, he felt, while *he* still hadn't. He therefore weighed his every word, fearful that he would not impress them. His self-conscious attempt to be more like his admired peers was anything but authentic. (He is now an attorney, and after four decades I am still in touch with him. I'm pleased to announce that in his various spheres of endeavor—as a husband and father, as a church leader, and in his profession—he has long transcended what once caused him to be so lacking in self-confidence.)

Admittedly, at some point the serious engagement of the mind entails a degree of introspection that may risk becoming neurotic. An authentic intellectual may spend an entire lifetime vacillating between such neuroticism and a hard-won emancipation from oversensitivity or inordinate concern about some matters. The main thing, I suppose, is to overcome one hurdle before encountering the next.

Here are three statements by students who last year applied for highest honors status, with which each of you will, I believe, readily identify. Interestingly, each evidences a thread of increased self-understanding, preceded or accompanied by a certain disillusionment with our institutionalized approach to learning. Here too each of us may detect a further clue with which to assess our own education. To realize, finally, that professors and courses can at best only motivate us to learn by our own effort, and that if we do not transcend the requirements they impose then little will come of that effort, is to begin to operate as genuine scholars must.

The author of the first statement has begun to sense that in the future, his intellectual life will entail more of the same dissatisfaction, that he may never come by a complete panacea for his frustration. In his own words:

> My college career is perhaps most characterized by its total insusceptibility to any concise description. It is a bizarre mixture of frustration, enlightenment, confusion, excitement, disillusionment, and general growing up. . . . I find it hard to speak of "turning points" or "landmarks" in my educational experience. My experiences seem to resemble a color spectrum—with no clear lines of demarcation, yet clear

> indications that change has taken place. One such change has been my acceptance of an ever-increasing amount of responsibility for my own learning. Through numerous experiences and through encounters with other students, I came to realize that I was missing the boat if my only objective was to fill the expectations of my teachers and that I had better start clearly defining what I wanted to learn and setting about to learn it by whatever means available.

The author of the next statement asserts that one should not cease questioning or blindly accept whatever she is told—reminiscent of Plato's maxim that "the unexamined life is not worth living":[3]

> I lack discipline, but I can drive myself on a schedule if I must. My attention span is sporadic. I am easily set-off in ecstatics over not much at all, which is of course an inefficient energy expense, and often I am not accessible to what is happening around me. This means I am not "living in reality." What has any of this to do with going to lectures, and writing papers, and making good grades? All of those proper activities I undertake with the least amount of pain and disturbance. Which is not to say that I am not affected by what I study. I have had many intellectual peak experiences. . . . I don't have any answers, but I am attuned to deceptions, and I don't like dishonesty. If I can help a roommate see the difference between a plastic flower arrangement, however perfect, and a few stray wildflowers in an old teacup, I feel like I have accomplished something in the practical sphere. If I can make up enough monster stories to keep me accepted by my friends under seven years old, then I have accomplished something creatively. If I can ever write a long poem that doesn't rely on wit or allusion, then I will have accomplished something intellectually. . . . I think I shall have to become a teacher. . . . What should I teach? Appreciation based on thorough scholarship. When should I teach? After I know something of both.

The third student may strike you as both skeptical and neurotic, but he is also sensitive, analytical, and ruthlessly honest—one of the most thoroughly honest people I have ever known. At the end of four years at BYU, he had the following to say:

> During college, I have come to realize that my threshold for tentativeness is unusually high (at least for BYU). For me, relativity is not an intellectual game; I simply have no interest in easy answers. . . . I have lost my innocent trust in the untested underpinnings of implicit assumptions. I will never again tread with such glib confidence. . . . I realize that to many this is a sign of personal weakness, but I count it a strength nonetheless. What I do acknowledge as a personal weakness is my very difficult acceptance of those who try to force my allegiances. I can find little love for those who compel me to justify myself to selection committees, to prostitute personal beliefs and experiences for grants of aid, awards, or admissions to graduate programs. . . . I am leaving BYU (and the honors program) with some disappointment and perhaps some resentment. I am disillusioned that many who espoused great confidence in the power of truth, reason, and the enquiring mind did not really have faith in what they taught. . . . Perhaps my disappointment stems largely from the tendency to expect too much of that in which one really believes.

All these students in their own way bear out Professor Edmund Morgan, who, in addressing the entering Yale freshmen in September 1959, contended that a university is essentially "a place where the world's hostility to curiosity can be defied" and that "dedication to curiosity should not end in indecision. It should, in fact, mean willingness to follow the mind into difficult decisions." In his charge to the Yalies, Morgan further added:

> We want you to be forever discontent with how little you know . . . and with how little we know. . . . We want you to back us into corners, show us up, make us confess we don't know. Does this sound formidable? It is not. We may tell you what we know with great assurance, but push us and you will find the gaps. . . . If you learn anything, it ought to change your minds, and hopefully it will change ours too. It will be a sign that we have both wasted four years if you leave here thinking pretty much the same way that you do now or if you leave us thinking the same way *we* do now.[4]

In summary . . .

As all these statements suggest, a quality education largely rests with the individual student—particularly his or her attitude toward learning. That attitude is complex. It entails a certain courage and independence of mind as well as humility and moderation. It bespeaks a kind of nonchalance, a taking of things in one's stride; a readiness to be disappointed and to settle for a dampened level of personal expectation, combined with a fearless loyalty to and hunger for the truth. It presupposes an ascetic attachment to one's task, a perfectionist bent, and a discriminating sensibility—or at least their assiduous cultivation. Such, incidentally, are what we must also cultivate and apply in the realm of faith as we initially acquire and then maintain what we call a testimony.

When so disposed, we are heirs, I believe, of a certain sacred power. Brigham Young alludes to that power in a definition that has never been surpassed. "Education," he said, "is the power to think clearly, the power to act well in the world's work, and the power to appreciate life."[5] May our aspirations remain that comprehensive and may we do them fuller justice in the coming academic year.

Notes

1. Karl G. Maeser, "History of the Academy," in *Educating Zion*, ed. John W. Welch and Don E. Norton (Provo, UT: BYU Studies, 1996), 2.

2. Aleksandr Solzhenitsyn, *The Gulag Archipelago*, trans. Thomas P. Whitney (New York: Harper & Row, 1973), 1:145, 405.

3. Plato, "Apology," in *The Dialogues of Plato*, trans. B. Jowett (New York: Oxford University Press, 1892), 2:131.

4. Edmund S. Morgan, "What Every Yale Freshman Should Know," *Saturday Review*, January 23, 1960, 13–14.

5. Quoted by George H. Brimhall, "The Brigham Young University," *Improvement Era*, July 1920, 831.

On the Need for Both Greater Spontaneity and Authenticity in Our Religious Life

Written in 1979, two years after my service as director of the BYU Honors Program, this essay is essentially a manifesto in behalf of both free inquiry and genuine academic freedom. It also demonstrates the rich influence on my own thought of the many extraordinarily brilliant and sensitive undergraduates with whom I interacted during the course of that privileged assignment. Nearly two decades later, I had the temerity to share it with members of the BYU administration who had convened several faculty members for feedback to help improve their and our relationship as well as our common enterprise. Years earlier, this particular essay had also come to the attention of faculty members in the College of Fine Arts, where I've been told it was widely circulated.

> For behold, it is not meet that I should command in all things; for he that is compelled in all things, the same is a slothful and not a wise servant; wherefore he receiveth no reward. Verily I say, men should be anxiously engaged in a good cause, and do many things of their own free will, and bring to pass much righteousness; For the power is in them, wherein they are agents unto themselves. And inasmuch as men do good they shall in nowise lose their reward. But he that doeth not anything until he is commanded, and receiveth a commandment with doubtful heart, and keepeth it with slothfulness, the same is damned.
>
> —D&C 58:26–29

> All truth is independent in that sphere in which God has placed it, to act for itself, as all intelligence also; otherwise there is no existence.
>
> —D&C 93:30

> Complete, unlimited freedom of expression for every sort of opinion, without the least restriction or reserve, is an absolute need on the part of the intelligence. It follows from this that it is a need of the soul, for when the intelligence is ill-at-ease the whole soul is sick. . . . When the light of the intelligence grows dim, it is not very long before the love of good becomes lost.
>
> —Simone Weil[1]

The need for openness

In October of 1978, the BYU audience was addressed by the ambassador from Sri Lanka, W. S. Karunaratne. Dr. Karunaratne, a Buddhist trained in philosophy, discussed his views regarding the proper religious attitude. With his Mormon audience in mind, the ambassador argued the need for a "critical outlook" that "gives us the open mind and the open society characterized by tolerance and understanding. The way to wisdom is to uncondition the mind regularly and unceasingly."[2]

The relevance of such remarks is echoed in a recent review of Douglas Thayer's *Under the Cottonwood and Other Mormon Stories*:

> His unsettling insights and style challenge the assumptions of modern urban Mormonism: our ignorance of and insensitivity to nature and history, our religious justification of acquisitiveness and materialism, our inhuman programming of youth for secular and religious "success," our knowing indifference to life and death, our intolerance of ourselves and others who deviate from Mormon perfectionism.[3]

Both comments bring to mind our ever-increasing pedagogical tendency in areas of religious instruction—whether in seminary or Sunday School—to provide an overabundance of outlines and reference materials, presumably so the teacher will stay safely in line and the discussion not too dangerously digress from the prescribed topic or interpretation. In my experience as a teacher in various church and church-sponsored educational contexts, this "overkill" has tended to dampen the sense of discovery which, I contend, would lead to greater conviction and stronger testimony if minds were left more to themselves to wrestle for answers. Of course, some might not respond so positively. But it seems to me that the sorry alternative is the generally halfhearted, half-awake participation we often experience in the religious classroom. This may also account for the common tendency of so many, particularly among the youth, to resort to secondary materials and a safe, clichéd impersonal rhetoric when addressing us from the pulpit. (One thinks of the hamstrung scholasticism of the medieval Catholic Church or the equally stagnant tradition of Confucianism.)

A survey of some of the better novels dealing with nineteenth-century Mormon life[4]—each faithfully reflecting the immediate family heritage of its particular author—reveals a similarly sluggish response, a dull, indifferent submissiveness on the part of many early church members to the challenges that came their way—whether colonization, the United Order, polygamy, or the Manifesto. A further telling clue comes from the comment of a friend regarding my attempt to deal in dramatic terms with a controversial figure in early Mormon history, the infamous John D. Lee:

> You never have Lee wonder about personal responsibility vs. authority. Should he not, in retrospect, have some misgivings about so easily "following orders"? . . . Did he die without ever reaching a higher moral development?
>
> I wrote this paragraph over a year ago. Since then our reading group has just finished reading Juanita Brooks's biography. She gives the same impression—he never raised the authority question. Perhaps it was that way.[5]

These circumstances may well indicate that the challenge of the LDS way of life is, after all, just that tough. Because, like all humans, we are such fallible creatures, we will naturally fall short. Still, a better understanding of the issues at stake might reduce confusion and reconcile or even encourage us to continue striving in the face of such perplexity.

Submitting to authority

It might, in fact, help to recognize and acknowledge the church's distinctively authoritarian nature. Professor Jan Shipps, a distinguished non-Mormon scholar who has nonetheless made a deep study of Mormonism, has pointed out to what extent on the Christian denominational spectrum the LDS Church stands next to Judaism. Already associating itself with the pre-Christian era through two of its exclusive sacred texts, the early restored church drew "biblical parallels," she points out, "every step of the way." "They had such a vivid perception of themselves as God's people," she adds,

> that the past and present were joined. Prosaic and matter-of-fact, they made the symbolic so tangible that a direct link was forged between their own day and the days described in Old Testament and New. Mormon theology's emphasis on the Family as the redemptive unit, its patriarchal blessing in which each individual's membership in the household of Ephraim or Manasseh or Judah is solemnly intoned and its "restored" priesthood all work to strengthen the Hebraic connection.

Shipps goes so far as to insist that Mormons are a "neo-Judaic people so separate and distinct that new converts must undergo a process of assimilation roughly comparable to that which has to take place when immigrants adopt a new and dissimilar nationality."[6]

The implication—which may only rarely occur to most Latter-day Saints—is that in contrast to the other more ecumenical Christian denominations, the church of our affiliation, while decidedly Christian, is also much more. Other Christian groups, even twentieth-century Catholics, are far less rigidly authoritarian—a tacit admission, from the LDS viewpoint, that their claim to divine authority is less substantial. For Mormons, the import is clear: without precedent in earlier Christianity (at least as generally perceived) and challenged by our conditioning in liberal secular institutions, we are nevertheless expected to adopt an attitude and posture of complete subordination. This creates ground for potential conflict and raises the need for personal adjustment in many individuals.

The conflict is nevertheless universal. As one scans its representation in literature, one is struck for instance by the resemblance in the plight of Goethe's perhaps most autobiographical hero, Torquato Tasso, who, as an artist, seems irreconcilably torn between following his impulse and submitting to his benefactor's wishes.[7] One also thinks of Goethe's twentieth-century successor, Thomas Mann, most of whose fiction reflects the same conflict between *Künstler* (artist) and *Bürger* (citizen).[8] Artists may have their own reward but also suffer from hypersensitivity. But that is the artist's problem—and most Mormons are not artists. Or is it *only* the artist's problem?

The value of spontaneity

My recent exposure to the work of one of the world's foremost avant-gardists has led to a heightened appreciation of the basic LDS tenets of perfection and eternal progress. To the theatricians of our day, the name of Jerzy Grotowski is well-known. The latter's Teatr Laboratorium in Wrocław, Poland, serves as the beacon or mecca to actors and directors that was once the province of Stanislavsky's Moscow Art Theatre. For the dynamic, revolutionary Grotowski, the term *poor*, as expounded in his handbook *Towards a Poor Theatre*, implies that to achieve true authenticity of expression, the artist must—instead of adding effects and refinements, instead of developing a particular technique—divest himself or herself of all pretension and eliminate all artifice, a tenet that strikes me as akin to the kenotic self-divestment attributed to Christ in Philippians 2:5–8.

Grotowski's intent is that his actors discover and then exert their own individual impulses. *Discovery* is, for Grotowski, a key term. One arrives at this kind of authenticity only by sacrificing comfort and struggling against some obstacle, some form of resistance—like an athlete who constantly pushes to surpass his or her previous record. Grotowski thus encourages the artist to explore what is as yet unconventional and unfamiliar—to avoid at all costs the banal, clichéd illustration of a particular text. Concrete reality, he argues, is always paradoxical and surprising. To be alive to the sense of discovery, which is how we all authentically respond in real life, the artist must always take a new and different route, then be curious about the outcome. Thus, for

Grotowski, another key term is *spontaneity*, which must nevertheless be carefully balanced with rigorous discipline.

What did I learn from this esoteric artist that is relevant to how we Mormons conduct our lives? During two weeks in the summer of 1977, I and other Americans trained with the Laboratorium's actors. We were privileged to witness how, in their work, these dedicated artists so thoroughly exemplify Grotowski's philosophy. As they strained both themselves and their pupils with the most demanding physical and vocal exercises, they demonstrated and profoundly understood, it seemed to me, what it means to strive for eternal perfection. (It should not be surprising that Grotowski and his associates later moved beyond stage productions to what they characterize as "paratheater"—an investigation in terms of the principles they previously applied as artists to life itself, a kind of religious quest.[9])

What Grotowski revealed to me was a fuller consciousness of the need, in all we experience, to discover its significance for ourselves and to undertake whatever we do with freshness, curiosity, and a sense of mystery—in other words, a sense of controlled spontaneity. Grotowski adamantly argues that the alternative is a stagnation and deadness that all too often characterize the performance of professional actors (and which Mormons might in turn meaningfully equate with the condition we refer to as "spiritual death"). This in turn echoes—does it not?—the Sri Lankan ambassador's credo regarding openness of mind, our need to "uncondition the mind regularly and unceasingly."

Not being too certain

This points to a kind of tenuous restraint in areas of ambivalence or uncertainty—an attitude toward life for which, in less than ideal personal circumstances, the poet Keats coined the expression "negative capability": as critic Lionel Trilling puts it, "the faculty of not having to make up one's mind about everything."[10] In a letter to his brothers, Keats recalls the exact instant when, in conversation with his friend, literary critic Charles Wentworth Dilke, "several things dovetailed in my mind & at once it struck me, what quality went to form a Man of Achievement especially in Literature . . . I mean, *Negative Capability*, that is when man is capable of being in uncertainties, Mysteries, doubts, without any irritable reaching after fact & reason."[11] But Keats is no nihilist or inveterate doubter. By settling at times for less, Keats seems to suggest, one can in fact know more than those who, like Dilke and their renowned contemporary Coleridge, are incapable of "remaining content with half knowledge."[12] Such a person, paradoxically, "will never come at a truth as long as he lives; because he is always trying at it."[13]

But what is the essential application for those of us who are something less than avant-gardists or striving poets? Perhaps there is a clue in even Grotowski's audacious assertion that the "transgression of the myth renewed its essential values"[14] and that "an element of menace reestablished . . . derided norms."[15] "We are talking about profanation. . . . a kind of tactlessness based on the brutal confrontation between our declarations and our daily actions."[16] Is this so very different from what Elder Hugh B. Brown said on one memorable occasion on the BYU campus?

> We have been blessed with much knowledge by revelation from God which, in some part, the world lacks. But there is an incomprehensibly greater part of truth which we must yet discover. Our revealed truth should leave us stricken with the knowledge of how little we really know. It should never lead to an emotional arrogance based upon a false assumption that we somehow have all the answers—that we in fact have a corner on truth. For we do not.[17]

Pondering this issue in an earlier essay, I wrote about "our paradoxical need to balance our sense of the actual and imminent, of what seems real, with our idealism."[18] (This was before I had read Robert Pirsig's *Zen and the Art of Motorcycle Maintenance*, which makes the same basic assumption though more profoundly.)

Acting in good faith

While wrestling even earlier with an aspect of the problem, I had observed (mostly to myself) that

> it is terribly demoralizing for those who in fact manifest loyalty and good intent and are therefore trustworthy not to be

> trusted. The natural response is a hurt which, if it persists, finally lapses into a kind of apathy and numbness. Under such circumstances the productivity of those so maligned diminishes, so that, particularly in a hierarchical setting, no one wins—subordinate or superior. This would seem to be a fundamental of organizational behavior, irrespective of its deep-seated moral implications.[19]

A student acquaintance, caught as a missionary in what struck him as a dilemma of conscience, finally settled on this pragmatic stratagem: "In matters of belief, follow what your conscience tells you; in matters of action (including public utterance of belief), follow what your leaders tell you; and in the matter of emotions and hurt feelings, forgive and forget."[20] The position so thoughtfully argued by yet another former student impels one to assert his or her independence of mind all the more hesitantly:

> We create the stress and the frustration ourselves by having to deliberate on each specific question because we have not made the more fundamental decision of choosing between our will and [God's] will. The frustration comes because we do not use our ingenuity to find the ways to keep the commandments, given our special circumstances. Instead we let our special circumstances convince us that we are an exception to the rule and thus rationalize our lack of obedience. . . .
>
> Herein lies one of the crucial keys to our relationship with Jesus Christ. When confronted with the decision of following our own selfish desires or living a commandment that seems difficult or even irrational, we make our decision according to our real desires. . . .
>
> The decision to follow the commandments rather than to be the exception is a manifestation of real faith. . . .
>
> Whether the question be integrity in business, missionary work, birth control, or sabbath slothfulness, if we are inclined to view those commandments through eyes tainted by self-interest, then we will not be able to obey them.[21]

How well this comports with the dictum from the *Lectures on Faith*, presented in the School for the Elders in Kirtland, Ohio, that "a religion that does not require the sacrifice of all things, never has power sufficient to produce the faith necessary unto life and salvation."[22]

Reconciling structure and spontaneous growth

But is the perennial conflict between faith and reason and the ongoing effort to keep the two in balance the ultimate formulation or even the only way to view the perplexities life poses? In this regard, the restored gospel itself suggests a profound epistemological breakthrough, whose clearest utterance occurs in various statements by Brigham Young, second prophet of the new dispensation, and by Hugh Nibley, who has been particularly sensitive to Brigham's insights regarding the intellect. I refer here to the excellent analysis of still a third former student:

> In both their works I think we can see a conception of intelligence which reconciles the notions of reason and revelation by transcending them. . . . A spiritual experience, Nibley says, is a communication of intelligence. More important, he insists that there is no final distinction between spirit and intellect. Even spiritual knowledge must be worked for actively; it does not just plop down on our brains. Brigham Young tells us likewise that revelation is necessary to correct reasoning. He also stresses that the acquisition of knowledge is not easy. Most strikingly, he tells us that we may ourselves become "fountains of revelation." . . . Yet this knowledge, or revelation, seems to flow through us as much as from us; it is not wholly ours though we are its source. . . . All this suggests to me a kind of openness which is something more than passivity, than resignation. It is as much an openness to ourselves as to anything else. Indeed, it seems in a sense to presuppose a basic harmony between the human mind and the world. . . . We can choose a world which tends toward life, or one which tends toward death. As we choose life, we become fountains of life-principles, we reveal the world we have chosen. What kind of world is it? The agreement between Nibley and Brigham Young is striking on this point: it is a whole which is at once orderly and expanding. This is a world which is above all open, creative. It thus requires a conception of reason-revelation always ready to transcend itself. . . . Brigham Young himself would rather

> admit that God has something yet to learn than to accept that he is no longer involved in man's greatest activity, the acquisition of knowledge. . . . The reasonable man whose orientation is basically open is always ready to transcend himself; in him reason willingly accepts the truths which rise up in him as in a fountain, content to follow just a half-step behind faith. For faith expresses a profound choice at the center of one's being, a center which can never be captured in the abstractions of reason, a center in which worlds are given birth before they can ever be dissected. . . . Both Brigham Young and Hugh Nibley clearly stress the individuality of revelation; they clearly do not ask us to depend on the revelation of the "authorities"; in fact they both leave lots of room for free movement around the "official" revelations, for they acknowledge that no revelation is perfectly true as it is expressed to us.[23]

It would thus seem that despite the church's authoritarian structure and the undeviating loyalty required of its members, there *is* a way to transcend regimented norms and to experience, even within the church's elaborate institutional framework, a sense of personal autonomy and individual creative growth.

An amazing application of this principle occurs in one of the church's most structured institutions: the Missionary Training Center (MTC). There, in Grotowski-like fashion, missionaries struggle with the intensive learning of languages and with a truly Spartan regimen of activity. At the same time, they generally experience—many for the first time in their lives—an overwhelming outpouring of the Spirit. This they manage to do by first bending to a myriad of personal constraints, then transcending them in their concern for one another's mutual welfare, as I have explored in depth elsewhere.[24] Despite the MTC's extensive hierarchical structure, there is room—utmost need in fact—for autonomy as well as the exercise of individual initiative, in addition to harmonious collaboration. My experience serving there as a branch president suggests to me that it is possible to quicken the activity that, in a more conventional church context, we so often undertake apathetically or out of a sense of half-reluctant obligation.

Why then are we in practice often so stultified? Why do we so often feel hamstrung by excessive programming, so alienated from the full exercise of our latent creative powers? The church, it would seem—at least in the echelon of highest leadership—is perhaps less inclined to inhibit our initiative than are the intermediate functionaries who, in their insistence on regimentation and arbitrary conformity, zealously seek to satisfy what they imagine to be their leaders' expectations. But this may be equally true of many individual members. In a perceptive essay, a fourth former student (sadly now a critic of the church) argues as follows:

> We know we have weakness of character, a sometimes plastic integrity, and we don't want it confirmed by the judgments of others. This is the fear that causes us to retreat after we have opened ourselves to someone. . . . After an intense conversation, it is awkward to return to the friend, for we fear we have depraved ourself in his eyes. . . . If we *are* able to return, we do it incriminating the selfishness of having been so preoccupied with ourself. Feverishly, we swear that this time we will be more unselfish, more concerned with others, to speak less and listen more, and, in short, to cut them off from the strength and reassurance of knowing us. . . . We do this because our difference makes us feel like a misfit, and, threatened with social rejection, we think of it as only negative. . . . We are so afraid of what others are thinking of us, when the others are not thinking of us at all, but only of what we are thinking of them. . . . That is why it is so hard to love others when they are drowning in the myths of artificial conformity; we simply can't find them. . . .
>
> Just as the traditional cavemen invented gods to explain things like the eclipse of the sun, we as traditional Mormons are prone to invent heresies to explain the holes in our religious understandings. Whether these myths are pure heresy or only over-generalizations, they ease the anxiety of not knowing, and more particularly the anxiety that we may be condemned for not doing something about it. . . . The danger of over-rationality is more than a mere threat of delay in our progression. It can kill the sense of life itself. Its tight control leads to a repression in which we learn to ignore all that we are not immediately sure of. We become so obsessed with order and control that we lose spontaneity and are unable to feel the

> essential joys of living. . . . Alienation from self leads to a second alienation from others. . . . Instead of seeing brothers and sisters all with individualities of fears and weaknesses, talents and strengths, we see only missionaries, home teachers, inactives and nonmembers. They are divided into two categories, the believers and the unbelievers. . . . Our inhibition can make us so judgmental that we can only see others with alternating conceit and covetousness. . . . Life becomes a silent burden of struggle unrelieved by the reassurance of others and because we are so careful about what we let out, many of the beautiful aspects of our personality never reach others either.[25]

If, then, because of fear or timidity, many have lost sight of the spiritual dynamics that need to attend our religious life, instead observing its conventions in a fossilized, mechanical, impersonal fashion—if it takes a Buddhist diplomat or a Polish avant-gardist to remind us of the kind of open, spontaneous, ever-seeking response of mind and heart we need to exemplify—we ought to heed them, for the difference is the difference between life and death. And who of us, aspiring to eternal life, would hesitate in our choice between such alternatives?

Notes

1. Simone Weil, *The Need for Roots: Prelude to a Declaration of Duties toward Mankind*, trans. Arthur Wills (Boston: Beacon Press, 1952), 23, 28.
2. W. S. Karunaratne, address given at BYU, October 19, 1978.
3. Kevin Barnhurst, review of *Under the Cottonwoods and Other Mormon Stories*, by Douglas H. Thayer, *The New Messenger and Advocate*, preliminary issue (1977): 24.
4. Maurine Whipple's *Giant Joshua*, Vardis Fisher's *Children of God*, Lorene Pearson's *The Harvest Waits*, Virginia Sorenson's *The Evening and the Morning*, and Herbert Harker's *Turn Again Home*.
5. Douglas D. Alder to Tom Rogers, October 12, 1978.
6. Jan Shipps, "The Mormons: Looking Forward and Outward," *Christian Century*, August 16–23, 1978, 764.
7. Goethe, *Torquato Tasso*.
8. See especially Thomas Mann's *Buddenbrooks*, *Tonio Kröger*, and *Death in Venice*.
9. For more on the later development and ultimate dissolution of Grotowski's Teatr Laboratorium, see the essay "'Interconnecting' at Home and Abroad" in this volume.

10. Lionel Trilling, "The Poet as Hero: Keats in His Letters," *The Opposing Self: Nine Essays in Criticism* (New York: Viking Press, 1955), 37.

11. John Keats, *The Letters of John Keats*, ed. Hyder Edward Rollins (Cambridge, MA: Harvard University Press, 1958), 1:193.

12. Keats, *Letters*, 1:194.

13. Keats, *Letters*, 2:213.

14. Jerzy Grotowski, *Towards a Poor Theatre* (New York: Simon and Schuster, 1968), 121.

15. Grotowski, *Towards a Poor Theatre*, 121, quoting L. Flaszen.

16. Grotowski, *Towards a Poor Theatre*, 52.

17. Hugh B. Brown, "An Eternal Quest—Freedom of the Mind," May 13, 1969, 12, *BYU Speeches of the Year, 1968–69*.

18. Thomas F. Rogers, "Where Is Reality?" unpublished essay, 1977.

19. Thomas F. Rogers, journal entry, 1976.

20. Gordon Wilson, student paper, fall 1978.

21. John Adams, "The Exception or the Rule," *Century 2* 2/5 (1978): 23–24.

22. Lecture 6:7, in the 1835 edition of the *Doctrine and Covenants*, http://josephsmithpapers.org/paperSummary/doctrine-and-covenants-1835.

23. Ralph Hancock to Tom Rogers, October 1, 1978.

24. Thomas F. Rogers, "An Insider's View of the Missionary Training Center," in this volume.

25. Student paper submitted in the late 1970s.

"Bumping": On Reconciling Contemporary Views of Knowledge and Causation with the Restored Gospel

This discourse must have been written for a presentation to students and fellow scholars. However, I can't recall any such occasion. In it, I attempt a reconciliation of numerous sources reflecting the contemporary zeitgeist with the restored gospel: a considerable, if in this case disputable, achievement. Sometime after its writing (in 1989), the campus was introduced to chaos theory, which for a time persuaded me that perhaps all phenomena and all events are random. Then Merriam and I traveled to Russia to meet the church's new converts there, and the fervent conviction some of them voiced to me that nothing is accidental made me reconsider. Later, my acquaintance with the Mandelbrot set and fractals led me to believe that at some deeper level, there is also a pattern of design and causation in all creation.

WHO, BESIDES MUSICOLOGISTS, HAS EVER HEARD OF Holzbauer, Monn, Wagenseil, Dittersdorf, or Süssmayr—all well-known and respected contemporaries of Mozart and Haydn? Salieri is more familiar—but only because of his prominence in Peter Shaffer's play *Amadeus* (later made into a movie) as a foil to the far more gifted Mozart. Similarly, almost no one today knows of Beethoven's contemporary Hummel, though he was illustrious in his own time. Just what has made these second-raters so second-rate and largely consigned their music to oblivion? My musician friends tell me it is because, craftsman though each of them was, there is never any "surprise" in what they turned out. Their work is all too predictable. And so we are not interested.

A creative misreading of British novelist E. M. Forster's classic critical essay "Aspects of the Novel" gave me a term for what he maintains all successful literary characters do to us: they "bump" us. As with the tantalizing progress of theme and variation in great music, they tend to defy our expectations. Because we cannot entirely figure them out, they both intrigue us and strike us as somehow all the more lifelike. (On later rereading Forster's essay, I discovered that his actual term is *bouncing*, which I find far less attractively suggestive. So "bumping" it remains.)

Think, in this regard, of the generally shocking and completely unexpected surprise that attended your personal discovery, whenever it was, regarding sexual reproduction and how you came to be physically. Or of what the artists and physicians must have thought and felt who first dissected corpses and systematically explored what lies beneath our skin.

Accidents, uncertainty, and unintended consequences

The present generation, it is commonly observed, no longer troubles itself to learn about its roots, let alone much revere them—to concern itself, that is, with history and tradition. But this may be due in part to the way history is mostly put to us: as something already well established, clearly understood and agreed upon by the experts, lacking much if any uncertainty, and leaving little in the past to be discovered. Hugh Trevor-Roper argues against this view in a remarkable essay titled "The Lost Moments of History." Citing an array of instances, Trevor-Roper suggests that significant historical outcomes are contingent and highly precarious—that much of the past as we know it could just as easily have turned out otherwise. He indicates, for instance, how close Mithraism or the worship of Hermes rather than Christianity came to supplanting the worship of classical Roman deities. "History," he insists, "is full of surprises, and if we lose the capacity to be surprised by it, we have lost the sense of it." Moreover, "results do not necessarily conform to intentions."[1]

Indeed, with but a few small alterations in the later course of events or the variable sanity and charisma of particular potentates, how likely it is we would now all be Muslims—or, if Napoleon had been more prudent, speakers of French; or, if Hitler had been more decent and humane (but equally ambitious and designing), of German. Such speculation—in which the review of events is "flexible, aware at every stage both of the alternatives and of the limitations"—makes history truly come alive.[2] Yet how few, even in the classroom, have ever allowed themselves to perceive it in such dynamically tenuous terms.

The distinguished elder statesman George F. Kennan voices similar reservations about historian Arnold Toynbee's vast generalizations. Kennan speaks of "the extreme variations in time and place from which such comparisons are drawn" and speculates on "Toynbee's failure to take full account of the element of the fortuitous—of pure chance—in the unfolding of human affairs, and his consequent assumption that everything that happened in those affairs had to have a reason visible and intelligible to the human eye."[3]

Current cumulative scientific understanding generally concedes a similar uncertainty about what is really "out there" and how much we really know. With increasing rapidity, physical and biological models are revised and updated as further discrepancies and incongruities come to scientists' attention. This is nowhere better perceived than by contemporary philosophers who base their assertions about the limitations and fallibility of our perceptions on the very constraints on thought that language itself necessarily imposes. In his landmark essay "Structure, Sign and Play in the Discourse of the Human Sciences," French philosopher Jacques Derrida speaks of "a series of substitutions of center for center" and states that particularly in the wake of "the Nietzschean critique of metaphysics," "the Freudian critique of . . . consciousness," and "the Heideggeran destruction . . . of the determination of Being as presence," any "center" must henceforth be seen as a "function" rather than a "locus" or "system of differences." Derrida traces this same process in the method of his ethnologist predecessor Claude Lévi-Strauss.[4]

Similarly, the contemporary American pragmatist philosopher Richard Rorty cites scientific historian Thomas Kuhn's influential hypothesis regarding the process of scientific discovery, while Harvard biologist

Stephen Jay Gould asserts that "our empirical world is a temporal sequence of complex events, so unrepeatable by the laws of probability and so irreversible by principles of thermodynamics, that everything interesting happens only once in its meaningful details."[5]

In a remarkably comprehensive treatise titled *That Noble Dream*, Peter Novick of the University of Chicago reviews for us how—in essentially all contemporary disciplines: history, science, philosophy, literary criticism, anthropology, legal studies, and psychoanalysis—"the center does not hold" (the title, in fact, of Novick's illuminating penultimate chapter, whose metaphor in turn clearly derives from Yeats's "The Second Coming").[6] As regards theology and scriptural exegesis, perhaps no one has more cautiously examined the essential foundations of Christianity than Loyola University philosopher Thomas Sheehan. In his book *The First Coming*, he affirms, "In the postreligious dispensation that Jesus inaugurated, faith—that is, living the present-future—means maintaining the *undecidability* of what is human and what is divine."[7]

We nevertheless already encounter this radically reconstituted view of Christianity in some of our most profound literature, beginning with Dante's unrivaled *Commedia*, whose daring conflations of the sacred and profane view hell as an inverse paradise and heaven in terms of the ancient world's most concupiscent commentary, Ovid's *Metamorphosis*. In Dostoevsky, we encounter an array of similarly paradoxical notions: salvation through the suffering that arises out of victimization and outright transgression; holiness and divinity in such "fallen" creatures as *Crime and Punishment*'s Sonya Marmeladova and *The Idiot*'s Nastasya Filippovna; faith and salvation in the prospect of one who, on the verge of murdering his neighbor, first prays and asks for forgiveness—thus acknowledging both God and his own wrongdoing in *The Idiot*.

With the public confession of the weak-willed Nikita in the stage play *The Power of Darkness*, Tolstoy's horrific depiction of peasant depravity, there occurs an equally sublime spiritual transcendence. Similarly, when in *The Death of Ivan Ilych* its tormented protagonist asks himself, "Why these sufferings?" the answer that comes to him—"For no reason—they are just so"—recalls nothing so much as the reply of Jesus to his disciples regarding the man born blind: "Neither hath this man sinned, nor his parents: but that the works of God should be made manifest in him" (John 9:3). The answer—if answer whatsoever—is one of tantalizing mystery, whose acceptance requires truly unprecedented faith in the essential rightness of this "undecidability," "uncertainty," "contingency," or whichever of several current buzzwords one chooses for such lack of cognitive certitude and closure. Echoing Christ's final words on the cross, the dying Ivan Ilych's last verbal encounter involves another character's comment, "It is finished!" and Ivan's own corresponding thought—so opposite our common apprehension of death's finality: "Death is finished."[8]

We might also note writer Simone Weil's profound meditations on the spiritual aspect of reverent submissiveness to—however violent, evil, and seemingly impersonal the forms it takes—pure Necessity, a submissiveness that presupposes and further acknowledges one's inevitable place in God's universe.[9] Such understanding also echoes in the declaration of Catholic writer Flannery O'Connor's perhaps most enigmatic character, the serial murderer of "A Good Man Is Hard to Find":

> "Jesus thrown everything off balance. It was the same case with Him as with me except He hadn't committed any crime and they could prove I had committed one because they had the papers on me. . . . I call myself the Misfit . . . because I can't make what all I done wrong fit what all I gone through in punishment."[10]

As for our own religious discourse—whether the approved rhetoric of our incessant mutual instruction or our personal, idiosyncratic formulations—what is any of it besides so much "head noise," needful, it would seem, but equally arbitrary: a welter of constructs whose significance may well lie far less in what is logically denoted than in the spirit that attends it and that manifests itself, more often than not, "between the lines"? Regarding such constructs, we ought perhaps to recognize that part of caring enough about and believing a thing is to feel free to exercise one's own imagination to the point of making that construct one's own. Also, when any construct strikes us as sufficiently "elegant" and "compelling" (terms common, I believe, to the criteria mathematicians apply to an acceptable if ultimately unprovable hypothesis), we will more readily acknowledge, even accommodate it to our own belief system. Derrida's expression, *play,* also seems to fit here. And surely it is only a matter of courtesy not only to respect the sacredness of another person's being, but also to respect whatever strikes that person as ontologically persuasive—the ritual or code of symbols with which he or she personally and reverently identifies.

Otherwise, as one commentator puts it, "we are all somehow specimens, driven by forces of which we have muddled awareness and over which we have small control."[11] Or as the poet Robert Browning puts it in "Bishop Blougram's Apology":

> Our interest's on the dangerous edge of things.
> The honest thief, the tender murderer,
> The superstitious atheist[12]

What of personal relations and the roles we're assigned in others' lives? What of the individual and his or her quest for self-fulfillment? What does life require of us? How many there indeed are who have set out to "change" this rather hardy but fairly intractable planet, yet sooner or later must give up, their efforts generally unrealized and of no account. How many of us feel the compulsive necessity to "make something of ourselves" or "make a difference" in others' lives—to control, manipulate, reform—and always with the best of intentions? Yet how often such efforts only prove self-defeating, even counterproductive: an excess expenditure of energy and concentration, when—like the current of a swift stream—life's broad sweep carries us where it will, despite our wishing otherwise. This also appears to be the position of Yale scholar Paul Kennedy toward historical outcomes in the bestseller *The Rise and Fall of the Great Powers.*[13]

Citing Machiavelli, the sociologist Daniel Bell in turn forcefully argues that "'men commit the error of not knowing when to limit their hopes.'"[14] Another critic, commenting on *In Pursuit: Of Happiness and Good Government* by political scientist Charles Murray, makes the following observation:

> A proliferation of studies guided by rational-choice models of action has emerged in the last 20 years that has revealed and empirically probed numerous "rationality traps" in which

> well-intended private action produces unintended and undesirable outcomes. This literature . . . demonstrates that self-interested, well-intended, good, private persons do not necessarily produce positive social outcomes.[15]

Present satisfaction and unlimited possibility

But we are *here, now.* That is nothing to minimize or apologize for. We exist. Our existence fills a purpose all its own, and in it we should take supreme satisfaction. We should rejoice and revel. And doing so should suffice, or nearly. If we are meant to "change" anything or anybody, it must be our individual selves. The most radical change may well be to accept and wholly delight in who we are. In doing so, surely we acknowledge, appreciate, and manifest our affinity with all creation and its Creator in a way not matched by any amount of anxiety-filled, duty-obsessed, sometimes all-too-wheedling and whining formal petition. We sense such soulful resignation in the Old Testament psalms and even in lyrics like those from LDS composer Lorin Wheelwright's "Oh, May My Soul Commune with Thee":

> From worldly care and pain of fear,
> Please bring me sweet release. (LDS hymns, #123)

What, then, are some possible implications for an LDS believer? It seems to me that the restored gospel's striking emphasis on both agency and eternal progression is remarkably consistent with the worldview that has here been endorsed and so extensively elaborated. Many of the concepts bequeathed to us through Joseph Smith—the metaphysical and epistemological vision with which the Doctrine and Covenants and the Prophet's sermons are replete—in many respects reflect this same openness and sophistication. The restored gospel's very here-and-now earth- and human-centeredness responds well to Sheehan's insistence that "the message of the kingdom of God is about Jesus of Nazareth—but only insofar as it is about every man and woman," as well as to Sheehan's final allusion to "the kingdom's 'protestant' moment of calling faith back to its origins" and his admonition that "the task is to make it so."[16]

Beyond this, Mormonism's cosmic definition of deity (not unlike the theophany in the *Bhagavad Gita* or that of Dante's *Paradiso*)—God's literal identification as a Supreme Intelligence with light, the power of creation, the life force—and the corollary definition of human beings as coequal intelligences and heirs do much to affirm the ultimate purposefulness and rightness of whatever Necessity (in Weil's sense) we may be forced to endure. The straightforward consolation for and reconciliation with suffering that Joseph Smith apprehended at Liberty Jail further affirms the potentially fortuitous role of tragic experience. And notice the contingent wording—"If thou art accused . . . And if thou shouldst be cast . . . if . . . if . . ."—all "if" (D&C 122:6–7).

We are usually disinclined to think in contingent terms. We seek the assurance that obedience guarantees immediate, tangible blessings. But when circumstances prove otherwise, we can and do resort to the same kind of stoic reassurance that sustained Joseph Smith. At the funeral of one of the LDS Church's most saintly and humane teachers of religion—a man taken at a too-early age by brain tumor, assured of recovery the week before by a high priestly blessing[17]—the survivors were reminded of Habakkuk's declaration:

> Although the fig tree shall not blossom, neither shall fruit be in the vines; the labour of the olive shall fail, and the fields shall yield no meat; the flock shall be cut off from the fold, and there shall be no herd in the stalls: Yet I will rejoice in the Lord, I will joy in the God of my salvation. (Habakkuk 3:17–18)

As Mormons, we often—perhaps too lightly—assert that it is God's inviolate respect for agency that causes him to maintain a needful ethical distance and avoid too much intervening in the here and now. It is on such baffling occasions as the foregoing that the reality of divine restraint—or respect, if you will, for contingency—most forcefully impresses itself upon us.

In yet another respect, the restored gospel can be viewed as reflecting Rorty's sense that any given rhetoric involves a particular vocabulary that is in a sense contextually specific and must needs be superseded. Revelations, we are told, are given in the idiosyncratic speech of the individual recipient—in the recipients' "weakness" and "after the manner of their language" (D&C 1:24). God communes, we are told, with "all nations, of their own nation and tongue" (Alma 29:8)—the implications of which we too seldom allow for in other traditions. Moreover, like few other religious traditions, Mormonism does permit the continuing revision of its "vocabulary" through the principle of ongoing revelation. In a certain sense, Mormonism is remarkably doctrine-poor—or, if you will, doctrine-free. While it attests to the reality of certain events—Lehi had a dream and traveled to the Americas, Joseph Smith saw the Father and the Son—the implications are left for each of us individually to interpret and recognize through *personal* revelation. The all-important role of the individual—of the "working out" of one's own salvation, as we say (see Philippians 2:12)—is thus a fundamental tenet of Mormonism, correctly understood.

We might even go so far as to concede Rorty's observation that

> the social process of literalizing a metaphor is duplicated in the fantasy life of an individual. We call something "fantasy" rather than "poetry" or "philosophy" when it revolves around metaphors which do not catch on with other people. . . . Conversely, when some private obsession produces a metaphor which we *can* find a use for, we speak of genius rather than of eccentricity or perversity.[18]

But this does not preclude the possibility that inspiration of a universal order underlies such "fantasy" or "obsession." In addressing graduates at the University of Chicago, Wayne Booth, a literary critic with Mormon roots, has made a useful distinction:

> If we define truth not as man's formulations of reality but as the basic principles of reality itself—the fundamental laws which make the world what it is and man what he is, whether discovered by man or not—then clearly truth is universal and absolute in the sense that it depends on neither times nor circumstances nor man's formulations for its existence as truth. Though truth in this sense—which has sometimes been considered one aspect of God's nature—presents itself to us in an unlimited number of perspectives, to say this is far from saying that truth is relative to our own private, subjective

> preferences. It is relative only to the world of discourse we have chosen to operate in.[19]

Nor does any of this suggest that we are not in need of each other or of supernatural support in realizing our utmost potential, or, as the scriptures put it, in sharing the divine "fulness" (e.g., John 1:16; Ephesians 3:19, 4:13; D&C 76:20; 93:4). But in all of this, individuality remains sacrosanct. (The notion of the collective, a body politic, is itself, we should recall, a fiction.)

A concept in acting called "the idiosyncratic gesture" attempts to convey credibility through what is distinctive to a given character, as reflected in the personality and mannerisms of the actor portraying him or her. Paradoxically, without such a stamp or flavor of uniqueness, the sense of verisimilitude—hence of authenticity and ultimate human relevance—diminishes. The brilliant Polish theatrical innovator Jerzy Grotowski has even gone so far as to insist that we must deride sacred norms in order to rediscover them.[20] Perhaps this is why events, and individuals too, are "unrepeatable," to use Gould's term. Hence, as Rorty puts it—echoing the notion of literary "bumping"—"the point of writing well is precisely to break the crust of convention." Hence, also, Rorty's definition of freedom as "the recognition of contingency."[21] In the restored gospel and in the pristine concepts of Mormonism, there is room, I believe, for such an interpretation.

Open-mindedness and religious faith

Besides all this, there is something else that (in my observation) more nearly links the sincere religious life—the life of faith—with this same postmodern tentativeness than with the overconfident, mind-made-up position of many who so totally disparage the religious disposition. All too often, I see in those who would rail against whomever they consider superstitious, deluded, and sentimental an unconscious and terribly negative emotional component—a harboring and magnifying of deep-seated personal resentments against those with whom they intellectually differ, often far out of proportion and with no conceivable benefit to either their own well-being or their relationship with others. This can also prompt them, with facile and often superior articulateness, to assail personalities, sometimes quite viciously.

Those who are so sure of themselves and of where by contrast others mistakenly stand—an attitude that admittedly all too often besets the pious—*choose* to operate from broad underlying assumptions, their own special premises. These premises allow them to arrogate to themselves the unfounded right to think the worst of and condemn others, often blanketly and with the most cruel, indiscriminate labels. This raises the questions: Who is least malleable—the "broad-minded" liberal or the provincial he or she so disdains? Who is most dogmatic? Most stunted and stratified? Most intolerant? Most disposed to taking adversarial "cheap shots"? Least secure and, again, least open to learning what most needs to be learned, to growth, change, personal refinement, and—ever hallmarks of civility—concord, goodwill, and genuine mutual supportiveness rather than their primitive opposites?

In contrast—and contrary to the notion that religion is by definition oppressive—I see the truly religious more readily presupposing that if there are wrongs, injustices, and misunderstandings, it is not so much for them to scapegoat and project blame as to look to themselves, change their own uncharitable viewpoint, and—irrespective of who is most culpable—still accept, forgive, and nonjudgmentally commit to resolving differences. In this mode, believers are, I submit—both emotionally and spiritually—far more flexible and open to change, to be worked upon and to work upon themselves, as well as more amenable to future contingency. Their very realistic premise about themselves is that they are still raw, unfinished material, not so very superior or grandiose and in need of further refinement.

In a remarkable presidential address before the American Psychological Association, Donald T. Campbell declared that "sophisticated behavioral scientists . . . relapse into an epistemic arrogance and literalism when dealing with religious claims for truth. . . . They hold up for religious discourse the requirements for a direct realism, a literal veridicality even though they may recognize that this is impossible for science itself." In compensation, he urges upon his fellow practitioners "a thoroughgoing epistemic humility . . . that would make them more sympathetic to social system truths when packaged in nonscientific or metaphorical language."[22] As another who has also rethought his former position, anthropologist Robin Horton writes that "the tradition-bound thinker is *more* critical and reflective, and *less* conservative, than I make him, and . . . the modern, scientifically trained thinker is *less* critical and reflective, and *more* conservative, than I make him."[23]

No one—no matter how learned or clever—is immune from an inhumane yet all too common reactionary tendency. The confidence and sense of superiority that stem from an impressive or acclaimed intellect is particularly vulnerable to such unjustified arrogance. Still, it is such persons, more than those of simple faith, who are, at least in theory, most disposed to appreciate the worldview now current. Its application in the realm of religion could in turn bring all the more alive a compelling sense of mystery, open-endedness, excitement, and, yes, reverence for life in all its aspects.

As for that ultimate and inevitable prospect, Death—that perhaps greatest of all Life's mysteries—even the believer is sorely tested. But what, by extension and like Ivan Ilych, we each need to be prepared for—particularly as a matter of faith—is that, like everything else, Death too will, when it comes, somehow marvelously "bump" us.

Notes

1. Hugh Trevor-Roper, "The Lost Moments of History," *New York Review of Books*, October 27, 1988, 61, 62.
2. Trevor-Roper, "Lost Moments of History," 67.
3. George F. Kennan, "The History of Arnold Toynbee," *New York Review of Books*, June 1, 1989, 20.
4. Jacques Derrida, "Structure, Sign and Play in the Discourse of the Human Sciences," in *Writing and Difference*, trans. Alan Bass (Chicago: University of Chicago Press, 1978), 279–80.
5. Thomas S. Kuhn, *The Structure of Scientific Revolutions*, 3rd ed. (Chicago: Chicago University Press, 1996); Richard Rorty, *Contingency, Irony, and Solidarity* (Cambridge: Cambridge University Press, 1989); and Stephen Jay Gould, "Mighty Manchester," *New York Review of Books*, October 27, 1988, 32.
6. Peter Novick, *That Noble Dream: The "Objectivity Question" and the American Historical Profession* (Cambridge: Cambridge University Press, 1988).
7. Thomas Sheehan, *The First Coming: How the Kingdom of God Became Christianity* (New York: Random House, 1986), 225.
8. Leo Tolstoy, "The Death of Ivan Ilych," in *The Death of Ivan Ilych and Other Stories*, trans. Aylmer Maude (New York: New American Library of World Literature, 1964), 149, 156.
9. James P. Holoka, ed. and trans., *Simone Weil's* The Iliad *or the Poem of Force*, 3rd ed. (New York: Peter Lang, 2006).

10. Flannery O'Connor, "A Good Man Is Hard to Find," in *A Good Man Is Hard to Find and Other Stories* (New York: Harcourt Brace & Company, 1992), 20.

11. Arthur C. Danto, "No Island Is an Island Anymore," *New York Times*, October 23, 1988, www.nytimes.com/1988/10/23/books/no-island-is-an-island-anymore.html.

12. Robert Browning, "Bishop Blougram's Apology," in *Men and Women* (Boston: Ticknor and Fields, 1856), 160.

13. Paul Kennedy, *The Rise and Fall of the Great Powers: Economic Change and Military Conflict from 1500 to 2000* (New York: Random House, 1987).

14. Daniel Bell, *The End of Ideology: On the Exhaustion of Political Ideas in the Fifties*, rev. ed. (New York: The Free Press, 1962), 393.

15. William Julius Wilson, "The Charge of the Little Platoons," *New York Times Book Review*, October 23, 1988, 12.

16. Sheehan, *First Coming*, 226–27.

17. James R. Christianson, 1932–1989.

18. Rorty, *Contingency, Irony, and Solidarity*, 37.

19. Wayne C. Booth, "Knowledge and Opinion," in *Now Don't Try to Reason with Me: Essays and Ironies for a Credulous Age* (Chicago: University of Chicago Press, 1970), 90.

20. See the discussion of "the dialectics of mockery and apotheosis" in Jerzy Grotowski, *Towards a Poor Theatre* (New York: Simon and Schuster, 1968), 22.

21. Rorty, *Contingency, Irony, and Solidarity*, 46, 167.

22. Donald T. Campbell, "On the Conflicts between Biological and Social Evolution and between Psychology and Moral Tradition," *American Psychologist*, December 1975, 1120.

23. Robin Horton, "Tradition and Modernism Revisited," in *Rationality and Relativism*, ed. Martin Hollis and Steven Lukes (Oxford: Basil Blackwell, 1982), 210.

Part 3

The Greatest of These Is Charity

One of life's most important purposes and functions—its greatest source of fulfillment, at least for me—is to commune, to "connect" with others at ever deeper levels of understanding, mutual acceptance, sharing, and identification by merging into one another's lives. And yet, how we tend to stifle our inclination, our need to do so, therewith missing the satisfaction and joy—the very nourishment to our souls—that alone derive from such communion, such connection. We do this largely, I think, from fear—fear of rejection. It is easily the most tragic tendency in human affairs and leads not only to emptiness and depression, but to resentment, hostility, and vengeful scapegoating. It lies at the root of the psychology that engenders and exacerbates all conflict and war, whether public or domestic, at every interpersonal level. If the devil inspires anything in us, it is our fear of and disregard toward each other, and hence ourselves. There are doubtless practical reasons—limits of attention and energy and time and availability—that preclude our attaching ourselves to or demonstrating our affinity for other than a certain number. But this should never serve—as it mostly does—as a pretext for our not universally caring for and about everyone of whom we become aware or who sooner or later enters our presence.

—InterConnections, from *Huebener and Other Plays*

Following page: Thomas F. Rogers, *Merriam*, oil

Discovering Ourselves in Others

This presentation, delivered in 1980, was requested for their lecture series by personnel at Brigham Young University's Harold B. Lee Library. The topic was of my own choosing. Its several anecdotal illustrations, largely drawn from my experience with others at BYU, prompted my own process of discovery regarding that same topic and its importance.

Our relationship with God

In all we might explore, it is most important, I believe, to discover just *who* we really are. In that context, I especially like BYU professor and clinical psychologist Allen Bergin's observation: "Relationships permeate existence. Personal qualities emerge in part from interaction with other identities. Without relationships, the existence of an identity would have no meaning."[1] In other words, it is our relationships with others that in turn define us. Is this not why that ultimate personal relationship to which the Savior made reference in his great high-priestly prayer—"And this is life eternal, that they might know thee the only true God, and Jesus Christ, whom thou hast sent" (John 17:3)—is so significant? Notice that the Savior speaks of *knowing* as a necessary aspect of that relationship, requisite for deriving full satisfaction from it.

Another scripture brings home the glorious destiny to which, as God's literal sons and daughters, all humans are heir: the potent promise that to those who qualify, the Lord will give "all that my Father hath" (D&C 84:38). This includes, if I understand it right, joint ownership and codominion over the entire universe. Besides raising anyone's vision of his or her personal worth, dignity, and divine potential, such a promise is itself a powerful witness that God is literally our Father, with the same generosity toward his offspring that is so instinctive in all but the most narcissistic or deranged earthly parents and the same inclination to bequeath his all to those who wish it and will learn to handle it. "What man is there of you, whom if his son ask bread, will he give him a stone? Or if he ask a fish, will he give him a serpent?" (Matthew 7:9–10). The Savior thus characterizes mortal fathers. His and his father's far greater magnanimity is nowhere so profoundly underwritten as in that glorious vision, afforded in the temple, of what men and women may become.

Relating to others

But in addition to the communion we should cultivate with God in prayer, in contemplating scripture, or in the temple, our devotion to him needs demonstration above all in our relationships with each other. He has said so in many places. And if we are indeed his vessels—individual "temples," as Paul insisted (see 1 Corinthians 3:16)—we will also come to know deity, and hence ourselves, in and through each other. Thus to know God better and know ourselves fully, we need to relate well to others—to so empathize that we can even identify with those who misuse us, because divinity is in them too. The Savior, it seems, had to learn this same lesson during his mortal sojourn. He had to take upon himself our "infirmities, that his bowels [might] be filled with mercy . . . that he [might] know . . . how to succor his people according to their infirmities" (Alma 7:12). He had to descend "below them all" (D&C 122:8).

There are doubtless other profound reasons why we are blessed for "bear[ing] one another's burdens" and "mourn[ing] with those that mourn" (Mosiah 18:8, 9). For example, unless the desires by which we are all driven express themselves in behalf of others, they turn destructively inward. "Consciousness is a poison when we apply it to ourselves," Zhivago tells his dying mother-in-law in Pasternak's novel *Doctor Zhivago*. "Consciousness is a light directed outward, it lights up the way ahead of us so that we don't stumble. It is like the headlights on a locomotive—turn them inward and you'd have a crash."[2] By contrast, when we manage to place ourselves vicariously in another's shoes, we are—by virtue of the comparisons this affords us—powerfully forewarned about what, for our own best good, we ought or ought not to do. This is surely part of the rationale that underlies the emotional catharsis that, according to Aristotle's theory, should occur when we experience aesthetically depicted tragic events.[3]

I also like to believe that great literary works such as *Hamlet*, *Lear*, and *Othello* not only alert us to our own vulnerability but unite us in concern and compassion with other sufferers—even with those who in their shortsightedness provoke others' suffering: the Claudiuses, Regans, Iagos, and Macbeths. Driven by desperate greed and merciless ambition, they are also manifestly unhappy. Legitimate tragic readings of men's and women's lives indeed raise our awareness, at least for a time, about what in this life is really most important and of lasting value, and are therefore spiritually therapeutic. (We should not expect them to do more than this—to change our lives, for example. That would be too easy.) War and other disasters can raise our awareness in this same way. It is about the only positive consequence of war, and its cost is much too high.

Even at one remove, adversity can impel us to overcome our normal lassitude and rise to valorous levels of performance. A recent incident in the branch over which I preside at the Provo Missionary Training Center (MTC) may serve as a meaningful illustration. One of our elders received word just two weeks before his pending departure for Italy that his younger brother had been found several minutes after sinking to the bottom of the municipal pool in Orem. The missionary, who only a year earlier had felt so estranged from his family that he had left home to live with friends, told me tearfully while keeping vigil at the Provo hospital with those same family members that his only concern was to live worthily enough to enjoy his angel brother's company in the next life.

This missionary would hold the other boy's limp hand for hours on end. He would have stayed through the night if he had not been required to return by curfew time to the MTC. His fellow missionaries were in turn struck by the remarkable faith and oneness that sustained this missionary and his family during their vigil and after the younger boy's death, just days before the missionary's departure for Italy. During that time, the elder never wavered regarding his mission and continued to memorize his discussions. In consequence, a firm resolve took hold among the entire branch to devote their best effort to the Lord's work. With "an eye single" (D&C 4:5), all eighty or so missionaries intently settled down to their immediate task. Personal problems largely ceased. On leaving for Italy weeks later, the majority of these young men and women had memorized all eight missionary discussions, where earlier only one or at most four of the dozen and a half or so who flew out together would have made such progress.

Reconciliation and forgiveness

The discovery of ourselves in others also bears upon the theme of reconciliation and forgiveness that recurs, I find, in much of the literature that most deeply moves me. There are, for instance, what for me have long been the transcendent moments in those peerless novels by Tolstoy and Dostoevsky—*War and Peace*, *Anna Karenina*, and *The Brothers Karamazov*. Besides the occasion when Priam embraces the knees of Achilles in the *Iliad*, there are in all literature few like the moment when in *War and Peace* Prince Andrey commiserates with his dastardly rival Kuragin as the latter undergoes an amputation during the Battle of Borodino; or when, across his wife's sickbed, thinking her about to die, Anna Karenina's husband takes Vronsky's hand and forgives his wife's seducer; or when, having nearly lost his faith and ready to lose himself in debauch, Alyosha Karamazov is so touched by the courtesan Grushenka's restraint that in a sublime vision he subsequently encounters his deceased spiritual mentor, whose death had so disillusioned him, in a setting—that of Christ's first miracle at Cana—which restores in him the capacity to reunite with Father Zosima in forgiveness and love. All of these remarkable scenes illustrate that ultimate Christlike mandate to empathize with and love one's ostensible enemy.

It is in turn gratifying to reflect that what drew me to the protagonists in several plays I have written was Helmuth Huebener's willingness to forgive the branch president he mistakenly presumes betrayed him to the Gestapo (*Huebener*); John D. Lee's expression of unwavering love for Brigham Young, conveyed to George A. Smith at the prison in Beaver in 1875 (*Fire in the Bones*); and Arthur Robison's final recognition that he must not hold against his old church colleague nor himself whatever it was that induced his brother Fred to take his own life or Arthur's son Larry to die in Vietnam (*Reunion*). My pursuit of this theme wasn't conscious, but it is gratifying, even in retrospect, to recognize a recurring pattern and hidden motive that bespeaks such a noble ideal or aspiration on the part of those mistreated characters.

One of the most meaningful consequences of seeing my plays produced and having some of my views appear in print is the people who have subsequently made themselves known to me, often people with distressing personal problems—some of whom have become my dearest eternal friends. There are many within Mormon society who are terribly lonely and alienated, who yearn for deeper interpersonal communion but find their conversation and relationships with fellow Latter-day Saints far too superficial and unfulfilling. Perhaps some of them need to communicate better with deity, to be less critical and more other-directed, but they still have this real need.

It is, of course, possible for us to wrongfully and destructively serve that need by inadvertently encouraging such personal dissonance and exacerbating their grievances, resentful carping, and self-pity. In so doing, we need to examine our own motives. As Brother Bergin reminds us, "Appropriate balance requires that love and affection not be dispensed indiscriminately, without reference to guidelines governing time, place, person, extent, etc."[4] Despite such risks, which can lead to manipulation by mutual consent for self-justification, we still need to commune, meaningfully and righteously, with each other. Nor is it always easy to deal with those who "kick against the pricks" (D&C 121:38) and in paranoid fashion refuse to recognize their truest friends.

My first teaching appointment eighteen years ago was at Howard University, an institution founded for and still largely patronized by black Americans. This was at the outset of the Civil Rights movement, just before the 1963 March on Washington. I shared offices then with an accomplished woman my age—the former prodigy of Howard's Department of Theatre, who had earned a master's degree in German when her husband attended Harvard. While trying to blend into the society of my colleagues and students, I'd been fairly reticent about discussing black–white relations until one day the subject somehow arose between Mary and me as we sat at neighboring desks during the consultation hour. I had innocently commented that I was glad to see people like myself finally "accepting" black people. Mary's sudden and intensely bitter rejoinder was: "We don't need your 'acceptance,' Whitey. We just want the same privileges you've had all along." More recently, I've encountered a similar resentment toward men in the attitude of some feminists. While I concede that such people have legitimate grievances, I also believe their disavowal of others' concern or good intentions is illusory and wrong. As Mother Teresa says of the dying poor in India, "It is not very often things they need. What they need much more is what we offer them. . . . Being unwanted . . . is the worst disease that any human being can ever experience. . . . For being unwanted, except there are willing hands to serve and there is a loving heart to love, I don't think this terrible disease can ever be cured."[5]

But what is it that too often keeps us from having the perspective we need to view others, even our enemies, with the affinity and mutual concern both we and they require? What are some of the impediments? And what role, if any, does education play in all of this? I have three surmises.

Letting superficialities divide us

The first is that without education, we are more easily inclined to take some things that are in fact quite arbitrary as literal and sacrosanct. We imbue them with such unnecessary importance that we are more inclined to censure or even condemn those who may not take them as seriously as we do.

Languages present that kind of arbitrariness. Some of us believe it an extremely useful step, in getting closer to those who do not speak our own language, when we familiarize ourselves with the (to us) nonsensical streams of sound that are their innate mode of self-expression. Only as we learn another's language and make it ours do we fully penetrate that person's strangeness, confirm that the other person also thinks and feels as we, and enable ourselves to communicate more than superficially.

But the assumptions we make about others, then reinforce with rhetoric—even within a common language—are equally divisive. I still vividly remember an evening before the fall of the Soviet Union when I sat in the lobby of the Kirov ballet theater in Leningrad (now St. Petersburg), talking to an amiable old usher who, when he discovered I was an

American—doubtless the first he had ever spoken with—immediately interrogated me about my salary, if I owned a car, etc. He then wistfully concluded, "Yes, you Americans are much better off than we. If you only had our freedom."

In this instance, distortions and an impasse in understanding had been deliberately imposed by political propaganda. Here is the confession of an early promoter of the writing of Solzhenitsyn, a former Red Army Major who, for protesting his soldiers' wanton rape and pillage at the end of World War II, was in turn sentenced as a political prisoner for "agitation against vengeance and . . . sacred hatred of the enemy."[6]

> With the rest of my generation I firmly believed that the ends justified the means. Our great goal was the universal triumph of Communism, and for the sake of the goal everything was permissible—to lie, to steal, to destroy . . . all those who were hindering our work or could hinder it, everyone who stood in the way. . . . Good and evil, humanity and inhumanity—these seemed empty abstractions. I did not trouble myself with why "humanity" should be abstract but "historical necessity" and "class consciousness" should be concrete. The concepts of conscience, honor, humaneness we dismissed as idealistic prejudices, "intellectual" or "bourgeois," and, hence, perverse.[7]

Or as philosopher Eric Hoffer puts it, the intellectual "has made the 20th century a century of words par excellence. In no other century have words become so dangerous. A failure to recognize this fact can have disastrous consequences."[8]

It is indeed "the tyranny of abstractions" that accounts for so much enmity-ridden prejudice.[9] Why, for example, has Russia for so many centuries, and likely centuries yet to come, been so routinely subjected, in the words of one observer, to a "lack of tolerance in its political affairs, of humility in its leaders, of proportion between glittering ends and sordid means, of honesty in assessment of its problems"?[10] One might wish that all of this were somewhat compensated for by the Russians' remarkable sense of communality. But that too has been perverted by their power-obsessed rulers—and thoroughly exploited.

I don't enumerate these depressing circumstances so much to point the finger at those whose minds and spirits are clearly shackled as to suggest wherein, without an ongoing broadening of viewpoint and vigilant self-awareness as to what we do not fully or accurately know, we ourselves can be similarly prejudiced. The increased recognition among many Mormons that many of our own Anglo-Saxon Wasatch Front mores are quite arbitrary and at variance with the traditional and sacred in other cultures—as our own Lamond Tullis, Spencer Palmer, and Lynn Tyler, among others, have made us increasingly aware—is indeed a hopeful sign.[11]

There are still numerous assumptions, equally arbitrary, that tend to divide those of us who live in close proximity and whose background is otherwise similar and homogeneous. A partial list of such tenuous assumptions might include the following:

- That the contemplation of evil and its consequences is not needful and cannot be useful or instructive
- That the bounty and the goods of this world, including what delights our senses, are not ordained by God for human pleasure
- That we need not be equally prepared and willing to renounce such pleasure at will or whenever called upon and to practice doing so
- That religious taboos and the observance of prescribed religious practices are not important
- That observance of prescribed religious practices by itself makes a man or woman sufficiently religious
- That one can grow spiritually (or remain spiritual) without internalizing faith, seeking personal revelation, exercising personal initiative, sacrificing, and constantly pushing beyond prior limits in so doing
- That individuals long conditioned to a certain degenerate lifestyle or pattern of thought cannot radically change or, after doing so, must still forfeit our full acceptance and respect
- That it is not important to heed the counsel of living prophets

- That we do not need to think through, discover and verify for ourselves, or obtain a personal witness of saving truths and how we individually need to apply them
- That there is no latitude for diverse opinion on more speculative points of doctrine over which authorities themselves have differed, and that it is not possible to respect and fellowship those whose interpretation of such matters fails to coincide with our own
- That we cannot tolerate someone whose views we consider to be in error
- That some human beings are infallible
- That people tend to be either all good (usually "our kind" of people) or all bad (usually some other kind)
- That Mormons have a monopoly on Christlike virtue and wisdom
- That affluence and social or family prominence imply greater righteousness
- That those whose politics are not conservative or even reactionary are not in tune with the Spirit
- That those with conservative political views lack compassion
- That we are not all liable to temptation, error, defensiveness, and rationalization
- That testimony is an inviolable acquisition rather than a tenuous, ongoing process

We err, I fear, in failing to distinguish between what is tentative, arbitrary, or nonessential and what is essential. We have a paradoxical need to balance our sense of the actual and imminent—of what seems real—with our idealism. The two often as not appear in contradiction, but the only effective way to cope with either, I believe, is to keep them both before us in tension and give each its due, without compromising either. I believe this is possible as well as necessary. Alternatively, we can embrace solely what we take for pure reality and thus lapse into self-centered cynicism and despair—or ignore perceived reality, becoming naive, narrow, and ultimately out of touch with this world, neither "in" nor "of" it. Maintaining the right perspective and equilibrium in the face of this fundamental paradox is, I believe, one of the ultimate challenges life affords us. It is the principal theme of some of our most provocative literature; it is, for instance, what makes both *Don Quixote* and *Madame Bovary* so timeless and so significant.

I see no other way to cultivate the wisdom we need than by remaining more tentative about some matters than we are generally prone to be: to retain a hardheaded view of immanent reality while, with uncompromising devotion, pursuing our high ideals. To do so, we must also be amenable to paradox, to which few thinkers have ever taken instinctively—Christ, Plato, and Dostoevsky being notable exceptions. I used to wonder how it was possible to think in such terms. Now, I can see no other way. I no longer presume to know the definitive answers to what is not given me to know in this life. To settle for that much blissful uncertainty unburdens and emancipates. I only pity all who still struggle with our inescapable ignorance and mask it with hasty, biased, clichéd assumptions.

There was a certain satisfaction in having sensed these things prior to reading their aesthetically profound expostulation in writer and philosopher Robert Pirsig's *Zen and the Art of Motorcycle Maintenance*.[12] A similar statement also recently appeared in what I consider a landmark essay titled "Living with Opposition in All Things" by Marvin Rytting, a BYU alumnus and psychologist. Rytting's perception reads as follows:

> It would take an entire issue . . . to discuss all of the paradoxes that I have come to accept, but the ultimate one may be the expectation that Mormons are supposed to be "in the world but not of the world." This injunction creates an overriding ambivalence about practically everything. We should be blessed with riches but not be materialistic. We are supposed to enjoy life but not too much. Our theology exalts the body, but the flesh is suspect. We need to know good and evil through experience but never do anything wrong. I think that we really have not solved the puzzle of being in the world but not of it. I know that I have not. At BYU, it seemed that not being of the world meant being five years behind it, but somehow I do not think that is what God has in mind.[13]

The ultimate benefit from such sensitivity about the ambiguity and complexity of so much that confronts us each day but which we so readily oversimplify, categorize, and then dismiss from our minds—the ultimate benefit to our relations with each other, so that we might in turn know ourselves—was well understood by the following outstanding mentors:

Joseph Smith:

> I [do] not like the old man being called up for erring in doctrine. It looks too much like the Methodist[s], and not like the Latter-Day Saints. Methodists have creeds which a man must believe or be kicked out of their church. I want the liberty of thinking and believing as I please. It feels so good not to be trammeled. It does not prove that a man is not a good man because he errs in doctrine.[14]

Brigham Young:

> I am more afraid that this people have so much confidence in their leaders that they will not inquire for themselves of God whether they are led by Him. I am fearful they settle down in a state of blind self-security, trusting their eternal destiny in the hands of their leaders with a reckless confidence that in itself would thwart the purposes of God in their salvation, and weaken that influence they could give to their leaders, did they know for themselves, by the revelations of Jesus, that they are led in the right way. Let every man and woman know, by the whispering of the Spirit of God to themselves whether their leaders are walking in the path the Lord dictates, or not.[15]

Hugh B. Brown:

> Preserve, then, the freedom of your mind in education and in religion, and be unafraid to express your thoughts and to insist upon your right to examine every proposition. We are not so much concerned with whether your thoughts are orthodox or heterodox as we are that you shall have thoughts.[16]

Aleksandr Solzhenitsyn:

> The line dividing good and evil cuts through the heart of every human being. And who is willing to destroy a piece of his own heart? . . . Our cellmate . . . explained it to me: "Cruelty is invariably accompanied by sentimentality. It is the law of complementaries." . . . Theirs were the same sincerity and honesty, the same devotion to the Party, the same lack of the moral strength needed to fight back, because they had no *individual* position.[17]

> The people is not everyone who speaks our language, nor yet the elect marked by the fiery stamp of genius. Not by birth, not by the work of one's hands, not by the wings of education is one elected into the people. But by one's inner self. Everyone forges his inner self year after year. One must try to temper, to cut, to polish one's soul so as to become *a human being*. And thereby become a tiny particle of one's own people.[18]

Some may object that the "tyranny of abstractions" I've been discussing is unavoidable whatever ideology one embraces, even that of the gospel. My response is that for all the understanding of life it affords, and like no other religion I can think of, the restored gospel avoids intellectual constructs. Instead, it largely views the statements it makes—its teachings or theological propositions—as descriptions of actual historical events. The first vision was such an event, as was its revelation regarding the nature of the godhead. They were witnessed at first hand by the boy prophet. The Bible, Book of Mormon, and Pearl of Great Price are in turn authentic historical records that offer us, as role models and object lessons, accounts of the individual lives of select forebears interacting in concrete historical settings with deity—personal histories that we, like Nephi, are to "liken" unto ourselves "for our profit and learning" (1 Nephi 19:23). No other religious body is, to my knowledge, so historically conscious, so reality-centered, even in its exponents' most daring speculations. And what we are to make of those speculations, what metaphysical significance we ascribe to them, is largely left to each of us to work out, along with our personal salvation.

As an incidental note, the charge to learn from the example of the scriptures has profound implications for the way we unavoidably learn from each other and thus, for better or worse, shape ourselves—by modeling each other's behavior. There is an analogy here to the way we first learn to speak through exposure to and immersion in our parents' vocabulary, syntax, and sentence intonations. Such is the power of example that, to some degree, the discovery of self inevitably involves discovering the nature of and becoming like those with whom we associate.

There is a final twist to this matter of feeling right toward those who entertain arbitrary points of view that may differ with or even contradict our own (because to some extent we all indulge in such opinions). An important letter, issued some three years ago by the First Presidency to all who conduct worthiness interviews, urged that those interviewed be told that in responding to the appropriate questioner it is "as if" they were replying to "the Lord himself." I relate this to our sacred obligation to sustain and deferentially relate to "the Lord's anointed"—who, as I take it, include all those who have been endowed in the temple, including those who have been married there and all who have served missions. Have you ever put yourself down, failed to "sustain" yourself out of excessive fear, worry, or self-pity? Such a response is sinful and tantamount to violating a covenant.

Don't we all fall short of the deference we owe one another, without which we cannot achieve that mutual concord so essential to knowing ourselves? Do we sufficiently refrain from judgmentalness and guile? It is well if we at last weary of our own or others' carping about this or that church leader. Our complaints are seldom important and invariably canker the soul—interfering with other matters that are much more vital and that, for their realization, depend upon the views and behavior of no other man or woman.

We cannot be made to think differently about a thing than we are inclined at the time—and this is a great guarantee of the sacred autonomy of intelligence: ours, the Russians', and everyone else's. But there is a way, even if at times our views differ from another's, to accept and sustain and love that person by virtue of his or her sacred office—or, even more so, by virtue of his or her sacred status as a fellow human.

Knowing and caring about others

My second postulate is even simpler: if you know someone well enough, you can't be nearly so prejudiced or indifferent toward that person.

One of those special friends I mentioned who first approached me after reading something I had written died last year, not yet forty. I know of no one who had a more Job-like existence. Stuart was never very well, or so it seemed. He couldn't hold a job. His keen sense of integrity communicated itself to others who were, like most of us, less thorough and perhaps more practical but also more disposed to compromise. Consciously or not, he reproached others, including his employers, with his ultrahigh standards. They in turn perceived him as a stubborn perfectionist and something of a hypocrite—a hypochondriac and slacker.

Stuart was also, incidentally, a genius who doubted himself—a man of the purest and most tender sentiments, but easily manipulated. He was often deeply depressed, particularly during periods of illness. I spent the entire summer after we first met helping him reconstruct and write his personal history so he could defend himself against charges raised against him in both civil and ecclesiastical courts. I served as a witness in his behalf when he was disfellowshipped by his bishop—and six weeks later when that decision was reversed by his stake high council. The day he died, his wife told me he considered me his very best friend.

I awoke one night recently, thinking of Stuart and all the other Stuarts I know. The list is long. I told my wife that if what Stuart thought of me were true, then it was a pitiful thing. I certainly wasn't the best friend he deserved to have. With my busy daily schedule, I gave little thought to his welfare, and for long periods of time, especially toward the end, he seldom came to mind. There were also times when I began to wonder if anything were really wrong with him. His case seemed so bafflingly borderline. And there were times when, chiding him for his stubbornness and impatience, I too became impatient. Worst of all were the times—too many—when, with this or another Stuart, I resented the intrusion on my time and, while feigning interest, really cared only about what I'd hoped to be doing instead.

I marvel at my high school peer and colleague Gene England. Because he is so open and understanding and because he so committedly believes in "dialogue" as essential to meaningful fellowship, he has over time attracted many who are disaffected, justifiably or not—those many of us would snub or feel uncomfortable around, fearing condemnation from others who view themselves (and, we hope, us) as "orthodox." I too have befriended some who murmur, who consider themselves displaced and find themselves on the fringe. But I haven't always been so patient or concerned, deep down, or generous as Brother England.

No, I haven't always made others my first priority, even when they've come to me in desperate need. In fact, had I cared more, I would at times have been *less* ingratiating. I would have commiserated less, cut some short and risked a confrontation by telling them what they might not care to hear, but what in my view they most needed. With enough concern, I might have reached some of them—if not at the time, then once they'd had time to reflect. Instead, I have too often felt like the author of this poem, a perceptive honors student who graduated last August:

Sometimes I feel smug because
I am such a good actor.
No one knows me deep inside.

I keep people out of my inside space
with a sophisticated facade.
I'm a pretty good manipulator of appearances.

You said you have seen the real me,
several times.
"Tell me," I said, "When did the real me show through?"

You told me of a time—
You—transmitting intense pain over the phone
me—wishing I could hang up and go to sleep;
You thought I was transparent, really open,
But few times have I been as two-faced:
acting like I cared when I really didn't.

You said you knew I cared
(You desperately needed to believe that).
I fooled you.

Somehow I don't feel so smug anymore.
I feel tight and boxed up.
I feel that in hiding myself

from even close friends,
I have hidden it even from myself.

I have been having second thoughts about my acting career.[19]

I suspect most of us are all too often that kind of actor. Even within our ecclesiastical stewardships, we sometimes condescend, assuming either that what we're doing is more important than someone else's need or that (without carefully weighing the other person's dilemma) we already know better than that person what he or she should do about it. When we treat others this way—or make them feel so insecure they expend all their energy trying not to displease us, instead of moving forward creatively on their own initiative with our sustaining respect, faith, and confidence, free even to make mistakes—we really do not esteem our brothers and sisters as ourselves. We are guilty of a subtle form of "unrighteous dominion," and even mental cruelty. Especially in our stewardships, we need to be wary of "the habit of always believing the worst of others," as one Russian dissident put it—speaking of how East Europeans have had to cope in the absence of genuine civil rights and democratizing institutions.[20]

It seems to me that at such times what really stands in our way isn't so much that we don't know each other well enough—which, according to my theory, closer familiarization ought to correct—as simply our unwillingness to consider others important enough to respect and take seriously in the first place. This suggests a major caveat about what traditional education by itself can (or cannot) automatically achieve. The benefit we derive from what we learn about others depends totally on our motive. We often say as a kind of put-down that in lashing out at others, people betray their own insecurity. But it is equally true of *us* whenever we are standoffish, condescending, impatient, or indifferent, or otherwise fail to accept others in full fellowship. How tragically we are thus diminished—we more than they. Nor is it a question of having cause. We all have ostensible cause whenever we take offense. "It must needs be that offences come" (Matthew 18:7). But nowhere is it written that we must or ought to *take* offense.

Is it not that other things get in the way—our greed, our pride, our selfishness? In light of our multitude of competing, difficult-to-prioritize obligations to ourselves and others, how can we justify our long lists of self-centered goals—such as the time so many of us too obsessively devote to being "beautiful" people and always looking our best? Or our slaving for well-appointed surroundings, for the perfect floor plan—such ephemeral ego crutches, in the long run debilitating, demeaning, and impressive only to ourselves? Or almost everything advertising persuades us to take with such deathly seriousness, like the shape of next year's latest model car? Isn't our yearning for power, for reputation, for sensual self-obliteration, for material possessions, not after all the most desperate of ploys, the seeking of an illusory refuge from what we most need to face in ourselves or our circumstances? (Since this was first written, I would readily add the narcissistic self-absorption of so many in online recreations and texting.)

I know a number of eligible and extremely capable young women who have had to learn great patience because a number of young male returned missionaries, equally impressive in a number of ways—you know some of them, you may be one of them—think too highly of themselves to settle for a slightly too thick calf or attached earlobes, at least until other prospects run out. They too are losers. They too know themselves imperfectly and, as the months and years go by, less well. It is insidious and tragic when, while theoretically espousing certain ideals, we so betray them by halfhearted application. As a Polish exchange professor pointedly told me after spending a year in this community, "The people here are sincerely trying to be artificially better than they are."[21] It was the word "artificially" that leapt out at me then and still does. Is it because we too inconsistently think through our priorities? As my wife recently observed, "People aren't going to be exalted for forcing themselves not to think."

As the two of us talked of these matters into the early morning on one of the rare occasions when, since the children came, we have managed to commune uninterruptedly, I recalled those special mentors in my own life, men who were "fathers" to me in the absence of my own father's beneficent influence. There were not many. And that is my point. There are far too few who make themselves available to others or do so in the proper spirit. But those few men who have strategically influenced my life had this in common: they always made me feel that just then, as I sat across from them, I was more important than anything or anyone else. They could do that because they had learned, as the prophet Joseph admonishes us, to "enlarge" their souls.

With the same limitations as the rest of us on their time, energy, and resources, such individuals have acquired a seemingly endless capacity to bless others. And they are, whether officially or extracurricularly, those most in demand. One wonders how they ever manage. Something must give. Something must be neglected—but it is never other people, including, as best as I can tell—and this is most significant—their own families. We all can and should be more like them. The formula, if there is one at all, is really very simple. As one individual recently put it—a BYU faculty member and former mission president, who in his spontaneous befriending of Israelis, Yugoslavians, and all who meet him strikingly exemplifies those same qualities: "We have to take the time and really love them."[22]

The discipline of discipleship

My third supposition draws a particularly close analogy to the process of learning and relates the discipline and concentration required by scholarship to getting outside ourselves, the resistance to immediate gratification, the sacrifice and courage which are in turn requisite to other-directedness and spiritual growth. We can, I think, so interpret the essentially negative injunctions of the Sermon on the Mount—that we rid ourselves of carnal compulsions ("Whosoever looketh on a woman to lust after her hath committed adultery . . . in his heart"), of the yearning for what "moth and rust doth corrupt" (materialism), of false piety and impure motives ("Do not your alms before men . . . When thou prayest, [do not] as the hypocrites . . . for they love to pray . . . that they may be seen of men"), of judgmentalness (seeing the "mote" while failing to notice the "beam" in our own eye), or indulging in worry and self-pity ("consider the lilies of the field, how they grow; they toil not, neither do they spin")—all of which diminish our capacity to "love [our] enemies": the acid test of love (see Matthew 5:28, 44; 6:1, 5, 19, 28; 7:3).

The working of such disciplined attention in Christian love is beautifully expressed by the profound religious writer Simone Weil, as follows:

> The capacity to give one's attention to a sufferer is a very rare and difficult thing; it is almost a miracle; it *is* a miracle. . . . The soul empties itself of all its own contents in order to receive into itself the being it is looking at, just as he is, in all his truth. Only he who is capable of attention can do this.[23]

In addition, everyone—every missionary, every Latter-day Saint—should read and reread Dietrich Bonhoeffer's *Life Together*, the most inspired handbook on Christian fellowship I know. In it, Bonhoeffer contends that "without Christ we should not know God" and that "without Christ we also would not know our brother"[24]—from which it follows that without Christ, who is our one peerless and fully reliable role model, we would also not know our best and most real selves. In this connection, there is considerable insight and wisdom in the theory of counseling subscribed to on this campus by BYU's Jonathan Chamberlain and others entitled "eliminating self-defeating behaviors."[25] It's a very useful notion that at the core of us all there is something divine and already perfected that, in the course of our lives, we then overlay with accretions of what is carnal, worldly, sinful—call it *karma* if you wish: something that is not really us, of which—as with faith and the assistance of the Holy Spirit we come to recognize that these accretions too are arbitrary—we can then divest ourselves, along with all associated pretensions, as we are urged to do in the Sermon on the Mount.

Surely no one more valiantly exemplifies the courage associated with Christian fellowship than the Moscow priest Dmitry Dudko, who, prior to his arrest in 1980, publicly contended that whatever might happen to him for preaching Christ would be, by contrast with the devastating consequences should men not have Christ's word, completely inconsequential. According to Dudko, "To endure, to experience sufferings—or at least to do so through compassion for your neighbor—*this* is the path of free faith in Christ's resurrection."[26]

A final caution about the discipline required of discipleship is offered by another Russian priest, Aleksandr Yelchaninov. He observes:

> The smallest atom of good realized and applied to life, a single vivid experience of love, will advance us much farther, will far more surely protect our souls from evil, than the most arduous

> *struggle* against sin, than the resistance to sin by the severest ascetic methods of chaining the dark passions within us.[27]

And thus . . .

All of this is offered in consideration of that simple but great commandment to love our neighbor as ourselves (see Mark 12:31), to which in turn attach great blessings. And yet how elusive that commandment is. Listen again to Eric Hoffer, who invokes it with this explanation:

> What I am going to advocate may seem far-fetched. But . . . as things are now, it may well be that the survival of the species will depend upon the capacity to foster a boundless capacity for compassion. In the alchemy of man's soul, almost all noble attributes—courage, love, hope, faith, beauty, loyalty—can be transmuted into ruthlessness. Compassion alone stands apart from the continuous traffic between good and evil proceeding within us. Compassion is the antitoxin of the soul. Where there is compassion, even the poisonous impulses remain relatively harmless.[28]

The Lord's Spirit, the Holy Ghost, is the spirit of love as well as the spirit of truth, and we simply cannot have it with us if we either dislike someone or are not honest. Our sense of right must always be tempered by an unqualified acceptance of, caring for, and ultimate love for others. Conversely, if we both love others and have integrity, we will care about our capacity to bless others, recognize our ignorance and ineptness, and hence be curious and seek to improve our knowledge and understanding. We will have the purest and best motives for wanting to study and learn.

When the Savior asserted that "whosoever will lose his life for my sake shall find it" (Matthew 16:25), he surely did not mean that we should lose ourselves either in our work or in pursuit of what is often called "the good life." It needs to be something far more vital—the life force itself, the *eternal* life force, as we can best come to know it in each other. We thus have reflected back to us a perception of that inner core of our own remarkable nature, which we cannot ourselves see and to which, on our own, we are necessarily oblivious. As we arrive at and maintain an awareness of who we and others really are, the proper value and purpose and use of everything else—including our own intellectual activity—assumes its right and harmonious role in the working of our lives; enriches, edifies, and in turn assists us to become increasingly less divisive, more sanctified and *one*.

We each assume therewith a certain burden. Often we are the only ones to know that is so—we and the Lord. But that burden is a great privilege, for it is the burden of life—our life with others—and the burden of divine love. In the words of a man I know only through what he wrote more than a hundred years ago as a young missionary, preserved for us in the *Millennial Star*:

> This, then, is true Priesthood—to be images of the living God, exhibiting in our characteristics his brightness and his strength; to be girt and endowed with the purity of his nature; to be unsullied in heart and mind; to stand by the strength of redeeming, saving qualities; to bless, and bless, and bless again, notwithstanding ingratitude in some—building, sustaining, and protecting . . . the weak, the downtrodden, and the helpless, till helping becomes our natural food—working on all principles that yield nourishment, support and strength—till our very presence is as the sun, cheering and blessing all. So shall God increase within us, refreshing our own spirits, and watering all around. And the characteristics of the holy Priesthood will grow out from us like the branches of a fruitful tree that yield shelter, shield, and fruit.[29]

Notes

1. Allen E. Bergin, "Bringing the Restoration to the Academic World: Clinical Psychology as a Test Case," *BYU Studies* 19/4 (1979): 460.
2. Boris Pasternak, *Doctor Zhivago*, trans. Max Hayward and Manya Harari (New York: Pantheon, 1958), 68.
3. Aristotle, "Poetics," *Introduction to Aristotle*, ed. Richard McKeon, trans. Ingram Bywater (New York: The Modern Library, 1947), 624–67.
4. Bergin, "Bringing the Restoration," 466.

5. Malcolm Muggeridge, *Something Beautiful for God: Mother Teresa of Calcutta* (London: Collins, 1971), 98–99.

6. Lev Kopelev, *To Be Preserved Forever*, trans. and ed. Anthony Austin (New York: Lippincott, 1977), 10.

7. Kopelev, *To Be Preserved Forever*, 11, 13.

8. Eric Hoffer, "Beware the Intellectual," *National Review*, September 28, 1979, 11.

9. William P. D. Wightman, "The Tyranny of Abstractions," *British Journal for the History of Science* 6 (1973): 233–46.

10. George Feifer, "The Dark Side of Solzhenitsyn," *Harper's*, May 1980, 57.

11. See, for example, F. LaMond Tullis, ed., *Mormonism: A Faith for All Cultures* (Provo, UT: BYU Press, 1978); Spencer Palmer, 1980 BYU address, "Why Study Asia?: Random Thoughts on Mormonism and the Oriental Faiths"; and the series of "Culturegrams" prepared by Lynn Tyler at the BYU Kennedy Center to enlighten Travel Study participants regarding foreign customs, ideologies and religious beliefs.

12. Robert Pirsig, *Zen and the Art of Motorcycle Maintenance* (New York: William Morrow, 1999).

13. Marvin Rytting, "Living with Opposition in All Things," *Dialogue: A Journal of Mormon Thought* 12/4 (1979): 110.

14. *History of the Church*, 5:340.

15. Brigham Young, *Journal of Discourses*, 9:150.

16. Hugh B. Brown, "An Eternal Quest—Freedom of the Mind," May 13, 1969, 9–10, *BYU Speeches of the Year, 1968–69*.

17. Aleksandr Solzhenitsyn, *The Gulag Archipelago*, trans. Thomas P. Whitney (New York: Harper & Row, 1973), 1:168, 202, 405.

18. Aleksandr Solzhenitsyn, *The First Circle*, trans. Thomas P. Whitney (New York: Harper & Row, 1968), 389.

19. Harold Walker, "Hiding in Myself Too Well," 1979. Published by permission.

20. Feifer, "Dark Side of Solzhenitsyn," 57 (citing the Russian dissident Vladimir Lakshin, author of *Solzhenitsyn, Tvardovsky, and* Novy Mir [Cambridge, MA: MIT Press, 1982]).

21. Visiting professor of computer science Bogdan Czejdo, personal conversation with the author.

22. James R. Barton, professor of civil engineering, BYU.

23. Simone Weil, *Waiting for God*, trans. Emma Crauford (New York: Putnam's Sons, 1951), 114–15, 146–50.

24. Dietrich Bonhoeffer, *Life Together*, trans. John W. Doberstein (New York: Harper & Row, 1954), 23.

25. See Jonathan M. Chamberlain, *Eliminate Your SDBs: Self-Defeating Behaviors* (Provo, UT: BYU Press, 1978).

26. Dmitry Dudko, *Our Hope*, trans. Paul D. Garrett (Crestwood, NY: St. Vladimir's Seminary Press, 1977), 196.

27. Aleksandr Yelchaninov, "Fragments of a Diary," trans. Helen Iswolsky, in *A Treasury of Russian Spirituality*, comp. and ed. George P. Fedotov (Belmont, MA: Nordland, 1976), 461.

28. Hoffer, "Beware the Intellectual," 11.

29. E. L. T. Harrison, "A Real Representative of the Most High," *Millennial Star* (October 9, 1858): 643.

Coping with Orthodoxy: The Honors Student Syndrome

This piece was written after my tenure with the BYU Honors Program, though whether presented in a formal setting or simply shared as a handout with selected others I no longer remember. Backed by the professionals I cite, this essay's association of emotional abnormalities with often precocious intellectuals leaves open the question whether those with such tendencies can nevertheless adequately accommodate the needs and interests of others. It may be that not all of them can do so. Since writing this, I have come to know several individuals who seem to fit the pattern of "bipolar" behavior—a term I didn't know at the time. My awareness of this syndrome has helped me to recognize in each the same familiar pattern and no longer expect more of them—or allow myself to be "used" for their self-centered purposes. I truly pity these individuals and trust that, on their malady's spectrum, some can still learn to cope with, if not entirely overcome, their propensity for the bald-faced grand delusions with which they often deceive others as well as themselves. Such individuals pose a test of our own charity—and a caution to all of us, particularly those with intellectual inclinations, about elements of our personality we may need to guard against.

Since serving as director of the BYU Honors Program and writing several mildly controversial plays, I have made the acquaintance of a number of people who tend to betray or openly express a profound and chronic personal distress. Initially, they arouse strong feelings of commiseration and challenge my sense of neighborliness. They make me feel useful and often flatter me by indicating that while others have misunderstood or rejected them, I have not. When they cry out for help, I readily lose sleep and come running, and I hope I will always be so inclined.

But more often than not, I begin to sense that I have not really managed to help them become more content. Instead, by offering such a sympathetic ear, I have at times unwittingly fed and perpetuated their distress. On the other hand, if I ever hint at the slightest doubt or reservation about what concerns them or dispute their view of it, they are immediately offended.

These individuals are invariably precocious, unusually sensitive, and amazingly insightful. I learn from them and find them interesting and lovable. That's what draws me to them—besides the praise and flattery with which (at least at first) they often shower me. With time, however, a recurring pattern of characteristics emerges that tends to suggest that the source of their discontent may be intrinsic to them. These include the following:

- Myopic obsession with what concerns them
- Lack of reciprocal interest in what concerns anyone else
- A tendency to dominate or steer all discussion toward what obsesses them, making communication essentially one-way
- Extreme defensiveness whenever their ideas and opinions are challenged or criticized
- An inordinate dependency on their few friends and confidants, while all the time asserting their independence. This dependency increasingly takes the form of imposing on others without considering or sufficiently caring what inconvenience this might entail and usually involves hours-long sessions of hearing them out. They almost seem to be testing our loyalty and friendship, ingeniously defying us to prove our good faith.
- Concerns that seem to be concocted or out of proportion
- A sense one develops that they *need* to have a cause to be distressed about that will attract the attention of sympathizers—or, lacking these, an adversary or two. They seem to have a special need to feel victimized, however seemingly

> traumatic the consequences, and would (one senses) rather hold onto their concerns than be rid of them.

I have never taken a class or read deeply about abnormal psychology, but I suspect these are symptoms of one or another recognized disorder. People I have known who exhibit these symptoms include my own father and other members of my family, representatives of each major profession, one or more offspring in the families of most faculty members I know, and far too many BYU honors students or former honors students I have known. Such traits also seem almost a given for artists who take themselves too seriously—as most artists do.

Many are no longer in the church. One—a former student, research assistant, and member of the BYU branch where I served (he taught the elders quorum)—is now a polygamist prophet. Another, his friend, wrote the following:

> It has been said that other universities have all the questions and none of the answers, whereas BYU has all the answers and none of the questions. This commentary evokes a smile because it typifies an all-too-prevalent emphasis at BYU on certainty to the exclusion of all areas of uncertainty. Perhaps because we place so much emphasis on testimony, on what we *know*, we have come to regard that which we do not know as threatening. Since we conceive uncertainty to be hostile, we seek to minimize it, to hide it, to destroy it. To suppose that uncertainty has no place in the gospel is to deny the place of faith in the gospel. Without faith no man is acceptable before God, and faith expressly denotes a state short of perfect certainty or knowledge. Certainly Mormons must recognize that the essential purpose of life is to learn to deal with uncertainty. Otherwise, why is a veil drawn across the knowledge of our previous existence?[1]

I quite like this and have, as you can see, kept a copy in my files. This individual too, I'm told, is no longer in the church. He apparently chose to ignore his own advice—or at least to deal with uncertainty by other means than the faith he once espoused. Both he and his polygamous former friend are returned missionaries, as are a number of others I describe.

Many of these people have experienced serious difficulty accepting or being fully reconciled to the church and remaining active in or fulfilled by it. But increasingly, I sense that whatever the issues they are reacting to—mindless conformity, the church's stand on the Equal Rights Amendment, the former policy on blacks and the priesthood, doubts about Joseph Smith, the dogmatism of some General Authorities, the intellectual blandness of editorials in the *Church News*, Mormon pop culture, the suppression or discouragement of thought in one or another area of inquiry—at root, each also suffers from an inability or disinclination to socialize and interact in a felicitous way with others. The same would be true in any highly structured society like that of the church that nonetheless includes a wide variety of personalities. Many, incidentally, have also had less than ideal personal relationships with one or both parents, often their father—a seeming substantiation of Freud's oedipal theory. They have a common tendency to react toward authority figures, including teachers, as they have at other times toward their parents.

I hasten to add that what I describe is doubtless to some degree true of each of us—at least at certain times in our lives. In that connection, I note some interesting observations by a research team attempting to formulate "a theory of adult male development over the age span of about 20–45," particularly about the so-called "mentor relationship":

> The presence or absence of mentors is, we find, an important component of the life course during the 20s and 30s. The absence of mentors is associated with various kinds of developmental impairments and with problems of individuation in midlife.
>
> The mentor is ordinarily 8 to 15 years older than the mentee. He is enough older to represent greater wisdom, authority, and paternal qualities, but near enough in age or attitudes to be in some respects a peer or older brother rather than in the image of the wise old man or distant father. . . . He takes the younger man under his wing, invites him into a new occupational world, shows him around, imparts his wisdom, cares, sponsors, criticizes, and bestows his blessing. The teaching and the sponsoring have their value, but the blessing is the crucial element. . . .

> The number of mentor relationships in an individual's life does not vary widely. Few men have more than three or four, and perhaps the modal numbers are none and one. The duration of the intense mentor relationship is also not extremely variable, perhaps 3–4 years as an average and 10–12 years as the upper limit. When this relationship ends, the pair may form a more modest friendship after a cooling-off period. The ending of the mentor relationship may take a rather peaceful form, with gradual loss of involvement. More often, however, and especially during the 30s, termination is brought about by increasing conflict or by forced separation, and brings in its wake intense feelings of bitterness, rancor, grief, abandonment, and rejuvenation in the mentee.
>
> The final giving up of all mentors by those who have had them tends to occur in the middle or late 30s. One does not have mentors after 40. . . .
>
> It is probably impossible to become a mentor without first having been a mentee.[2]

There are important implications here for parenting or surrogate parenting and what may be expected in its absence. I now recognize the special mentors in my own life, though I did not fully at the time, and know what a significant difference they made in my orientation and outlook. Such influences may be particularly important for those of us whose intellectual interests and outlooks make us fit in less well with our peers, potentially depriving us of important socialization experiences.

Let me share some further findings that shocked me when I first read them and still haunt me over a year later. Research by sociologist Douglas H. Heath published in *The Journal of Higher Education* found the following:

> SAT quantitative and verbal aptitude, achievement test, college grades, departmental chairman ratings of intellect, and the receipt of college honors were not found to predict several hundred measures of adult maturity and competence. However, the measures, particularly increasing SAT scores, were found to be directly related to a variety of measures indexing psychological, particularly interpersonal, immaturity. . . . Too exclusive an academic emphasis may actually interfere with

> the maturing of some men. . . . Academic success depends on the suppression of feeling. . . . The academic life reinforces the overcontrol and suppression of impulse and emotionality.[3]

Allow me next to cite the observations of Jackson Newell, dean of liberal education at the University of Utah, as they appeared in a recent issue of *Dialogue: A Journal of Mormon Thought*:

> The quest to balance personal needs and beliefs with church loyalties is not always waged with success. Some surrender to the institution, whether from faith or exhaustion, and find contentment in the obedient life while memories of the encounter fade dimly from view. Others opt for freedom in personal expression and abandon ship—eventually dissolving their ties with organized religion in favor of less constraining social groups. But there are others who, for one reason or another, refuse to allow either social needs or personal needs to predominate. Within this group, too, a simplified view suggests two extremes: the *unconscientious resister* (the foot dragger) and the *conscientious critic* (the loyal opposition). Although the former give every appearance of conformity, they make private accommodations of one kind or another. One common example is the member who accepts a calling from a sense of duty and then proceeds halfheartedly with the responsibilities. This approach is perilous to self-esteem and paralytic to community and institutional life. In the short run, however, it appears to be the route of least resistance, so its path is both well known and frequently trodden.
>
> Conscientious critics pursue a healthier course. They give honest but appropriate expression to their personal views, seeking changes they believe would strengthen the Church and culture, but remain committed to the institution and the way of life. Conscientious critics walk a tightrope, however, because both their motives and their ideas are regarded with suspicion by highly orthodox members as well as foot draggers. . . .
>
> It is my belief that Mormons have more freedom of expression and more latitude in behavior than most of them use. . . . A few members, however, make a show of their differences

> with the Church, or with orthodox members of it, simply to satisfy their own needs to be seen as independent-minded. Consciously or unconsciously, some seek to be ostracized. This behavior is regrettable because it intimidates some who would otherwise enjoy greater freedom within the faith. Even so, others may hold the same ideas, but will express them without threatening or offending fellow members. . . .
>
> E. E. Cummings is supposed to have said that most people can be put in one of two categories—those who define themselves primarily by what they are against and those who define themselves primarily by what they are *for.* Well-educated people, thinking people, often fall into the first group, and they make good critics because they have been schooled in analytical methods. But they are too seldom *constructive* critics and when they are not, they are notoriously ineffective in the Church. Those who genuinely seek the "space" to be intellectually honest in the Church will have a wider berth if they are of the second, positive type.[4]

I recently had a moving encounter with one of our exceptionally fine student instructors. She had been unusually affected by some literary stimuli—negatively so. I tried to reconcile her to the material. In her frustration, she indicated that she was prone to take some things more seriously than most and to be misunderstood by both family and friends. This same student had written essay exams of a quality far above that of her peers. I pointed this out to her and told her I felt she had special gifts that unavoidably set her apart, but that she should never hold that against herself or question her sensitivity because others don't always pick up on it.

The individual eccentricities and peculiarities that are part of what we uniquely bring to the service of others and of God can also act as barriers—internal and external—to positive, meaningful interaction with others. It is vital that we embrace these differences for their positive value, both in others and in ourselves, while at the same time recognizing when we need to make adjustments and even give up part of our individual point of view. It was the Savior himself, as I recall, who suggested—and also exemplified—our need to be not only innocent as doves but wise as serpents. This difficult balance is poignantly exemplified in "A Strange

Story" by Peter Taylor—a thoughtful and neglected non-Mormon writer. Its hero, very likely autobiographical, had throughout his childhood and early youth communicated with voices coming from various inanimate objects, among them chestnut trees. He knew those voices were real because they had on occasion predicted the future. And he was very at home with them. For that, he was ostracized and considered weird by friends and loved ones. Finally somehow realizing he had to choose between other people and his enchanting voices, he commanded them to depart. The protagonist then declares:

> Though I stopped hearing the mysterious voices one hears as a child that night in my room, at seventeen I was still learning to listen to the voices of people—still discovering just how carefully, for love's sake, one must always listen. And I was thirty before I felt that love's recompense was adequate. . . .
>
> After seventeen, I became obsessed with learning from people—about people and the world. I listened to everybody. I became a wonderful listener, and still am. Everybody says so. . . . Whenever I return to the scenes of my childhood and admire the pale beauty of the sycamore trees and the glossy leaves of the oaks—almost like magnolias, some of them—I understand how far, in my mind, I have had to withdraw from trees in order to learn to love them. I go for walks in the woods with my family sometimes, on my visits back home, and often I cannot help remarking on the absence of any chestnut trees in the woods. My family find it very curious that I remember the chestnuts at all and tell each other it is evidence of how much I have always loved Nature. But that isn't so. It is something I have learned. It is something strange and wonderful that I have learned to do.[5]

Montaigne perceived this problem in his own contemporaries, arguing that "aggressive and quarrelsome arrogance that believes and trusts wholly in itself" is "a mortal enemy of discipline and truth," insisting that too much "affirmation and opinionativeness are express signs of stupidity," and observing that the "sea of human opinions" is "unbridled and aimless." As an antidote, he recommends that we question our own judgment and earnestly listen to our "friends" as well as to our innermost "self."[6]

The poets have as much to say. Auden's "The Bard" should give us all pause:

> . . . They cried "It is a God that sings,"
>
> And honored him, a person set apart,
> Till he grew vain, mistook for personal song
> The petty tremors of his mind or heart
> At each domestic wrong.
>
> Lines came to him no more; he had to make them
> (With what precision was each strophe planned):
> Hugging his gloom as peasants hug their land,
>
> He stalked like an assassin through the town,
> And glared at men because he did not like them,
> But trembled if one passed him with a frown.[7]

I also admire these particular lines from Yeats's "A Prayer for My Daughter":

> An intellectual hatred is the worst . . .
>
> . . . all hatred driven hence,
> The soul recovers radical innocence
> And learns at last that it is self-delighting,
> Self-appeasing, self-affrighting,
> And that its own sweet will is Heaven's will; . . .
>
> And may her bridegroom bring her to a house
> Where all's accustomed, ceremonious;
> For arrogance and hatred are the wares
> Peddled in the thoroughfares.
> How but in custom and in ceremony
> Are innocence and beauty born?[8]

We all require custom and ceremony. But with it, as Professor Newell points out, "There is no substitute for introspection, at regular intervals, to sort out means and ends and measure our progress against the example of Christ." He also argues, "Conscientious critics need support from and association with others of like mind, not so much to bolster their strength as to nourish their commitment—to the Church."[9] If we sufficiently manifest the "broken heart" and "contrite spirit" the scriptures so frequently recommend, we will, I believe, manage to so support others—and receive support ourselves as needed.

I give the last word to another honors student who came to this fortunate conclusion in her senior year:

> Most unexpectedly, I find myself beginning to feel a vague "we" instead of "them" and "me" in reference to my fellow students. No matter how we differ in superficialities, we share the most important source of oneness. One cannot be at one with God alone. . . . There is no hope of reaching God, of knowing love, alone. So on the way to finding *me* I found a most important *you*. Others form the center of the Christian self. This was not easy to accept and harder still to live. People had come to mean very little to me. They were so disappointing, inconsistent and time consuming.[10]

May we all similarly come to recognize the value of commonality with others—both those who share our intellectual inclinations, and those who do not.

Notes

1. Self-evaluation from a student in the BYU Honors Program.
2. Daniel J. Levinson, Charlotte M. Darrow, Edward B. Klein, Maria H. Levinson, and Braxton McKee, "The Psychosocial Development of Men in Early Adulthood and the Mid-Life Transition," in *Life History Research in Psychopathology Volume 3*, ed. David F. Ricks, Alexander Thomas, and Merrill Roff (Minneapolis: University of Minnesota Press, 1974), 251–53. The authors' conclusions were expanded in *The Seasons of a Man's Life* by the same authors (New York: Alfred A. Knopf, 1978), and further research related to females of a comparable age was released in 1996 (Daniel J. Levinson, in collaboration with Judy D. Levinson, *The Seasons of a Woman's Life* [New York: Alfred A. Knopf]).
3. Douglas H. Heath, "Academic Predictors of Adult Maturity and Competence," *Journal of Higher Education* 48/6 (November–December 1977): 613, 629.

4. L. Jackson Newell, "Personal Conscience and Priesthood Authority," *Dialogue: A Journal of Mormon Thought* 13/4 (1980): 83–84, 86.

5. Peter Taylor, "A Strange Story," in *Miss Leonora When Last Seen and Fifteen Other Stories* (New York: Ivan Obolensky, 1963), 132–33.

6. Michel de Montaigne, "Apology for Raymond Sebond" and "Of Experience," in *The Complete Works of Montaigne: Essays, Travel Journal, Letters*, trans. Donald M. Frame (Stanford, CA: Stanford University Press, 1957), 387, 823.

7. W. H. Auden, Part VII of "Sonnets from China," in *Collected Poems*, ed. Edward Mendelson (New York: Random House, 1976), 152.

8. William Butler Yeats, "A Prayer for My Daughter," in *The Collected Poems of W. B. Yeats*, rev. 2nd ed., ed. Richard J. Finneran (New York: Scribner Paperback Poetry, 1996), 189–90.

9. Newell, "Personal Conscience and Priesthood Authority," 85.

10. Senior self-evaluation, BYU Honors Program, 1976; emphasis added.

The Difference

These reminiscences were published in a volume of stories by various contributors titled The Gifts of Christmas. *Including events from Merriam's and my mission in St. Petersburg, Russia, they remind us that our special attention to those in need can on occasion be life-giving and also deepen our own appreciation of life's purpose—that the benefit of such attention is often unexpectedly reciprocal. During an earlier Christmas season, when I was still a graduate student, my failure to contact someone as his home teacher possibly had the opposite consequence—a sobering object lesson.*[1]

Christmas is for most of us a season of delight—of nostalgic reunion with family and friends and special excitement for the very young. It is also a time when those with less firm ties are, by contrast, particularly lonely.

This, as we discovered on our mission to St. Petersburg, Russia, is no less so in northern cities where the almost perpetual and (for some) depressing darkness is compensated for by increased attendance at concerts, the theater, and the ballet as well as by extended festivity. For a full month, Russians celebrate both the Eastern Orthodox and Western Christmases and also two New Years, as prescribed by first the more recent Gregorian and then the old Julian calendar, whose dating of holidays is approximately two weeks later.

Unfortunately, in a country whose consumption of alcohol is already one of the very highest, heavy drinking invariably attends such dark winter distractions. It stands to reason that many a recent convert has had to overcome this debilitating habit before his or her baptism and that from time to time—with everyone around them, fellow workers and old friends, constantly toasting them at this particular time of year—some lapse.

One such, a relatively young man, had reverted to his former alcoholic ways. His condition, which involved self-destructive impulses, was particularly serious. Knowing this, his priesthood leaders—also relatively new in the church, as were all our Russian members at that time—nevertheless instinctively agreed that the young man required special tending. Until he had once more managed to overcome his addiction, they took turns sitting with him in his apartment and constraining his frequent attempts to resort to the bottle and, in despair, throw himself from the balcony outside his window. Like most city-dwelling Russians, he lived in one of the country's many strictly utilitarian high-rise structures—some of which house as many as a thousand families—and the floor he lived on was one of its highest.

This man's home teachers and the brethren in both his district and branch presidencies were as busy as you and I at that time of year. But for at least a week, on a rotating basis, each found the time to be with their unfortunate brother. And that made all the difference.

Learning of this incident, I couldn't help recalling the now distant occasion when, as a newly married graduate student approximately this same man's age, I found myself one early December in one of our own more northerly cities: New Haven, Connecticut. I was serving at the time in our elders quorum presidency and, it goes without saying, as a home teacher.

My home teaching companion and I had just been given the name and address of another young man, newly baptized, whom we'd so far not met. He'd already been in our community, it seemed, for a number of weeks but hadn't yet appeared at church. His recently arrived membership record indicated he was only seventeen and had previously resided in Florida. He had, for whatever reason, traveled north on his own, presumably looking for work. He wasn't, as best we could tell, one of the highly favored Yale undergraduates.

Besides helping with our small family's busy preparations for the forthcoming holidays, I had to complete my term papers during the month of December. So I suggested to my companion that we postpone our home teaching visits until just before Christmas and in that way also use the occasion to deliver a special season's greeting. That seemed reasonable, and my companion, another graduate student, readily agreed. We would therefore wait several more weeks, we decided, before contacting the young seventeen-year-old, about whom we knew next to nothing.

I'm sure we did not pray about that decision. While our plan worked out well enough with our other families, for whom the press of time was much like our own, this was not true for the young Floridian. On the very eve of Christmas, we finally located his New Haven address—a rented room in a shabby part of town. After several rings, the boy's landlady opened the door. Upon our mentioning his name, the woman gave us a quizzical look and for a moment remained fairly speechless.

"You're from his church, you say? Why, don't you know? We found him in his apartment just two weeks ago. He'd hanged himself from the light fixture. We called the police. They took over from there. No one knew where he was from or who his kin were. He never told us."

"Was there at least a funeral?"

"A service? I don't think so. Just a burial wherever they do that for the homeless."

We will never know if, by earlier reaching one for whom we'd been entrusted with a sacred stewardship, we could have made enough of a difference. Could we have established sufficient rapport with our first visit? Could we have persuaded him to join with us at church the following Sunday? And would renewed contact with the Saints have made him feel enough better about himself and his future prospects to deter the irreversible violence he visited upon himself shortly after? If in dire need, would he have made that clear enough while mingling with us for the very first time? Would our branch president have sensed that need and somehow found the time for an unscheduled interview? Would any of us have even discerned the young man's desperation enough to come to his aid? And would our assistance have made, again, enough of a difference?

Those questions remain unanswered. We will never know, in this life anyway. But one thing is certain: whatever might have been done for him was *not* done because none of us were there when we should have been. And why was that? Because, I fear, we viewed our assignment as home teachers all too perfunctorily. Yes, we were dutiful. We'd managed to visit our families each month. But we didn't appreciate what a literal lifeline our assignment could be and doubtless often is, more than any of us can ever know.

I wish I could say that since then, I have looked after my home teaching families, always guided by the Spirit and not just the letter. But I am still haunted, years later, whenever I think of the difference between our default back then toward a lonely, perhaps altogether friendless seventeen-year-old and the self-sacrificing concern for "the one" exemplified years later by certain Russian Latter-day Saints, all of them very young in the kingdom. I suspect they took their assignments and their relationship to one another much more seriously. Why? Perhaps in part because, not long before, many of them had also "been there."

That is surely one of the great blessings of living and serving in the mission field and interacting with investigators and new members. They don't attend meetings and involve themselves with the church just because others expect them to. Often the only converts in their extended family, they may even encounter severe opposition from family and acquaintances. Why do they bother? Why inconvenience themselves? Because, with their newly acquired testimonies, sparked by those of the elders and the sister missionaries, they keenly understand what a remarkable difference their new outlook has made—the difference between life and death, spiritually and sometimes literally. By rubbing shoulders with them, we too become more acutely aware of that particular difference. Missionaries are perhaps the most richly rewarded by this symbiotic process, witnessing the new members' fervent and whole-souled response on a daily and almost hourly basis.

This reminds me of another Christmas in St. Petersburg, just six months before my wife and I would be released and return home. Christmas day itself is a time when, with families tightly gathered, missionaries have less than usual success going door to door or finding many prepared to hear them on the street. (That in itself may be ironic: the Savior's messengers find a relatively bleak reception on the very day the whole Christian world commemorates his birth.)

In any event, missionaries too need a special boost on that day. So, as on the Fourth of July, we pursued what had already become a mission tradition: gathering all our missionaries in one place, usually a hotel restaurant, and, along with a festive meal, enjoying a holiday program together. On this particular occasion, something prompted me to recall a remarkable short story by the Russian author Anton Chekhov and read it to those assembled.

The story takes place during the cold, still-dark Russian days before Easter. Returning to his village home, the protagonist, a young seminarian, stops to warm himself at a fire tended by two destitute peasant women, a mother and daughter, both widows. The student recalls for them the account of Peter's denial of Christ, which he has probably just been assigned to read at the seminary, perhaps for the very first time—an account whose setting is also that of a dark, cold night by a similar fire. As he does so, the women, sensing the Savior's loneliness and travail more deeply than the student, begin to weep. Their response triggers in him the recognition that he, the women, and the characters in the biblical account all share the same travail. With unexpected joy, he feels one with them and, beyond them, with all creation. In Chekhov's words:

> He thought that truth and beauty which had guided human life in the Garden of Gethsemane and in the high priest's courtyard had gone on uninterruptedly to this day, and must always have been the chief thing in human life and in all earthly life . . . ; and the feeling of youth, health, vigour—he was only twenty-two—and an inexpressible sweet expectation of happiness, of unknown mysterious happiness, took possession of him little by little, and life seemed to him enchanting, marvelous, and full of lofty meaning.[2]

Reading the story aloud to our 130 missionaries, I could hardly get through it, so struck was I by the parallel to our own situation. Without saying more, I hoped the missionaries could sense how like the young seminarian they were. Their investigators, whose faith and appreciation for their message had in turn strengthened the missionaries' own faith and brought them so much spiritual insight, were not unlike Chekhov's two women.

Since then, I've thought even more about the story's rich implications—particularly how the contemplation of others' spiritual frailty and consequent sorrow, as with Chekhov's allusion to Peter's denial of the Savior and, implicitly, our own inadequacy as well, can nevertheless unite us with one another in bonds of sympathy, bringing unanticipated joy and a renewed sense of wonder about life itself. That seems a fair description of the gospel in action.

The women's abject existence witnesses to their lifelong oppression. They could well resent the rest of mankind and could, if Chekhov wished it, turn on the seminarian with spite and curses. Instead, they weep in sorrow and compassion. Their response provokes in the young man a deeper appreciation of the gospel event and of life itself: Peter's life, by implication Christ's at the time of his passion, the women's, and lastly his own. It thus affords him a vision of the connectedness of all God's creation through shared experience, in this instance of betrayal and consequent sorrow—engendering in the student an unexpected affinity with the suffering that all have cause to know. And he rejoices in that connectedness. Shared suffering—"mourn[ing] with those that mourn" (Mosiah 18:9)—ennobles him, enabling him to identify more readily with oppressed and sinful "others." "All these things shall give thee experience, and shall be for thy good" (D&C 122:7). Shared compassion leads to a sense of goodness, beauty, and the purposefulness of all existence. And this brings joy.

Whether he knew it or not, Chekhov here describes the very process by which—as missionary, investigator, or long-term disciple—each of us is spiritually quickened. It often begins with a certain sadness, so effectively conveyed by his story's mood and setting, that comes from dissatisfaction with oneself or with one's circumstances. It involves regret, a desperate desire for change, and a consequent searching and openness to altered understanding.

Recounting the New Testament incident, the student unwittingly testifies of it to the women. Their tears in turn profoundly testify to him of that event's authenticity and spiritual import. This, it seems to me, is not unlike what all of us experience as, however feebly, we testify to and serve one another.

Notes

1. Originally published in slightly different form as Thomas F. Rogers, "The Difference," in *The Gifts of Christmas: Essays, Stories, Poems, and Recipes* (Salt Lake City: Deseret Book, 1999), 104–12; © Deseret Book Company. Used by permission. The final episode recounted in this essay is also mentioned in Thomas F. Rogers, *A Call to Russia: Glimpses of Missionary Life* (Provo, UT: BYU Studies, 1999).

2. "The Student," in *The Chekhov Omnibus: Selected Stories*, trans. Constance Garnett, ed. Donald Rayfield (London: Everyman, 1994), 298.

Insights from a Patriarch's Journal

From 2007 to 2014, I had the honor of serving as an LDS patriarch in the church's Europe East Area (comprising, besides Russia, nine former Soviet satellite countries). After twenty-five trips and the bestowal of over 2,600 blessings, my journal account ran to several hundred pages. What follows are excerpts from only a few of its entries, highlighting what I have learned from the faithful and inspiring Latter-day Saints I served in that capacity—what they taught me. (Full names have been omitted as needed to protect confidentiality, as well as for safety's sake in this again-dangerous part of the world.)

Softened hearts

While both the patriarch and those receiving his blessings should be worthy, prayerful, and in tune with the Spirit, it is equally important that during their blessing, recipients sense their Father in Heaven's great love for them.

This insight vividly occurred to me in 2008 during my first tour to the Russia Moscow Mission. In one instance, an especially stern middle-aged brother came to the Europe East Area office for his blessing. I had never before encountered such a grim demeanor. Before his retirement, he had been a career officer in the Red Army, and he was now a recently set-apart branch president. During the preliminary interview, he also indicated that he and an adult son had a very strained relationship, but gave no details. I wondered if I could sympathetically enough relate to this brother to offer him a proper blessing. Then a quiet prompting entered my mind: "You were not called to judge this man by his gruff exterior. He has come to you, trusting that you would be a conduit for the inspiration he needs."

After laying my hands on his head, I was prompted to tell him he would be more successful as both a branch president and a father if he strove to emulate the Savior's kinder, more gentle nature. That evening, I put a rhetorical question to my liaison in the area presidency, Elder Larry Gibbons: "What single personal quality do you think a patriarch most needs to fulfill his calling?" I then shared my new insight: "Worthiness and being in tune with the Spirit are both essential. But *most of all*, one needs to love them. That's what I discovered earlier today."

Three years later, again in Moscow, a much younger man came for his blessing. He had been baptized only the year before after overcoming a habit of heavy drinking. He was now elders quorum president in the branch where he resided. I looked once more at his name: "Are you by chance the son of the branch president I gave a blessing to a few years back? Now serving with him as a priesthood leader?" He answered in the affirmative. In the intervening three years, a true miracle had transpired: A father's heart had turned to his child, which had been fully reciprocated. Divine love had intervened, reflecting itself in their now close, amicable relationship. Healing had taken place and their former estrangement had reversed itself.

The people we serve

There is exceptional diversity among those who come to us for blessings. Blessings have been declared upon those from at least four strains of Mongolian descent: Tatars on the Volga River in and around Kazan, Russia; Crimean Tatars in Ukraine; Bashkirs centered in Ufa in western Siberia; and Buryats, whose center is Ulan Ude in eastern Siberia. (The LDS Church has erected impressive facilities in each of those far-flung locales.) I have also given blessings to those of Uzbek and Azerbaidzhani descent; gypsies in Varna, Bulgaria; Iranian refugees in Armenia, doctors and other professionals whose personal courage and commitment to the restored gospel are unsurpassed; and several young Africans, many of them studying medicine, including some from Nigeria, one from Cameroon, and another from Zambia (who had also served an LDS mission in South Africa). Two of them, already married, have

LDS Russian wives. Like gypsies and those from the Caucasus, blacks are subject to the prejudice and maltreatment so traditional in Eastern Europe toward those with a darker pigment. Unprecedentedly, all the Abrahamic lineages have been identified and declared by the itinerant patriarchs assigned to the church's Europe East Area (all the tribes of Israel, plus those declared on rare occasions to be of the lineage of Abraham without specifying a tribe).

Many who join us have lived unusually desperate lives, but they are neither fatalistic nor complacent. The Greek tragedian Aeschylus took as his motto "wisdom through suffering," which the Russian spiritual genius Dostoevsky morphed into "salvation through suffering." The gospel, as we know it, asserts that suffering can best be understood and accommodated with an eternal perspective and the application of the cardinal Christian virtues—faith, hope, and charity. Assisting these Latter-day Saints has been a rare and sacred privilege.

Among those who stand out for me are some with serious physical disabilities. These include a branch president in Yaroslavl, near Moscow—a man in his forties who, due to degeneration of his spine, is bent over at a forty-five degree angle but whose angelic countenance radiates unusual serenity and joy. They also include a dynamic and beloved former district president in Pleven, Bulgaria, who has used a wheelchair for over a quarter century, and two paralyzed young men in Yerevan, Armenia—one a victim of the severe earthquake that devastated his country two decades ago, in which he also lost his wife. In despair, he tells me, he several times attempted to take his own life; but since their baptisms, both men are reconciled to leading a purposeful life, and the prospect of eternal kinship and still serving others now supports them. There is also a young brother in Vladivostok who at age twelve was severely crippled by a drunk driver (before encountering the church, and himself already a drug addict and alcoholic). Though he can no longer engage in athletics and walks with great difficulty, he is now a serious student, intent on becoming a lawyer and establishing a center for those similarly disabled.

Then there are the sisters, many of them older, who, like too many women, have been victims of violent or negligent, often alcoholic fathers, husbands, even sons. While not holding any priesthood office, these women—with their humble, devoted, largely behind-the-scenes service and maternal devotion—are the backbone of both their branches and their families. I tell them they are our "glue." For many, the opportunity to socialize and serve is most fulfilling. Those who have never had the opportunity to marry are comforted by the assurance that by living worthily and compassionately serving others, they can in the eternities be part of a complete family with a loving spouse and righteous descendants. Their blessings echo the consoling assurances of numerous latter-day prophets and apostles.

During 2013 in Ukraine, just prior to the disturbing civil war there a year later, I was particularly glad I could bestow patriarchal blessings upon a number of older sisters—some of them "pioneer" members who had joined the church as long as two decades earlier when it first came to their communities, a number of them early Relief Society presidents who had still not had the opportunity to receive their blessings. Among them were several who for one reason or another had long been inactive, but were now returning to the fold. Their blessings assured them that their adult children and subsequent posterity would over time and in the eternities be profoundly blessed by their having done so. I was glad I could provide this assurance to so many, some of whom may no longer be with us the next time an LDS patriarch is able to visit their area.

As I return to various missions, members often remind me that I previously conferred blessings on them. This includes couples whose unions I was privileged to seal when my wife Merriam and I were missionaries at the Stockholm Sweden Temple. Even so, I've observed that the relationship between otherwise outstanding couples (both in Russia and here at home) is often seriously tested by temperamental discord and the tendency for one or both—not always the husband—to dominate decision making. Prior to sealing marriages in both the Stockholm and Bountiful temples, I've taken to urging that both husband and wife be willing to accommodate the other's distinct needs and wishes at least fifty percent of the time—and not keep score, as Merriam wisely adds.

Remaining faithful

Home and visiting teaching efforts remain weak throughout the Europe East Area's missions, where distances and tradition are an impeding factor. Apart from their own family members, people are less inclined to visit one another in their homes (invariably apartments). But there are notable exceptions, especially among the sisters.

As a disadvantaged, impoverished minority since the fall of Soviet occupation, the Russian sisters in Tallinn, Estonia, are an inspiring case in point. Members of their Relief Society testify of the close-knit, loving association that, since joining the church, so vitally sustains them. During the occupation, relatively few of these mostly older women needed to learn Estonian, so their employment is now quite limited. One of them, a scrub nurse who cleans the floors in a hospital's operating rooms, tells me that before her baptism, the abuse she'd endured had induced her to swim far out into the Baltic Sea and not return to shore; but before she got that far, a "voice" prompted her to change her mind. Shortly afterward, she met the missionaries, was baptized, and, despite her still-bleak material circumstances, her life changed forever. I heard a similar account from a young girl in Vladivostok in the Russian Far East who accidentally fell several stories from a tall building and who—having never thought of God before then—while in free fall, called upon him. Her coat miraculously caught on a balcony's ledge, and she suffered no serious consequences. Shortly thereafter, her family met the missionaries and were baptized.

Among my special heroes are the rare husbands and fathers who come for blessings but whose other family members, I sometimes notice, have already been church members for a number of years. When I further inquire, I'm told something like, "I finally decided I needed to give up drinking in order to save myself—for my family's sake." The incidence of alcoholism in Eastern Europe is astoundingly high. I've observed more than once that it is Satan's most effective weapon in destroying marriages in this part of the world, at least seventy percent of which, I'm told, end in divorce.

Equally rare but noticeably present in every branch are a few young men who—lacking the influence of like-minded peers, experienced priesthood leaders and, often as not, the example and encouragement of a member father—have nevertheless managed to withstand the pressures and temptations of their adolescent peers, remaining active in the church and preparing to serve missions. These young men and the young sisters who also serve missions are truly the future of the church, blessed by the prospect of temple marriage to a worthy and equally devoted spouse and the raising of children and, through them, further progeny who follow their example. (While serving at the Stockholm temple, Merriam and I already saw such continuity where Swedish families have joined each other over successive generations. The same is now occurring among our Russian members.) Sadly, as a mission president recently told me, too many young Latter-day Saints are so subject to social pressure that even on a first date with a nonmember, they are expected to become physically intimate. Unmarried couples frequent every hotel where I stay—not to mention the revealingly attired young women who wait for patrons at the elevator on every floor.

I think of Dmitry Prokovtsev, an older teen and recent convert in Riga, Latvia—a seemingly nonchalant Russian who had seriously considered the missionaries' message only after, in the space of two years, three of his buddies had separately gotten drunk, gone swimming in the Baltic Sea, and drowned. His blessing encouraged him to consider serving a mission, even though he struck me at the time as still "green," his sticking power uncertain. Three years later at a gathering of members in the Siberian city Novokuznetsk, I encountered a seasoned Russian missionary who told me he was about to return to his home in Riga. He had to remind me that it was he who had received that same blessing three years earlier. I believe I did not at first recognize him because, unlike the tentative young man I remember from the time of his blessing, Dmitry now radiated so much confidence and happiness, full of beaming smiles. He will be a great strength to the church when he returns home. Such encounters are the priceless pay one receives from making these trips. (As an update, during my final tour about two years later, again to the Baltic Mission, I once again encountered Dmitry with his wife and their infant child during Sunday services in Riga. He was still beaming, just as I remembered him while serving on his mission.)

Mission drivers

The drivers who serve the Eastern European missions are all skilled and able. These include the Ukraine Kyiv Mission's Aleksey, who doubled as his mission president's executive secretary; my own former missionary Igor, also Ukrainian, who earlier drove for the Russia St. Petersburg

Mission; and Roman, a non-Mormon who for nearly eighteen years now has driven for the Russia Samara Mission and whom, when we last parted, I challenged to investigate what over the years so many of us have traveled so far to represent to his people. The church badly needs such expert drivers: major highways are still often only two undivided lanes, dominated by large lumbering trucks which it is always a calculated risk to pass. It's questionable if the frequent fatalities ever make the evening news.

The Ukraine Dnepropetrovsk Mission's driver, Pasha, is, for me, an especially memorable figure. Like Aleksey in Kiev, he had served an English-speaking mission (Pasha in London, Aleksey in Canada) and is a fabulous translator as well as coordinator of numerous mission-related activities, even while on the road. Both are working on advanced degrees in economics, and both have young families. In the evenings, Pasha would sit with his laptop researching his dissertation, while I read Doug Thayer's novel, *The Conversion of Jeff Williams*, whose protagonist's conscientious and ultrarighteous cousin unexpectedly dies from kidney failure just as he is preparing to serve a mission. Pasha's whole-souled dedication to his family and his various callings reminded me of that character. Pasha's wife was just then bedridden with a precarious pregnancy. Each evening he tenderly, encouragingly talked with her on the phone.

Though our acquaintance was brief, I respect and love Pasha as much as any Latter-day Saint I've ever known. We'd spent nearly a week together in very close quarters as I traveled throughout southeast Ukraine bestowing blessings, sharing rooms in a series of hotels and rented apartments. Respecting my companion's need for solitude as he pursued his research, I'd avoided watching TV. However, I one evening asked if he knew how to activate the set where we were staying so that—after several weeks without any news about the outside world—I could catch up on events in Syria and on the drawn-out but ever-fascinating political campaigning back home. Pasha willingly complied. Remarking that the TV set accommodated over sixty channels, he began to surf them for me, remote in hand. As he did so, I noticed that, oddly, he'd turned his back to the screen, only identifying each transmission as he searched for BBC or CNN by its sound. He explained that he did so in order to avoid any offensive images that might cross the screen.

It was still early in the evening when particularly salacious advertisements and programs are less likely to appear. Even so, Pasha didn't want to take a chance. I wondered if perhaps even the ads' skimpily clad models inordinately disturbed his sensibilities—like, say, the effect of sugar on some diabetics. At that moment it struck me that he and I were the products of two quite different, almost opposite cultures: not Ukrainian and American but something far more universal. If such extremes were our only option, there is no question that this young man's heightened caution is what we ought to aspire to and settle for.

As we traversed our southward course, the early spring's leafing of trees noticeably progressed, and I saw more of Ukraine's flat, fertile countryside than on past occasions. Farther north the earth was darker—the famous several-feet-deep topsoil known as *chernozyom* ("black earth"), historically the breadbasket of not only Russia but much of Europe. As we drew nearer the Black Sea, the soil, though still rich and fertile, became decidedly brown. "*Korichnevozyom*" (brown earth), I quipped—a term I suspect I'd just invented.

Siberia (Novosibirsk and Yekaterinburg Missions)

In Novosibirsk, I met President Daniel B. Gibbons, a former Salt Lake City judge. Assigned to a Russian mission just a year before, he had worked hard on Russian and told me he conducts interviews without the aid of a missionary interpreter. He had two copies of our published missionary journal, *A Call to Russia*, which he said he had already read four times. I told him that with such an endorsement, it should by now be a bestseller. (His father, Francis Gibbons, now a former Seventy who served as executive secretary to several LDS First Presidencies, had as a young law student been my deacons quorum advisor. I told Daniel about our connection, who in turn mentioned it to his father in a phone conversation. His father's endearing reply: "I remember little Tommy.")

After Moscow and St. Petersburg, Novosibirsk is said to be Russia's third largest city. The daily (sometimes twice daily) walk from my hotel to the mission office was—except for the fierce traffic and polluted air—quite invigorating.

A particular middle-aged couple from a small outlying village are among the most "on fire" members I've ever encountered. The story of the dreams (mostly hers), promptings, and impressions that had earlier caused them to leave Siberia and with their sizable young family travel first to Moscow, then to St. Petersburg to seek and find the church is astonishing. They returned to another city in Siberia where the husband was later called to preside over the local branch, which grew by fifteen members in just the first year. Like President Gibbons and the branch president in Tomsk, this brother is by training an attorney, equally dynamic and other-directed. (I may soon need to retire my shopworn lawyer jokes.)

Besides bestowing blessings, I've often been asked to speak at firesides for the local members. On one such occasion in Novosibirsk, my presentation appeared to be well enough received. Afterwards, I spoke with a brother who is my personal nominee for Novosibirsk's future stake president. His remarkable son, to whom I'd given a blessing before his mission to Moscow—now married, a father and branch president—also came up to me. I recalled his excellent translation skills when just the year before I'd addressed his congregation. Sadly, I detected that though still handsome, his mouth was turned down on one side—suggesting Bell's palsy or a recent stroke, young though he is. Later, a missionary told me that this was apparently the consequence of his too strenuously pursuing his many obligations at work, in the church, and as head of his new young family. (Can we sometimes be too conscientious?) I wanted to remind him of the scripture about not running faster than one has strength—as I did the sister who, at forty-one, had come for a blessing to have a fifth child, despite the health hazards she'd encountered with her previous pregnancy and the death of her last, stillborn infant. That's Russians for you—a people of extremes! (Since then, I'm told, the former missionary and branch president has had a full recovery and is now employed at the church's area office in Moscow.)

Among the last to receive blessings in Novosibirsk were two young men, recent converts—one eighteen, the other twenty-eight, though they looked the same age. Both radiated love, goodwill, and joy. I wonder why there aren't more like them. I was also told about a Chechen who joined the church here about six years ago, then, filled with missionary zeal, returned to his homeland to convert others and was subsequently executed, presumably for his missionary efforts. Another rare but ill-fated exception!

Omsk is a large, very spread-out city on the Irtysh—a major tributary of Siberia's Ob River, one of the world's longest, which flows to the icebound Arctic. Once more, I've encountered older sisters, many of them among the very first members here, with both tremendous personal faith and in almost all cases a family history of violence and abandonment exacerbated by the use of alcohol on the part of husbands and fathers. In one instance, a woman's brother stabbed their father to death while defending their mother against him. He then served time and, like his sire, became an alcoholic and died from its consequences. In my blessings to the survivors, I'm often prompted to assure them that such loved ones were victims of a disease from which they are now free and that this will be taken into account in their final judgment.

Another woman's son lived with a nurse who provoked her own mother's death, then prevailed on him to take the blame because of the emotional condition that might exonerate him. Sent to a psychiatric facility, he received such harsh treatment that he became incapacitated and resorted to tobacco to calm his nerves. (One thinks of the incarceration with hardened criminals here in Omsk that, we're told, led Dostoevsky to resort to vodka and the strong tobacco he addictively rolled into cigarettes that he constantly smoked as he wrote all night, afflicting him with the emphysema that finally killed him. If all the church had ever done for us was bring us the Word of Wisdom, that alone would be a great boon!) At his mother's request, we met with the son and arranged for a blessing of health, which, while I stood in the circle, I made sure was voiced by his local priesthood leader. Of the six admirable older sisters I gave blessings to here on my last Sunday—many of them among our earliest members—the only child of one, her son and also a church member, had taken his life in his early twenties. Another's only child, a daughter, had been murdered at the time of Perestroika. Such is the harsh backstory to many of these Russians' lives.

In firesides, I have testified that our families will endure and remain united if, as parents, we love our children enough and if, as children, we love our parents enough (see Malachi 4:5–6). I first made that assertion in blessing a young wife and mother in Ufa in the Russia Yekaterinburg

Mission, in the presence of her less-active husband. That challenge seems particularly apt where so many of these dear people and their marriages are concerned. We need to offer them better instruction and counsel regarding courtship and marriage. How badly they need to consider the simple but important teaching I encountered in a course from Lowell Bennion—that friendship (and with it fundamental compatibility) must precede blind infatuation, leading to a complete commitment. Otherwise, in many instances, the relationship does not last.

The fireside in Omsk went well except for one heckler, a non-Mormon whose attire reminded me of a Hell's Angel and whose outbursts I calmly but firmly tried to deal with: "This is not a *dopros* [interrogation]—by you of me, but a talk, a sermon, in a religious setting." At one point the same young man stomped out of the chapel, then returned as the meeting ended, accompanied by one of the older sisters (his mother?). As they approached, I wondered if he might be carrying a weapon, but through his alcohol breath, he asked me to forgive him for his outbursts. The woman by his side then whispered, "He has problems"—drinking clearly one of them.

One heartbreaking incident in Siberia involves two amazingly spiritual and committed twin brothers, now in their early twenties, whose blessings (which I had bestowed three or so years earlier) had prompted both to plan on serving missions. When I'd seen them again at a previous fireside, I'd praised them to those in attendance, but I only now learned that after their mission calls had reached their former Soviet-style district president, he'd notified them that due to charges brought against them by an unspecified third party, he had rescinded their calls. (If back home such charges were leveled against a young prospective missionary, unless they involved transgressions as grievous as murder, robbing a bank, or fathering an illegitimate child, his priesthood mentors would still work with him, encouraging him to repent and hoping to set him on the right path: that is, still heading for a mission.) Their district president's verdict and concomitant refusal to convene the disciplinary council they had immediately requested in order to defend themselves and clear their reputations had been endorsed at the time by the distantly located mission president. During this latest, third visit to the mission, I learned about this from one of them and immediately informed President Gibbons. Apprised of the circumstance, he intends to investigate the matter and afford them the due process built into all civilized judicial protocols, including those of the church. His words to me: "I believe you were meant to make me aware of this situation."

Meanwhile, these brothers have completed their schooling and established themselves in good jobs. (Their father now works for one of them and would likely lose his employment were his son to serve a mission.) I am satisfied that the charges are unfounded, though the brothers are now less active than earlier and have turned down various callings. Earlier, the one I spoke with had, he tells me, already served the equivalent of two years on "mini-missions." I asked his excellent new and fairly young branch president (who had been unaware of the circumstances) if he personally felt their treatment was justified, and he agreed it was not. In the young man's presence, I asked if *he*, the branch president, had served a mission, which he hadn't. I hoped this might suggest to these brothers that while a mission is an invaluable experience, it is not a prerequisite to further meaningful service as a priesthood holder.

The foregoing still heavily weighs on me. I wonder if at times our long-suffering efforts to convert others aren't nullified by the careless, unfeeling way we—particularly those in authority—may subsequently treat them. When those of us who are assigned sacred stewardships too cavalierly, indifferently, and uncaringly discharge our responsibilities, we become empty vessels who default in our callings and damage rather than support and lift those we are meant to serve. We need to know those we shepherd individually and deal with them justly and compassionately, not by fiat.

In one Siberian hotel, both the grandson who accompanied me and I were practically eaten up by bloodsucking midges, smaller than mosquitos, that made their way through a window screen. After we complained, the hotel staff explained the purpose of a particular apparatus into which we were to insert a tablet of insecticide, then plug it into an electric outlet to keep the creatures at a respectful distance. I wondered what its effect might be on humans.

Russian Far East (Vladivostok Mission)

A middle-aged sister, who had been institutionalized as a mental patient and now lived with her sickly mother, had fears (real or otherwise) that after their mother's death her married brother would recommit her, acquire power of attorney, and sell their mother's apartment—her only place to live—for his own gain. This all-too-common circumstance—disputed living space—has forced people to marry, divorce, and continue to coexist with alienated spouses: a situation often described in Soviet-era stories and novels. In her blessing, this sister, like a number of others, was urged to share her plight with her priesthood leaders and turn to them as needed allies—a notion that seems to have thus far eluded her and others like her.

An outstanding man in his twenties who came for his blessing seemed in every way "on fire." He was already well established professionally (like so many others in Yuzhno-Sakhalinsk, working for one of the "Big Oil" firms) and anticipated a temple sealing with a sister from Yekaterinburg whom he met at a gathering of LDS youth in Siberia. But he is, sadly, an all-too-rare exception in his broader society's male population. Far more typical are the stories I hear about the too-common default of men, their abuse and abandonment of women that leaves so many families dysfunctional or incomplete. Truly this fulfills that key prediction in Malachi that unless the hearts of the children turn to their fathers (and especially the reverse), the Earth will be cursed—not because the Lord wants it that way, but because God's offspring have brought it upon themselves. Who are most accountable for the world's deficient families and, for that matter, its many wars? Clearly, those most imbued with testosterone.

The final blessing bestowed here evoked a number of unexpected literary associations, especially the spirit of Dostoevsky. A striking man in his early thirties, a member for less than two years—extremely serious but flashing an occasional smile—shared with me his story. He has the same first name as the hero of Dostoevsky's *Crime and Punishment*, Rodion—the first live Russian I believe I've encountered with that name. Not unlike the suspiciously manipulative pawnbroker in Dostoevsky's novel but with far more evil intent, a particular old woman tragically impacted his earlier life as well as those of his older brother and a male cousin. For a time, Rodion had attempted to mediate between his brother and that woman's daughter—his brother's wife—but then sensed that his interference had only worsened the situation. After his brother decided to separate from her, the mother, a sorceress, placed a curse on the three men. (Yes, we are in that Siberia where the occult still companionably flourishes together with traditional Christianity.) The upshot was that his cousin was killed in a car crash, his brother took his own life, and Rodion was haunted by Raskolnikov-like nightmares involving the sorceress. He blamed himself for all of this until, at the time of his baptism, he was assured that any inadvertent responsibility on his part was forgiven. He now had the urge to approach the sorceress and express his forgiveness; however, in his patriarchal blessing, he was cautioned to avoid any further contact with *tyomnye sily* (dark forces).

Connecting with others

With the assistance of a particularly sensitive and caring senior missionary couple in the Russia Samara Mission, I had an unexpected and especially edifying experience involving two brothers. In the mission office, I'd interviewed one young man of missionary age we'll call Andrey, then bestowed his patriarchal blessing. Before we began, however, I'd noticed another young man, slightly older, sitting outside the door. Andrey informed me that this was his own blood brother. Did he want his brother present for the blessing? No, his non-Mormon brother only wanted to talk to me about how he could stop smoking.

Speaking with both young men after Andrey's blessing, I realized I had little background or knowledge with which to assist the older brother. Then I happened to recall a conversation with the mission president and his wife just the night before. They'd had the candor and humility to go beyond a polite, superficial presentation of themselves and tell me about one of their offspring, a son now in his thirties for whom the gospel never seemed to "take" (as with one of ours). Their son had been deeply addicted to many substances throughout his adolescence and subsequent adult years. Learning not long ago, and in their parents' absence, of his worsening near-death condition, this son's adult siblings had flown to be at his bedside. They brought him to a detox center and arranged for a program of closely monitored, supervised care to which he is, thankfully, at last responding.

Recalling what the mission president and his wife had so recently shared, I halted my conversation with Andrey and his brother, asking them to wait while I went next door to phone the mission president. He wasn't in, but I explained to his wife our need for more expert counsel. As I finished my call, the office couple, who had overheard my plea, spoke up: "We are trained to offer courses in overcoming all kinds of addictions. We've done this before. We can offer such a course to anyone who's interested, even a single person, member or nonmember." They dropped what they were doing and joined Andrey, his brother, and me, bringing with them copies of the church's manual *Opredelevaya Zavisimosti* (*Overcoming Addictions*). They briefly explained what the course would entail and arranged to meet with Andrey's brother in the future. They also made clear that to successfully overcome an addiction, one must have a close friend who will routinely monitor and verify one's progress. In our previous interview, I'd asked Andrey if he and his brother were close. "Not particularly," he'd told me. Before we parted, I thought to ask him, "Will you be your brother's friend?" (*"Are you your brother's keeper?"*) Andrey eagerly nodded.

This example illustrates what, in our often bungling fashion and while encountering frequent rejection, we attempt to achieve by reaching out across the world in a team effort. Was this experience merely serendipitous, or were we somehow guided? If the mission president and his wife hadn't shared with me their own family concern, which I may in turn have invited by telling them about one of ours, I'd never have gone to that outer office to call the mission president and there be overheard by those with the expertise to do something for Andrey's brother.

I later received a letter from the missionary couple informing me that Andrey's brother has been making significant progress. Their observation that "addiction is the chief reason for the sudden inactivity of so many brand-new members" corresponds with what I too have witnessed. What meaningful service, often beyond their express assignment, is given by our missionary couples—surrogate grandparents to needy young people, so often with dysfunctional family backgrounds. How badly such missionaries are needed.

Bulgaria

Two contrasts: on the same day in Plovdiv, Bulgaria's second largest city, I first conferred a patriarchal blessing upon its long-revered district president as he sat in his wheelchair. In our preliminary interview, before I could ask a single question, he interrupted me to declare: "I am a sinner, and I don't judge others." The next party was a newly baptized middle-aged sister who, after I asked if she had any particular personal concerns, immediately responded: "No. I'm not a sinner."

Another sister told me she is still stalked by a non-Mormon former lover who ingratiates himself with her relatives and friends, including other church members, persuading them of her mental instability. I have to take what people tell me about themselves at their word. In this instance, I told her that she badly needs to share her concerns with trusted members of the church, particularly her priesthood leaders, and have them as her allies. (If she was only imagining this, I felt they would be able to discern it and properly address her concerns in the best possible way.)

A lovely sister's member husband had dissipated himself with alcohol, leading to their predictable divorce, but wanted to marry her again. I had given blessings both to her and to their fairly young daughter before he showed up, she later told me, for a sacrament meeting at which I spoke with some pointed comments that also applied to their situation. At meeting's end, she approached me and said she felt that he was still playing her along. Much as she wanted a married life, she was now inclined not to remarry him but instead to wait for a more reliable future relationship. Their innocent daughter certainly deserves better than the violence her father previously injected into their life.

My final blessing during one trip here was to an elderly brother who had endured numerous painful surgeries. With his non-Mormon daughter's permission, he brings his young grandson to church meetings. He wanted to know if he shouldn't simply refuse further surgeries and pass from this world. In his blessing, I was prompted to suggest that he needs to stay alive as long as possible for the sake of his grandson.

Armenia and Georgia

I was privileged to bestow the first blessings ever given to citizens of Georgia, a number of them Armenian. Historically, Armenia was the first nation to declare itself Christian, soon followed by Georgia. Armenians have tended to marry their own rather than those of other nationalities. This may be reflected in the fact that in the blessings I have given, most Armenians share the same Abrahamic lineage. I've also noticed that they mostly join the church as entire families rather than individually. Forced to produce weaponry during the Soviet occupation and lacking abundant natural resources, most of Armenia's population, like the Jews before them, have emigrated to other countries to sustain themselves. We find many Armenians in Russia and elsewhere in Eastern Europe, among them some of our finest church leaders and full-time missionaries.

Before the church organization in Armenia recently became a stake, it was led by Zhan Pogosyan, an impressive district president, now a member of the stake presidency. While a young student, he had joined the church in St. Petersburg at the same time we served there. His wife has been one of the faithful transcribers of my and the other patriarchs' blessings.

A brother of missionary age who came for a blessing was embittered because, due to a hereditary impairment, he walked on crutches and was thus physically unable to serve a full-time mission. Before the blessing, I pulled in his discerning and sympathetic mission president, Ronald J. Dunn, to learn more about the case. He consoled the young man's distraught mother and vowed as well to intervene with a disaffected older son. The young man is now serving a mini-mission with an American elder and enjoying it immensely.

On my last evening, President Dunn, his wife, their excellent office senior missionary couple, and I enjoyed a delightful change of fare at a local Indian restaurant. Our young waiter from Bombay, recognizing us as religious representatives, unexpectedly addressed us with the request that we offer a prayer, not on the food but in his behalf—that he might find better employment. We all bowed our heads, and the mission president voiced such an entreaty. No self-consciousness here—only respect on the part of a likely non-Christian for what and whom we represented, prompted by his obviously deep-felt personal need.

Reconnecting in St. Petersburg

During the sixth year of my calling, I took a week-long side trip to show the city's fabulous sights to my grandson and to a former BYU colleague, Walter Rudolph, who joined us there. For me, it was also a kind of pilgrimage. I doubt I will ever again have the stamina to do all the walking our greedy sightseeing entailed. Even Wally's feet gave out. But it was most gratifying to have him with us, especially when certain unforeseen challenges abruptly confronted us.

Once, as we boarded a bus, a team of slick pickpockets blocked my entrance, diverting my attention while an accomplice neatly extracted both coin purse and wallet, which I only detected after we'd alighted from the bus a few stops later. For me, the most egregious and irreplaceable loss—more than cash, credit cards, and ID—was two laminated calling cards I'd carried with me for several decades as nostalgic mementos of significant others.

More than compensating for the theft, our visit the next day to two back-to-back fast and testimony meetings was not unlike what we would hope for on the joyful dawn of Resurrection Day—a reunion with loved ones that I could never have anticipated. I've summarized what miraculously occurred that Sunday in the following letter to an old acquaintance then serving in the St. Petersburg mission office:

> Dear Natasha:
>
> Tomorrow will be a week since my grandson, my colleague, and I attended the two fast and testimony meetings at the Central Branch facility and after each meeting briefly saw and spoke with you and so many others. Those encounters were not unlike the "celestial reunions" Merriam and I enjoyed at the Stockholm temple when so many of you came there. Some say that since our time with you many have become inactive—*ushli*—but there clearly remains a solid core of faithful members from the past, from even the very beginning, and others we don't know who have meanwhile joined you. Nor will all who have departed stay away forever, as I discovered last Sunday. It was, for me, truly a day of miracles. In particular, two showed up whom I'd hardly expected to see again. In fact, I did not at first recognize either of them and did not realize

who V [an early young branch president who later became disaffected] was until after we had departed. Someone finally had to tell me that the other young man was A, the one-time dynamic young president of the Ploshchad Muzhestva Branch and, though briefly, our missionary at the Provo Missionary Training Center, who until that very day—last Sunday—had not visited the church since 1994. In our brief exchange, A nevertheless bore to me a strong testimony: "I never doubted Jesus Christ or that this is his true church. I only doubted my own behavior" (whatever that might have been). Those were his exact words.

So A taught me a great lesson, as did V's friendly, timid smile: that we must never close the door on those who have strayed and that—like the lost sheep, the lost coin, and the prodigal son—many will, in due course, return to the fold. Some have their own timetable, and we must always be there with open arms to receive them. Such surprising and thrilling reunions will surely take place both in the future and in the next life, where the Savior will mercifully unite all who together bend their knees to Him. The loss of my wallet the day before to a thief on Nevsky Prospekt was well worth coming to St. Petersburg and being with you all again on Sunday. In fact, the effort required to bestow so many blessings over the past several years has—besides the great privilege it has been to serve so many others—been well worth it, including all the jet lag—if only because of last Sunday.

With love and gratitude to all of you for the witness you have been that has so strengthened my and Merriam's faith and testimonies and in turn blessed our family—sincerely your brother,

Thomas Rogers

Before we flew home, I also spoke with L, my great actor (the lead in church productions of my play *Huebener* and a stage adaptation of *The Brothers Karamazov* while I was mission president), who, although an electrical engineer, is at heart a poet. I already knew that his marriage had been contentious. He now told me that he had decided to return to his family out of love for their children and because, as he put it to me, without the gospel "life would be *beztolkova* (meaningless)." These unexpected but wholly welcome reconciliations bring to mind Lutheran pastor Dietrich Bonhoeffer's sage observation: "Our brother's ways are not in our hands; we cannot hold together what is breaking; we cannot keep life in what is determined to die. But God binds elements together in the breaking, creates community in the separation, grants grace through judgment."[1]

Immediately after the two fast and testimony meetings and those astounding reunions, we traveled just three subway stops to the memorable Dostoevsky *dommuzey*—his last of twenty-three St. Petersburg residences, in which before his death Dostoevsky completed *The Brothers Karamazov.* As our excellent English-speaking guide, herself a professor and Dostoevsky specialist, reviewed for us Dostoevsky's major fiction, I thought of the extremities of feeling and behavior that so many of my dear Russian friends (or their family members) had passed through. It is as if they too were Dostoevsky's characters—projections of his astute observations and profound psychological insights, clear proof over a century later that they were no exaggeration.

Why did I ever study, then teach Russian, along with the great literary culture of the Russian people? Reconnecting that Sunday morning reminded me that there was ample and good reason. And if the Russians are a fair sample of all humanity, then I can only loudly exclaim, "How glorious we all are in our imperfection!"

After returning from what has by now become our sacred second home, I wondered if this might be my final visit here. Just a week later (unknown to me at the time), Elder Russell M. Nelson of the Quorum of the Twelve Apostles would organize the new St. Petersburg Russia Stake. The stake's new patriarch now bestows all the mission's blessings. (Three years later would witness my own release from this assignment.)

Future of the church

During 2013 and with the lower missionary age limit, I became more aware of many young men and women near missionary age who are eager and determined to serve missions. As I interviewed each for his or her patriarchal blessing, I was deeply impacted by their strong testimonies. They have withstood social pressures from schoolmates and others their age and are destined to be the future of the church in their respective locations—influential spiritual leaders and heads of their own future families. One family with four such sons, whose father is in the Ukraine Donetsk Mission presidency, especially stood out for me. Each son was "on fire" about his church membership and eager to serve a mission since attending a country-wide conference of Ukrainian youth in the Carpathians. I wonder how those four young brothers have fared since Donetsk became the epicenter of a horrific civil war.

Though conversions are now fewer than at the outset, the younger adults who have served missions should bring an extra measure of experience, stability, and long-term commitment to the church's ministry and to their very own families—much as we witnessed in the wards we attended ten years before in Sweden.

I often think of several others—such as Emil, the young adult gypsy in Varna, Bulgaria, who, because he was lame and unemployed, feared he could never marry and support a family. Yet contrary to the tradition of his fathers, he is a giver, not a predator, serving in a branch presidency. With his excellent English, he is also a valuable liaison between his people and the senior missionaries. One reason he is so altruistic and free of acquisitive tendencies is doubtless that as an orphan, he was institutionally raised—truly a mixed blessing in his case. (More recently, I've learned that a senior missionary couple who served in Varna have found sponsors and arranged for Emil to have needed surgery by specialists in Tel Aviv so he will be more able-bodied and more likely to find employment or training for some profession.)

I think as well of Timur, a young man of Uzbek heritage whom I first met in Rostov, where he was already serving in a branch presidency before his mission in Moscow, where he eventually was an assistant to the mission president. Timur's story is filled with both shadow and light. His father, I'm told, had been the wealthiest man in postcommunist Rostov until someone who owed him money took his life rather than repay him. This was when Timur was still a young child. Fortunately, an uncle took him in hand and joined the church, leading to Timur's own conversion. He is now a businessman in Moscow. His returned missionary wife wonderfully served for a period of time as the area office coordinator for patriarchal blessings.

There is also Vlad, the piano prodigy from Far East Arctic Magadan (the site of a notorious Soviet extermination camp for political prisoners who only lasted six months, on average, in its freezing gold mines). As a young adolescent, alone at home and contrary to his parents' instructions, Vlad opened the door to two strangers—missionaries. He, his mother, and his sister later moved to Moscow, where local members paid for his training at a conservatory. He had asked for a blessing when I first met him in St. Petersburg, but was doubtful about what the disruption of army service and then a mission might do to his artistic career. Prompted by his blessing to venture forth, he was already completing his service as yet another assistant to his mission president at the time of my later tour to one of the Siberian missions.

I think of Aleksandr Mosenkov, a returned missionary and St. Petersburg–based astrophysicist who was just a little boy when we knew his family twenty years ago. His father, a doctor, was an outstanding branch president and has authored an engaging historical novel featuring events depicted in 3 Nephi.

And I recall Boris Leostrin, who, during our earlier mission, as a quiet young teenager would eagerly volunteer to go out teaching with the missionaries and on Saturdays would help shelve supplies in the St. Petersburg mission office. When we departed for home, I announced to our staff, "This young man must serve a mission someday." At that time, we weren't aware of his family background and did not know that his mother was also a member. A decade later, we met his parents, who had also been called to serve as fellow missionaries at the Stockholm Sweden Temple. We then learned that Boris's father was not yet a member during our time in St. Petersburg. However, before entering the army—a prerequisite to serving his mission—Boris had asked his father to consent to be baptized by him. Boris is now a counselor in the St. Petersburg stake presidency.

And then there's the young Sasha Nepomnyashchy, who, also not yet a member back then, was recruited by his sister as a supernumerary in our stage adaptation of *The Brothers Karamazov.* After his baptism, Sasha, like Boris, served a mission, then served as a counselor in the St. Petersburg district presidency. Since that time, he has coordinated the mission's seminary and institute program.

Finally, I think of Viktor Bogutsky, the missionary from the Pacific island Sakhalin in the Russia Vladivostok Mission who so impressed me at the time of his patriarchal blessing at the Provo Missionary Training Center. In the second year of his mission, he and a Russian companion were riding in a taxi in the Tatar city, Kazan, in the Samara mission. For some reason, Elder Bogutsky suggested that he and his companion trade places. Shortly after, they were hit head-on by an oncoming truck. Elder Bogutsky was the sole casualty. Two years later, again on Sakhalin Island, I arranged to visit his mother and a married older brother, then serving in the local branch's elders quorum presidency. At that time, their mother shared with me the missionary journal and letters of her impressively charismatic and enthusiastic missionary son in which he nevertheless repeatedly mentioned his foreboding that he would not complete his mission alive.

And I continue to think about and pray for the twin brothers in Siberia.

There are such outstanding youth in practically every branch of every mission: noble spirits, moving against the grain of the society around them—"pilgrims in a strange land" helping to lay the foundation of Zion for themselves and for their needy people. As I revisit the sites of previous blessings, I acquire a more in-depth appreciation of the members and their circumstances—and, with it, of our common humanity. In some cases, it is with sadness as I encounter those I've come to know and love whose lives (especially marriages) have in one way or another fallen apart. But hopelessly or forever? That is not for any of us to presume or say.

One most important lesson I've learned is exemplified by the apostles in our day. Taxed as they are, such special witnesses exemplify what the Savior taught about the value of souls. A case in point is Elder David A. Bednar, who, while presiding over the Europe East Area, toured the St. Petersburg mission. (This was conveyed to me by our former area president, Elder Paul Pieper, who, before being called as an LDS General Authority, in turn presided over the St. Petersburg mission.) Together, the two traveled to the residence of a former branch president—in his day a wonderful, beloved priesthood leader—who had since forfeited his church membership. Elder Bednar took the time to meet and plead with this brother to mend his ways and reclaim his young family. Such in the Lord's eyes—as it should be in ours—is the value of "the one"—*everyone.*

Over time, three things will, I believe, further fortify our members' ongoing commitment to the church: temple attendance, the experience of full-time missions, and patriarchal blessings.

It has been a spiritually vivifying experience to interact with these brothers and sisters. In the process, the superficial barriers of cultural, linguistic, and ethnic difference slough off and fall away. We are one, as close as our family members back home and sometimes even closer. This is the great blessing of the restored gospel to humankind. Of this I testify.

Note

1. Dietrich Bonhoeffer, *Life Together*, trans. John W. Doberstein (New York: Harper & Row, 1954), 108.

What Is Love?

When in the 1970s I presided over BYU's 101st Branch, most of its male members were returned missionaries, seriously searching for an eternal companion. In our second year there, a third of our members became engaged, and a third of these to another member of the same branch. Despite their eagerness, many were still unsure if the party they were deeply smitten by was Mister or Miss Right. In that very year, the Mormon musical Saturday's Warrior *was taking everyone by storm. Its thesis—that marriages are "made in heaven"—left everyone concerned to know if his or her infatuation with someone else was in fact foreordained. Since Zeus's thunderbolt had failed to manifest itself, quite a few couples were—despite their mutual compatibility and the attraction they felt for each other—still waiting for a spiritual confirmation. My pragmatic counsel tilted a number of the engagements I've mentioned as well as others beyond our branch's confines as that counsel was shared across campus. So many came to me with the same concern, in fact, that I finally offered it as a printed handout. Among the perplexed couples who considered and acted on the advice that follows, I'm aware of two subsequent LDS General or Area Authorities and several past or current stake, mission, or temple presidents and their wives, many of whose sons and daughters have now served missions and also married.*[1]

> Verily, verily, I say unto you, Except a corn of wheat fall into the ground and die, it abideth alone: but if it die, it bringeth forth much fruit.
>
> —John 12:24

Some have suggested that the classical varieties of love—charity, friendship, affection, and *eros* (romantic or sexual love)—are aspects of one and the same emotion, entailing in each case empathy, goodwill, and the extension of oneself in behalf of others. There is doubtless wisdom in so viewing the subject rather than stressing the differences. Although what follows is written with *eros* in mind—the kind of love generally associated with the feelings that occur between a man and a woman, a husband and a wife—the other kinds of love are fundamental to it. This sheds further light on what can be expected of conjugal love and what it, in turn, requires of us.

Frequently—after being drawn to someone who strikes us as a potentially desirable life's companion—we despair that the relationship lacks sufficient infatuation, is no grand passion, and that the one essential ingredient, genuine *love*, appears to be lacking. We crave a greater certainty, an overwhelming conviction that we are truly fated for one another. And because that undeniable conviction doesn't come—as in the majority of cases it does not, you may be relieved to know—we are frustrated, hesitant, and noncommittal. Unfortunately, this uncertain state can indefinitely persist if we do not, sooner or later, recognize it as a very normal circumstance. With more realistic expectations, we can confidently move ahead—to the point of commitment and beyond.

Love, as the Savior defines it in the scriptures, is both integral and consequent to our giving and sacrificing ourselves in behalf of others. How then can it be manifested to any significant degree before we commit ourselves to a significant other and consciously exclude other prospects? That is the first sacrifice a meaningful relationship demands of us, and for many, it is not easy. The choice of one good prospect out of many may seem arbitrary, but it represents a meaningful kind of self-denial—and the more one is required to exclude, the greater a test such decision making becomes. After thoughtfully committing ourselves, we may still be tempted to reconsider, but with sufficient resolve—and an understanding of the stakes involved—we can and must put such temptation behind us.

You may feel disillusioned that the pursuit of romantic love involves such conscious calculation. But we would do well to ask ourselves why the Lord instituted marriage vows in the first place. Surely almost every bride and groom sincerely *intend* to be faithful to each other. But the Lord knows better than we how fickle and capricious we can be. He knows that only by conscious, pledged effort will we stick to our intent to love each other consistently and forever. Only with such effort will our love increase and remain in force. This is why we are expected to *marry* and *declare* our intent, preferably before God, angels, and witnesses.

No love can be as meaningful before marriage as after, because—like everything else in life—its outcome depends not on who we are or what we've already done but on what we *will yet do* with it. Our love for a companion is mostly potential—eternal potential—and what we make of it will be one grand, glorious, creative act, made up of countless daily smaller thoughts and acts. Initial infatuation, though momentarily reassuring, can be terribly misleading. Witness the outcome of so many early high school engagements. Witness the serial marriages and divorces of so many movie stars. The point is that there can be no guarantee. If the Lord could guarantee that our choice would end in success, it would deny us our agency to choose to make it right or successful on our own. And that would contradict the whole purpose of our creation.

But can we at least have some initial reassurance? Is it unfair to ask for that? Yes, we can, and no, it isn't. But we often seem to expect such reassurance in a form so overwhelming that only a prophet might be privileged to receive it. In this connection, I suggest rereading Alma 32, substituting for *faith* the word *love*. Truly the way love for others grows in us is not that much different. Because it depends on our works and future expectations, it is as much a product of faith as is a testimony. We should ask ourselves the following modest but telling question: "Do I so much as desire to love that person?" If the answer is affirmative, the most formidable barrier has already been overcome, and we are—or can be—well on our way to loving her or him. If all we feel is peacefulness when we consider committing ourselves to someone—only a warmth (which is after all a degree of "burning")—that is all the confirmation the Spirit sends to many. When one thinks about it, however, that is all we really need.

Two additional criteria are nevertheless indispensable and should be investigated, discerned, and fully corroborated before the relationship moves toward commitment: (1) spirituality, including spiritual potential, and (2) overall compatibility. The latter can be assessed in terms of how well we share each other's interests, how well our personalities complement each other, and simply how lonely we feel when the other isn't around. If we can be satisfied on these two points, there is very little more we ought to expect. The rest is up to us—even the love that emerges from our relationship: a love that, if truly authentic, can only be earned, not given.

God wants all his sons and daughters to experience the culmination of such love in marriage. Brethren who hold the Melchizedek Priesthood know that their eternal blessings, including exaltation, are directly predicated on sharing that priesthood with a worthy sister to whom they have pledged themselves for time and all eternity. The Lord does not want us to delay this blessing unduly—and with good reason.

Whom we marry is as important as *that* we marry, and in the manner and place the Lord has ordained. In moving toward that eternally consequential moment and searching out an appropriate partner, we should apply the most meaningful criteria but not encumber the process with nonessential or irrelevant expectations. For one thing, that takes the fun out of it. As with most good things, love, when it strikes, should come as a certain unexpected surprise, that we might be all the more "surprised by joy," as C. S. Lewis would say: that joy which—as with the reunion with loved ones and the Lord beyond the veil—will be all the more profound because we could not anticipate it in all its glorious detail.

Love must remain enigmatic and mysterious, even if this creates occasional frustration. Like personality and life itself, it would lose much of its force and dignity if we could totally account for it or produce it at will in some kind of test tube. Even so, we must believe that—as creatures of God's love, his eternal offspring—we are capable of love for any and all creatures, in all their diverse forms. This can, of course, lead to love's perversion (see the beginning of C. S. Lewis's discussion of *eros* in *The Four Loves*). That is why the Lord has felt it necessary to place appropriate bounds on the manner and degree with which we give expression to such love.

Such limitless capacity should reassure those—mostly sisters—who may not have the opportunity in this life to experience love in marriage. They are still expected and, for their own further self-development, must learn to channel their love in other ways that are both acceptable and needed. This they can do—to their personal satisfaction—because love is basically the same, whatever its context. Love is essentially selfless and other-oriented. Only as such can it truly bless either the lover or the beloved. While some may miss out on the love we all hope to find in marriage, the love they extend in other contexts can be a real satisfaction in this life, and can be a valuable preparation for those eternal bonds that prophets of God have said will ultimately not be denied any who desire and are worthy of them.

A final thought: doesn't it seem reasonable that there are forces at work trying to discourage righteous individuals from getting together and founding an eternal family? If, therefore—even when all the essential signs are positive—we still feel periodically uncertain and confused about committing ourselves, we should perhaps consider the possibility of such an influence at work and, recognizing it for what it is, make sure we don't give in to it.

In much of life, we seem unable to avoid committing ourselves either to the Lord or to Satan. Where eternal bonding is concerned, can there be any question about where we owe our total allegiance? Then let us make sure our deeds and decisions do not contradict our good intentions, nor be surprised if this requires an act of faith. When did we ever suppose that in this life we would need to dispense with living by faith? And where should it be more applicable than in such decisions of eternal moment?

Note

1. My thinking on this topic has been influenced by the inspired insights of Lowell Bennion, who, as director of the LDS Institute of Religion at the University of Utah, was an important spiritual mentor to both myself and my wife.

The Vietnam Veterans Memorial, Washington, DC

Powerful sentiments attended my first visit to the Vietnam War memorial on the Capitol Hill mall in Washington, DC. Shortly thereafter, in 1989, I attempted in this poem to capture the mood it conveys by matching the memorial's stark simplicity—a lesson for all aspiring artists.

Approaching the massive effigy of our Greatest President—
there to contemplate his words about the sacred worth
of all people and the price he paid for so believing—
our path suddenly slopes below the mall's green turf.

No imposing, eye-arresting structure, no fanfare, virtually
no announcement until we see by our feet against the vertical
excavation a first black granite slab, triangular, and, in plainest
white inscription, one or two modestly carved names—then
an adjoining partition, larger now as our path still gradually
descends, with more names streaming, one after the other,
row upon row.

Then ever-larger slabs—each still below the level where grass
and dandelion sprout; small children chase and tumble; picnickers
spread quilts, then sprawl, leisurely sigh, reminisce and laugh, make
love, or, lying meditatively prone, stare enchanted at cloud and sky.

Our descent proceeds below the highest partition and explosive
apex of ever more such names. Then the path continues,
a slightly perceptible rise—like, after his *descensus* and those three
tumultuous dark days, the Son of Man's *ascensus*—and the now
equally merciful diminution of those distinctive, though
unpretentious,
familiar-sounding combinations of given, middle and surname—
in all, nearly 60,000.

No special status accorded—no indication of duty or rank or unit
or branch of service. No suggestion of each man's size or age—
though most were young, boys more than men and young
as those who now, on the lawn above, romp and wrestle with
small children or at twilight lie with girlfriends and young wives
or tightly embrace on the several benches lining the
paths that spread across this vast and solemn park.

No indication of those further accidentals—race and color—
fulfillment of that Tall, Gaunt Man's vision, now eternally
framed in stately white abode, sadly staring at this same ground
and with bowed head honoring these and (we imagine) many others
he would sooner than himself have seen honored. For them only this
simple recognition: the roll call, the assertive listing of their names
below the earth where they now lie—and where we must go to
read them,

Names brought prematurely low by the folly of elders who did not
well enough understand that this earth and the flesh upon it are
no one's to possess or commandeer: fitting memorial to human
folly, as to the tragic nobility of innocent and wasted lives.

Inspired designer, who set here those names, each unlike the other,
to remind us that these were, like ourselves, precious, unique,
irreplaceable souls—so separately named and addressed by mothers
and sires, wives and children who tenderly claimed and loved them—

Who put them where they now are, below and
within the earth—barrier, reproach, enticement, and reminder to those
still alive that these no longer access sight, hearing,
touch, our accustomed contact with grass, sky, manmade
structures, the rush and novelty of public and private events,
choice of movement and direction, purposeful labor, play, the forms
of pleasure, contemplation, or one another—

Who with these names reminds us that we
are also ONE, all connected, and must all be superseded, yet—
wherever there is sufficient caring and introspection—may be
similarly thought upon with wistful, tender kindness, sympathy, and awe.

"Interconnecting" at Home and Abroad

Written at the request of Sunstone's *editor, this "travelogue" discloses my often feeble, even failed attempts to bridge cultural differences with mostly foreigners in Germany, Russia, Poland, Bulgaria, Armenia, Syria, India, and China. (I've left out similar encounters in Austria, Italy, France, and the former Yugoslavia, involving further attempts to communicate with local citizens in their native language.) My focus and concern was to overcome the artificial barriers and arbitrary impasses that retard the recognition of our common humanity, with the sad acknowledgment that similar suspicion, mistrust and—perhaps worst of all—indifference can and do as much arise in the streets and neighborhoods of what we think of as "home."*[1]

> Let your hearts expand, let them be enlarged toward others. . . . The mind or the intelligence which man possesses is coequal with God himself. . . . All the minds and spirits that God ever sent into the world are susceptible of enlargement.
>
> —Joseph Smith[2]

As a self-styled polyglot, I have, for some reason, tended to pursue the language of "the enemy." Don't ask why.

Postwar Germany

My first mission call to Germany, headquartered in Berlin, occurred only ten years after the end of World War II, and, obviously, I had no say about where I was called. In fact, I'd earlier studied French and was secretly hoping that would recommend me for the land of our former allies. But I'd also already studied almost three years of Russian, for which in 1955 there was not the slightest chance a missionary would have much use.

While in Germany, I got to know Erich Krause, devoted genealogical director for the North German Mission and a former devotee and SS bodyguard of the Führer himself. His alter ego was surely another Krause—Walter—who had escaped a death sentence at the hands of the Nazis only by fleeing prison during the Allies' fiery bombing of Dresden and whose own father, an ardent East German communist, had later denounced him for being less political and embracing Mormonism. Walter Krause lived into his nineties and was the first to be called as patriarch for all of eastern Europe.

I doubtless encountered many former Nazis and Nazi sympathizers during that two-and-a-half-year sojourn. Many had probably fled from the Russians to Schleswig-Holstein, an early mission area of mine; and then, of course, there was Berlin itself. But discussing politics wasn't part of a missionary's job description, and, blessedly, we were mostly oblivious to the earlier background of our fellow church members and those to whom we brought the "word."

Cold-war Russia and its aftermath

In the early 1990s, as a mission president in St. Petersburg, Russia, I could not help but be keenly aware that a number of our outstanding priesthood leaders, some of whom had been highly responsible professionals in the Soviet enterprise, must have been Party members only two or three years before. One of these—the late Vyacheslav Yefimov—particularly stood out for me. He was the street-smart but deeply spiritual president of our mission's largest district and later the first native

Russian to be called as a mission president. A few years earlier, he had been the supervisor of more than five hundred employees in the St. Petersburg transportation system. Brother Yefimov saved me from making a number of grievous mistakes and naive judgment calls as I first took over the reins there.

Those who live under global alignments opposed to our own are simply, like us, mostly subjects if not victims of where and—since those alignments so readily alter—when they were born. We should always keep this in mind, though I have not always done so. I painfully remember, for instance, disputing the solemn pronouncement of a venerable tour guide in 1957 at the Lenin Museum on Red Square. I was still an LDS missionary, not yet released nor returned home, and, yes, there all by myself. I'd received the permission of my exceptionally indulgent mission president to a most presumptuous request: to take advantage of an unprecedented *Gesellschaftsreise* (group tour) advertised to Germans wishing to visit the Soviet Union. As it turned out, no German as yet cared to, and I went all by myself for ten days, the distance from San Francisco to New York and back, with the finest hotel accommodations, restaurant meals, guide service, and more—all for $400. *Inturist* was just then rolling out a bargain "red carpet" to promote Western tourism. Moscow is now considered the world's most expensive city. Those were indeed—and in more than one sense—"the good old days."

My gray-haired guide was, for what seemed the nth time, pointing out another portrait of Lenin and reciting one of his gems of wisdom: "Serve your fellow men, and you will know great joy" (or words to that effect). So I impertinently rejoined—I was still a missionary, don't forget—that someone else had said the same thing almost two thousand years before. My guide, who had, with all the dedication of a secular nun, taught herself English just the year before in order to serve at the first postwar international conference of communist youth, was scandalized. After all, I was standing on her sacred turf, and she was, clearly, a true believer.

Former Yugoslavia

Have I as yet learned the important lesson I've here been preaching? I'm not so sure. Earlier this year, while waiting for the Paris metro with a grandson, I noticed a woman reading a newspaper in Serbo-Croatian and could not refrain from trying on her a few phrases from the time I'd spent in her homeland decades earlier. Somehow I readily remembered the sentence, "*On vech veliki momak*"—"He's already a big boy"—and, though somewhat out of context, handily spoke it, pointing at my grandson. The lady, a recent émigré, was flattered at my attempt to speak her language until we told her that we were Americans. She then made it clear that she was Serb, not Croatian, and still deeply resented our bombing Belgrade during the UN action against the forces of Miloshevich and Radzich. My sense (not to mention the rest of the world's) that the Serbs had perpetrated blatant and horrific genocide in Bosnia made no difference. In her eyes, America was the hated enemy, and the conversation suddenly terminated.

While I held nothing against the woman personally, I was reminded of just how deeply historic resentments run in many people. During my time in Bosnia in the 1970s, while the communist dictator Tito still reigned, citizens often conjectured that after his demise, in this artificial country no larger than the state of Wyoming, there would arise a cataclysmic civil war involving Serbs, Croatians, Bosnian-Herzegovinians, Macedonians, and possibly Slovenians, each egged on by centuries-old grievances. How prophetic this proved to be just a few decades later. Those in the United States who still insist on flying the Confederate flag may come closest to such a perpetuation of inherited resentment.

Cultural contrasts

During the Cold War, I was, through the arts, afforded further opportunity to appreciate cultural differences between "the other" and myself. After my German mission, I was for several years an actor on Second Avenue in Salt Lake's own Deutsches Theater, a little cultural marvel no longer in operation. There for at least a quarter century, Siegfried and Lotte Guertler, themselves professional émigré thespians who had during World War II made films for the Nazi regime, annually produced on their own living room stage an average of five full-length classical German plays. But our audience was almost entirely comprised of elderly German émigrés. We seldom saw there any native-born Americans, not even those who had once served missions in the *Heimatland*.

During my numerous sojourns in Russia, I have always tried to visit a Russian Orthodox service—not so much for the liturgy as simply to bask in the choir's glorious a cappella singing. While I consider that church's ethical stipulations and spiritual community grievously lacking, its music, icons, and incense mesmerizingly convey a genuine mood of solace and consolation. I also respect the deep reverence its worshippers invariably demonstrate.

Poland under the Soviets

In Poland, where I've had lengthy residences to study both its language and theatre, I've been enthralled by the Krakow Franciscan basilica's marvelous art nouveau stained glass depictions of deity and various saints, the creations of my favorite Polish artist, the marvelous portraitist Stanisław Wyspiański, himself also one of Poland's noted playwrights.

Just as while in Vienna I learned that Austria's foremost "religion" is classical music, in Cold War Poland I discovered that the thrust of that nation's fiercely patriotic Catholicism has been the memorialization of its defenders through centuries of suffering and defeat at the hands of occupying powers. Given their flat, defenseless terrain along what cultural geographers have called Europe's "shatter belt" and their military vulnerability due to factionalism and political disunity, the Poles have been forced to commemorate their defenders' *failure* to withstand foreign aggression. Although a seventeenth-century Polish king, Jan Sobiecki, is credited with repulsing the Ottoman Turks outside Vienna, preventing further Islamic inroads into Europe, Poland long disappeared from the map after other powers partitioned it. Poles also suffered the proportionately greatest loss of life in World War II, approximately one of every seven citizens. During the Soviet occupation, tour guides would slyly tell us that when on one occasion a Russian general stood before an image of Sobiecki on Krakow's central square, he inquired about the imposing figure's name. "Sobiecki," his guide promptly affirmed. The general's rejoinder: "Of course he's *sovietsky*, but what's his name?" With similar wry humor, citizens in Warsaw will tell you that the best view of their city is from the very top of its tallest building, the Palace of Culture and Science, presented at war's end as a gift from the Russians to the Polish people, though built (as the Poles I spoke to insisted) by conscripted Polish labor and modeled after Moscow's own several high-rise "ziggurats," including the University of Moscow. (Russian dissidents would refer to their style as "Stalin birthday cake" or "Stalin dust catcher.") "And why does this building afford the best view?" "Because then you don't have to look at it."

Celebrating Poland's brave but unsuccessful defenders was the prevailing leitmotif I encountered in all forms of Polish artistic expression during my two fairly lengthy residences there in the 1970s. During a memorable tour with theatre professionals (and amateurs such as myself), I was introduced to films and stage productions by Poland's foremost avant-gardists. I had, for instance, a privileged interview with the country's veteran filmmaker, Andrzej Wajda, whose films had paid tribute to both the protesting Gdańsk shipyard workers clandestinely massacred in the early 1970s and those who launched the Solidarity movement a decade later in the same locale. In turn, the world-renowned performances by Jerzy Grotowski's Teatr Laboratorium in Wrocław (formerly the German city Breslau) focused on the ordeal and sufferings of those interned in the Nazi camps.

In the film *My Dinner with André*, an actual New York–based director, André Gregory, tells the actor Wallace Shawn about undergoing a mock live burial in Poland as a participant in a metatheatrical activity. This was the sort of thing Grotowski was now into, and a number of the more impressionable members of our group had similar experiences during the two weeks we were with his actors. Others of us underwent grueling vocal and physical exercises—intended to free up our innate visceral emotions so that our onstage responses would be all the more primal and authentic.

Grotowski's actors had already ceased performing plays as such; but for a documentary film by Wajda, they had revived their last one—*Apokalypsis cum Transfiguris*—an imagined account of rivalry and disputation among Christ's first disciples, leading to his rejection and abandonment before the crucifixion. Our group was allowed to view two successive rehearsal performances in preparation for the filming.

The show's idea had been suggested by personal clashes among Grotowski's actors, who consented to expand on them for the purpose of his production. The emotional intensity of the play was almost unbearable. I felt transported, as though actually there—nearly persuaded that such dissension might in fact have occurred among Christ's first followers. Christ's desolation and loneliness were, under such circumstances, all the more vivid. A year or two later, the troupe, who had lived together like monks and nuns and whose sole purpose in life had been their art, broke up.

With the LDS Church's extensive outreach to individuals both within and outside the fold (home teaching, missions, humanitarian aid), the LDS outlook on both everyday life and human destiny is notably positive, optimistic, and mutually supportive. Thus, I was not at first prepared for this almost opposite perspective or the historical conditioning that underlies the social mentality and worship of Catholic Poland. But, like the decor of Poland's churches, which so darkly focuses on Christ's suffering, these unforgettable expressions of courage and dignity wrested from oppression and defeat helped explain to me an unfortunate nation's perpetually stoic survival against greatest odds. Though I could not fully identify with that legacy, I was indelibly affected.

After returning home, I staged for the BYU Department of Theatre a reconstruction of images, gestures, and scenes from Grotowski's and others' avant-garde productions. As our audience entered the Pardoe Auditorium, they were forced to walk over empty, worn shoes scrounged from Deseret Industries, reminiscent of the exhibits of liquidated inmates' confiscated belongings on exhibit at Auschwitz since the end of World War II. Like our largely wordless reenactment, the effect was eerie and, I imagine, unlike anything BYU audiences had previously encountered.

Armenia

But I am not always so unruffled—as was the case when, at the end of a recent month-long stay in Armenia, I went with the mission president there to the Genocide Museum in Yerevan. I already knew about the Ottoman Turks' horrific slaughter of Armenians during World War I, but the tour helped clarify the circumstances. This time, our guide was younger and very knowledgeable. As we followed her from one exhibit to the next, I noticed that a swarthy young man in blue jeans had attached himself to our party, standing a little behind us but clearly following the guide's English. On an impulse I turned and asked, "Are you also an American?" upon which he abruptly vanished. I asked the guide who he might be. Her answer: "He's probably a Turk. They sometimes come like that to listen in but don't want people knowing who they are." I understood, but I felt bad that I'd provoked such discomfort.

The very next day after I boarded the plane from Yerevan back to London, a British seatmate, a middle-aged woman, whispered in my ear that the bald-headed man sitting just in front of me, with his wife, teenage son, and daughter in adjacent seats, was "the former president here who, in protesting the recent elections, fomented riots in which scores of people were killed. He's a very bad man." Although we were already heading for London in a British Midland carrier, I thought it prudent to change the subject. My seatmate, an investigative journalist, found that agreeable enough until my reply to her question, "What are you doing here?"—"I'm with the Mormon church"—immediately brought down the conversational shutters. There was not a peep more from either of us for the rest of the flight. A "reality check" and strong reminder that, like Turks in Armenia, Mormons are not always so endearing—particularly at a time when America is far from admired and, in this instance, just after the media had given widespread attention to Warren Jeffs's Texas fundamentalists.

An ongoing challenge

That old difficulty again: How do we reach out to others with the certainty and conviction of our faith and values without counting on any personal acceptance or even respectful acknowledgment? But let's turn that question around: How willing are we to extend to "the other" equivalent respect and appreciation while not compromising our testimony or standing at a comfortable remove from our own energizing faith? Must we simply view the world's various religious philosophies and systems of belief as interchangeable and relatively the same?

This ecumenical challenge was brought home to me when in the 1970s my daughter and I toured and, for a length of time, resided in India. While in Kashmir, we found ourselves literally snowed in and unable to fly back to Delhi. My daughter Krista was laid low with the flu, so for three days, I traveled to a nearby Muslim restaurant and carried back our meals. The young waiter there finally asked if I were a Christian and then exclaimed that he could not imagine anyone's being other than a devotee of Allah. (It reminded me of the time in the 1960s when the young student body president at the University of Moscow clandestinely visited me, asked several wondering questions about American affluence, then abruptly declared, "I can't imagine living anywhere besides the Soviet Union.") I think my response this time was fairly inspired: "Whatever you and I choose to call him—Allah or Jehovah—surely we can agree that he created each of us and is the Father of us all. Isn't that what's really important?"

Encounters with Muslims

More recently, and closer to home, my encounters with Muslims have proved similarly perplexing. After retiring, I took up an intensive study of Arabic, the language of our ostensible enemies and geopolitical rivals, auditing two year-length Arabic courses at the University of Utah. My last teacher was Abdullah, though that had not always been his name.

Born in New England and raised in Salt Lake City, Richard Lux was a full-blooded Caucasian American. Responding as an engineer to an offer from the University of Utah Medical Center, Richard's father had brought their family to our area. Though Richard was not a Mormon himself, his best school friend and playmate was a "straight-arrow" Japanese-American Latter-day Saint. Together, he tells us, they played pranks and got into the typical scrapes of young men their age. They were inseparable until one day, in high school, this friend told Richard that a certain seminary teacher had advised his charges not to associate with nonmembers. Richard says that from that moment, he detested Mormons. Later, while pursuing Arabic at Columbia University, he converted to the Muslim faith.

I have seldom encountered a more delightful or dynamic teacher. The irony is that—now a devout Muslim—Abdullah's opinion of Mormons has considerably softened because he sees us in terms of his and our shared ethical standards and our respect for the transcendent: "We have so much in common." I wistfully suspect that had they remained friends, his Mormon neighbor might have eventually prevailed on him to seriously investigate and accept a religion he now highly respects from an almost unbridgeable distance.

Then there was my Arabic tutor Hussein, an Iraqi refugee in his midthirties who lives and works right here in my Bountiful community. A Shia from Basra, Hussein was recruited as a teenager to fight the Iranians in Saddam's earlier US-backed offensive against Iran. Unlike Abdullah, Hussein was not a very good teacher, but I was a far-from-apt pupil. One day in the middle of a lesson and without any explanation, he stood up and announced that he had to leave. He never came back, and that proved to be our final lesson. It was, I suppose, a face-saving way to let me know he'd had it with this dull pupil. Maybe, though, such a response reflects the sort of politeness that, in being so direct, we Americans have little sense of—another cultural difference and barrier to overcome.

In any event, on a previous day Hussein and I had been poring over my dual-language text of, believe it or not, *The Count of Monte Cristo*, when he began to reminisce:

"There was a great man who had to live for several years in Paris but finally returned to his people."

"Are you possibly talking about the Iranian imam, Khomeini?"

"Yes."

"But you fought against Khomeini as one of Saddam's soldiers."

"He was a very great man."

"Do you happen to know, Hussein, that Khomeini sent to China for cheap plastic toy keys and distributed them to young boys, telling them this was their key to Paradise, then urged them to go ahead of his troops against you to clear the minefields with their own bodies?"

"Oh, but they wanted to do that. They wanted to go to heaven."

Sadly and paradoxically, my contact with Muslims during the time I spent in Damascus was slight and superficial. By chance, I ended up in its Old City, considered the world's oldest still-inhabited community, and for centuries now a Christian enclave. In Arabic it is called *Bab Tuma*—meaning "The Gates of [the Apostle] Thomas," who, according to local lore, came there preaching the gospel. My hosts and their son, my excellent tutor Basil, were Roman Catholics, and their compound is not far from a number of renowned biblical sites—the house of Ananias, for instance, who cured Paul's blindness—silted over in the course of two millennia but excavated and now a subterranean Franciscan chapel. Suggesting the common juxtaposition of sacred places and shrines from various religious traditions, Syria's largest and most prominent mosque lies not much farther in the opposite direction: the burial place of Saladin, the great Iraqi warrior who put an end to the Crusades in Jerusalem. But that's not all. Within the mosque proper is an especially ornate structure that houses, as legend has it, the remains of none other than John the Baptist, though here he bears an Arabic name. His relics are honored by agreement with the Christians whose own church stood earlier on the same ground—a striking accommodation by those who at times are far less tolerant of other religions.

I've yet to fully comprehend the children of Allah.

Kashi

Doubtless the most exotic country I've ever visited is India. Even a good quarter of a century later, my impressions of it are quite vivid. India still has one of the most totally religious cultures on the planet—the majority of its people fully accepting of Hindu tradition. As a Westerner, I felt slightly uncomfortable with the general fatalistic assumption that one's hardships and suffering were earned in a previous life. But I also noticed that even the *achhuti*—untouchables—sitting on an ash heap and sorting discarded paper and plastic for a few sustaining grains of rice seemed so essentially calm and accepting of their condition that few if any in that society appear to suffer from ulcers or require a psychiatrist. I suspect, however, that since I was last there, with India's burgeoning, more westernized and relatively prosperous middle class, much has changed in that regard.

For the first two months, Indrail passes in hand, Krista and I literally "rode the rails," superficially taking in the entire subcontinent with the exception of Nepal. Everywhere were beggars—the more freakish, the more effective. At a seashore temple site in the Dravidian south, we were amazed to see a quite young girl carrying a full-grown turbaned man, his withered limbs wrapped, snakelike, around her waist. During a long train stop in Puna, encouraged by her father and brother, each with an amputated arm, another young girl—strikingly beautiful—approached our train car. She went for the Arab men sitting at an opposite window, enjoying a repast of fresh fruit, imploring them with the uplifted stubs of her own arms, from which both hands had been deliberately removed. The Arabs laughingly held out a single grape which, somehow, she managed, tweezerlike, to grasp between the stubs and bring to her lips. Then they turned their backs on her. In Mumbai, while crossing a long bridge, we were swarmed by a pack of well-trained urchins who, for all the world, reminded us of the similarly organized young gypsies who now everywhere in Europe descend on the unsuspecting traveler—reminding me that a thousand years ago, the gypsies' ancestors, speaking the Sanskrit language they call Romish, came from this same place.

Almost any morning in either Mumbai or Calcutta, where millions live on the sidewalk, doing their ablutions and preparing food with the help of fire hydrants and the open gutter, fresh corpses lay on the sidewalk, always discreetly covered by a thin cloth. Crossing the country from Calcutta to Delhi through the relatively poor and wild Bihar Province, we were accosted in our compartment by young men who compelled us to surrender our reserved seats to them; we'd already heard of the Wild West–type banditry on trains, knives sometimes slashing through the partitions dividing one compartment from the next to reach the bandits' victims.

By contrast, we were, as total strangers, often invited by our Indian traveling companions to attend a lavish family wedding celebration at a forthcoming destination, which on one occasion we in fact did. Our presence as foreign guests seemed to add a certain prestige to the occasion.

Unlike the prominent body odor still frequently encountered in public places in Russia, I never detected anything but total cleanliness—thanks to Indian natives' much lighter apparel and the worshipful practice of daily bathing. After our first landing in Calcutta, we had taken an evening stroll to a nearby marketplace. The variety and condition of apparel amazed us: the locals seemed not the least style-conscious or ostentatiously self-aware—whatever might barely cover their nakedness would do. Finally, visiting the famed temples of Kajuraho in the jungles of central India, we had a sense in the many bas-reliefs of the erotic abandon of an earlier mode of worship, called *tantra*.

Having located two able and willing tutors, I finally settled to study, first in Jabalpur, Madhya Pradesh, center of the Thugee criminal cult that strangled its victims with silk cords, from which English derives the word *thug*. Eventually, I returned alone to India's ancient holiest city, Varanasi (corrupted by the British to Benares), formerly known as Kashi, where, with the help of my phenomenally dedicated tutor Virendra Singh, a Kshatriya (one degree below a Brahman), I rented for forty dollars a month a two-story building overlooking the sacred Ganges.

For coolness, like everyone else at that time of year I slept on my building's flat roof. The sights and sounds that awakened me at sunrise presented an unforgettable tableau: streams of pilgrims passing by on their way to the river and salvation, shouting "Ram! Ram!"—invoking the deity and protagonist of their most popular scripture, the *Ramayana* (like the Book of Mormon for us)—and beggars lining the path, hands extended for coins or a few grains of rice. *Dhanyawad*, the common word for *Thank you*, was here studiously avoided: it was understood that the giving of alms is a saving act for which the bestower and not the receiver should be especially grateful.

My attention was nevertheless quickly diverted by the hawks and vultures that swooped ever closer, checking me out in case I'd expired overnight and was ripe enough for devouring. I had only a few minutes to gather my effects and descend from the roof before swarms of wild monkeys, the newborn babies often still clinging to their mothers, descended to steal anything in sight—eyeglasses, reading matter, bedclothes. In one instance, I defiantly shook my fist, in turn receiving a still more defiant grimace. Don't aggravate wild monkeys: they have sharp teeth and often carry rabies (if not, as we've since discovered, AIDS).

On a corner outside my window sat another deliberately amputated beggar, near naked, who ecstatically invited one of the many nearby sacred cows to lick the salt off his perspiring skin—his particular mode of ablution. Once the enchanting voice of another such pilgrim beggar whom I could not see came wafting from below. We later learned that though he did not speak Hindi, this old man had come from Calcutta to end his life at the Ganges. The language he used, Bengali, was what everyone agreed was *Bharat mei bahut, bahut mitya bhasha*—India's most beautiful language. Virendra in fact engaged the man to serenade us on the evening of my departure. The other guests and I passed the hat so that he had enough to keep him in rice for the next several months, a fee well earned.

Life in India is certainly filled with its own distinct contradictions. I eventually learned not to post my letters in official street-side receptacles—they never reached their destination. Apparently the postal workers who collect them peel off the postage and throw the letters away, so it is only safe to bring mail directly to the post office and witness, with his rubber stamp, a more reliable clerk performing the requested cancellation.

Meanwhile, openly published statistics—India, unlike Russia, is a viable democracy with freedom of the press—indicate that annually thousands of young wives are, through the connivance of mercenary spouses and mothers-in-law, burned to death in staged kitchen fires so the husband can find another wife with a new dowry. Exposés further suggest that far too many widows of all ages are cast onto the street, even by their adult children, to spend the rest of their lives as either beggars or prostitutes. Many seem to accept their fate stoically enough: "It's my karma. It's obviously my punishment for misdeeds in a previous life." Devoted widows are even still occasionally praised for committing suttee (or sati)—outlawed during the British occupation—in which a woman willingly throws herself upon her deceased husband's funeral pyre.

"The body is just an empty shell, while death frees the soul from its imperfections." Despite this common sentiment, funeral rites are, like weddings, elaborate and costly. Virendra kindly invited me to witness part of an eleven-day ceremony conducted by his friend, chair of Benares Hindu University's civil engineering department, who, as his mother's oldest son and a Brahman, presided at her funeral. With shaved head and wearing a single sacred string—his "garment"—the professor was at one point instructed to bring the string from his left to right shoulder. On another occasion, I was privileged to sit on the man's veranda floor for a funeral feast—the guests ushered there in shifts, our food served in banana leaves while monkeys clamored through the grillwork.

As a modern scientist, the professor had, Virendra told me, been particularly concerned about the raw sewage and diseased corpses that have brought the Ganges to an unimaginable coliform level—despite which, claiming to have immunity, most pilgrims and lifelong residents still freely drink from its waters and bathe in them. Some years later, I once more encountered the professor in a full-page photographic spread in an issue of *Life,* fully immersed in the same holy river, his head barely rising above its waves. He too must have considered himself impervious to its harmful physical properties.

As nowhere else, there are in India a multiplicity of gods. One day I observed Virendra's wife sitting on their cold concrete floor intensely reading and reciting from the holy epic, the *Ramayana*. Virendra explained that she was doing so as a rite of mourning for her recently deceased father. With its supernatural mythological setting, the *Ramayana* eulogizes the virtues of its heroine, who is willing to commit suttee and do all else that would honor her paramour. Having several times noticed on their wall the portrait of Ganesh, the elephant god, I at last had the temerity to ask Virendra, himself well educated, if he could really take such a deity at all seriously. "It's for my wife," he confessed. Such animistic deities are, apparently, far more popular with the masses, while Virendra and the more scholarly tend to view them as symbolic, favoring a more abstract and sophisticated line of worship. It's the Indian equivalent of, say, our own culture's contrasting Unitarians and born-again evangelicals.

In my ongoing search for striking ritual and theological parallels between Hinduism, this oldest of all extant world religions, and Mormonism, I felt richly rewarded when I came across the German Indologist Max Mueller's rendition of the Vedic *soma* ritual, which, with its washings and anointings, I leave for anyone who has been through an LDS temple to read about and ponder. Then there is the common presence of a water source—often an outside pool or vat—on the site of most Indian temples, which Hindus also consider their holiest edifices. This architectural use of water in sacred spaces reminds me of the landscaping around LDS temples. I've already mentioned the sacred thread. Speculative as all this must be, it is perhaps helpful to recall that Hinduism is an at-least-four-thousand-year-old Aryan transplant from the plains of Central Asia, with commonalities between the Indians and the Sky God–worshipping Scandinavians.

Two high moments stand out from my month-long stay in Jabalpur. First, my all-too-brief interaction with Shri Matiji Pandit, a most gifted tutor, from whom I tried to acquire the rudiments of what may be the most difficult of all ancient languages, Sanskrit. With a PhD in Vedic Sanskrit (the language's oldest form) from Benares Hindu

University, Dr. Pandit had been engaged by my hosts, American and English professors at the local Methodist seminary, to teach Sanskrit to young Indians preparing for the Christian ministry. Despite her commitment to Hinduism, she was often confided in by these young future Christian preachers, who sought counsel regarding occasional impasses with their Western mentors.

One day, having read that there had once been practically a separate god for each devotee, I asked Dr. Pandit if, in her vast knowledge of Hindu lore, she had ever encountered a deity who had either preached love for one's enemies or voluntarily given his life for all humankind. After a long pause, she quietly answered, "No." This conversation—now a quarter century old—was a defining moment for me, providing a further, unexpected foundation for my conviction that Jesus Christ and his mission are truly distinctive, as they must be if he is the world's one and only Savior.

While in Jabalpur, I enjoyed the hospitality of a most gracious member of the seminary faculty, Dr. David Scott, who, though American, had grown up in India, the son of missionary parents. A year earlier, I had made initial arrangements to travel there, and though we were total strangers, Dr. Scott and his wife had kindly offered to have Krista and me as his houseguests. However, only a week before our departure, they sent us a telegram with the warning that others at the seminary would not welcome us because we were Mormons. While in the United States, his dean—a native Indian—had received a highly unfavorable impression of our missionaries. Nevertheless, the first time we found ourselves in Jabalpur, I phoned Professor Scott, half expecting to be stoned. His curiosity piqued, he decided to come see us at our hotel. After meeting us, he at last declared that he would, after all, arrange both a tutor and accommodations for us at a recently vacated missionary bungalow with a staff of five servants. Such accommodations were then still fairly affordable. It soon became clear, however, that neither the Scotts nor any of their Western Methodist colleagues wanted to hear a word about our suspect religion.

Then, one day, Krista became acquainted with a venerable Indian gentleman who resided in a neighboring bungalow. A former Muslim, he had, in his youth, stowed away on a ship to the United States. Before returning to his native community and clan, he had earned a PhD in theology at Princeton. After converting his extended family, he became Jabalpur's now highly revered first native Methodist minister, long retired. Upon learning from Krista about our own religious background, he leaped up and returned to the room with various photo albums featuring LDS temples. Until that moment, we had imagined that no one within a 1,000-mile radius (except perhaps the faculty members at the seminary) had ever even heard of Mormons. Later, the man's married daughter, a local high school teacher and the source of his photographs, came to see us. As it turned out, she and her husband had previously served for two years as Hindi translators at the LDS Church College in Samoa, where she'd acquired a glowing impression of our church.

One evening the week before Easter, her father invited me to join him on his way to the Methodist chapel for their daily Lenten service. Because of the heat, I had by then gone native and was, like him, wearing a diaper-like *dhoti*. So together we took off, walking arm in arm past sacred cows and peasant carts along a dusty road. After we arrived at the chapel, he escorted me to a prominent pew, reserved in his honor. I don't remember much about the service, but I'll never forget the astonished and slightly distressed looks on the faces of the entire seminary faculty, all of them in their own allotted pews. Some time later, the old minister's daughter asked to speak to me, earnestly declaring, "I want to join your church." I informed her that she would not only need her husband's permission but would also probably have to wait until missionaries and a branch of the church came to Jabalpur. I'd be pleased to know—and not terribly surprised—if that is by now the case.

Also while at the Methodist bungalow in Jabalpur, we briefly made room for a British couple who had for years served in Africa and India as missionaries for the Assemblies of God. Civil as they were, their attitude toward us reflected that of our hosts, so we never discussed religion. Later, however, the local minister for the Assemblies of God—a former Brahman—paid a call, requesting that I preach to his congregation, which I did. It was an exhilarating experience, and, subtly, I tried to insert in my remarks a little of the restored gospel. Afterward, it became clear why I'd been so eagerly requested to hold forth before the man's vivacious, young congregation—energetically singing their hymns from memory to the accompaniment of his tambourine: "Could you arrange to send us a portable electric organ?" he asked just before we parted ways. In reply, I asked for his mailing address and promised to be in touch with his religious counterparts in Utah, which promise I later fulfilled.

Beijing

On the surface, China seems less compatible with my perhaps more transcendent outlook. According to religion scholar Huston Smith, China—despite its ancient grounding in Taoism, Confucianism, and Buddhism—is noteworthy for a literati class that traditionally valued practical social skills and organizational management more than lofty spiritual yearnings.[3] My wife, Merriam, and I went there in 2001, the year after my retirement, at the behest of BYU's China Teacher Program, where we spent a full ten-month academic year. I returned the next year to Nanjing University to study second-year Mandarin with a student group from BYU.

The regimentation of Chinese life was clearly in evidence throughout, and hardly a surprise. The world's impression at the 2008 Olympic games of masterminded synchronization was no exaggeration. Though we mostly effete old fogies had been required to take doctor-certified tests for AIDS before traveling there, we were apparently still under suspicion, and one day, with very short notice, all the foreign teachers at Peking University were herded into buses and brought to a medical facility for further testing. I wondered if the same precautions are taken with the young women who adorn every barbershop, ostensibly to give massages. Their services, I've read, account for at least three percent of the entire Chinese economy, as available women are in short supply due to the nation's one-child policy and the systematic abortion of female fetuses.

One thing especially struck me: unlike anything I've yet to witness in Eastern Europe, the Chinese seem to eagerly lean into wherever they are going, whatever they are doing (so many up early in the morning on their bicycles). Construction projects take shape overnight with round-the-clock, antlike shifts. The at-least-three-hundred-million "surplus labor" pool (i.e., unemployed) are that eager to earn another day's bowl of rice and pass on a portion to their family.

Beijing, like Moscow, interminably extends itself. Its high-rise facades are nevertheless graced by a variety of styles with curved gabled rooftops, a nod to ancient Chinese tradition. One could wish for such a flair for individuality in the monolithic structures of Eastern Europe. In Moscow and other Russian cities, I've more recently noticed a greater attempt toward individuation, perhaps inspired by or in imitation of the Chinese. Recent structures in Khabarovsk at the far eastern end of Russia, for instance—only thirty kilometers from the Chinese border, whose construction crews are clearly "guest workers" from across the Amur River—very much resemble those in Beijing.

Red lanterns line many a street for blocks on end, denoting the presence of restaurants. Somehow the Chinese manage to eat out a lot. Though I'm still told that our Chinese restaurant fare in the United States is not the real thing, I'm hard put to see much difference—except that, as a student once put it to me, "We Chinese eat anything that creeps or crawls." Unlike in Russia, nightlife is vibrant. Also, unlike Russians, who seem to do little more than export their mineral, oil, and natural gas wealth, the Chinese are, as we all know, extremely resourceful at producing just about *everything*—particularly cheap fake goods in perfectly duplicated foreign packaging. Sometimes their translated labels are, like those of the Japanese during their earlier industrial boom after World War II, quite amusing. I once purchased a classical CD whose English title ought to have been "The Maiden's Prayer" but which, due to a misspacing, sounded more like an ad for a female douche: "The Maiden Sprayer." An invitation to a Christmas season performance by the Peking National Ballet of Tchaikovsky's perennial *Nutcracker* was billed in English as "The Walnut Clip."

We were privileged to teach a huge number of graduate students—all PhD candidates—at Peking University, the nation's Harvard. Its ornamental grounds, with running streams, lily ponds, and bridges, had actually been laid out and paid for by American Protestant missionaries prior to World War II and the advent of communism—a fabulous showplace with a most inviting ambience. Our quite adequate housing was in a dormitory reserved for foreign faculty, which, we learned through the grapevine, had been the site of Madam Mao and the Gang of Four's house arrest prior to their execution. We were told that none of the indigenous faculty at the time dared look in the building's direction, and we sensed a spooky aversion to the place on the part of various locals.

Apart from the unreasonable workload—eight separate two-hour sessions each week with a total of 160 students, and in my case, a weekly composition and two journal entries from each of them to read and comment on—we found our students an eager delight. Mostly of peasant origin, they earnestly hoped to secure for themselves a challenging profession and decent living standard. For many, we were their first native English-speaking instructors. As representative Americans, we may have also conveyed to them, along with the language, a certain fashionable prestige. In any event, they seemed to enjoy and highly respect us. They often told us, "You are my parent," a traditional Chinese response to one's teacher. Maudlin as that was, they seemed to mean it, despite the fact that a number of them were no longer young adults, many married, and some already in their forties. Except for rare holiday visits to their home villages, most had to live apart from their families, including spouses and children. Some already had important and prestigious positions in Chinese society.

A month into the second semester, while standing one morning before one of my classes, I was suddenly afflicted with a particularly searing abdominal pain. I did not hesitate to announce that I would have to end the class and immediately go to a hospital. A student I'd not seen earlier and who, in fact, had joined the class that very day promptly arose and declared, "I am a banker. I have a car just outside this building, and I will drive you there." This was unheard of—student transportation on campus was limited to the ubiquitous bicycle. But I took advantage of the good banker's offer. As it turned out, I was afflicted with epididymitis, a serious urinary tract infection, consequent to the TURP operation I thought I'd already recovered from. I have never felt closer to the veil than during the subsequent several days I lay in Beijing's only Western hospital, whose staff had just been joined by its first Western-trained urologist the day I was admitted.

Then there was the manager of one of China's five boxcar factories, who weekly flew to Beijing from Dalien on the Pacific Coast just for our class. Later, on separate weekends, both he and the banker flew Merriam and me to their respective cities, where they housed and dined us. In Dalien, I requested that we visit our student's boxcar factory, which, starting with hoops of steel sheeting, turns out a new boxcar every half hour, adorned with the purchaser's freshly painted logo. They sell for an unheard of $15,000. When our supervisor learned that we'd accepted these lavish invitations, all she could imagine was that we were taking a bribe, but I tried to assure her that both students would receive the grades they deserved. I have no doubt that the grades of party functionaries and their dependents are routinely changed if they prove not high enough.

One of our students was already the editor of a legal publication. Another lovely young student, already a justice, periodically excused herself to travel on assignment and join a panel of other judges to adjudicate various state trials. One day, I thought to ask her if she had ever had to sentence someone to death. Her too-calm answer, after citing what was for my Western sensibilities a shockingly high number: "I interpret the law as conscientiously as I can."

Besides teaching our graduate students, I earned extra pay by taking on a number of undergrads for a conversation course. These far-younger students differed from the grads in their more privileged socioeconomic background, better foundation in English (clearly the products of prestigious schools), and greater sophistication. They reminded me of the confident, well-heeled undergraduate Yalies I'd once rubbed shoulders with who wore scuffed blue jeans and worn sneakers—their elite uniform—by contrast with more formally attired grads like me who were there only due to generous fellowships. My Chinese undergrads had already seen pirated versions of films that had not yet come out at home, and I could tell they were confidently looking forward to joining the nation's ruling class. By now, they are all, I imagine, very well entrenched.

Proselytizing is illegal in the People's Republic of China. Wisely, the LDS Church has forbidden its functionaries to so engage. While we were in Beijing, only expats could assemble for LDS Church services. Since then, hundreds of native Chinese members who converted while abroad and later returned to their homeland have been permitted to assemble together, but not with their foreign counterparts. One area authority, Elder Chia Chu-Jen, himself Chinese with a Hong Kong passport, was long allowed to serve as a liaison with native Chinese Latter-day Saints. Despite the legal restrictions, various foreign evangelical Protestants—including some of our own colleagues at Peking University (who, incidentally, viewed us much as had the British journalist in Yerevan and the professors at the seminary at Jabalpur)—have openly preached to their students, and baptisms have ensued. This seems to be tolerated because such groups allow their local leaders to be appointed by the PRC government, something the LDS Church would never allow.

Despite the fact that we studiously avoided any discussion of religion, an amazing thing occurred between us and almost all of our Chinese students: a one-on-one bonding, in this case with individuals whose racial, linguistic, cultural, and political traditions differed markedly from our own and despite relatively brief weekly contact. These connections were as personal and endearing as I can ever remember with my former students, missionaries, or even in some cases our own children. How does one account for that?

During two successive semesters—with a totally new group of students showing up after the first—I required that, among other things, they write about their family history. I already knew that during Mao's Cultural Revolution most genealogical records had been destroyed, so I asked them to phone home to a grandfather or maiden aunt if they could not return to their village during the intervening midsemester holiday and learn more about their forebears: in other words, to become oral historians.

My sample of brief but moving accounts—particularly of the sufferings of parents, grandparents, great-grandparents, aunts, and uncles, under first the occupying Japanese and then the ruthless forces of their Revolution—were often horrendous and deeply poignant. The Chinese people's suffering has known no bounds. It is in every way equal to the millennia-long oppression of average Russians. This particular assignment and the idea of it were entirely new to our students, something they weren't much conditioned to think about, close as they all were to their immediate, still-living family members.

Those who presided over the branch of the church we attended for expatriates were remarkably gracious and generous on our behalf. Most were former missionaries or mission presidents who had served in

Taiwan and who, because of their rare language facility as Westerners, were now the CEOs of major legal, accounting, and consulting firms that had arrived in China on the commercial ground floor after the normalization of relations under Deng Xiaoping. These individuals were now multimillionaires, two of whom who have since been called to leadership positions in the Quorum of Seventy. On one occasion, at a conference of the mainland China District, one of these brethren dutifully translated for the government official who frequently dropped in on our meetings, while the presiding church leaders from Hong Kong quickly adapted their remarks to the spirit of the twelfth Article of Faith. The Chinese official kept nodding his head in vigorous agreement; we knew the congregation's immediate interests had been deferred for a greater, long-range cause.

During my return to China the following summer as an auditing student at Nanjing University, an American friend and I managed to visit a nearby Buddhist monastery and converse there with several novice monks who spoke surprisingly good English. With the earnestness and openness of his countenance, one of them particularly stood out for me. From a group photograph, I isolated his striking image and have, in my postretirement avocation as a portraitist, tried several times to capture, both in oil and pastel, what for me has become a kind of icon—much as various fashionable images of the Savior inspire many Mormons. I feel I have fallen short but keep trying. This young Chinaman's radiant, beatific gaze still eludes my ability to depict it. Does this say something about my own spiritual deficiency? Or is all of this just some erratic obsessive-compulsive fetish—a figment of my all-too-mortal imagination? I know very little about this earnest young true believer, who might have so easily chosen his peers' far more materialistic and conventional way of life, especially in a society where such ascetic religions are generally viewed as antiquated anathema. But something about his face resonates with me, and—whatever it is—I consider it China's spiritual gift to me. (One of my several attempts to convey this young monk's likeness is reproduced on page 70 in this collection.)

Conclusion

Years ago, in a particularly thoughtful essay on ecumenicism and the Mormon missionary experience, Tancred I. King, a student at Columbia University's Center for Japanese Legal Studies, wrote the following:

> Christianity can gain from Islam a heightened awareness of the majesty, the grandeur, and the absoluteness of God. From Hinduism, Christianity can gain greater respect for meditation and reflectiveness. From Buddhism, Christians can understand the impersonal side of ultimate truth. The Confucian emphasis on humanism, social order, and filial piety can enhance Christian life. From Taoism and Shintoism, the Christian can more fully realize the sacredness of nature.[4]

Already in 1978, the First Presidency had memorably suggested as much: "The great religious leaders of the world such as Mohammed, Confucius, and the Reformers, as well as philosophers including Socrates, Plato, and others, received a portion of God's light."[5]

King's observations seem easy enough to apply. In practice, however, difficult ironies often abound as we attempt, bewildered, to reach across boundaries and interconnect. This is no less the case here at home between ourselves and others who see things quite differently: in my own case, former students and colleagues who, now disenchanted, have left the Mormon fold; and at the opposite end of the spectrum, friends, neighbors, and relatives whose political philosophy so markedly differs from my own. On one or another of those same two counts, even some of our children and closest kin do not see things as we do. But we must all still engage in *vzaimnoe sosushchestvovanie*—mutual coexistence—as Soviet propagandists used to put it. And, while remaining as forcefully committed as ever to what gives our own lives special meaning and motivation, we must at the same time respect the other's right to his or her position with sufficiently empathetic understanding of his or her reasons for it.

While once waiting for a plane in the Istanbul airport, I looked up from my hard metal chair at the row of seats facing me. There sat eight or nine Middle Eastern women, all swathed from top to toe in their heavy, suffocating burkas. I thought they were elderly, though it was hard to tell. Then, looking a little beyond them, I spied four Hasidic gentlemen, ringlets dangling beneath their black fedoras, each wearing a phylactery on his forehead and a large striped prayer shawl about his shoulders. The men were standing sideways in a passageway behind the women, bobbing up and down as they recited their morning prayers. Though in such close proximity, each group was entirely oblivious to the other.

If I'd dared, I'd have taken a picture. The juxtaposition of these two colorful yet so contrasting human clusters was uncannily reminiscent of their (or their counterparts') uneasy coexistence in Israel. The fact that neither deigned to notice the other suggested the certainty each had of its own superior self-contained world—prompting me to wonder if what they projected might not reflect more than just the impasse between Jews and Muslims on a planet where by circumstance of birth alone so many different ethnic, cultural, and religious alignments keep us at such an aloof and suspicious distance, all offspring of the same Creator yet strangers to each other.

Quite by contrast, I once chaperoned a group of ten American students on a memorable odyssey to Yugoslavia. Most were Jewish, from New York City. Under the auspices of the Experiment in International Living, they would each become the adopted member of a Yugoslavian family, the "brother" or "sister" of that family's counterpart their same age and gender. Just days before their departure, they learned we had been assigned to an all-Muslim community in Bosnia-Herzegovina. In fear and trembling, my six or so Jewish wards ventured eastward—as if to their doom. But not to worry! As we shortly discovered, the Bosnian Muslims—inheritors of four hundred years of Turkish cultural and religious conditioning—were nevertheless as indifferent to events in the Middle East as they were to Tito's communism. About the only danger my students faced was the Turkish coffee their hosts served at every meal—so thick one had to eat it with a spoon; so strong, it actually provoked heart palpitations in some of my charges. The overall relationship was placid, with not the slightest shade of cultural clash.

Which circumstance, I've since asked myself, was more ideal: the studied mutual disdain of those older parties in the Istanbul airport or the calm indifference to the other's ethnicity on the part of our hosts and my students in that small Muslim town?

Should we not try for greater awareness, even engagement with each other—with all the awkwardness, risk, even danger that might entail? If others view us with undue suspicion, shouldn't we—with faith emboldened by the restored gospel's perspective on universal kinship—look beyond those differences with broader understanding and the earnest yearning to bridge them? Finally, might we not feel as much impelled to reach out—despite our very real differences—to all within the fold of the Lord's church? That may well be our most imposing and most needful obligation.

Notes

1. A slightly different version of this essay was published in *Sunstone*, February 2009, 24–37.
2. Joseph Smith, *Teachings of the Prophet Joseph Smith*, comp. Joseph Fielding Smith (Salt Lake City: Deseret Book, 1976), 228, 353, 354.
3. Huston Smith, "Transcendence in Traditional China," *Religious Studies* 2/2 (April 1967): 185–96.
4. Tancred I. King, "Missiology and Mormon Missions," *Dialogue: A Journal of Mormon Thought* 16/4 (1983): 48.
5. Statement of the First Presidency regarding God's Love for All Mankind, February 15, 1978.

Part 4

Out of Zion, the Perfection of Beauty, God Hath Shined

> We constantly need to remind ourselves—despite our idealistic striving—of our humanity, our flawed natures. . . . Such narratives can serve us in a cautionary fashion, both individually and as a society. . . . By its very nature, drama deals with conflict and with what is problematic—if successful and relevant, addressing real life, not necessarily offering solutions but raising issues and related questions.
>
> —From "A Playwright with a Passion for Unvarnished Depictions"

> Whereas with faith we can direct our gaze, as the beasts never do, from the ground upward, the objective scrutiny of our earthly surroundings nevertheless reminds us of our ongoing need to reach heavenward, while remaining united through compassion with those who—whether or not by their own doing—have cause to mourn. . . . Such verbal art . . . points to, touches upon, and indeed serves what is most sacred.
>
> —From "The Sacred in Literature"

Following page: Thomas F. Rogers, *Turkish Woman*, pastel; reference photograph courtesy of Owen Clark

The Sacred in Literature

Delivered in 1981 as a BYU forum address, these remarks represent one of several public pronouncements on my part regarding the ability of serious fiction—both in tragedy and in humane, discerning depictions of real life—to sensitize audience members or readers to the suffering of others, especially those who markedly differ from us in their personal histories, vicissitudes, attitudes, and values. Such writing can help us be more understanding and compassionate. Even the portrayal of dissolute behavior and sin can serve as a useful object lesson. That, at least, is the position I took—and still endorse.[1]

I WOULD LIKE TO CITE AS AN EPIGRAPH the following excerpts from talks given a week ago by two missionaries just before they departed for Italy. The first: "There is a receptacle behind my house that is full of garbage, but I don't have to wade through it to know what is there." The second: "We must have unhappiness to know happiness. . . . It is on the days when we feel that the whole world is against us . . . that we get on our knees and pray harder. . . . Those are the days when we learn and grow in maturity, spirituality, and love for our neighbor and ourselves."

These statements arise from personal struggle, increased self-awareness, and profound growth, and both are very meaningful. As just the other day I scanned a recent anthology of short stories by John Updike, I thought how applicable both statements are to so much he has written. These particular stories, which I suspect are highly autobiographical, trace the dissolution of a marriage that ends in divorce. Even the first of them suggests with what guiltless abandon Updike's young couple seek amorous adventures outside their marriage. For all their cleverness, and Updike's in describing them, they saddened me. At Updike's expense, notwithstanding his brilliance and stylistic grace, my own values—and blessings—blazed forth in more bold relief than ordinarily.

Fallibility in fiction

I have read few stories so poignant and properly terrifying as one in that collection entitled "Separating." Written on the eve of Updike's own divorce, it ends with a teenage son's unanswerable question to a father who is about to leave his family:

> "Listen. I love you so much, I never knew how much until now. No matter how this works out, I'll always be with you. Really."
>
> Richard bent to kiss an averted face but his son, sinewy, turned and with wet cheeks embraced him and gave him a kiss, on the lips, passionate as a woman's. In his father's ear he moaned one word, the crucial, intelligent word: "*Why?*"
>
> *Why.* It was a whistle of wind in a crack, a knife thrust, a window thrown open on emptiness. . . . Richard had forgotten why.[2]

This story tells me there is something terribly sacred about the union of a man and woman and the family they found, that its disruption for any reason brings terrible anguish at a price that even those who perpetrate that disruption should recognize is much too high. Or take Joyce Carol Oates's haunting story, "Where Are You Going, Where Have You Been?" We know what nightmare a thrill-hungry fifteen-year-old girl will face and may never live through (certainly never be the same afterward) as she yields to the enticements of the leering stranger who stands outside her screen door, coaxing her to undo the latch and ride off with him into the night. How devastating, we sense, will be the consequences of her disregarding that great fifth commandment and the equally great seventh, about which, in violating the first of them, she may no longer have much choice. Oates spares us those consequences, but what we are left to imagine is all the more grim.

My remarks tend toward the position of the second missionary, though I believe both perceptions are important and valid. As my title suggests, I restrict what I am saying to literature that is philosophically provocative—that addresses life's mysteries and what most puzzles and concerns us. Such literature raises questions and poses problems, without necessarily presuming to have all the answers; yet it is this literature that evokes the strongest feelings from most teachers of literature and the arts, to which I and others have devoted nearly a lifetime of thought and attention. My BYU colleagues and I feel very deeply about such literature and have long since reconciled with it our understanding of the gospel and our spiritual lives. Its implications thrill us, satisfying our minds and spirits as fully as the periodic table of elements, nuclear theory, or the wonder of DNA thrill our counterparts in the sciences. What I will say about this literature is a principal justification for our assigning students to read it in our classes.

The authors and works I discuss may nevertheless surprise some of you because each of them describes some person or situation it would be better to avoid rather than emulate. One or another character in these works—usually the chief character, the protagonist—is tragically unwise, even sinful. Nevertheless, I hope to demonstrate that such writing, when sufficiently objective and honest, can be instructive, even edifying. I will try to suggest how, in speaking to our experience, such writing also reminds us of our aspirations. I do not include here works that are billed as "realistic" only because of their shocking, sensational appeal—like the publicity hype for practically every R-rated movie. Nor do I endorse what, however skillful and sophisticated, concerns itself with "the ugly and pathological"[3] for its own sake; nor that which views life as utterly hopeless and self-defeating.

By contrast, the body of writing I here endorse, which emerged so notably in a few great nineteenth-century prose novels, offers us not only the realism of carefully catalogued physical detail (an aspect of its style) but also a realism that is ultimately and predominantly ethical, psychological, and spiritual. This kind of realism posits universal norms whose violation, we sense, brings negative consequences for us all—a realism, in other words, that affirms (if often only between the lines) that we are each still in control of our eternal destinies and of what will bring us lasting joy.

We who are accustomed to art that addresses actuality (or pretends to) cannot appreciate how long it took before writers thought to treat the life of common people in a contemporary setting, to emphasize character over plot, and to view human beings, whether heroes or villains, as both more or less virtuous and more or less flawed—in other words, as all of us know ourselves to be. If, in the literature we are dealing with, our fallibility receives special attention, we must not misconstrue the reason why. In the words of one of the twentieth century's most respected critics: "Of course . . . we don't call evil itself, or division, or conflict, desirable things. We only call facing up to them . . . a desirable and mature state of soul and the right model and course of a mature poetic art."[4]

Realism in the scriptures

Regarding this "facing up" to ourselves, we have a remarkable precedent in the scriptures—particularly in the way so many of God's prophets, the leaders of various dispensations (or their scribes), allude to their own inner struggles. We need only recall Moses's hesitancy to serve because he stuttered; Joseph's lack of tact in dealing with his brothers; and Paul, that former persecutor of the saints. There were also Moses's rashness when, not without some provocation, he slew the Egyptian; David's sins with Bathsheba and against Uriah, his indulgence of Absalom, and his vengefulness toward those like Joab who disagreed with his capriciousness; Peter's cowardice in denying the Savior to avoid persecution; and Thomas's incredulity before the resurrected Savior. And, lest we overlook the women, the wiliness of the patriarchs' wives who, by deception, advanced their favorite sons, or the example of Martha, who was too busy tending her hearth to listen to the gospel, even from the lips of the Master. The Book of Mormon, too, is replete with confessions from prophets who struggled with temptation and unrighteous choices.

Why, we may well ask, is the word of God itself fraught with so many instances of human frailty? Why is imperfection so boldly depicted, especially in the elect of God and in the early saints? Why, in their accounts of these otherwise admirable figures, didn't the evangelists and those who compiled the scriptures simply censor all but the most favorable details? However much it may disturb us to learn about the frailties of God's chosen servants, we had better believe there are good reasons the Lord wanted us to know them. Do these flawed elect of God inspire us any the less? Of course not. In fact, they are all the more credible because they are so human. They are people with whom we can more readily identify.

We don't, for the most part, fully appreciate how unusually realistic the scriptures are as literary phenomena. The idea of accurate documentable reportage had, as yet, somehow not penetrated the ancient mind. This became clear to me when I first read a chapter or two in a remarkable work of literary criticism, Erich Auerbach's *Mimesis*. The word *mimesis* means imitation or the attempt to duplicate reality, and I commend these chapters to you. They deal with the episode in the Gospel of Mark in which, as Christ is taken prisoner, Peter feigns not to know him, and they also discuss the nature of Old Testament narrative in general. Here are Auerbach's dispassionate comments:

> A scene like Peter's denial fits into no antique genre. It is too serious for comedy, too contemporary and everyday for tragedy, politically too insignificant for history—and the form which was given it is one of such immediacy that its like does not exist in the literature of antiquity. . . . Different as Petronius and Tacitus may be in a great many respects, they have the same viewpoint—they look down from above. . . . Here [in the New Testament] we have neither survey and rational disposition, nor artistic purpose. The visual and sensory as it appears here is no conscious imitation and hence is rarely completely realized. It . . . is attached to the events which are to be related, because it is revealed in the demeanor and speech of profoundly stirred individuals and no effort need be devoted to the task of elaborating it. . . . And the story speaks to everybody; everybody is urged and indeed required to take sides for or against it. Even ignoring it implies taking sides.[5]

How did Mark and the other authors of the New Testament manage to break through all the literary stereotypes that preceded them to convey so directly and forcefully what they had to say? And why, again, didn't they take more pains to "gild the lily," to adorn the good guys, *their* team, and more vividly contrast to them the bad guys, their enemies? Self-aggrandizement is a natural human tendency, but the evangelists clearly did not resort to it. They did not even try to put a tidy face on their subjects' fallibility. And with what results? Auerbach explains:

> Because [Peter's] faith was deep, but not deep enough, the worst happened to him that can happen to one whom faith had inspired but a short time before: he trembled for his miserable life.[6]

However, adds Auerbach,

> It is only through this experience that the significance of Christ's coming and Passion is revealed to him.
>
> A tragic figure from such a background, a hero of such weakness, who yet derives the highest force from his very weakness, such a to and fro of the pendulum, is incompatible with the sublime style of classical antique literature. . . . Viewed superficially, the thing is a police action and its consequences; it takes place entirely among everyday men and women of the common people; anything of the sort could be thought of in antique terms only as farce or comedy. Yet why is it neither of these? Why does it arouse in us the most serious and most significant sympathy? Because it portrays something which neither the poets nor the historians of antiquity ever set out to portray: the birth of a spiritual movement in the depths of the common people. . . . All this applies not only to Peter's denial but also to every other occurrence which is related in the New Testament.[7]

Auerbach also contrasts the prose of the Old Testament with that of the Hebrews' contemporary, Homer:

> Domestic realism, the representation of daily life, remains in Homer in the peaceful realm of the idyllic, whereas, from the very first, in the Old Testament stories, the sublime, tragic, and problematic take shape precisely in the domestic and commonplace. . . . In the Old Testament stories the peace of daily life in the house, in the fields, and among the flocks, is undermined

> by jealousy over election and the promise of a blessing, and complications arise which would be utterly incomprehensible to the Homeric heroes. . . . Abraham, Jacob, or even Moses produces a more concrete, direct, and historical impression than the figures of the Homeric world—not because they are better described in terms of sense (the contrary is the case) but because the confused, contradictory multiplicity of events, the psychological and factual cross-purposes, which true history reveals, have not disappeared in the representation but still remain clearly perceptible. . . . Such a problematic psychological situation as this is impossible for any of the Homeric heroes, whose destiny is clearly defined and who wake every morning as if it were the first day of their lives: their emotions, though strong, are simple and find expression instantly. . . . In Homer, the complexity of the psychological life is shown only in the succession and alternation of emotions; whereas the Jewish writers are able to express the simultaneous existence of various layers of consciousness and the conflict between them. . . . How much wider is the pendulum swing of their lives than that of the Homeric heroes![8]

Auerbach says of the Hebrews:

> They are bearers of the divine will, and yet they are fallible, subject to misfortune and humiliation—and in the midst of misfortune and in their humiliation their acts and words reveal the transcendent majesty of God. There is hardly one of them who does not, like Adam, undergo the deepest humiliation—and hardly one who is not deemed worthy of God's personal intervention and personal inspiration.[9]

The great realistic literary tradition

If there are other heroic characters who come at all close to those of the scriptures in their raggedness and complexity, they are those, I contend, that first appeared in the plays of fifth-century-BC Athens (their origins, by the way, are also religious); those we encounter over a millennium later in Elizabethan England; and most recently and prolifically, those in some select modern novels and short stories of the last two centuries. Allow me to mention some of the novels and other works of prose that have meant much to me, recognizing that we all have our own special lists.

One busy semester in graduate school, I started to read Proust's great seven-volume novel *Remembrance of Things Past*. To the jeopardy of Old Church Slavonic and Serbo-Croatian, I could not put it down. In its evocation of an entire epoch and civilization, at least among the aristocracy, there has never been anything quite like it. But at least four others precede Proust, and an acquaintance with each belongs to everyone's general education: Stendhal, Balzac, Flaubert, and Zola. It may not be a very sophisticated thing to say, but the one who means the most to me is Zola. Like his idol Flaubert, Zola thought himself totally detached—a naturalist of the first order. But Zola deceived himself, as did Flaubert in *Madame Bovary*, because, for all their meticulous analysis of their contemporaries and the social classes of their day, they were at heart, like all the great realists, deeply moral and idealistic.

Despite himself, we catch Zola editorially bemoaning the characters' self-destruction in his horrifying study of the effects of drunkenness—*L'Assommoir*, the name of an actual Paris tavern. Other important novels by Zola, all dealing with social ills that still beset us, include *Nana*, which traces the ruin of individuals and families in consequence of a double standard of morality for men and women, and prostitution; *Germinal*, which, as powerfully as the writing of Marx, describes the exploitation of workers in the industrial age; and *La Terre*, which with a plotline similar to that of *King Lear* explores the degeneracy of the wealthy but unrefined landed gentry.

Then there are the great novels of adultery, magnificent novels—*Madame Bovary*, Tolstoy's *Anna Karenina*, and Theodore Dreiser's first and best, *Sister Carrie*. Why do I recommend them? Because, apart from their artistic excellence, they powerfully dissuade. They warn us again and again of the consequences of certain choices, consequences which, if we are still sufficiently young and innocent, we might not fully anticipate; and they help us understand how it feels to suffer those consequences without actually having to do so. In evaluating the moral stature of a literary work, we can profitably apply this plain and simple criterion: does a work glamorize or justify what it describes? Or does it imply that evil is illusion and that "wickedness never was happiness"?

If the latter is true, then the work is not prescriptive, and it is *not* enticing you. It has a purpose, but that purpose is not to make evil appear attractive.

Modern realism

I have so far mainly alluded to novels written on the European continent in the later nineteenth or early twentieth centuries. We should not overlook the British literary tradition. Significant authors in terms of what we have been discussing include at least two women, Jane Austen and George Eliot; two men who were born outside of England, Henry James (America) and Joseph Conrad (Poland); John Galsworthy, E. M. Forster, and perhaps Graham Greene; but not many others.

There are also some extraordinary contemporary writers, many of whom write in English and essentially in the realistic vein. A good half are women. At BYU we honored one of them, Eudora Welty, with an honorary degree just a year ago. There is also Anne Tyler, who, while in her thirties, authored a number of prize-winning novels that ever so subtly trace the heartache and yearning for human ties in a range of characters. Her best novel, I think, is *Searching for Caleb.* And there is the British short story writer (and more recently author of acclaimed science fiction) Doris Lessing. Lessing was, I understand, a close contender for the latest Nobel Prize, and she deserves such recognition.[10] Her stories display perceptive and provocative psychological insight, exposing the moral flabbiness in each of us. Peter Matthew Hillsman Taylor's stories, less well-known, are anthologized in several collections. His characterizations are equally subtle. In some respects I prefer him to John Cheever, whose deft satire largely restricts itself to the empty worldliness of the suburban upper class on the eastern US seaboard.

Then there are such gems of novels as *A Death in the Family,* James Agee's now vintage look at mortality and childhood, truly an American classic; Reynolds Price's *A Long and Happy Life*; Larry Woiwode's piercing vignettes about married life in *Beyond the Bedroom Wall*; and William Gibson's moving *A Mass for the Dead.* In addition, there are the important American-Jewish writers—Saul Bellow, Bernard Malamud, and Isaac Bashevis Singer, two of them Nobel Prize winners—and our perhaps most profoundly religious twentieth-century writer, Flannery O'Connor. My list is, as I indicated, highly personal and limited.

There are a few works, equally realistic in their handling of character and treatment of suffering, which also celebrate life's transcendent mysteries and depict with remarkable ecstasy and persuasion that greatest miracle of them all: forgiveness and reconciliation between contentious brothers or between fathers and sons, and, in an instance or two, the reunion of estranged loved ones after death or a long, deathlike earthly separation. We readily sense how sublimely these works exemplify the greatest commandment and the kind of faith that attends miracles of every kind. I think particularly of key scenes in Tolstoy and of Dostoevsky's last of four extraordinary novels, *The Brothers Karamazov*. I keep it on my shelf of "semisacred" books, along with a superb short story by Aleksandr Solzhenitsyn titled "Matryona's Home" that recounts the hallowed, self-sacrificing life of a nondescript elderly woman on a Soviet collective farm.

An example of Mormon fiction that powerfully offers a presentiment of celestial society and kinship both here and beyond this existence appears in *Bread and Milk and Other Stories*, a deceptively slight and simple volume of vignettes by Eileen Kump, who once taught English at BYU, about the life of her pioneer grandmother. I am especially moved by the grandmother's sentiments as, on the occasion of her husband's funeral, she studies their young grandsons and, in her mind, reflects about them to her deceased companion:

> Those sacred, half-grown, unknown quantities, not quite spitting images of their dads or any other human creature, not happy about their granddad dying but not unhappy either. There they stood and the way of their standing, awkward as it was, sent praise to heaven, praise for the dead man whose blood flowed in their veins and whose stature added height to theirs. . . .
>
> "The blood was there so of course the tribute to you was there, but, Sweetheart, that day I saw glory! I saw an eternity of sons!"[11]

(Other significant authors of Mormon fiction who had already emerged at the time of this address or have done so since then include

John Bennion, Jack Harrell, Levi Peterson, William Reger [as yet largely unpublished], Douglas Thayer, and Brady Udall—among several others. Most have written a number of arresting short stories and one or more novels, and have also been associated with BYU either as students or as members of the English faculty. Harrell, who now teaches at BYU–Idaho, is, in my opinion, perhaps the most provocative and foremost among them. Although I had no influence on their writing, I was privileged to have both Reger and Jonathan Langford, author of the singularly poignant novel *No Going Back*, in my BYU classes. An array of memorable short stories by other writers has also appeared over the ensuing decades in both *Dialogue* and *Irreantum*.)

The value of negative examples

Among all these works, as in the scriptures we have considered, there are few that depict a totally ideal circumstance or condition of life. Again, why should that be? What benefit can come from dwelling on failure or depraved lifestyles, however uninviting their depiction? First of all, the works cited are cautionary and instructive; they warn us what to avoid. In the words of the widow and biographer of a great Russian poet who died in Stalin's death camps, "Pain warns a man of illness and thus gives him the chance of healing himself."[12] Many scriptures, speaking of the Lord's chastening, say the same thing. It was Milton, no less, who said, "I cannot praise a fugitive and cloistered virtue, unexercised and unbreathed, that never sallies out and sees her adversary, but slinks out of the race. . . . That which purifies us is trial, and trial is by what is contrary."[13] Or, in a saying attributed to Joseph Smith: "By proving contraries, truth is made manifest."[14]

Second, such literature consoles us and helps us better accept our own adversity. There is something to the saying that "misery loves company." We are more inclined to endure affliction and vicissitude when others suffer with us, or at least commiserate. Isn't that why we are admonished to "bear one another's burdens" and "mourn with those that mourn" (Mosiah 18:8–9)?

Third, such writing helps us better understand and empathize with those less fortunate than we are. I recall a conversation I once had with a colleague who asked me for a definition of dramatic irony. I indicated that I thought an aspect of it involved the recognition that "there, but for the grace of God, go I." My friend astutely qualified my answer: as we view the fate of a particular tragic hero, he suggested, we might well say instead, "There, *with* the grace of God, go I—in that same man's shoes." One of the most memorable moments in all my reading has to be the day I first read Dostoevsky's account of the old pawnbroker's murder in *Crime and Punishment*. Though we quake in fear and trembling at the horror of the deed, you and I, as readers, are nevertheless made to join with Raskolnikov as he brings down his axe on the defenseless old woman's head and feel somehow far more sorry for him than her. Without condoning failure or evil, such writing points up life's ambiguities and causes us, viewing others, to be less judgmental. In a saying attributed to Jacob Burckhardt, the famed Renaissance historian, "The essence of tyranny is the denial of complexity."

Fourth, by the very default in its characters' lives and their frequent tragic resolutions, this literature points to the need for and desirability of something better and more ideal: a profound "subtext" or "deep structure" to which we are enticed by its absence or opposite. The dosage is not so great that we feel it to be overly sentimental or unreal in terms of actual experience, or that we are being preached at. If it is sufficiently subtle, we are allowed to arrive independently at the conclusions it points to, so that they are *our* conclusions—and all the more credible and convincing because we arrived at them through our own discovery. Those writers who most engage us always leave us room to speculate about their meaning. This is one of the important reasons, I believe, for indirection and ambiguity in art—whose analogue in the scriptures, as in life itself, is their sense of paradox, humanly perceived. If we cannot fully appreciate this important aesthetic principle, much of the significant art of both the present and past will elude us. We encounter it as dramatic irony, or metaphor of situation, in both tragedy and certain works of realistic prose. We also encounter it as the irony of unexpectedly juxtaposed forms, or the metaphor of appearances or effects, in modern art and the tragicomic absurd theatre. This sense of paradox—so fundamental to everyone's experience when we probe that experience deeply and honestly enough—accounts for life's ongoing mystery. It impels us to seek solutions beyond our limited ability to understand and cope by means of reason alone. In the face of life's paradoxes, our logic sooner or later fails us. Life's ambiguities should break down our self-sufficiency and prompt us to turn beyond ourselves for transcendent answers. Literature that brings this to our awareness can thus serve a profound religious purpose, prompting an awareness of our spiritual poverty and leading each of us to cultivate a "broken heart" and a "contrite spirit."

Fifth, this literature tells us that beauty is a manifestation of goodness. In his lectures at Harvard in the late nineteenth century, the philosopher George Santayana declared:

> Beauty . . . seems to be the clearest manifestation of perfection, and the best evidence of its possibility. If perfection is . . . the ultimate justification of being, we may understand the ground of the moral dignity of beauty. Beauty is a pledge of the possible conformity between the soul and nature, and consequently a ground of faith in the supremacy of the good.[15]

I like to think that in words chosen not to alienate his fellow professors, Santayana here implies that beauty is a pledge of eternity. The great twentieth-century poet W. H. Auden made the religious connection even more explicit:

> Every beautiful poem presents an analogy to the forgiveness of sins. . . .
>
> Through its analogies, the goodness of created existence, the historical fall into unfreedom and disorder, and the possibility of regaining paradise through repentance and forgiveness are recognized.[16]

Just as the greatest art is the art of living, so the beauty we encounter in the fiction I have mentioned is the beauty of lives that aspire, or should aspire, to what is noble and right, even in the face of ongoing misery and affliction. The valiant, if often fatal, stance of the tragic hero and the belated recognition of the error of his or her ways by many a modern novel's protagonists—even if only fully sensed in the mind of the reader—are noble and edifying illustrations of beauty of character, or at least of its desirable potential. Experiencing this recognition, even vicariously, can provide each of us perspective on ultimate, transcendent values.

Conclusion

Such literature strongly implies—and more effectively because it *only* implies—the need for brotherhood and sisterhood, mutual forgiveness, and reconciliation between alienated neighbors, parents and children, and husbands and wives; for such alienation is one of its characteristic themes. Just as the scriptures afford us such a rich array of role models and object lessons, we can also benefit from testing life's fundamental principles, if only in their breach, in literature. Both tragedy and significant prose fiction bring to our awareness a proper sense of values and the correct moral response to extremes of circumstance that in the murky twilight of normalcy are rarely tried or truly tested.

In spirit, such literature is not only humane or vaguely spiritual. It is also Christian. Whereas with faith we can direct our gaze, as the beasts never do, from the ground upward, the objective scrutiny of our earthly surroundings nevertheless reminds us of our ongoing need to reach heavenward, while remaining united through compassion with those who—whether or not by their own doing—have cause to mourn. I submit that in the instances I have mentioned and many others, such verbal art—though it is not the word of God—points to, touches upon, and indeed serves what is most sacred.

Notes

1. An earlier version of this essay was originally published in *Literature and Belief* 1 (1981): 57–69.
2. John Updike, "Separating," *New Yorker*, June 23, 1975, 41.
3. Erich Auerbach, *Mimesis: The Representation of Reality in Western Literature*, trans. Willard R. Trask (Princeton, MA: Princeton University Press, 1953), 505.
4. W. K. Wimsatt, "Horses of Wrath: Recent Critical Lessons," in *Hateful Contraries: Studies in Literature and Criticism* (Lexington: University of Kentucky Press, 1965), 32.
5. Auerbach, *Mimesis*, 45–48.
6. Auerbach, *Mimesis*, 42.
7. Auerbach, *Mimesis*, 42–43.
8. Auerbach, *Mimesis*, 22, 20, 12–13, 18.
9. Auerbach, *Mimesis*, 18.
10. Lessing ultimately received the Nobel Prize in 2007.

11. Eileen Gibbons Kump, "God Willing," in *Bread and Milk and Other Stories* (Provo, UT: BYU Press, 1979), 90.

12. Nadezhda Mandelstam, *Hope Abandoned*, trans. Max Hayward (New York: Atheneum, 1974), 414.

13. John Milton, "Areopagitica," in *Prose Selections*, ed. Merritt Y. Hughes (New York: Odyssey Press, 1947), 223–24.

14. *History of the Church*, 6:428.

15. George Santayana, *The Sense of Beauty: Being the Outline of Aesthetic Theory* (New York: Dover, 1955), 269–70.

16. W. H. Auden, "The Virgin and the Dynamo," in *The Dyer's Hand and Other Essays* (London: Faber and Faber, 1963), 71.

Cokeville

It is my abiding sense that important art mirrors life, however disguised—and its creator's personal history, if only in surrogate fashion. I spent many a childhood summer in the quiet town of Cokeville, Wyoming, whose first white settler was a mysterious great-grandfather, Sylvanus Collett. When each school year ended, I'd be driven there from our small apartment in the center of Salt Lake City to stay with an aunt and uncle and play with the kids my age. Still-vivid memories of those idyllic visits and of events both before and after have melded in this nostalgic poem-of-sorts, originally written in 1989—with the addition of an imagined dramatic final flair that may yet happen, but let's not rush it.

Cokeville was also the site of a near-atrocity in 1986, when a former town marshal and his wife took hostages at a local elementary school—leading to their own deaths, though fortunately not those of any schoolchildren or other adults. Sadly, such occurrences are nowadays all too commonplace.

Swooning in sweltering summer sun, the young boy stands,
tempted to slip beneath the endless train and keep
walking to join his favorite cousins and float grass blades and
chips of bark, watch water beetles sprint like
catamarans on their meadow's ditch or, with them,
plunge fraternally naked into its water hole from the old
tire that sways from a sagging branch of cottonwood into
cool, oblivious depths. To his young boy's

mind all's secure and safe in this dusty cow town where
every day is just the same.

The closest thing, he thinks, to danger are the gang wars with
slightly older boys the other side of these same tracks, who
boisterously display their notched sticks, clothespin
triggers, and ammo—cross sections of old inner tubes—that
could, if you're hit too close, raise welts or—if you're not
careful, mothers keep warning—put out an eye. Plus
the one tomboy, Lu Ann (the bane of their adventures), who
always joins them—mayor's daughter, he the
one dealer in new cars, Chevrolet—and who with her still
baby-talk in the frenzy of battle screeches: "I am the
enema!"

Still he stands—the rusty freight cars forever
extending in both directions, too far to walk around—when
all he need do is duck beneath the one before
him—"Pacific Grove" its alluring letters beckon—and
in two seconds be on the other side and off to
his cousins. But against this too their mothers constantly
inveigh with cases of hoboes cut in two—those shy,
mysterious creatures who twice a week stop at his mother's
door for ham sandwich or leg of chicken.

He doesn't know—she hasn't told him—that, when
she was slightly past his age, working in the local bank,
they held a gun on her, then locked her in the safe—
not hoboes, but two young men who at school just
the year before sat next to her around the firewood stove,
knew and didn't want to hurt her. Later, trying to
rob a train—traversing the corridor of a particular
car, now muzzling the ladies and gents, demanding their
baubles and bills—they themselves were gunned down by a
grizzled fed who—pretending he was another sleeping
penniless bum—slumped in his seat until, their backs to him,
they'd passed him by.

That's maybe why she looks out for these other now fatherless
souls, just passing through, and never turns them down. They too
sat once in someone's classroom. They were known,
liked by some, loved at least by their mothers. And maybe
it's good protection. Word gets 'round. The boy can't know—
because his mother hasn't told him—that her own granddad,
himself a kind of outlaw, settled this place before standing
trial down south in Utah for—in his early twenties then, already
with three wives, as a Mormon Danite, deputy to a
man named Rockwell—gunning down two other men.

And he cannot know, this same young boy, that decades later,
living elsewhere with children of his own—this town now the
faintest of recollections—another freakish life-threatening
moment would jolt the place's stillness as a desperate man
and woman take the school kids hostage, then,
pressed by lawmen, blow their own brains out.

But now—at last resolved to risk a dive beneath the train—
he hears the sudden rattling collision of distant boxcars at
one far end and, seeing in front of him the wheels begin to
roll, thanks his stars or God or whomever, deep down in
their guts, frightened young boys pray to that he still
stands there, not cut in two, and that, for reasons he will
never know, this and other terrors that, like a rare
earthquake, have every fifty years or so wrenched this
sleepy know-nothing, do-nothing town—and must surely
wrench it again when you least suspect—have passed and will
a while yet pass him by.

Until on another sweltering summer day—now himself a granddad,
standing on a fifth-floor veranda in a distant city—he too
will be gunned down, not by sections of inner tube,
bandits' or Danites' bullets or some manic hobo or
deranged interloper and his moll, nor run down by a
locomotive. But
dispatched by another kind of accident, which in his day
physicians will
euphemistically call "cerebral."

A Playwright with a Passion for Unvarnished Depictions: An Interview with Tom Rogers, by Todd Compton

Following are excerpts from an in-depth interview with Todd Compton that appeared in the spring 2008 issue of Dialogue, *exploring what prompted me to write plays about the mostly tragic subjects I settled on, many of them based on the biographies of famous persons. Not discussed here is another theme of which I was less conscious when I wrote them: the classic oedipal rivalry between a man and his father or father-surrogate, which is readily apparent in all three Mormon-related plays on which the interview focuses.*[1]

One day when my BYU Greek class was awaiting the arrival of our teacher, Tom Rogers popped his head in the doorway and talked to us for ten or fifteen minutes or so. (One of my fellow students must have been a friend of his.) At that point, he was well-known for his plays Huebener *and* Fire in the Bones, *which dealt with two conflicted tragic heroes in Mormon history, Helmuth Huebener and John D. Lee. Someone asked him why he wrote about such problematic figures. His answer, as I remember it, was, "Those kinds of situations are just so interesting!"*

Recently, I've been preparing an article on problems in Mormon history as an avenue toward faith. That made me think of Tom Rogers's response, and I thought it would be worthwhile to probe further, in an *informally written email interview (summer 2006), how he came to write his three plays on Mormon subjects—*Huebener *(1976),* Fire in the Bones *(1978), and* Reunion *(1979).*[2]

TODD: *How did you get interested in being a dramatist? Your field of study, Russian literature, focuses more on novels.*

TOM: I was, as an actor, already involved in plays while in high school and at the University of Utah. At the time, I was bent on majoring in international relations and a likely future career with the foreign service. Debate seemed like good training, so—along with my peers Gene England, Bob Bennett, Doug Alder, Steve Covey, and Hal Eyring—I was active in debate at East High and later during my freshman year at the University of Utah. Meanwhile, I had a few roles on the U of U stage and even more challenging ones at the Barry Lynn Theater on Salt Lake's lower avenues. However, scheduling conflicts finally forced me to choose between debate and theatre, and I opted for the latter—eventually fulfilling the requirements for a BA in both theatre and political science. I think what led me to prefer the stage to debate was the sense that we get closer to real life when we involve ourselves in its affective side rather than in often artificially staged polemics that are more abstract and theoretical. The psychological and often irrational emotional causes of human action struck me as both more instructive and more intriguing.

I also began studying Russian as a freshman, considering that particular language a critical and useful adjunct to political science. It was during the outset of the Cold War and the nadir of the McCarthy era, and we knew so very little about our former World War II allies, by then our demonized enemies, the Russians. The current parallel with Arabs and the Muslim world seems obvious. Russian was taught extensively back then in the Salt Lake City public schools. It seems unbelievable that the same cannot be said as yet for either Arabic or Mandarin Chinese.

Only after my mission to Germany and while I was in graduate school did I become fully aware of the wonders of classical Russian literature, which, like drama, I found both aesthetically appealing and psychologically compelling. It further underscored for me the universality of all human experience rather than its purported divisiveness, and it eventually served as the core subject matter I ended up writing about and teaching.

Earlier, simply because it was offered then, I took my first course in playwriting during my initial freshman quarter from the incomparable Robert Hyde Wilson. Out of it came my first full-length script, later directed by Professor David Morgan at the U of U's small "auxiliary" theater, the Play Box. Although that play, *Nest of Feathers,* was an inferior script and far too imitative of William Inge, its production whetted my appetite to try again—particularly with submissions to a playwriting competition then sponsored by the LDS Church's Mutual Improvement Association. Later, due to a misunderstanding regarding my qualifications for studying a language on the graduate level, I applied for Yale's DFA program in playwriting and dramatic literature instead of Russian, which I pursued for the first two years there, turning out more uninspired scripts because I hadn't yet connected my writing either with my own psyche or with truly significant and fascinating Mormon concerns. In the meantime, I more fully discovered the profundity of Russian literature, which prompted me, while only a year away from completing that DFA, to switch disciplines. I've never regretted it, though it cost me another six years of graduate study.

TODD: *I'm sure any list of the top ten plays written by Mormons would include your* Huebener. *How did you get the idea for writing about Helmuth Huebener?*

TOM: My first mission was in northern Germany, with headquarters in Berlin. Hamburg, Huebener's hometown and the site of his clandestine activity, was one of our cities. I recall a fellow missionary there on one occasion mentioning Huebener's story. He'd heard about it from a local member. This was fairly unusual, since our members and investigators were rather tight-lipped about their personal experience during World War II, which had ended just a decade earlier. I was only dimly aware that a number of those we worked with had been members of the Nazi Party.

After my mission, I put the whole thing out of my mind. It was almost two decades later, while I served on the BYU faculty, that my colleague Alan Keele gave a presentation to our college faculty about Huebener's impact on important postwar German authors, notably Nobel Prize winners Heinrich Böll and Günter Grass. Knowing of my prior interest in playwriting, Alan singled me out during the same lecture and challenged me to write a play on the subject. Alan and history professor Douglas Tobler generously shared with me their research about Huebener, which became the play's principal source.[3] Till that moment I'd almost forgotten I'd ever written plays—so immersed had I meanwhile become in my career discipline, Russian literature.

Alan's unexpected challenge forcefully revived the creative juices. The gracious interest and support just then of the BYU theatre faculty was also an important catalyst.

Todd: *Could you tell the basic Huebener story for readers who might be unfamiliar with it?*

Tom: Helmuth Huebener, who during his show trial in Berlin was characterized by the prosecution as having the mind of a thirty-year-old professor, was—despite the existing law protecting minors—condemned to death and beheaded at the age of seventeen. While listening to BBC shortwave accounts of the war (itself an illegal act), he'd become convinced that Hitler's propaganda machine was lying to the German nation about the war's progress. He was also strongly persuaded of the Nazi regime's tyrannous aggression against other peoples. As the trusted clerk to the LDS Hamburg district presidency, Huebener had access to a mimeograph machine, which he subsequently used to run off leaflets attacking Hitler and official Nazi accounts of the war. Recruiting two other young Latter-day Saints, Karl-Heinz Schnibbe and Rudi Wobbe, he then proceeded to distribute the leaflets throughout Hamburg.

Later, he approached other youth to assist, including a coworker at the state welfare office who eventually informed their supervisor, a loyal Nazi. The young men were arrested and brought to trial. To protect Schnibbe, who was technically no longer a minor, Helmuth took full responsibility for their deeds. Clearly, their dissident activity placed the LDS Church, which was already viewed as an American entity, in great jeopardy. Huebener's conflict—to choose between his conscience and the loyalty required of him by those in power—is the common dilemma of classical tragedy, perhaps its most notable exemplar being Sophocles's Antigone, whose fatal heroism closely resembles Huebener's own. In part to protect the church in Germany, Huebener was immediately excommunicated by his local priesthood leaders. After the war, when his story came to the attention of church leaders, Huebener's membership was reinstated by the First Presidency.

TODD: *What themes attracted you in the Huebener story?*

TOM: As I've suggested, it had the depth and proportion of a classical tragedy. I find similar dramatic impact in Mormonism's still most imposing novel to date, Maurine Whipple's *Giant Joshua,* whose plot uncannily resembles the Hippolytus myth, first treated by Euripides, then brilliantly reworked in Racine's *Phaedra.* In a historical setting that would surely interest Mormon audiences, Huebener's story simply cried out for dramatic treatment. That was my only consideration at the time. It was also a story of which few Latter-day Saints were aware.

TODD: *In the actual writing stage of the play, did you ever think, Oh-oh, my bishop (or brother, or conservative colleague) isn't going to like this?*

TOM: No. Unlike Huebener and the outcomes he doubtless anticipated from his own authorial projects—his anti-Nazi pamphlets—I all along presumed that the play would receive a positive reception, which for the most part it did. My bishop was actually one of its most enthusiastic viewers.

The play was written during the heady period when LDS historians, particularly Leonard Arrington and company, were boldly moving forward with their own stimulating accounts and interpretations of our culture's past. Deseret Book had, for instance, just brought out Jim Allen and Glen Leonard's *The Story of the Latter-day Saints,* intended, I'm told, for courses in the church's seminaries and institutes and only subsequently critiqued and not reprinted because of its allusions to nineteenth-century polygamy.

At the same time, in almost unprecedented fashion, my views as BYU honors director were featured in a two-page centerfold of the university's alumni magazine, *BYU Today,* under the heading "Mormon Scholars: Thoughts from a Person Who Believes in the LDS Intellectual," with a large cover photo of yours truly sporting his ubiquitous Richard Nixon five-o'clock shadow. Even the otherwise extremely cautious theatre faculty were, at that time, strong champions of new plays like *Huebener* that dealt with LDS heritage and present-day Mormon life. About that time, Lael Woodbury, then dean of the College of Fine Arts, together with Charles Metten, department chair, and Ivan Crosland, *Huebener*'s director, eagerly petitioned Academic Vice President Robert K. Thomas for permission to move ahead with a campus production of *Fire in the Bones,* a first-ever literary treatment of the Mountain Meadows Massacre. In a two-hour discussion, Thomas, who had keen instincts about political correctness, explained to the four of us why it would be imprudent to perform that play at BYU. At the time, even allusions to historical polygamy, which prominently figures in the play, proved taboo. *Fire in the Bones* was subsequently produced in the Salt Lake Valley by the short-lived Green-Briar Theatre, made up of former BYU student thespians. I was out of the country at the time and never saw it.

Todd: *You compare the moral conflict in* Huebener *to the conflict in* Antigone *in which the heroine has to choose between two admirable ideals: loyalty to family and loyalty to state. I was struck by how sympathetic and reasonable you make both Huebener and his branch president Zoellner, and their opposed ideals. You can argue that both are completely right and completely wrong. Would you say your play treats the difficulty of finding absolute right or wrong in many situations?*

Tom: That is what makes the situation such an intriguing dramatic dilemma: competing "goods," only one of which one can be settled on. I agree that I probably idealized both Huebener and, for sure, his branch president. I've been told the branch president was a fanatically loyal Nazi and would have been far less sympathetic toward Helmuth, had he at all known about his activities prior to the latter's arrest. In fact, I've been told on good authority that when the branch president did find out about Huebener's activities, he exclaimed, "If I'd known, I'd have shot him myself!" Some have also suggested that the play's Helmuth is almost too fearless and self-composed. Sensing this, I've tried to encourage the actors who portray him to reflect with body language, furtive looks, etc., what would be normal apprehension about what he was undertaking.

I also gave him a line in which he admits his fear. On the other hand, our best source about Helmuth's truly unusual personality, his close friend Karl-Heinz Schnibbe, who has, over the years, generously attended and fielded questions at a number of postperformance discussions in Provo, Bountiful, and elsewhere, has always contended that Helmuth *was* unusually determined and courageous—clearly a motivating inspiration for Karl-Heinz to this very day.

There is no question that Huebener's position vis-à-vis Hitler and Hitler's war machine was the only morally correct one. What he could have ever really accomplished that would make a lasting difference by so openly defying it is, nevertheless, moot. Huebener's prospects were limited and put the church and its members in great jeopardy. But who can fully foresee such things? His cause was both noble and extremely heroic; but its outcome, where both he and others were concerned, was disastrous.

TODD: *You say that in 1976, you (including Alan Keele and Douglas Tobler) were asked to desist from further productions or publications on the subject of Huebener. Could you talk about that?*

TOM: A few religious dissidents have here and there made more of it than they should have, but the play had immense appeal for the general public. Glowing reviews in the Salt Lake newspapers apparently alerted certain church leaders to possible unfavorable fallout affecting certain members and the church's welfare in distant places. I've never been sure why in 1976 we were asked to desist from further productions or publications on the subject. Some have speculated that it might have somehow interfered with plans to erect a temple behind the Iron Curtain in Freiberg, Germany. I've looked into the matter with those East German Latter-day Saints of my acquaintance to whom authorities of the DDR (Deutsche Demokratische Republik) first recommended the church's doing so. However, the timing doesn't exactly coincide.

We also had a number of members living in other countries under authoritarian regimes. It may have seemed possible, if unlikely, that if the example of Huebener had come to the attention of church members in those countries, one or more of them might have been incited to emulate his actions, with dire consequences for the church. We will never really know.

TODD: *I was struck by that quotation from BYU President Rex Lee on the back of your collection* Huebener and Other Plays *with reference to his ancestor John D. Lee, the only person convicted and executed for participating in the Mountain Meadows Massacre. He said: "I have always struggled with why any rational human beings could have done what my great-grandfather and others did on September 11, 1857. I still don't understand it. But I get more of an insight from your play than I ever had before. It's not that you present any more facts. I knew them all. . . . I doubt you could have written an essay that would have re-created the dynamics that may have existed in Cedar City on that Sunday evening quite as helpfully as did your play." How did that blurb on your book come about? Did Rex write you a letter?*

Tom: I had the temerity to share the play with President Lee when I read about the conciliatory event he had helped organize at Mountain Meadows between his own clan and that of the Fanchers. His response was the gracious letter of acknowledgment you cite, which he then gave me permission to use on the anthology's back cover.

Todd: *How would you advise Mormon playwrights to deal with problem issues? Will this be healthy for the Mormon community?*

Tom: We constantly need to remind ourselves—despite our idealistic striving—of our humanity, our flawed natures. We as much as others need existential humility as we represent the restored gospel and its fullness. Such narratives can serve us in a cautionary fashion, both individually and as a society. All that we have to share, which is so vital and precious, would have even greater appeal if we operated on a more horizontal level, both with one another and with everyone else. Otherwise, we are less than genuine: we play a hypocritical role and are self-deceived. In this regard, the Savior was, as in all else, our finest, purest, most reliable role model.

I also resonate to the following: "The belief in God does not guarantee the knowledge of God's wishes. This is the most elementary lesson of the history of religious faith. The believer lives in the darkness more than he lives in the light. He does not wallow in God's guidance, he thirsts for it" (writer and critic Leon Wieseltier).[4] "The spirit of liberty is the spirit which is not too sure that it is right" (jurist Learned Hand).[5] "With or without religion, good people can behave well and bad people can do evil; but for good people to do evil—that takes religion" (physicist Steven Weinberg).[6] "Any religious symbol, so interpreted that it refers not to a thought-transcending mystery but to a thought-enveloping social order, misappropriates to the lower principle the values of the higher and so (to use a theological turn of phrase) sets Satan in the seat of God" (comparative religion scholar Joseph Campbell).[7] And, finally, from my wife, Merriam: "Consideration can't be legislated any more than morality can be."

TODD: *Would you explain, then, how you see Lee as a scapegoat, and heroic?*

TOM: We use the term *hero* in more than one way: first, simply, for a protagonist or principal literary character. Then (not always the same) for someone who is particularly self-sacrificing and noble in character. I view Lee more in terms of the former definition—like Arthur Miller's Willy Loman in the play *Death of a Salesman*, circumstantially more sinned against than sinning but certainly not of flawlessly saintly stature.

Lee's sacrifice and service as an early missionary and as the chief provisioner of the first Mormon pioneers was valiant and truly noteworthy. On the other hand, his involvement in the Mountain Meadows debacle was unfortunate and deeply tragic; there, his response was confused and weak because he lacked what Solzhenitsyn refers to as an essential "individual position" or conscience, which we might relate to what we call the influence of the Holy Ghost.[8]

In the strained circumstances of 1857, I very much doubt that the voice of the Spirit was sufficiently sought or listened to. Then again, there's the matter of competing goods or, in tragedy, vicissitudes, where choosing the high road is fraught with loneliness, pain, and immediate peril. The branch president as depicted in *Huebener* is less flawed than Lee because he has not, in fact, betrayed that play's protagonist but only disagreed with him. The actual person on whom he is modeled was, in fact, not involved in Huebener's arrest, though as I've already mentioned, his response after learning of the event was far less empathetic.

After all the time that has elapsed since the initial production of *Huebener*—thirty-two years, in fact—it only now occurs to me why the story and the play's treatment of it have had such universal appeal. Plotwise, the reason is almost purely situational: although there is a decidedly external enemy—the Nazi regime—the play's real conflict occurs within an otherwise ideologically unified church congregation and, beyond that, within individual characters. The presumed dichotomy of more righteous Mormons versus less enlightened or less valiant nonmembers isn't even implied. Instead, we witness a welter of confusion, disagreement, and viewpoints—as in any body of believers. The same dynamic also takes place in both *Fire in the Bones* and *Reunion*.

Such an approach is, I believe, closer to real life and something with which viewers, whether insiders or the uninitiated, can more readily identify. Such an approach to religious subjects also avoids preaching or special pleading. Any spiritual "lesson"—or sense of inner struggle on the part of earnest believers—comes through subtly and between the lines and is therefore less obtrusive and more forceful. Such treatments of ourselves and our religious tradition strike me as far more winning in the long run—sparking both broader and keener audience interest because, again, they are that much truer to how things really are.

TODD: *Turning again to* Fire in the Bones, *how closely would you say your play follows the actual chain of events in the Mountain Meadows Massacre and its aftermath?*

TOM: That play is a fairly faithful account of John D. Lee's involvement in the massacre. I based it almost wholly upon Juanita Brooks's critically acclaimed history of the event and her biographies of both John D. Lee and his youngest wife, Emma.[9] For dramatic effect, its beginning and concluding scenes reprise the moment of his execution. (Curiously, the noted author Judith Freeman used a similar narrative frame in her recent novel on the same subject, *Red Water.*) Lee, of course, is a complex character because, while he took a principal part in the massacre, he is generally regarded as having been unjustly singled out in 1877 for punishment.

Interestingly, my own great-grandfather, Sylvanus Collett, went to trial in Provo in 1878—accused, in concert with the recently deceased Orrin Porter Rockwell and two other men, of having dispatched four ill-fated emigrants from California, the Aiken party, a month or so after Mountain Meadows. I've written a play on that subject titled *First Trump* (not yet produced) and also recently completed the draft of a related first novel whose working title is *The Book of Lehi.* However, when I wrote *Fire in the Bones,* I was only dimly aware of my ancestor's escapades. So there was no personal motive in writing a play about the Mountain Meadows Massacre—except that, like *Huebener,* that event struck me as, in addition to its historical interest and fascinating moral complexity, ideal material for dramatic treatment.

TODD: *I read over your first three plays recently, and in the first two plays, I was struck by the theme of excommunication. The experience of actual excommunication must have been overwhelming for a true believer like Huebener. Was this a theme that you were drawn to, or would you say it simply happened to occur in both* Huebener *and* Fire in the Bones*?*

Tom: It is strictly coincidental that the protagonists of my first two important plays—Huebener and John D. Lee—were excommunicated and, in both cases, had their membership posthumously restored. Naturally, that very circumstance added special poignancy to their stories. Only after both plays were written and received productions did I realize that plotwise, I'd fallen into a rut. In order to right what seemed like a kind of thematic imbalance or too limited focus in what I'd so recently explored as a playwright, I then conceived of *Reunion,* in which two brothers square off regarding their diametrically opposed viewpoints about life and the gospel. They are, if you will, the thesis and antithesis whose synthesis—articulated and personified by their dying father, a former institute teacher—is that ultimate truth transcends both of their passionate and so universally human positions.

Todd: *Was* Reunion *easier or harder to write than your former two plays?*

Tom: *Reunion* wrote itself. I recall having heard practically every line out of the mouth of one or another acquaintance, or having said it myself on some occasion.

Todd: *Could you summarize the main characters and main dramatic conflicts in the play?*

Tom: *Reunion* is mostly an *agon* [Greek: "competition or contest"], an argument between two brothers who represent what LDS historian Richard Poll suggested were the Iron Rod versus the Liahona mentalities among church members.[10] It's a sort of dialectic in which the Robison family's dying patriarch transcends his sons' bickering with a more Christlike perspective, insisting that ultimate truth and wisdom surpass the partisan disputations we are so prone to as we mutually contend about our righteousness and which moral stance is correct. The disputants' father Arthur Robison urges reconciliation.

Intuitively, his less articulate wife conveys the same transcendent perspective. A younger brother is momentarily dissuaded from serving a mission; but during a blessing requested by their father, he is possibly persuaded to reconsider his options—as is a hitherto wayward sister. I've rather facetiously called this play the first Mormon "soap."

Todd: *You performed in* Reunion *and so did some of your personal friends, such as Marden and Harlow Clark. Can you tell us about those early rehearsals and performances?*

Tom: I recruited the cast largely from the BYU English faculty. They all felt a ready affinity with the play's characters and the issues it explored—which, I believe, made their acting so persuasive and credible. They were wonderfully supportive during the play's frequent staged readings in the BYU law school auditorium. Harlow, who portrayed the youngest son, had recently returned from a mission, and his father Marden read the part of the father with deep and sensitive understanding—reflecting, I suspect, his own past experience with students and members of his own family. For ten years after his retirement, he served as a campus bishop in a married student ward.

Todd: *On the phone, you told me about varied reactions to* Reunion. *Could you repeat what you told me?*

Tom: At the end of each reading, we held a lively discussion with audience members. Quite often someone would first say that he or she found the characters artificial and a caricature of real Latter-day Saints. Invariably, someone then popped up and declared, "No. That's my family." Or "That's my mother." Et cetera. For most, the discussion seemed cathartic—a recognition that we are all flawed, vulnerable, and limited in perspective, even as we earnestly attempt to live gospel-oriented lives. Acknowledging our common human detritus seemed to encourage those present to feel they were on an even playing field with everyone else, that they were more accepted, more capable of persevering and fighting the good fight. During one such discussion, an associate dean from the school of business disparaged the play as "a slur on the Mormon family," but his response was atypical. The fact that the play so viscerally involved its audience was, I felt, an indication of its effectiveness as a "think piece."

Todd: *What is the value of looking at dysfunctional families and relationships?*

Tom: To humble us and help us recognize that dysfunctionality and find encouragement in the realization that we all partake of the same human condition.

Todd: *Sam Taylor tells the story of having characters in his fiction that were widely criticized as unrealistic. So in his next novel, he included a character drawn totally from life. And the critics pounced on that one as the least lifelike character of all!*

TOM: Truth, as we often say, is indeed stranger than fiction—to which some wag has quipped that art is less strange than real life because art has to make a certain sense. I suspect, however, that there are readers and viewers (including some critics) who are comfortable only with stereotypes and would therefore tend to react in the way you describe. For me, an effective idiosyncratic trait or gesture individualizes and consequently brings a character all the more to life.

TODD: *I liked the ending of* Reunion, *in which the very active son (flawed) and the liberal, inactive son (flawed) come together under the leadership of their father (flawed). Why did you choose a ritual to end the play?*

TOM: It wasn't calculated. It just occurred to me and felt right—much as I often feel uncomfortable hearing actors mouth prayers on stage. On such occasions, I've even seen BYU audience members close their eyes and bow their heads in unison. You'll notice that in *Reunion,* the stage directions indicate a dimming of lights and "Curtain" before any words can be spoken. However, I admit to a penchant on my part to conclude this and other plays with a kind of ritual. As I wrote in the preface to the first anthology of my plays, *God's Fools*: "The ritual—be it a toast [as in *Huebener*], an execution [*Fire in the Bones,* also *Huebener*], or a blessing [*Reunion* and *God's Fools*]—is foreshadowed early in each play and, in each case, concludes it. The nature of this ritual, or at least the use made of it in its particular dramatic context, serves and was motivated, I'd now like to think, to affirm some transcendent, postmortal connection between the hero and his eternal destiny."[11]

TODD: *Would you say that the ending of the play leaves us with a family that is not necessarily different in their church activity, but is more loving?*

TOM: Yes, probably so. But that's already a great step forward, wouldn't you say? As important as a formal commitment or any amount of affirmative rhetoric. Words alone are cheap.

TODD: *You could interpret* Reunion's *ending as a statement about church activity versus love. How do you see the interplay of love and the institutional church at the end of the play?*

TOM: Well, the blessing by a patriarch (in this case, husband and father) is, as such, prescribed and encouraged by the church. Without such an institutional incentive, I doubt it would even occur to any of the family members. But note this particular blessing's intimacy, its spontaneity. Although impelled by Arthur's desperate calculation to bring his children together, the home teachers, for instance, who also appear as characters in the play, did not suggest it. Nor did any other ecclesiastical leader.

TODD: *As a writer of Mormon history, I see the need to look frankly and carefully at problems in Mormon history, practice, and scripture, in order to view them with full, authentic faith and come to resolution with them. Would you say that's a dramatic theme in all three of the plays we've discussed?*

TOM: By its very nature, drama deals with conflict and with what is problematic—if successful and relevant, addressing real life, not necessarily offering solutions but raising issues and related questions. In a Mormon context, therefore, dealing with such problems is unavoidable. And, yes, I agree with you that awareness of the facts as we can best know them is a firmer and more honest foundation for faith. If we appear to have something to hide, doubts readily arise.

Besides, the historical or biographical nitty-gritty, once you delve into it, is far more fascinating than airbrushing or spin. If properly apprehended, it also fosters even greater admiration for the very human struggle all men and women, including our idols, have been through. Think of President Spencer W. Kimball's marvelous biographies,[12] Elder F. Enzio Busche's refreshingly candid autobiography,[13] the Bible's frequent depiction of personal flaws in Old Testament patriarchs and kings as well as Christ's apostles, the confessions of youthful waywardness by various Book of Mormon prophets, not to mention Joseph Smith's self-effacing personal history in the Pearl of Great Price and the reproaches and admonishments he receives from the Lord in various revelations in the Doctrine and Covenants. These unvarnished depictions encouragingly help us identify with such figures and render them even more heroic—as do the circumstances and portrayal of character that underlie all viable tragedy and realism.

I was called to serve as a director of BYU's Honors Program about the time I started writing these plays. I was also, simultaneously, a campus branch president. Perhaps I was naive at the time, but in those days there appeared to be a seamless relationship between free intellectual inquiry and faith. That was, of course, before the culture wars and before more widespread radical dissent descended upon us. I will add that in the late 1960s, I was induced to further pursue my teaching career by moving to BYU from a state institution, in part because I felt that my students at the latter school were extremely self-assured and their minds were already fairly well made up, often skeptically, about life and its ultimate purposes. In contrast, it seemed to me that many a more committed LDS young person, as at BYU, was in considerable need of humanistic broadening—which, in turn, gave me a personal sense of "mission" that I felt less at the University of Utah. Though largely subconscious, I think that same impulse underlay my urge to write the plays we've been discussing.

TODD: *Here's a general one. If you were to pick the five plays that have influenced you the most, what would they be? Feel free to add other plays, but start with five.*

TOM: That's hard. I'd rather just mention particular playwrights. In my early years I fell under the sway of the three leading contemporary American playwrights, Tennessee Williams, Arthur Miller, and William Inge. With my penchant for biographical and historical subjects, I am probably closest to Miller, whose Willy Loman in *Death of a Salesman* is based on an uncle of his, whose *After the Fall* revisits his marriage with Marilyn Monroe, and whose *Crucible* is an allegory for the McCarthy era "witch hunts." Of the more recent English language playwrights, I have often cited as our finest the British absurdist Harold Pinter (*The Homecoming, The Caretaker*), the Irishman Brian Friel (*Dancing at Lughnasa*), the American black August Wilson (*Fences, The Piano Lesson,* etc.) and the, for me, utterly amazing Sam Shepard—whose actual surname, incidentally, is also Rogers (*Buried Child, Fool for Love, A Lie of the Mind*).

For me, Shakespeare has always been something of an enigma. I admire him from a distance but more readily relate to his earthier contemporary, Ben Jonson. Late in the day, critics like Yale's Harold Bloom, Harvard's Stephen Greenblatt, and Oxford's late A. D. Nuttall have helped me better fathom from the subtle clues that relate various plots and seemingly disparate characters the pattern of Shakespeare's ultimate sympathies and worldview. As Nuttall keeps insisting, Shakespeare "'did everything.' . . . It is remarkably hard to think of anything Shakespeare has not thought of first."[14] Everyone should read Nuttall's very recent *Shakespeare the Thinker.* Additionally, as I believe Harold Bloom observed, the Bard was the very first writer in all human history to portray characters debating within themselves a course of action.[15] That strikes me as, in turn, what playwrights do when they assign this or that opposed viewpoint to various characters. They are really just debating within themselves the issues that so fascinate and compel them.

Of the classic Greek triad, I prefer and resonate most with Euripides, who, with his larger number of extant plays, was clearly the most popular of the three in the ancient world. If more sensational than Aeschylus and Sophocles, he is also psychologically the most profound, the most modern. In a number of respects, Euripides is, for me, a supreme model. I believe that his frequent female protagonists are also emblems of his beloved city-state, Athens, and that in ways hard to fathom, their tragic destinies reflect that nation's decline. His last play, *The Bacchae,* is an amazing commentary on political hubris as well as on the perils of both spiritual and artistic pretension.

In conclusion, allow me to say just this much more about truly serious literature—realistic fiction and tragedy—which, despite Aristotle's claim for the latter's "purgation of the emotions," seems so off-putting to many. Just recently, in fact, another emeritus scholar chided my enthusiastic endorsement of Cormac McCarthy's latest profound if predictably stark novel, *The Road,* indicating that as an ordained LDS patriarch, he could not recommend it to others. His declaration was a reminder that temperamentally we are all different, but it left me wondering how he handles the Book of Mormon's depictions of slaughter and carnage. Does he see in them any elevating purpose? How would he respond to Joseph Smith's "Thy mind, O Man, if thou wilt lead a soul unto salvation, must stretch as high as the utmost Heavens, and search into and contemplate the lowest considerations of the darkest abyss, and expand upon the broad considerations of eternal expanse"?[16]

For me, if not for everyone, the honest depiction of tragic events has important spiritual-ethical import. Besides serving as an object lesson, it arouses Christlike compassion for those less fortunate and also conveys to us—even in its default and frequent absence—the nobility of self-sacrificing behavior as, when necessity dictates, the greatest of goods and the most beautiful thing imaginable. If we can catch tragedy's transcendent vision and allow it to inspire us, then we, too, will strive for that same nobility and cherish its beauty above all else that self-indulgently lures us. If we can respect it sufficiently, it might just "save" some of us.

Notes

1. A complete version of this interview was published in *Dialogue: A Journal of Mormon Thought* 41/1 (2008): 67–90.

2. All three plays, together with others by Tom Rogers, are available through the website of BYU's Maxwell Institute at publications.mi.byu.edu/rogerscollectedplays.

3. See Alan F. Keele and Douglas F. Tobler, "The Führer's New Clothes: Helmuth Huebener and the Mormons in the Third Reich," *Sunstone* 5, November–December 1980, 20–29; Karl-Heinz Schnibbe, with Alan F. Keele and Douglas F. Tobler, *The Price: The True Story of a Mormon Who Defied Hitler* (Salt Lake City: Bookcraft, 1984); and *When Truth Was Treason: German Youth against Hitler: The Story of the Helmuth Hübener Group Based on the Narrative of Karl-Heinz Schnibbe*, comp., trans., and ed. Blair R. Holmes and Alan F. Keele (Urbana: University of Illinois Press, 1995).

4. Leon Wieseltier, "The Elect," *New Republic,* November 22, 2004, 14.

5. Learned Hand's swearing-in speech before some 150,000 new US citizens in New York's Central Park, 1944, in Gerald Gunther, *Learned Hand: The Man and Judge* (New York: Alfred A. Knopf, 1994), 549.

6. Steven Weinberg, "A Designer Universe?," *New York Review of Books,* October 21, 1999, www.nybooks.com/articles/archives/1999/oct/21/a-designer-universe/?p=2.

7. Joseph Campbell, *The Flight of the Wild Gander: Explorations in the Mythological Dimension* (New York: Harper Perennial, 1990), 206–7.

8. Aleksandr Solzhenitsyn, *The Gulag Archipelago,* trans. Thomas P. Whitney (New York: Harper & Row, 1973), 1:405.

9. Juanita Brooks, *The Mountain Meadows Massacre* (Stanford, CA: Stanford University Press, 1950); *John Doyle Lee: Zealot, Pioneer Builder, Scapegoat* (Glendale, CA: Arthur H. Clark, 1961); and *Emma Lee* (Logan: Utah State University Press, 1975).

10. Richard D. Poll, "What the Church Means to People Like Me," *Dialogue: A Journal of Mormon Thought* 2/4 (1967): 107–17.

11. Thomas F. Rogers, *God's Fools: Plays of Mitigated Conscience* (Midvale, UT: Signature Books, 1983), vi.

12. Edward L. Kimball and Andrew E. Kimball Jr., *Spencer W. Kimball: The Early and Apostolic Years* (Salt Lake City: Deseret Book, 2006); and Edward L. Kimball, *Lengthen Your Stride: The Presidency of Spencer W. Kimball* (Salt Lake City: Deseret Book, 2005).

13. F. Enzio Busche, *Yearning for the Living God: Reflections from the Life of F. Enzio Busche,* ed. and comp. Tracie A. Lamb (Salt Lake City: Deseret Book, 2004).

14. A. D. Nuttall, *Shakespeare the Thinker* (New Haven, CT: Yale University Press, 2007), 265.

15. Harold Bloom, *Shakespeare: The Invention of the Human* (New York: Riverhead Books, 1998). See, for example, pages xix, 7, and 401–5.

16. Joseph Smith, in Dean C. Jessee and John W. Welch, "Revelations in Context: Joseph Smith's Letter from Liberty Jail, March 20, 1839," *BYU Studies* 39/3 (2000): 137; spelling and punctuation standardized.

Why I Wrote *Huebener*

The work for which I will probably be best remembered is Huebener, *a play about a real-life seventeen-year-old LDS youth during World War II who produced anti-Nazi propaganda and was caught and subsequently executed. He was also excommunicated from the church by his local branch president, but his membership was reinstated by the LDS First Presidency after the war.*

The play had an extraordinarily successful first run. Parents brought their young sons and Aaronic Priesthood advisors their quorums. Huebener *enjoyed one of the longest extended runs in BYU theatre history and was seen by an estimated one-fifth of the 1976 BYU campus community.*

At the time, I was not aware of any negative reactions. However, during its continued run I was asked by LDS Church authorities not to make the play available for further performance, and others working for BYU and I were also requested not to publish material related to Helmuth Huebener—a prohibition that lasted until 1992.

Some have speculated that the reasons may have had to do with negotiations regarding a temple in East Germany during the years of Soviet occupation. However, other events of the time—including my early release as director of the BYU Honors Program—led me to worry that some who had not seen the play but had only heard about it might believe it reflected a lack of faith (or faithfulness) on my part. The following essay draws on thoughts from that time, shared (in a perhaps paranoid gesture) with my then-bishop and my department chair—now modified and updated based on forty years' perspective since the events in question.

Why write a play like *Huebener*? One might as well ask: why write plays at all? Or why write anything that reflects upon our experience or that of others? I cannot be sure. The urge is largely subconscious, but it must have something to do with sorting out and making sense of that experience, particularly when there is a clash of wills and opinions.

Writing about human conflict

There are, I am aware, two schools of thought that in turn reflect diverse kinds of temperament. The first would suppress the literary treatment of whatever appears unsettling and problematic in human relations. The second would not. Those in the second camp are generally styled "intellectuals." They tend to take literature seriously and to include the masterworks of fiction among their "best books" (see D&C 88:118). I doubt if many in this camp would ever ask the question "Why did a man write . . . ?" any more than they would ask, "Why did he live and breathe?"

Before becoming a teacher of Russian, I had spent several years at playwriting—from 1951 to 1955 while an undergraduate at the University of Utah and from 1958 to 1960 as a pupil of John Gassner at the Yale School of Drama. Except for a long dry interval from 1960 until the 1970s, playwriting has been my principal avocation. I wrote *Huebener* while serving at BYU as an LDS branch president. My spiritual condition and devotion to the church were then, as best I can judge, very strong. Indeed, it was my devotion that found resonance in Helmuth Huebener's story.

First of all, I found Huebener's example truly inspiring. I had originally heard about his valiant discrediting of Nazi propaganda and his consequent trial and execution while serving as a full-time missionary in the East (later North) German Mission. Like others, I was deeply impressed by this young Mormon who had taken a moral position that, in the aftermath, no one would deny was the only correct one, even though he was almost alone in so doing.

Huebener's story was highly dramatic as well as poignant and psychologically arresting—particularly because of the censure to which he was subjected by fellow Mormons and the misunderstanding that arose between them. Without taking sides, that is the stuff of great drama. I am inclined to explore such predicaments, not to distort or sensationalize but because that is the way relationships—even between well-intended persons and close kin—often are.

The impact of *Huebener*

Regardless of the author's intention, it is, I suppose, legitimate to ask about a work's ultimate impact on the beliefs and attitudes of readers or an audience. Had *Huebener* shaken the faith of even a small portion of those who saw it, there might be cause for alarm. But for the overwhelming majority, as far as I knew, it *did not* have that effect.

While it would be unrealistic to expect that the play pleased each of the more than 5,000 who saw its initial performances, I received very few negative responses. (One isolated case was a student who felt we made the German Mormons look too good by identifying Huebener as one of them.) The generally overwhelming response to the play from such a cross section of BYU's campus community provided considerable reassurance about our ability as church members—our need, in fact—to face historical truth, however problematic, and come away somehow cathartically strengthened. To feel, on the other hand, that there are things we must not know can only raise doubt and suspicion and ultimately erode the credibility of those who would act as censors. (This is, in fact, an essential point of the play itself—at least as concerns Huebener and Dr. Goebbels.)

I personally believe that because audiences felt it was actually possible to recognize head-on that we are all fallible and that there are certain areas of controversy for which there are no easy, pat answers—we all know from personal experience that this is so, more than we often care to admit—they came away not disillusioned but strengthened and reassured. Agency and the right and need individually to discern truth by independently testing it with our minds had been affirmed—and the result was positive.

Doubts and consequences

My experience with *Huebener* corroborated the saying: "If the church is really true, we should be able to handle the truth about the church." Even so, I wondered if the early release from my position with the

BYU Honors Program and its unusual public announcement, even in the Salt Lake media, signaled some sort of ecclesiastical or at least administrative displeasure—particularly in light of the request I had received not to make the play available for further performance. My apprehension seemed confirmed when I heard that a church official had asked a former cast member about my reasons for writing the play. The sympathetic reactions to my release by other faculty and by several students made me wonder if they knew something I didn't. At the time, it was hard to imagine that I would ever again receive high church approval for any assignment for which I might conceivably be recommended. I even thought my position at BYU might come into question or a disciplinary council regarding my church membership might be convened.

Thankfully, nothing ever came of these concerns, though they were real enough to me at the time. Contrary to my expectations, I have since been asked to serve in several positions indicating considerable trust, including a call to preside over the Russia St. Petersburg Mission in the early 1990s and a recently concluded calling as a patriarch to the same part of the world. My employment at BYU was never jeopardized (so far as I know), and other plays of mine continued to be produced there. Nevertheless, my concerns at that time point to an impasse that still faces some intellectuals in the church. I do not believe this impasse is at all necessary. Rather, it derives, I feel, not so much from any real conflict involving the gospel or the church per se as from the way—with more fear, suspicion, mistrust, condescension, and deference to institutional expediency than is warranted—some tend to view others.

Despite the anxiety I experienced back then, the play's enthusiastic reception—which in turn led to the revival of my playwriting efforts and the creation of many more plays, as well as eventual performances of *Huebener* in places as far distant as Russia and Finland—was well worth it for me, and hopefully for others.

Lessons learned

Many LDS artists tend to believe that only what is noncontroversial and clear to the weakest or most unsophisticated is likely to be sponsored or condoned. My experience doesn't completely refute that suspicion.

To the extent this *is* true, art that is officially endorsed by the church will probably never be great art. If, by chance, the non-Mormon world is first favorably impressed by what one of us brings forth at his or her own initiative and risk that turns out to be "of good report and praiseworthy," then perhaps it will ultimately receive due recognition. But that was ever so. While we are urged to do many things "of [our] own free will" (see D&C 58:27), priority and preference often appear to be accorded to those who are less original but predictably safe. It may be that some of us would have more respect and approval if we did less—or did it less well.

I draw several corollaries from this entire experience:

First, it is usually better to consult directly with the subject of any controversy. Too many secondary sources and too much hearsay result in sloppy investigation and poor institutional and interpersonal relations.

Second, the more adverse concern we pay some phenomena—a play, an article, or a piece of art—the more publicity we are likely to bring to it. The withdrawal of *Huebener* from production became an unwitting *cause célèbre.*

Third, there are times in *any* institutional setting when one must negotiate between the Scylla and Charybdis of individual autonomy versus group expectations while striding a razor's edge. Personally, I have not always sensed that need as quickly as I should have. It is not so much a question of virtue as of sagacity and having an agreeable nature, that willingness to defer to one's "betters" we call *sustaining.* Since (and partly as a result of) the production of *Huebener* and its aftermath, I have gained a far deeper understanding of the need to subordinate one's will to a greater purpose—and can readily be brought to do so if convinced of the inspiration and necessity of such deference.

In spite of our human failings, Latter-day Saint artists and writers *do* in fact have great potential to "bring to pass much righteousness" through our creativity when we are "anxiously engaged in a good cause." Through Joseph Smith, the Lord promised: "For the power is in them, wherein they are agents unto themselves. And inasmuch as men do good they shall in nowise lose their reward" (D&C 58:27–28). We can spiritually benefit from our efforts and from their deferential, sometimes delayed promotion even when the church itself does not always or immediately recognize or appreciate their potential and good intent.

For the Cast and Production Staff of *Huebener*

I wrote this "love note" to the first cast of Huebener *in 1976 on the eve of its premiere performances in BYU's Margetts Theatre, after realizing during the play's dress rehearsal that our fine actors, all too aware of their story's outcome, were already—inappropriately—mourning the protagonist's eventual death with their very first lines. The late Ivan Crosland, the play's marvelous director, agreed and urged the cast to lighten up. It made all the difference in what turned out to be a memorable "event." As a playwright, I will likely be remembered only for* Huebener, *but the play's startling success and general appeal prompted me to keep at it, turning out close to thirty scripts, including adaptations from the novels of Dostoevsky and other beloved authors.*

I HAVE LEARNED MANY WORTHWHILE THINGS from the rehearsals that have preceded our show's opening. In a technical sense, I have become increasingly aware of what I would call the need for dynamics in art. I think we have all discovered (or rediscovered) the need for these dynamics, not only in the course of the overall production and performance of a play, but also in the individual actor's interpretation of a role. They are not easy to grasp or to remember. That is one reason why a director is so needful. From his or her distance, the director can bring objectivity and perspective to a view of the show's overall effect that the actors and crew cannot. The director can more readily sense what is needed in terms of the show's rhythm and tempo, the counterpoint and synthesis of its multiple parts. Directors are as needful to the whole as conductors to an orchestra. When the latter call for more crescendo, more pause, or a quickened pace, the musicians readily respond, trusting the conductor's judgment, however unusual or arbitrary those instructions may strike them individually.

So it is with the stage director, except that the actor is his or her own instrument. This leaves a degree of autonomy and a range of personal interpretation which, with the director's concurrence, the actor must nevertheless creatively fulfill as a unique contribution. In doing so, utmost imagination, sensitivity, good judgment, and self-discipline are called for.

There is a tendency, I believe, for all of us—writer as well as actors—to conceive our characters too simplistically and one-dimensionally. We try to establish their basic attitude and emotion, then portray these as faithfully (hence as literally and straightforwardly) as we are able. But in doing so, we often discover that our performance, for all its conscientiousness, is monotonous and unconvincing. This is because our reading of characters and how they would most likely present themselves to others is, as it turns out, anything but lifelike.

In real life, we tend to represent ourselves in ways that conceal the true state of our feelings. Because of the disparity in our minds between how we actually feel and how we *ought* to feel or relate to someone else, we bluff, role-play, put up facades, even deceive ourselves and do so with good intentions. These contradictions in mood and consequent manifold levels of feeling and expression provide the actor with a rich and varied source of expression. But they have to be analyzed and justified. Hence the value of what Stanislavsky called "subtext," which would at times dictate that the actor project the very opposite of what the words themselves convey. Somehow, Chekhov's dialogue makes these personal contradictions so apparent, so innate, that actors ignore them only at their peril. Ever since Stanislavsky, we have tended to respect such nuances in Chekhov—and been mesmerized by them. But they are as applicable to all human beings and to any playwright's characters. That is in fact what gave Chekhov's characters the power to so mesmerize us—because we could so readily identify with them, because they are so universal.

Another important but easy-to-overlook principle is that just as effective comedians are deadly serious about themselves and the characters they portray, so the actors playing tragedy should rarely feel sorry for themselves or take themselves as seriously as their situation warrants. They should be fairly oblivious to their story's tragic outcome. They need to be cheerful, hopeful, optimistic, even while heading on a collision course—or else they would in most cases do more to avert their impending catastrophe. The contrast between their confident naiveté and what the audience may anticipate makes their plight all the more poignant, the irony of their predicament all the more delicious.

These principles describe, I believe, how we are as real people much of the time. We are anything but consistent, so it is hardly a mistake for a character at one point to express one thought or intention and at another its opposite. To do so will make that character seem all the more fully fleshed, all the more *real*. It is also likely that the more truly dramatic and fraught with inner conflict a character may be, the less frequently his or her true feelings will tend to surface. They will appear only sporadically, unintentionally, and—in all they *haven't* disclosed, all that *hasn't* been said—represent only the tip of an iceberg. The actor must trust the audience to recognize those few illuminating clues—which will be all the more powerful and revealing because they haven't been overdone. This is also an excellent way to "tease" one's audience by keeping its members in suspense about how a given character will ultimately assert himself or herself.

This leads to another principle that is hard for actors always to apply: the principle of understatement, by which we can often much more forcefully convey an intense emotion using *less* movement, *less* gesture, *less* volume, *less* intonation. There is probably no more intense mode of vocal expression than a hushed monotone—except silence itself. And yet there are those moments when, to realize the needed dynamics and be more lifelike, an opposite mode is called for. Select lines must be gushed, intoned, delivered with direct and unmistakable passion. Voices must crack and quaver. Screams must be prolonged. Here the director, again, is in the best position to know what will and won't work.

Which leads me to say something about Brother Crosland. Any director who takes on the production of a new play and agrees to work face-to-face with the playwright assumes a formidable burden (as does the cast)—including the possibility of considerable conflict and additional personal strain. Brother Crosland is unusually amenable to such risk taking and prospective torture. He is not only an outstandingly conscientious and sensitive director, so instinctively right about those dynamic principles I've alluded to, but also an exceptionally gracious, thoughtful, and kindly disposed human being. I don't believe he has raised his voice once during any of our rehearsals. But that is strength, not weakness. With his patient, encouraging, confident smile, he wins our allegiance far more readily than he could ever demand it with ultimatums, impatience, or a hot temper. Even more miraculous: he and I have, as he himself has attested, been in almost total agreement about the many specifics we have called to your attention. I don't really know why that is. I didn't expect it. But it is a most fortunate circumstance—for all of us and for the production. He needn't have been so magnanimous in inviting me to comment as extensively as he has. I didn't expect that either. He is just that fine and open a man. He exemplifies qualities almost unheard of in the stereotypically temperamental, egotistical artist. The harmony we have all consequently enjoyed together—and the unusual good feeling—are what at all times ought to typify our relations with one another as Latter-day Saints, even in an artistic enterprise, but too seldom do. I think you realize, as I do, just how lucky we are to have Ivan as the director of this production. He has already invested so much extra in it that he didn't need to.

But so have you. I can't remember ever working with so dedicated or talented a cast and production staff, particularly one so large. I am, despite my many minute criticisms, still amazed at how readily you learned your lines and how you have all grown so impressively in your roles. You still need to improve and perfect, but I know how intent you still are in doing so and am most grateful. As a group, you have deeply endeared yourselves to me, and I only hope that my presence and my comments have not too much intimidated or annoyed you. If they have, I apologize. I have great faith in what you will make of this show before our live audiences, and I do encourage you never to cease exploring your characters or remaining open to the sudden inspiration that will keep your performances fresh and lead to those electric moments of charged, authentic emotion we felt a week ago in the encounter between Helmuth and Zoellner and in the cell scene with Emma, and that Brother Crosland and I have for some time consistently experienced during the trial and execution. On those occasions, I have been brought close to weeping, and I'm sure your audiences will be also.

I hope the performances will give you that kind of personal satisfaction as you work your magic upon your audiences and that, in the aftermath, you will benefit from the same insight and improved skill this experience has afforded me. I also hope the reviews will give you your due—as the show's advance publicity, fine and extensive as it was, did not. I know you believe, as I do, that *Huebener* is more than just another play—not because of its writing, but because of the people and the important principles it addresses. I think any calls for "Author!" on the opening night would be a sacrilege. The only ones we should honor are the teenage boy who gave his life, thus enabling his story to inspire the rest of us, and those whose lives in turn influenced him: the Prophet Joseph Smith and the Savior. I also want to assure you that your first-night audience will be a very special one that will be rooting for you all the way, an audience that will be critical but also badly want you to inspire and move them. These include, as you know, the real Schnibbe and Wobbe, as well, we hope, as Huebener's two stepbrothers and the mission president, Brother Wunderlich, who prepared and argued the appeal that led to Huebener's posthumous reinstatement as a church member.

Thanks, each of you, for your special contribution, of which I am not unmindful.

(At the end of the play's first performance and again on the anniversary date of Huebener's execution, the stage was darkened; then spotlights disclosed two middle-aged men standing at the center of the stage—the real Karl-Heinz Schnibbe and Rudi Wobbe. A third spotlight illuminated the empty space between them, commemorating their long-absent boyhood friend, Helmuth Huebener.)

The Gospel of John as Literature

Whether as a poem or a literary narrative, the Gospel of John wins the Booker or the National Book Award, hands down. How specially inspired were the New Testament's compilers when they chose to settle for more than a single account of the Savior's life, death, and resurrection. How particularly forceful John's masterfully crafted version—itself a strong witness to the inspiring role of artful expression in chronicling and testifying to sacred events. I express my gratitude for the influence of BYU faculty members C. Wilfred Griggs and John F. Hall on my understanding of the scriptures in general and the Gospel of John in particular.[1]

If I were challenged to name my favorite literary work, my thoughts would quite naturally turn to those remarkable novels by Russian authors—Dostoevsky's *The Brothers Karamazov*, Tolstoy's *Anna Karenina*, or Pasternak's *Doctor Zhivago*—which, in my opinion, have no equal and even rank among the world's semisacred books. If pressed to choose among them, I would probably settle for *The Brothers Karamazov*, whose epigraph, incidentally, is from the Gospel of John.

Each in his or her unique way, our greatest writers and the lives they depict cry out, often tragically, for a mediating, comforting, inspiring voice that might assure us the universe is not cruelly indifferent to our circumstances and our ultimate fate. Intentionally or not, their works point to the Savior. But there are other writings from which his very voice calls to us. (See D&C 18:34–36.) These of course are the scriptures. And if I were cast upon a desert island with only one book to sustain me for the rest of my days, I would want that book to be the Gospel of John. I would choose it because, beyond any other work I know, it is both a literary and a spiritual masterpiece, as lovely and compelling as any Sophoclean tragedy or the verse of our greatest poets, yet also a profound testimony to the divine mission of Jesus Christ.

The poetry of the Gospel of John

Viewing the Gospel of John aesthetically, we can say first of all that it is richly poetic, yet at the same time the simplest in its vocabulary of all the books of the New Testament. It is also a slim book. (With some embarrassment, I note that my commentary is easily as long as the book itself.) John tells us in his very last verse, "And there are also many other things which Jesus did, the which, if they should be written every one, I suppose that even the world itself could not contain the books that should be written" (21:25). If John knew more, why didn't he give us more? Did his stylus run dry? Did he lack the means to buy more ink and parchment? Possibly. But John's style, we are told, was essentially gnostic, meaning that he wished in cryptic fashion to allude to the gospel's deep mysteries without betraying their essence to the unreceptive or as yet uninitiated. These are the hallmarks of poetry too: brevity, compression of meaning, and obliqueness or indirection. So much is nevertheless given—intimated between the lines or in the form of pithy clues that, if we are sufficiently thoughtful and sensitive, conjure a wealth of feelings and associations. We are so engaged—given so much space to thinkingly, feelingly react—precisely because the text is so understated. Less is truly more.

If this work were not scripture, I'd be wary of its sway on me. Its precepts strike with the force of mathematical axioms. They are like compelling music, whose ethereal harmony and pure pitches convey distilled intimations of eternal truth and divine love. Like the very greatest verse or music, this gospel provokes a sense of awe, a tearfulness, a quiet euphoria, a ready intimacy with its subject, a "peak experience" (to borrow a term from the psychologist Abraham Maslow), a spiritual "high" or "fix." It makes us feel the way we sometimes feel in the presence of a masterpiece or in very holy places. Those who have beheld Michelangelo's *David* at the Accademia Gallery in Florence or visited the Van Gogh Museum in Amsterdam or traveled to Christ's alleged tomb in Jerusalem or the Sacred Grove in New York know what I mean.

The Gospel of John is also basically lyric. Like the most ecstatic love poem, it celebrates the goodness, truth, beauty, and above all the love of God for his principal creations, you and me: "For God so loved the world, that he gave his only begotten Son, that whosoever believeth in him should not perish, but have everlasting life" (3:16). The author openly acknowledges the forces of darkness and destruction, and the work's protagonist entertains no illusions regarding the threat they pose: "If I had not done among them the works which none other man did, they had not had sin: but now have they both seen and hated both me and my Father" (15:24). But unlike the great tragedies or the finest realistic novels, the Gospel of John does not brood about the human condition. Nor does it condemn: "I judge no man" (8:15), Christ declares. And to the woman taken in adultery: "Neither do I condemn thee: go, and sin no more" (8:11). John earlier confirms this divine restraint by telling us, "For God sent not his Son into the world to condemn the world; but that the world through him might be saved" (3:17). Instead, the Savior affirms—without the slightest reservation—"I love the Father" (14:31) and "the Father loveth the Son" (5:20). Then he prays that his disciples may know the same love: "that the love wherewith thou hast loved me may be in them" (17:26). The Gospel of John is in this sense the ultimate love lyric: a paean of universal affinity like no other. It affirms the Lord's full, unqualified acceptance of us all—something many a Christian has a hard time understanding, particularly about himself or herself.

Understanding the Son of God through metaphor

Where his immediate hearers are concerned, perhaps the chief mystery in the Gospel of John is the Lord's identity as the Son of God, the true Messiah and Savior of this world. It is this to which the book's striking metaphors largely have reference. And how many there are—how rich their imagery. John begins by enigmatically referring to Christ as "the Word" (1:1), alluding, as the New Testament rarely does, to the Savior's premortal existence and his role as Creator. (In Greek the term is *logos,* which bears an array of further associations, not the least of which are the concepts of *order* and also *intelligence*.) Then, in one of the book's most pregnant and recurring images, John calls the Savior "the true Light, which lighteth every man that cometh into the world"

(1:9). How marvelously this metaphor ties in with all the connotations of vision or lack of it that later arise as Christ heals the blind man. The double entendre and the greater figurative significance of the following lines—so reminiscent of what Sophocles does with the very same image in *Oedipus Rex*—require no further comment, though they appear to be totally lost on the learned Pharisees. The blind man's parents, in their effort not to be implicated by the disapproving officials, also fail, it seems, to recognize the spiritual import and the tremendous irony in their very own words: "We know that this is our son, and that he was born blind: But by what means he now seeth, we know not; or who hath opened his eyes, we know not" (9:20–21). In powerful though perhaps unwitting testimony, the blind man himself provides the key:

> Then again called they the man that was blind, and said unto him, Give God the praise: we know that this man is a sinner.
>
> He answered and said, Whether he be a sinner or no, I know not: one thing I know, that, whereas I was blind, now I see.
>
> Then said they to him again, What did he to thee? how opened he thine eyes?
>
> He answered them, I have told you already, and ye did not hear. (9:24–27)

If we question what is ultimately being conveyed by this intricate play of words, Christ lays the issue to rest just verses later:

> And Jesus said, For judgment I am come into this world, that they which see not might see; and that they which see might be made blind.
>
> And some of the Pharisees which were with him heard these words, and said unto him, Are we blind also?
>
> Jesus said unto them, If ye were blind, ye should have no sin: but now ye say, We see; therefore your sin remaineth. (9:39–41)

Across the broad spectrum of Indo-European languages, incidentally, there is a close correlation between the basic roots for "to see" and "to know." We see this in the Slavic *videti* (to see) and *vedeti* (to know). (*Bear* in Russian is *medved*, the "honey-knower.") In Sanskrit we have the oldest sacred texts, the *vedas,* and the science of wisdom, *vedanta,* with obviously the same root. For a fuller elucidation of this central image of light and vision in relation to Christ and the spirit of truth, reread the remarkable vision in Doctrine and Covenants 88—equally poetic in its expression.

Other metaphors in the Gospel of John are similarly profound in what they tell us about Christ and his role in the destiny of all humanity. In chapter 1 and many times thereafter, the Savior refers to himself as "the Son of Man." (Even in 9:35, where the King James Version reads "the Son of God," the Greek has "the Son of Man.") In chapter 2, Christ refers to his body as a "temple" (2:19, 21), inviting profound reflection upon this striking notion that Christ's body and ours are in fact temples of the Spirit. In chapter 3, he both is "the bridegroom" (3:29) and also describes himself as the analogue of the brass serpent that Moses raised to preserve his people in the wilderness (3:14). In the dialogue with the Samaritan woman, he is the source of "water springing up into everlasting life" (4:14); when teaching in the synagogue in Capernaum, he is the "living bread" (see 6:32, 35, 51).

As in other literary masterpieces, we encounter leitmotifs that unite images, lines, and the work itself with other texts. The symbolic ties to desert manna, to the unleavened bread of the Passover, and to the emblems of the sacrament are apparent. And there are further remarkable associations with this single image—the staff of life. As British journalist and religious commentator Malcolm Muggeridge suggests, "Bread, in his estimation, was to the body what the truth he proclaimed was to the soul. It had its own sanctity, and just for that reason could not be procured, as the Devil proposed, miraculously from stones."[2]

Consider this: after partaking of the fruit of the tree of knowledge of good and evil, Adam and Eve were thereafter prevented from partaking of the fruit of the tree of life (see Moses 4:31), at least while in a mortal, sinful state. The tree of Lehi's vision, which is finally reached only by those who enduringly hold to the iron rod, is in turn clearly interpreted as symbolic of "the love of God" (1 Nephi 11:22), while the tree of faith described by Alma (or are they all to some extent the same tree?) is described as bearing a fruit, for those whose faith sufficiently matures, that is "sweet above all that is sweet" and "white above all that is white" (Alma 32:42)—a fruit that fully fills and nourishes but that is accessible only when we satisfy certain conditions. I sense a further correspondence between the constraints placed on our access to the precious fruit of these several trees and the admonition that when we partake of the emblems of the atonement unworthily, we eat and drink "damnation" to our souls (see 1 Corinthians 11:29; 3 Nephi 18:29). Similarly, the beverage we drink in the sacrament as much evokes the Savior's reference to himself as the source of "living water" as it does the sacrificial shedding of his blood. What a deftly woven network of allusions and cross-references! How compact and seemingly endless the pattern of its imagery.

There are other metaphors I can barely touch upon. BYU humanities professor George Tate has pointed out that for him, "the feature that most distinguishes John from the other gospels is the overt, spoken comparisons Christ makes between himself and details of the exodus."[3] This in turn subtly identifies Christ as the very Old Testament Jehovah and Hebrew Messiah (see 3 Nephi 15:9). One such image appears in the announcement of John the Baptist, "Behold the Lamb of God" (1:29), with its obvious allusion to the unblemished lamb prescribed for sacrifice during the Passover. Challenged by the Pharisees, Jesus in fact refers to himself with one of the titles of the Old Testament Jehovah, "I am" (8:58; see Exodus 3:14). (I doubt that many Christians perceive all that this response implies about the overarching role of Christ in the history of humanity.) With equal import, Christ refers to himself in chapter 14 as "the way, the truth, and the life" (14:6), while in chapter 10 he is the "door" to the sheepfold (10:9) and also the "good shepherd" (10:11), pointing to a further scriptural antecedent in the Twenty-third Psalm. In chapter 11 he is "the resurrection, and the life" (11:25), and in chapter 15 "the true vine" of which we are the "branches," fruitful or otherwise (15:1–6).

An insightful discourse by Jeffrey R. Holland (not yet an apostle at the time of its writing) suggests a further reason for the use of such metaphors grounded in the familiar experiences of the Savior's listeners:

> They . . . needed the uncommon invitation commonly extended to lift up their eyes to higher purposes. . . .
>
> . . . Jesus spoke of TEMPLES and the people thought he spoke of temples. . . . He spoke of BREAD and the people thought he spoke of bread. . . . These were not merely parables in the

> allegorical sense. . . . They were in every case an invitation to "lift up your eyes," to see "heavenly things." . . . They are also repeated manifestations of his willingness to meet people on their own terms, however limited that understanding, and there lead them on to higher ground.[4]

The Gospel of John as drama

I have been writing of the Gospel of John as I might of a poem. Like the other three Gospels, it is also a drama with pathetic if not starkly tragic overtones in the depiction of its hero's earthly demise. The Savior's betrayal, arrest, crucifixion, and resolve to submit to the most painful of deaths are, at this point of his story and as pure plot, as nobly tragic as anything any dramatic hero ever had to face. And in the fact that Christ's predicament is occasioned by his own sense of principle and concern for others, there is a decidedly greater affinity with tragic heroines such as Antigone or Joan of Arc than with the victims of hubris and temperamental excess found in most Greek and Shakespearean tragedies.

The Gospel of John is also remarkable for the skill with which it characterizes various supernumeraries through dialogue. Think of the blind man's gutless parents, so unwilling to acknowledge the miracle of their son's healing and its obvious source. They must have been highly respectable citizens who valued their reputation above everything else. How vividly they contrast to the guileless Samaritan woman who, though she had lived with many men, hides nothing, readily acknowledging, "Sir, I perceive that thou art a prophet" (4:19). She then approaches her own people, urging them to "come, see a man, which told me all things that ever I did: is not this the Christ?" (4:29). The prevailing theme of these terse dialogues is, again, the discovery of who Jesus really is. These encounters embody all the tension and surprise, all the suspense and reversal of expectation of Sophocles's "recognition scenes" that Aristotle commended to dramatists in the *Poetics*. Consider three by now familiar episodes—each, in the unawareness and incredulity of its personae ("Who is this man?"), a gem of dramatic suspense. From the encounter with the woman of Samaria:

> If thou knewest the gift of God, and who it is that saith to thee, Give me to drink; thou wouldest have asked of him, and he would have given thee living water.
>
> The woman saith unto him, Sir, thou hast nothing to draw with, and the well is deep: from whence then hast thou that living water?
>
> Art thou greater than our father Jacob, which gave us the well, and drank thereof himself, and his children, and his cattle?
>
> Jesus answered and said unto her, Whosoever drinketh of this water shall thirst again:
>
> But whosoever drinketh of the water that I shall give him shall never thirst. . . .
>
> The woman saith unto him, I know that Messias cometh, which is called Christ: when he is come, he will tell us all things.
>
> Jesus saith unto her, I that speak unto thee am he. (4:10–14, 25–26)

After all the indirection and verbal parrying, that matter-of-fact last line takes my breath away, as it must have the woman's. It reminds me of perhaps the most compelling testimony recorded in modern times: again, terse, direct, unqualified, and unpretentious—straight reportage without need for the slightest speculation:

> And now, after the many testimonies which have been given of him, this is the testimony, last of all, which we give of him: That he lives!
>
> For we saw him, even on the right hand of God. (D&C 76:22–23)

There is a similar climactic directness in Jesus's words to the blind man:

> Jesus heard that they had cast him out; and when he had found him, he said unto him, Dost thou believe on the Son of God?
>
> He answered and said, Who is he, Lord, that I might believe on him?
>
> And Jesus said unto him, Thou hast both seen him, and it is he that talketh with thee. (9:35–37)

The voice of Jesus

Who was the reporter who stood by and took down these exact words? I cannot say. But as I read such passages, it is the Master's voice I hear in or between such lines. I'm reminded of something I once heard the great literary scholar René Wellek say about the Christ of the Gospels to a group of "sophisticated" Yale graduate students as we examined Dostoevsky's memorable legend of the Grand Inquisitor: "No man could ever duplicate that voice or that personality." Malcolm Muggeridge made a similar observation:

> The gospels convey no impression of how he spoke, the timbre of his voice, whether he used gestures and was given to declamation, though in their reports of what he said the style of his utterances is unmistakable. This was sharp, incisive, pungent, often ironic and never rhetorical. He was clearly very observant, both of nature and of men; very aware of how society worked, of the forces of cupidity and aggressiveness which shaped human behavior. Hence his great gift for vivid imagery, and for telling a story; his parables are little masterpieces of narration, and, like the best of Tolstoy's short stories . . . easily comprehensible at all levels of understanding. As a communicator pure and simple, I should say that Jesus was supremely effective—this quite apart from his special role and mission in the world. . . .
>
> . . . No one can fail to be aware of the teller; behind the parables one senses a perceptive, often ironic, brilliantly creative mind. Unmistakably, they are the work of an artist rather than of a thinker, or, in the narrower meaning of the word, moralist.[5]

Part of that voice's force and potency come from all the Savior says or hints at in so few words. Dostoevsky uncannily captured this quality in the Grand Inquisitor scene in *The Brothers Karamazov*, during which a bitter and condemning Spanish priest in medieval Seville harangues his prisoner in a pages-long monologue, then, when he stops, receives the most eloquent and irrefutable response imaginable: not a single word but a kiss of understanding, forgiveness, and magnanimous compassion from the condemned prisoner for the man who has decreed his imminent destruction in the fires of the auto-da-fé. In a letter he wrote while in Siberian exile, Dostoevsky, like Wellek, commented on the singularity of the Savior's voice as he had encountered it in the scriptures:

> I believe that there is nothing lovelier, deeper, more sympathetic, more rational, more manly, and more perfect than the Saviour; I say to myself with jealous love that not only is there no one else like Him, but that there could be no one. I would even say more: If anyone could prove to me that Christ is outside the truth, and if the truth really did exclude Christ, I should prefer to stay with Christ and not with truth.[6]

That same voice is taut, suspenseful, intrinsically dramatic in its reply to the Pharisees as recorded by John:

> Your father Abraham rejoiced to see my day: and he saw it, and was glad. Then said the Jews unto him, Thou art not yet fifty years old, and hast thou seen Abraham? Jesus said unto them, Verily, verily, I say unto you, Before Abraham was, I am. (8:56–58)

This took the Pharisees' breath away also—enough for them to pick up stones and attempt to take his life right then and there.

Jesus engages in similar repartee, deftly placing the burden of self-justification upon his accusers, even when he is seized by the authorities: "Jesus therefore, knowing all things that should come upon him, went forth, and said unto them, Whom seek ye? They answered him, Jesus of Nazareth. Jesus saith unto them, I am he" (18:4–5). Again before Caiaphas (this in the account by Matthew), in response to the high priest's demand, "Tell us whether thou be the Christ, the Son of God": "Thou hast said" (Matthew 26:63–64). And yet again before Pilate: "Pilate therefore said unto him, Art thou a king then? Jesus answered, Thou sayest that I am a king" (John 18:37). Note with what further dramatic irony—far surpassing even the comprehension of its instigator, Pilate—a sign to that effect is placed on the cross above Christ's head, unwittingly acknowledging over the objection of his enemies his just claim to that title. Similarly the scarlet robe, crown of thorns, and reed scepter with which the Roman soldiers adorn him. Here we see the kind of ironic confusion of mock appearances with reality that we have come to expect in the work of certain twentieth-century absurdist playwrights.

Other textual effects

In examining the text's overall narrative structure, we encounter another feature in common with the best dramatic scripts. Episodic as are all the Gospels, we reach a point in John where the pace of events nevertheless radically changes. In a scene whose action so retards that time seems to stand still—as it does during Shakespeare's soliloquies, certain operatic arias, and intimate and usually climactic cinematic moments when the camera slowly moves to a long, sustained close-up—the Gospel of John concentrates on the Savior's discourse to the apostles just prior to his arrest. This sermon, which in its significance rivals and beautifully complements that delivered on the mount in the Gospel of Matthew, extends over five chapters and treats subjects not dealt with in any other account: the sending of the Comforter and with him the Lord's peace; the striking parable of the vine and the branches; the great high priestly prayer invoking divine unity and love; and, at the outset, what must be an especially sacred ordinance—the washing of the disciples' feet: a visible gesture fully articulate in all it teaches about the Savior's unsurpassed humility and love for others. There must be a reason why John, of all the evangelists, was privy to that occasion and alone recorded it.

Others could tell us far more about the nuances of the Gospel's original Greek. (One wonders what we may be missing because we can't have the Savior's words in Aramaic—or, for that matter, Nephi's in Reformed Egyptian.) It was exciting for me to learn that the root meaning of our word *deacon* is simply "servant," of *angel* "messenger," that the English word *pneumatic* derives from the Greek for "spirit," and *martyr* means "to witness." (What heroic associations the two concepts bring together: "witness" and "martyr.") As with all fine writing, the exact choice of words and their subtle connotations are important and sometimes crucial. Here's just one example: in a scripture familiar to all returned missionaries—"And this is life eternal, that they might know thee the only true God, and Jesus Christ, whom thou hast sent" (John 17:3)—the Greek form of the verb *know* is present subjunctive, which makes the recommended action, to "know" God, a process and an ongoing requirement rather than a single completed act. Thus salvation is *not* just a matter of instant conversion, but a process of enduring and ever renewing our acquaintance with the Lord until we draw our very last mortal breath.

Spiritual insight

As much as I value the literary qualities I have been discussing, it is the fundamental themes of the Gospel of John that finally persuade me to prefer it to any other text. Christ is characterized in chapter 1 with the attributes of "grace and truth" (1:14) in the King James Version. The Greek word for *grace* has a still broader range of significance: it also stands for divine or spiritual love. These two qualities, love and truth, sum up all the other virtues. Many verses in the Gospel of John affirm to what extent Christ taught them and was their exemplar: "This is my commandment, That ye love one another, as I have loved you" (15:12); "And ye shall know the truth, and the truth shall make you free" (8:32); "And for their sakes I sanctify myself, that they also might be sanctified through the truth" (17:19).

Time and time again, Christ also stresses his deference to the Father in all he says and does: "I can of mine own self do nothing: as I hear, I judge: and my judgment is just; because I seek not mine own will, but the will of the Father which hath sent me" (5:30); "He that speaketh of himself seeketh his own glory: but he that seeketh his glory that sent him, the same is true, and no unrighteousness is in him" (7:18). With special concern he gives us this touchstone to his own credentials and, by extension, ours too when we act in his name. Then there is that plea for unity in his great intercessory or high priestly prayer, which must be the spiritual high moment in this or any other Gospel. (How fittingly—and how ironically—it occurs just prior to the divisive and conspiratorial playing out of his betrayal, arrest, trial, and execution.)

A further important corollary to the Savior's plea "that they may be one, even as we are one" (17:22) is the sense of joyful fulfillment to which, along with deity, humanity is potentially heir: "that both he that soweth and he that reapeth may rejoice together" (4:36). Already in that pregnant first chapter, the evangelist asserts, "But as many as received him, to them gave he power to become the sons of God" (1:12). And elsewhere: "I ascend unto my Father, and your Father; and to my God, and your God" (20:17). It is clear from the foregoing not only that the Father and Son are distinct personages, but that we too are invited to partake of all they enjoy. Yet for saying so, we are viewed by many as spurious or even non-Christians.

There are profound implications in the Lord's striking term of self-address, so frequently invoked in this particular scripture: "the Son of Man." I find here an undeniable suggestion that God the Father is indeed a Man (though written with a capital "M"): a perfect Man. The further implication is surely that we, too, being men and women, are at least potentially heirs to the same divinity and perfection. This recurring thesis is, to my mind, the philosophical apotheosis of the Gospel of John, its greatest so-called "mystery." Sadly, the glorious import of this very clear teaching has over time been overlooked or even denied by the majority of readers, who must think so little of themselves that they are unwilling to believe what the Lord has told them about their own potentially divine nature—or live for its full realization.

The Savior's discourse on the Holy Spirit in the Gospel of John is surely the most extensive in all scripture. Lest we become impatient and weary when the Spirit seems to elude us, we should all ponder Christ's statement, "The wind bloweth where it listeth, and thou hearest the sound thereof, but canst not tell whence it cometh, and whither it goeth: so is every one that is born of the Spirit" (3:8). And we should keep in mind the various blessings that he has promised us, through that Spirit, if we keep his commandments: comfort, discernment of truth, enlightenment, remembrance, and peace that passeth all understanding (see 14:16–27).

In his comments on the man born blind, the Savior also gives us a very important answer that separates his doctrine from all the fatalistic or deterministic theologies and -isms of this world. When even his disciples wonder, "Master, who did sin, this man, or his parents, that he was born blind?" (9:2), the Savior's singular reply is, "Neither hath this man sinned, nor his parents: but that the works of God should be made manifest in him" (9:3). Still later he deferentially and self-effacingly reaffirms, "And whatsoever ye shall ask in my name, that will I do, that the Father may be glorified in the Son" (14:13).

On the surface, some of the Savior's statements seem terribly discriminating: "No man can come to me, except the Father which hath sent me draw him" (6:44); and "I pray not for the world, but for them which thou hast given me; for they are thine" (17:9). Calvin must have cherished these verses, but he failed to see in them that impersonal statement of natural law to which even the Lord is bound. Surely those who fail to qualify as the Lord's do so by their own choice. As another verse so forcefully puts it, "And this is the condemnation, that light is come into the world, and men loved darkness rather than light, because their deeds were evil. For every one that doeth evil hateth the light, neither cometh to the light, lest his deeds should be reproved" (3:19–20).

Finally, there is the Lord's sublime plea for our sanctification in his great prayer to the Father, which ties this scripture to the final verses of the Book of Mormon. What does it mean to be sanctified? Do we sufficiently ponder that expression? A key to how we must go about doing so is provided in another striking metaphor, again in John, in that very verse Dostoevsky chose as epigraph to his great masterpiece: "Verily, verily, I say unto you, Except a corn of wheat fall into the ground and die, it abideth alone: but if it die, it bringeth forth much fruit" (12:24).

The Savior's compassion

The compassion shown by Jesus in the Gospel of John represents yet another aspect of the Savior's personality that transcends mere words—one that ties this Gospel to both the Book of Mormon and the Pearl of Great Price. First, there is the incident in a vision, recorded in Jacob, in which "the Lord of the vineyard wept, and said unto the servant: What could I have done more for my vineyard?" (Jacob 5:41). After addressing the multitude on the American continent, the Savior "wept, and the multitude bare record of it, and he took their little children, one by one, and blessed them, and prayed unto the Father for them. And when he had done this he wept again" (3 Nephi 17:21–22). It is interesting that in the description of Christ's emotional state the account in 3 Nephi differs markedly from the accounts of his sermons in Matthew,

Mark, and Luke. If John had included an account of the Sermon on the Mount, I would expect it to resemble 3 Nephi in what makes that version so distinctive. Another account of the Lord's weeping occurs in chapter 7 of the book of Moses. Speaking with Enoch several millennia before his mortal descent upon the earth, the Lord declared, "Behold, I am God; Man of Holiness is my name; Man of Counsel is my name; and Endless and Eternal is my name, also" (Moses 7:35). And then:

> The God of Heaven looked upon the residue of the people, and he wept; and Enoch bore record of it, saying: How is it that the heavens weep, and shed forth their tears as the rain upon the mountains?
>
> . . . How is it that thou canst weep, seeing thou art holy, and from all eternity to all eternity? . . .
>
> The Lord said unto Enoch: Behold these thy brethren; they are the workmanship of mine own hands, and I gave unto them their knowledge, in the day I created them; and in the Garden of Eden, gave I unto man his agency;
>
> And unto thy brethren have I said, and also given commandment, that they should love one another, and that they should choose me, their Father; but behold, they are without affection, and they hate their own blood. (Moses 7:28–29, 32–33)

How profoundly this elucidates the reason why Christ would weep while blessing the children of the Nephites—sensing, despite their innocence, a like potential for enmity, contention, and consequent affliction. A few verses later, we are told that the Lord

> told Enoch all the doings of the children of men; wherefore Enoch knew, and looked upon their wickedness, and their misery, and wept and stretched forth his arms, and his heart swelled wide as eternity; and his bowels yearned; and all eternity shook. (Moses 7:41)

How aptly all of this pertains to Alma the Younger's elucidation of the atonement—"that his bowels may be filled with mercy, according to the flesh" (Alma 7:12)—and his father Alma the Elder's characterization of true disciples as "willing to mourn with those that mourn . . . and comfort those that stand in need of comfort" (Mosiah 18:9). Through the gift of compassionate tears, God enters the hearts of humans, and humanity in turn unites, in affinity and in purpose, with the divine.

The account in John of the Savior's reaction to Mary's grief prior to the raising of her brother Lazarus similarly underscores that profound compassion that finally, as much as all he ever said, endears him to us and persuades us that, with all our fallibility, he truly understands and still stands by us:

> When Jesus therefore saw her weeping, and the Jews also weeping which came with her, he groaned in the spirit, and was troubled,
>
> And said, Where have ye laid him? They said unto him, Lord, come and see.
>
> Jesus wept.
>
> Then said the Jews, Behold how he loved him! (11:33–36)

The Savior's tears, described so explicitly nowhere else in the New Testament, are the most sublime token of his matchless love. To my knowledge, there are no passages in the world's many other sacred writings that so poignantly convey God's unfathomed love for humankind, his constant other-directed tenderness and sensitivity, and, most moving of all, the grief occasioned by his paternal and brotherly compassion—so human, yet so divine.

At this point aesthetic principles may no longer apply. Nevertheless, in common with only the greatest literary, musical, and visual masterpieces, such scripture touches our hearts and has its way with us in a manner that critical analysis cannot fully account for but that cannot be forgotten and leaves us never again quite the same.

Notes

1. This essay was originally published in *BYU Studies* 28/3 (1988): 67–80.

2. Malcolm Muggeridge, *Jesus: The Man Who Lives* (New York: Harper & Row, 1975), 52, 55.

3. George Tate, "The Typology of the Exodus Pattern in the Book of Mormon," in *Literature of Belief,* ed. Neal E. Lambert (Provo, UT: Religious Studies Center, Brigham Young University, 1981), 256.

4. Jeffrey R. Holland, "Lift Up Your Eyes," *Ensign*, July 1983, 12–13.

5. Muggeridge, *Jesus,* 43–44, 64.

6. F. M. Dostoevsky to Mme N. D. Fonvisin, Omsk, March 1854, in *Letters of Fyodor Michailovitch Dostoevsky to His Family and Friends,* trans. Ethel Colburn Mayne (New York: Horizon Press, 1961), 71.

The Image of Christ in Russian Literature

This essay starts by making a case for Dostoevsky's seminal role as a Christian writer—the creator, I contend, of literature's most full-blown "Christ figure." It also traces the spate of writers who followed in his wake and vein, especially (and perhaps surprisingly) during twentieth-century communism's heavy-handed suppression of such religious expression. I don't recall where I originally presented it—possibly at a Slavic literature section of the Rocky Mountain Modern Language Association. It was clearly written before Sinyavsky was released from prison and allowed to emigrate and before Solzhenitsyn was deported to the West in the early 1970s and has now been updated somewhat for this collection. Of possible incidental interest, I once had a private interview with Soviet author Vladimir Tendryakov in Moscow. Before he became a noted author of atheistic fiction, Tendryakov had been an ardent believer. His ethical critique of cowardly, self-serving fellow citizens struck me as not unlike that of his Christian contemporary, Solzhenitsyn. I believe I was the first American he had ever met or spoken to.

The image of Christ and the personality of Jesus have long informed the moral viewpoint of Russian literature and inspired its positive heroes. In this regard, Tolstoy's later protagonists—the contrite ex-philanderer Nekhlyudov in *Resurrection* and the saintlike characters of his several short parables—are no exception. However, a companion trend—less representational, more imaginative, even grotesque, and often concerned with subconscious motives and the theme of human evil—also frequently invokes not only the Christlike but Christ himself in a nevertheless moving contemporary setting. This tendency, profoundly introduced by Fyodor Dostoevsky, is surprisingly revived and gains momentum after the communist revolution and persists into the final decades of Soviet writing. By comparison with other national literatures, the number of such instances is impressive, suggesting to what extent the life of Christ has—despite over a half century of antireligious indoctrination—impressed the Russian national consciousness with that life's reality and intrinsic drama. For this, we must in part credit the religious idealism transmitted by a thousand years of Russian Orthodoxy, an influence that is obviously still felt.

The Dostoevskian archetype

Upon his return from exile and by then a devout Slavophile conservative, Dostoevsky first conjured a Christlike character in *Crime and Punishment*: the young girl Sonya, whose very name suggests the Byzantine Saint Sophia, a personification of divine wisdom. True to his taste for paradox, Dostoevsky makes of this paragon of spirituality and Christian conscience a nonetheless fallen woman.

Despite certain fundamental differences, Sonya's symbolic association with Jesus is nonetheless unmistakable. As literary critic George Steiner observes, Sonya "herself associates the skeptical blindness of the Jews with that of the hero and in a profoundly moving ambiguity links the image of the dead Lazarus to that of the murdered Lizaveta. Raskolnikov's spiritual resurrection foreshadows the ultimate resurrection of the dead."[1]

Subsequent novels by Dostoevsky deal even more directly and provocatively with the figure of deity. The recently published notebooks to these novels evidence the enigmatic evolution the divine personage undergoes in Dostoevsky's thought. Readers might not otherwise imagine that *The Idiot*'s protagonist—the clairvoyant, guileless, Quixote-like Prince Myshkin—was originally conceived as a benign and merciful alter aspect of the demonlike Stavrogin, whose amoral villainy is well symbolized by the title of Dostoevsky's next novel, *The Possessed* (literally, *The Devils*), for which Stavrogin in turn serves as the focal center. Earlier versions of *The Idiot* reveal a Myshkin whose behavior vacillates between superhuman benevolence and the outright diabolical. In *The Idiot*'s final form, this duality is resolved by providing Myshkin with another contrasting alter ego, Rogozhin, whose carnality and materialism lead to the heroine Nastasya Filippovna's ruin and violent death.

There can be no doubt that Dostoevsky envisioned both Myshkin and Stavrogin as approximations of Jesus. The symbolism of certain associated events is all too clear. For example, in a crucial subplot narrated toward the beginning of *The Idiot*, we learn that while recovering from a nervous collapse at a Swiss sanitarium, the "idiot" Myshkin had befriended and reconciled to her peers a previously disgraced young girl whose name is, significantly, Mary. Other allusions follow: to the donkey that brought Christ to Jerusalem (in Myshkin's case the donkey he observes when first traveling to Switzerland); Myshkin's later comparison of Nastasya to the face in an icon; his exchange of crosses with Rogozhin; Rogozhin's denunciation of Myshkin's other rival, Ganya, as a Judas (in essence, Ganya "sells" his claim to Nastasya for Rogozhin's money); Myshkin's meek submission when Ganya slaps his face; his title of prince; and even his designation as an "idiot," implying not so much imbecility as holiness in Russian lore—all of which further substantiate the archetypal divinity for which Myshkin figuratively stands.

Central to Dostoevsky's sublime spirituality and indicative of his profound grasp of Christian ethics are the parables that on one occasion Myshkin relates to Rogozhin:

> "As to faith, I had four different encounters in two days last week. In the morning I was traveling on one of our new railways, and I talked for some hours with a man I met in the train. I had heard a great deal about him before and, incidentally, that he was an atheist. He really is a very learned man, and I was glad of the opportunity of talking to a real scholar. He is, moreover, an exceedingly well-bred person, and he talked to me as though I were his equal in knowledge and ideas. He doesn't believe in God. One thing struck me, though: he didn't seem to be talking about that at all the whole time, and this struck me particularly because before, too, whenever I met unbelievers and however many of their books I read, I could not help feeling that they were not talking or writing

about that at all, though they may appear to do so. I told him this at the time, but I'm afraid I did not or could not express myself clearly enough, for he did not understand what I was talking about. The same evening I stopped for the night at a provincial hotel where a murder had been committed the night before, so that everybody was talking about it when I arrived. Two peasants, middle-aged men who had known each other for years—two old friends, in fact—had had tea and engaged a small room in which they were to spend the night. They were not drunk, but one of them noticed that the other was wearing a silver watch on a yellow bead chain, which apparently he had not seen on him before. Now, that man was not a thief. He was, in fact, an honest man and, as peasants go, far from poor. But he liked that watch so much and was so tempted by it that at last he could not restrain himself: he took out his knife, and when his friend turned his back to him, went up cautiously to him from behind, took aim, raised his eyes to heaven, crossed himself and, uttering a silent, agonizing prayer, 'O Lord, forgive me for Christ's sake!'—cut his friend's throat at one stroke, like a sheep, and took his watch. . . .

"In the morning I went for a stroll round the town. . . . There I saw a drunken soldier staggering about the wooden pavement and looking completely bedraggled. He came up to me. 'Won't you buy a silver cross, sir? I'll let you have it for twenty copecks. It's a silver one, sir.' I saw a cross on a filthy blue ribbon, which he had evidently just taken off, but it was really made of tin, as one could see at a glance, a very big, octagonal cross of a regular Byzantine pattern. I took out a twenty-copeck piece and gave it to him, and at once put the cross round my neck—and I could see from his face how pleased he was to have cheated a foolish gentleman, and he went off immediately to spend his money on drink—there could be no doubt about that! . . . So I walked away, thinking, 'I mustn't be too quick to condemn a man who has sold his Christ. Only God knows what is locked away in these weak and drunken hearts.' An hour later, on my way back to the hotel, I came upon a peasant woman with a newborn baby. She was quite a young woman, and the baby was about six weeks old. The baby smiled at her for the first time since its birth. I saw her suddenly crossing herself with deep devotion.

> 'What are you doing that for, my dear?' I said. . . . 'Well, sir,' she said, 'just as a mother rejoices seeing her baby's first smile, so does God rejoice every time he beholds from above a sinner kneeling down before Him to say his prayers with all his heart.' This was what a simple woman said to me, almost in those words—a thought so profound, so subtle, and so truly religious, in which the whole essence of Christianity is expressed, that is to say, the whole conception of God as our Father and of God's rejoicing in man, like a father rejoicing in his own child—the fundamental idea of Christianity!"[2]

In his study, *Dostoevsky: The Major Fiction*, Edward Wasiolek comments on these anecdotes as follows:

> The Prince's conception of the essence of religion is paradoxically contained in the gesture of a murderer, the words of an ignorant peasant woman, and in his own attitude toward a thief. The peasant is weak and cannot resist temptation, but he knows that he is doing wrong. In knowing he is sinning, he acknowledges God. It is not the act as such, but the movement of the heart toward God that defined the religious value of a man. Similarly, the first movement of the Prince's heart had been toward judgement of the solder, but he refrains from doing so. How can the Prince—or any man, Dostoevsky implies—know what lies behind the motive to deceive? How can anyone, except God, know the infinity of each man's soul? Prince Myshkin refrains from an act of judgement, for an act of judgement is an act of will and an arrogation of God's right. To judge is to lose one's faith in God. The essence of religion lies not in the act—not in the crime or the statement or atheism, or in the act of deception—but in the movement of the heart and soul toward God or in the free act of faith in which the soul turns its face from the self toward God. This is why Myshkin is so delighted by the words of the peasant woman. She sees correctly the essence of religion in man's face turned to God, as the baby's is turned to its parent.[3]

Myshkin's treatment of others is, however, his most benevolent, most Christlike attribute. As Wasiolek points out, "The Prince pays for the hurt that is visited on him by accepting it and suffering it, and by suffering it he breaks the vicious circle of hurting and being hurt, and by breaking the circle, he effects changes in others."[4] He thus fills the role of the kenotic or suffering, humiliated Christ so traditional to Russian Orthodoxy. The reader will look long and hard in all literature to find a comparable example of such guilelessness and forgiving.

Critics agree that except for his encounter with the children in Switzerland, Myshkin's positive influence is short-lived. He never permanently transforms but only tragically frustrates the sinners who surround him. But his "failure" in this respect underscores the way humans have so fully rejected Christ's gospel and denied its influence in their lives. Myshkin's return to the Swiss sanitarium at story's end may in turn fittingly suggest the retirement of Christ and his apostles to more celestial spheres after the world did them so much violence. In Myshkin's case, the violence is Rogozhin's murder of Nastasya—who symbolically ties these two so opposite men together:

> All night the Prince and Rogozhin lie by the side of the white figure, and in the morning when Rogozhin begins to scream and laugh, the Prince smooths his hair and cheeks, as a final gesture in his attempt to soothe the hurt and to take it upon himself. The Prince is a failure as Christ was a failure, helpless to check the hurt that we do to each other, but ready to take it upon himself and by his own faith to give all an image of the best of themselves. When critics charge him with being a failure, they seek what is dramatically unbelievable and morally impossible. The Prince cannot change the universe, but a universe of Myshkins might. The Prince is a success because for a moment he is able to kindle the faith in others of a truer image of themselves; for a few minutes he is able to quiet by his own suffering, the rage of insult upon insult. His faith, or the faith of anyone, can change another person only if the person accepts the faith, or accepts the forgiveness, or, what is the same thing, forgives himself—all the most difficult things in Dostoevsky's world.[5]

As a type of Christ, Stavrogin presents a far knottier problem. This hero serves as figurehead and inspiration to an entire gang of despicable petty socialist revolutionaries. He has in his time converted one of their number to Christianity, still another to atheism. At the end of *The Possessed*, Dostoevsky's corpse-strewn stage resembles nothing so much as that of an Elizabethan dramatist. Stavrogin is indirectly responsible for the tragic deaths of numerous other characters, including four of the five women he has corrupted, and also provokes three suicides, including eventually his own. Like Myshkin, he is in a sense unique to literature in that he is less the author of his own intentions than a reflection of the ideas and the desires of those around him. However, whereas Myshkin inspires men with a vision of their divine potential, Stavrogin mostly tempts them to realize their baser selves.

Yet despite—or indeed because of—his shocking moral apathy, Stavrogin illustrates an opposite side of divinity in Dostoevsky's conception: that of the false Messiah or Antichrist. The earmarks of Jesus are everywhere evident. His name derives from the Greek root for *cross*; he too is slapped and literally turns the other cheek; various characters wish to kiss his feet; one of the women in his life, his alleged wife in fact, is a cripple whose name is, again significantly, Mary; and—here the traditional confusion of Father and Son reveals itself—he fathers a son by yet another Mary, though he is himself at times referred to as a virgin. Steiner elucidates Stavrogin's complex symbolism:

> Many aspects of Stavrogin belie the notion of theophany, the idea that he performs, in some tragic and secret manner, the role of God in Dostoevsky's final mythology. He bears the marks of a false Messiah and is shown to us in the guise of Antichrist. . . . Verkhovensky himself draws a parallel between the orgiastic cult of the Skoptsi and the revelation of Stavrogin as the messianic Czarevich. In a moment of agonized intelligence, Marya Timofeyevna bitterly rejects Stavrogin's claims to authentic royalty. He is not the "Sacred Bridegroom" and the "Falcon" of the impending apocalypse, the hieratic redeemer of Byzantine iconography. He is "an owl, an imposter, a shopman." She refers to him as Grishka Otrepyev, the monk who pretended to be Dimitri, the murdered son of Ivan the Terrible. And this identification of Stavrogin with the false Czar—who plays so rich a part in Russian poetry and religious thought—is hinted at throughout *The Possessed*. In a tone of characteristic

> ambivalence, half in homage and half in derision, Pyotr salutes Stavrogin as Ivan the Czarevich. When Marya Shatov's son is born, she names him Ivan, for he is Stavrogin's child and secret heir to the kingdom. Like Antichrist, moreover, Stavrogin dangerously resembles the true Messiah; in him darkness itself burns with a peculiar radiance. "You're like him, very like, perhaps you're a relation," says the Cripple. It is she alone, with the penetrating gaze of folly, who sees Stavrogin's nakedness; he is wearing a false mask of brightness, he is a bird of night pretending to the soaring majesty of the falcon.[6]

Like so much else in Dostoevsky, Stavrogin is truly enigmatic. While Steiner feels that "few figures in literature draw us closer to the limits of understanding" and "none persuades us more forcibly that the consoling distinctions between good and evil, between the sacred and the monstrous, are of human contrivance and restricted application," he also concludes that "in his portrayal of the relations between Stavrogin and the other characters, Dostoevsky reverted to one of his arch-themes: the advent of folly and evil through the aberration of love. Where it is love of God that is being perverted, the folly and the evil are correspondingly greater."[7] As with other characters in this novel, readers reveal themselves more than Dostoevsky in the interpretations they bring to bear.

Myshkin and Stavrogin are the respective prototypes of two more characters in Dostoevsky's subsequent novel, *A Raw Youth*: Makar Ivanovich and Versilov. This double phenomenon of Christ versus Antichrist again recurs in Dostoevsky's monumental *The Brothers Karamazov* in the opposition between, on the one hand, Father Zosima and his novice Alyosha and, on the other, Alyosha's brother Ivan and his unwitting disciple, their half-brother Smerdyakov. It also emerges in Ivan's own profound composition, the legend of the Grand Inquisitor, in which the historical Christ, here appearing in sixteenth-century Seville, submits himself to vilification for failing to impose his will on humankind, then responds, eloquently yet without a word, with a gentle, forgiving kiss. For D. H. Lawrence, this kiss betokened not a reprimand but actual acquiescence.[8] Such is Dostoevsky's understatement and the appeal to various prejudices of the problems he poses.

Zosima's ethical doctrines, which constitute one of the novel's thirteen books and again sound the note of universal forgiveness, are—like Myshkin's demeanor in Switzerland and Alyosha's influence on a circle of young boys—an inspiring elucidation of the Sermon on the Mount. Analogous to Christ's fundamental appeal to simple, nonworldly people, it is only with children that either Myshkin or Alyosha wields any significant influence. Nor is it by accident that Alyosha's followers are twelve in number or that on the day they bury the young Ilusha, he preaches to them of the resurrection:

> "Karamazov," cried Kolya. "Can it be true what's taught us in religion, that we shall all rise again from the dead and shall live and see each other again, all, Ilusha, too?"
>
> "Certainly we shall all rise again, certainly we shall see each other and shall tell each other with joy and gladness all that has happened!" Alyosha answered, half laughing, half enthusiastic.
>
> "Ah, how splendid it will be!" broke from Kolya.
>
> "Well, now we will finish talking and go to his funeral dinner. Don't be put out at our eating pancakes—it's a very old custom and there's something nice in that!" laughed Alyosha. "Well, let us go! And now we go hand in hand."
>
> "And always so, all our lives hand in hand! Hurrah for Karamazov!" Kolya cried once more rapturously, and once more the boys took up his exclamation:
>
> "Hurrah for Karamazov!"[9]

So ends Dostoevsky's last and crowning creation.

Transitional figures: Merezhkovsky, Solovyov, and Blok

It should give pause to those who tend toward overfacile explanations that after Dostoevsky, the image of Christ is less exploited in Russian letters until the outbreak of the socialist revolution and thereafter. It is true, on the other hand, that already at the start of the twentieth century, numerous Russian philosophers and esthetes—doubtless infected by the changing times—were rediscovering, in fact reworking, religious concepts. Foremost among these Christian liberals was Dmitry

Merezhkovsky, whose renowned trilogy of historical novels titled *Christ and Antichrist* dealt with critical moments and personalities in both world and Russian history: *Julian the Apostate, or the Death of the Gods* (1893); *Leonardo da Vinci, or the Gods Resurgent* (1896); and *Peter and Alexis, or the Antichrist* (1902).

The original inspiration for the entire movement was Vladimir Solovyov (1853–1900), Russia's most heralded philosopher and, in his youth, an intimate acquaintance of Dostoevsky. Solovyov, who in his writing promoted St. Sophia and the notion of a world spirit, dominated the thinking of Russia's Symbolist poets and dictated the early themes of Symbolism's greatest exponent, Aleksandr Blok. In his early period, Blok devoted scores of poems to his "Beautiful Lady" and her later outgrowth, the "Strange Lady," both of them bearing mystically universal overtones. The figure of Christ is startlingly reintroduced in Blok's remarkable long poem *The Twelve* (1918), which invokes but hardly glorifies the recent revolution. At the poem's end, where a reckless patrol of Red soldiers saunter through dark wintry streets, their machine gun bursts are confronted by an invincible advancing specter:

> Rat-a-tat-tat!—And only an echo
> Resounds in the buildings . . .
> Only the blizzard with a long laugh
> Floods through the snow . . .
>   Rat-a-tat-tat!
>   Rat-a-tat-tat! . . .
>
> . . . And so they march with a commanding step—
> Behind them—a hungry mutt,
> Before them—with a bloody flag,
> And unseen in the storm,
> And untouched by their bullets
> With a light hovering step,
> In a field of pearly snow
>   In a white crown of roses—
>   Before them—Jesus Christ.[10]

At least a dozen interpretations have been suggested for Christ's appearance in this stirring coda—some prorevolutionary, some antirevolutionary. It has not gone unnoticed that there are exactly twelve in the patrol that Christ confronts. I have been told that Blok himself was unsure of his reasons but felt that this was the only appropriate conclusion.

Mayakovsky

Among those who followed Blok's lead—many of them likewise poets and writers in the nonrealistic Symbolist fashion—was Vladimir Mayakovsky, the most brilliant exponent of Futurist verse, an anarchic, anti-institutional rebel who was, ironically, eventually "canonized" as the patron saint of Soviet socialist realist poets. If *The Twelve* is the poem of the Revolution *par excellence*, Mayakovsky is its poet laureate.

Mayakovsky uses Christ—as he does communism—in service to his own private and egotistical purposes. Various critics have noted, for instance, that in an emotional and purely self-referential sense, Mayakovsky vilifies the precommunist status quo, instead glorifying the utopian socialist future because it augurs the prospect of his own immortality. In his excellent treatise, *The Symbolic System of Majakovskij*, Lawrence Stahlberger argues that

> the poet . . . applies many images from the "Passion" of Christ to his own situation. What are the aspects of the "Passion" that are emphasized? That the very ones who Christ would save are those who crucify him. Christ is the "Son of Man" crucified by men. The poet sees a similarity between his own position and Christ's, relative to the people. . . . In addition, Christ represents an invasion of the historical or temporal by the eternal. The poet . . . has a demand for the overcoming of time manifested in the orderly succession of days, by a leap into the future. Only the figure of Christ and the Christian view stress this overcoming of the temporal by the eternal.[11]

It is in this highly qualified, even paradoxical, context that one must read lines like the following:

> This led to my Golgothas in the halls
> of Petrograd, Moscow, Odessa, and Kiev,

where not a man
but
shouted:
"Crucify,
crucify him!"
But for me—
all of you people,
even those that harmed me—
you are dearer, more precious than anything.
. . . . . .
Where men's eyes stop short,
there, at the head of hungry hordes,
the year 1916 cometh
in the thorny crown of revolutions.[12]

His famed play *The Bedbug* is perhaps Mayakovsky's most literal expression of his yearning for Christian immortality. Here, however, he dispenses with the supernatural and instead posits the preservation of earthly human life by means of a scientific deep freeze.

True to his verse, Mayakovsky became so completely alienated and disillusioned by the Stalinist status quo that in 1930 he took his own life.

Olesha

Three years before, in a delightful short novel satirizing the bourgeois scruples of Soviet citizens during Lenin's "New Economic Policy" (NEP), which marked a return to private enterprise during the years 1921–1929, Yury Olesha portrayed a similarly disenchanted intellectual, another social misfit with messianic overtones. This is Ivan Babichev, hero of Olesha's masterwork, *Envy*. Critic and translator Andrew MacAndrew discusses Ivan's symbolism:

> Very significant . . . are three statements made about Ivan on three different occasions: the first, the tale of his turning wine into water at a wedding; the second, his exclamation, upon being arrested by the security police, that he is on the way to his Golgotha; and finally, the picture of him spread-eagled against a wall and pierced by the needle of his own machine.

> These are unmistakable allusions to Christ's miracle at the wedding in Cana (although in that case water was turned into wine), His capture by the soldiers, and His crucifixion. Ivan is a caricature of a savior, and Olesha feels perhaps that this is all the old world deserves.[13]

The allusion to Cana immediately reminds the scholar of a comparable incident in *The Brothers Karamazov* when, having suffered disappointment and doubt as an aftermath of his beloved Father Zosima's death (Zosima is castigated by rival priests as unholy because his corpse has too quickly decomposed), Alyosha dreams of reunion with Zosima on the occasion of Christ's first miracle. Wasiolek's commentary is again helpful:

> Alyosha needs help to bring him out of a bruised, self-pitying love which refuses to accept what is not his to judge. . . . The miracle he had wanted for his Elder is effected in his heart and symbolically in the dream he has of Christ's turning of the vessels of water into wine at the marriage of the Cana of Galilee. Here Christ creates a miracle for the joy of others, and not for himself, "not to show his own terrible power, but to visit gladness upon men." The miracle Alyosha experiences in his heart is the change from his own "hurt" feelings to the shared joy of others. The Elder, who has been humbled, takes the hand of Alyosha, who has rebelled against the humbling, and together they are wedded in Christ's joy, the joy of forgiveness by the acceptance of forgiveness. "All that is true is beautiful, and all that is beautiful is completely filled with forgiveness," Alyosha whispers to himself in understanding.[14]

Bulgakov

Employing an unconventional approach similar to those of Dostoevsky and Olesha, yet another novelist of the early Soviet years, Mikhail Bulgakov, dramatizes the human impact of Christ's passion. In a manuscript ostensibly written by one of his characters, Bulgakov's otherwise satirical fantasy, *The Master and Margarita*, treats the poignant recognition by Pontius Pilate that he has indeed killed a god. In vengeance on those who have forced his hand, Pilate orders Iscariot's subsequent assassination. The novel's title suggests another obvious aspect of its symbolism: The "Master" of the principal episode is the persecuted writer and Margarita, like Mary Magdalene, his faithful follower who had fallen into evil ways. Long suppressed, Bulgakov's novel finally acquired a rebirth of worldwide recognition with its reissue in the Soviet literary journal *Moscow.*

Pasternak

In certain ways, Bulgakov's masterpiece reminds one of Boris Pasternak's *Doctor Zhivago.* Both novels include the ostensible literary handiwork of a principal character, which then serves as a clue to that novel's interpretation and ultimate significance. Several of the Zhivago poems (a cycle of twenty-five at the novel's close) focus on the historical Savior as protagonist, including the first, "Hamlet" (despite its title), and the last and perhaps most impressive, "Garden of Gethsemane." Other titles—"Star of the Nativity," "Miracle," "Magdalene"—are also indicative. In "Hamlet," the speaker, sounding at first like an actor cast as Hamlet, says:

> The stir is over. I step forth on the boards,
> Leaning against an upright at the entrance,
> I strain to make the far-off echo yield
> A cue to the events that may come in my day.
>
> Night and its murk transfix and pin me,
> Staring through thousands of binoculars.
> If Thou be willing, Abba, Father,
> Remove this cup from me.[15]

The character Zhivago's central role as a lone, unpopular life-affirmer (the name "Zhivago" is derived from the Russian root for "life") is likened both to Christ's sacrifice and to Hamlet's painful indecision, as well as to the role-playing of the actor who must for a time be that Hamlet. (Prior to the appearance of his novel, Pasternak had translated and published a celebrated volume of Shakespeare's tragedies in Russian.) In Pasternak's story, the Jesus-Magdalene theme recurs in the relationship between Yury and Lara (another fallen woman); and there is much more elaborate symbolism, including numerous allusions to death and resurrection, that firmly establishes the kenotic, suffering Christ as an important correlative to Zhivago's character, brilliantly bringing together Pasternak's several inspirations: that death is necessary to rebirth and Christ to freedom, that nature affirms this as do love and art. This is the ultimate perspective his final verses shed upon Zhivago's own distraught career and many failures. Christ is again the speaker in the following poignant paean to eternity in "Garden of Gethsemane":

> "Seest thou, the passing of the ages is like a parable
> And in its passing it may burst to flame.
> In the name, then, of its awesome majesty
> I shall, in voluntary torments, descend into my grave.
>
> I shall descend into my grave. And on the third day rise again.
> And, even as rafts float down a river,
> So shall the centuries drift, trailing like a caravan,
> Coming for judgement, out of the dark, to me."[16]

In a monograph on Soviet authors, *Myth and Symbol in Soviet Fiction*, I comment as follows on the imagery of Christ's passion in *Doctor Zhivago*:

> Christ, who concerns himself with the individual and with all humanity, provides in his transfiguration, death, and resurrection a rich image of life's flow and change. In history these events are most strikingly manifest in political revolution. And because revolution is cataclysmic and fraught with tragedy and suffering, what is more fitting than to focus on the most kenotic point in Christ's life—his passion? Or again to locate the objective correlative of Christ's passion not in a single person but in a set of common experiences in which a whole people—suggested by a variety of secondary, hence more truly representative characters—must undergo the trauma of terrible, divisive choices ("Choose ye this day . . . ") and suffer the consequences? . . . The novel's mythopoeic imagery distributes itself in random but cumulative fashion throughout the book. All must suffer the "passion" of revolution—all are victims. But if there is victimization, there is also transcendence, for

> Pasternak sees the Revolution as an aspect of universal life in an ongoing cycle of death and renewal.[17]

Sinyavsky

Andrey Sinyavsky—a literary scholar who championed Pasternak's work—also followed in Pasternak's creative footsteps, writing at first anonymously under the pseudonym Abram Tertz. Like Pasternak, he was an "underground" writer who eventually paid for his clandestine novels with official calumny and, prophetically in his case, a sentence to Siberia. Before his disclosure, imprisonment, and subsequent exile as a dissident writer late in the Soviet period, Sinyavsky continued the unpopular tradition of associating concern for God with everyday life. In a collection of short essays and aphorisms titled *Thoughts Unaware*, Sinyavsky declares:

> We are so accustomed to urban comfort and technical progress, that we no longer believe in God. With all the things we have made about us, we have begun to regard ourselves the creators of the universe. . . . Enough discussion about man. It is time to think of God. . . . One must not believe on account of tradition, nor because of the fear of death . . . nor because someone commands or something frightens, nor from humanitarian principles, nor to be saved, nor to be different. We must believe simply because God exists.[18]

Sinyavsky's protest, like that of Mayakovsky's scapegoat-martyr, is dramatically registered in the words of his character Rabinovich—like Christ a Jew and, in the plot of *The Trial Begins*, a political prisoner. While digging a ditch in the frozen Siberian waste, Rabinovich unearths a long-buried weapon:

> It was a dagger, eaten away by rust and with a handle shaped like a crucifix.
>
> "How do you like that?" asked Rabinovich again. "A nice place they found for God—the handle of a deadly weapon. Are you going to deny it? God was the end and they turned him into the means—a handle. And the dagger was the means and

> became the end. They changed places. Ay-ay-ay! And where are God and the dagger now? Among the eternal snows, both of them!" . . .
>
> Seizing the dagger in both hands, he raised it like an umbrella and poked it at the sky which hung lowering over our ditch.
>
> "In the name of God! With the help of God! In place of God! Against God!" He really did sound like a madman now. "And now there is no God, only dialectics. Forge a new dagger for the new Purpose at once!"[19]

Might this not be Christ's own reaction to the insidious corruption in various times and places of his bequest to humanity?

Solzhenitsyn

Regarded in the West as Russia's greatest writer of his day, Aleksandr Solzhenitsyn frequently depicts as kenotic Christs the meek but principled victims of totalitarian oppression. The first of these to win him lasting recognition was Ivan Denisovich (*One Day in the Life of Ivan Denisovich*), followed by yet another semiautobiographical political prisoner, Gleb Nerzhin (*The First Circle*). Perhaps the most saintly is an elderly peasant woman, the retired collective farm worker Matryona ("Matryona's Home"). Like Dostoevsky's Sonya, Matryona exemplifies the proverbial goodness and long-suffering of Russia's common people. Generous to a fault, Matryona meets her death helping a group of men dislodge a sledge caught on the tracks before an oncoming train. In the aftermath, both kin and neighbors castigate her for her gullibility and for failing to reward each of them with her meager inheritance. But not unlike the hagiographer of some Byzantine saint, Solzhenitsyn's narrator then provides a deft perspective on Matryona's true, Christlike worth:

> It was only then, after these disapproving comments from her sister-in-law, that a true likeness of Matryona formed itself before my eyes, and I understood her as I never had when I lived side by side with her.

> Of course! Every house in the village kept a pig. But she didn't. What can be easier than fattening a greedy piglet that cares for nothing in the world but food! You warm his swill three times a day, you live for him—then you cut his throat and you have some fat.
>
> But she had none . . .
>
> She made no effort to get things round her . . . She didn't struggle and strain to buy things and then care for them more than life itself.
>
> She didn't go all out after fine clothes. Clothes, that beautify what is ugly and evil.
>
> She was misunderstood and abandoned even by her husband. She had lost six children, but not her sociable ways. She was a stranger to her sisters and sisters-in-law, a ridiculous creature who stupidly worked for others without pay. She didn't accumulate property against the day she died. A dirty-white goat, a gammy-legged cat, some rubber plants . . .
>
> We had all lived side by side with her and never understood that she was that righteous one without whom, as the proverb says, no village can stand.
>
> Nor any city.
>
> Nor our whole land.[20]

Tendryakov

Although in a purely secular context Vladimir Tendryakov, another late Soviet writer, differs from the foregoing authors in his standing as a committed Communist Party member and atheist propagandist, he similarly celebrates the personal heroism of maligned but virtuous individuals within contemporary Soviet society who are confronted with the difficult choices and the unjust condemnation that well-meaning persons must often bear. Illustrative is Dubinin, the supervisor of a remote lumber camp (*Three, Seven, Ace*), who, in befriending a malicious escaped convict, is unwittingly implicated in the latter's death and betrayed by his own cowardly men. Though in his less tendentious fiction Tendryakov avoids any reference, either overt or symbolic, to Christ as such, Dubinin's fate parallels and—who is to say?—may also reflect the Savior's Passion.

Rasputin, Aytmatov, and Tarkovsky

Three other towering literary figures who became especially prominent in the later years of Soviet domination were Valentin Rasputin, Chingiz Aytmatov, and Andrey Tarkovsky. Particularly in two of his short novels, *Live and Remember* and *Farewell to Matyora*, the Siberian Rasputin evokes Christ's atoning sacrifice in the person of two separate heroines: the wife of an unprincipled military deserter and the elderly Darya, who, with others, insists on remaining on their ancestral island home as it is flooded to accommodate the construction of a dam on the Angara River.

Though Aytmatov comes from the non-Christian Kirgiz culture, his late novel *The Execution Place* features a protagonist who is as exemplary a self-sacrificing Christian as any ever conceived in Russian letters. In an early story, "Dzhan," a young man becomes a living Eucharist, exposing his naked flesh to the attack of voracious eagles in an effort to protect his nomadic people.

Finally, the incomparable auteur filmmaker Tarkovsky portrays alienated protagonists who nevertheless pursue arduous and inspiring spiritual quests. These include the historic icon painter Rublyov (*Andrey Rublyov*) and the mystical guide who vainly tries to lead others beyond their modern obsessions to a mysterious "Zone" in a remote war-torn setting (*Stalker*). In *Sacrifice*, his final film—in my view the world's most spiritually profound allegorical movie—Tarkovsky portrays the desperate conversion and faith of a man bent on saving both his family and the entire world from a likely third world war and nuclear holocaust—like Dostoevsky's Myshkin, whom Tarkovsky's hero once played as an actor, another unforgettable Christ figure.

Conclusion

Fyodor Dostoevsky's profound spiritual legacy and its symbolic allusions to Jesus Christ have markedly influenced subsequent Russian letters. Despite Soviet ideology and its prescribed atheism, Christ's personality, the drama of his life, and his inspired, pristine teachings clearly exerted ongoing impact on the minds and hearts of Russians during the Soviet era.

Among those who followed Dostoevsky's lead in this regard are some of the most profound writers of the Soviet era. Such writers take full poetic license in adapting the image of Christ to their particular esthetic and philosophical ends. Like Dostoevsky himself, they depart from the traditional religious point of view. They also write in other than a strictly realistic or socialist realist vein.

That these writers found so much merit in the person of Christ as an element of literary interest—particularly in a time and place when Christian fundamentals (including such concepts as supernatural divinity and immortality, which these writers generally assume) were such an intellectual taboo—is striking. That these same writers should emerge in the course of well over a half century during which they were subjected to and conditioned by the antireligious arguments of "godless communism" is one of the seldom observed—but to the believer, easily comprehensible—ironies of our time.

Notes

1. George Steiner, *Tolstoy or Dostoevsky: An Essay in the Old Criticism* (New York: Alfred A. Knopf, 1959), 302.
2. Fyodor Dostoyevsky, *The Idiot*, trans. David Magarshack (London: The Folio Society, 1971), 256–58.
3. Edward Wasiolek, *Dostoevsky: The Major Fiction* (Cambridge, MA: The MIT Press, 1964), 106–7.
4. Wasiolek, *Dostoevsky*, 104.
5. Wasiolek, *Dostoevsky*, 109.
6. Steiner, *Tolstoy or Dostoevsky*, 313–14.
7. Steiner, *Tolstoy or Dostoevsky*, 316–17.
8. D. H. Lawrence, "Preface to Dostoevsky's *The Grand Inquisitor*," in *Dostoevsky: A Collection of Critical Essays*, ed. René Wellek (Englewood Cliffs, NJ: Prentice-Hall, 1962), 90–97.
9. Fyodor Dostoevsky, *The Brothers Karamazov*, trans. Constance Garnett (New York: The Modern Library, 1973), 821–22.
10. Aleksandr Blok, *Stikhotvorenija i poemy* (Leningrad: Sovetskij pisatel', 1961), 2:430. Translation by Thomas F. Rogers.
11. Lawrence Leo Stahlberger, *The Symbolic System of Majakovskij* (The Hague: Mouton, 1964), 70, 72.
12. Vladimir Mayakovsky, "The Cloud in Trousers," in *The Bedbug and Selected Poetry*, trans. George Reavey (New York: World Publishing, 1970), 83.

13. Andrew R. MacAndrew, introduction to *Envy and Other Works* by Yuri Olesha, trans. Andrew R. MacAndrew (Garden City, NY: Anchor Books, 1967), xviii.

14. Wasiolek, *Dostoevsky*, 179.

15. Boris Pasternak, *Doctor Zhivago*, trans. Max Hayward and Manya Harari (New York: Pantheon, 1958), 523.

16. Pasternak, *Doctor Zhivago*, 558–59.

17. Thomas F. Rogers, *Myth and Symbol in Soviet Fiction: Images of the Savior Hero, Great Mother*, Anima, *and Child in Selected Novels and Films* (San Francisco: Mellen Research University Press, 1992), 222. See also Thomas F. Rogers, "The Implications of Christ's Passion in *Doktor Zhivago*," *Slavic and East European Journal* 18/4 (1974): 384–91.

18. Abram Tertz, *Mysli vrasplokh* (New York: Rausen, 1966), 85, 87, 110. Translation by Thomas F. Rogers.

19. Abram Tertz, *The Trial Begins*, trans. Max Hayward (New York: Pantheon, 1960), 127–28.

20. Aleksandr Solzhenitsyn, "Matryona's Home," trans. H. T. Willetts, in *Halfway to the Moon: New Writing from Russia*, ed. Patricia Blake and Max Hayward (New York: Holt, Rinehart, and Winston, 1964), 90–91, ellipses in original.

Hearts of the Fathers, Hearts of the Children: Transcendent Familial Ties in Selected Films and in Works by Twentieth-Century Russian Writers

I was privileged to deliver these remarks (presented here in abridged form) in the Maeser Building auditorium as the 2011 annual BYU Honors Alumni Week lecture. In it, I recap the pathos of Russian life as depicted by some of the most gifted and courageous authors of fiction during the Soviet era. All were at least implicit critics of the regime; two died in the Soviet labor camps, while the work of others remained long suppressed. Arrestingly, the work of these authors has in common with several contemporary non-Russian films a common theme that is particularly dear to Latter-day Saints. Echoing the Old Testament's final verses, both the works I cite by Soviet writers and these equally remarkable films subtly, perhaps unwittingly, assert a postmortal connection between generations of kin, or their surrogates.

A PRECOCIOUS FORMER STUDENT AND TEACHING ASSISTANT, Sterling Van Wagenen—cofounder of the Sundance Film Festival and founding director of the Sundance Film Institute, who went on to produce and direct numerous fine films commercially and at BYU—first put me onto a number of intriguing foreign films, beginning in the 1950s, that evoke for me the universal if mostly subliminal human yearning for generational connection so sacred to Latter-day Saints and mandated in Malachi. I've since encountered a few other memorable films with that same aspiration. In each of them, a child plays a crucial role in carrying forward his or her progenitors' legacy, in some instances even intimating their ongoing association beyond this life.

This same theme of generational connection arises in the work of the Soviet authors who were the subject of my last scholarly monograph, *Myth and Symbol in Soviet Fiction*.[1] The work of all these writers is highly allegorical, which is the only way their critical assessment of twentieth-century Russian life could at all have come to the Soviet public's attention.

The Apu trilogy

Apu, the protagonist of a trilogy of Bengali movies directed by Satyajit Ray[2]—played in these films by different actors of increasingly older age—witnesses the deaths of his grandmother, sister, father, mother, and eventually his beautiful young wife, who succumbs giving birth to their child. At this point he becomes so bitter that he disowns his infant son and becomes a wandering beggar until encountering the boy several years later, when—responding to his innocent appeal at about the same age we knew Apu in the first film—Apu's heart turns to the boy, who does not know Apu is his father. The boy's maternal grandfather looks on as the two are reunited—thus reaffirming the cycle of generational continuity. Almost wordlessly, this moving moment also illustrates the vital theme of *reconciliation*.

Places in the Heart

More familiar to Westerners is the ending of the otherwise straightforward and realistically depicted 1984 American film scripted and directed by Robert Benton, *Places in the Heart*, set in a small Texas community sometime in the pre–World War II United States much like the town where Benton spent his own childhood. We hear a preacher address his congregation, probably Baptist. Trays are passed for communion. All are somehow present—black and white, both the story's protagonists and its villains (even members of the local Ku Klux Klan)—all assembled together. Also present are the late sheriff's widow and their young daughter and son. Then, inexplicably, we see the deceased sheriff himself. Next to him is the black adolescent, still almost a child, who, while drunk, had unintentionally shot his former benefactor, the sheriff—for which the young man was promptly lynched. Upon partaking, members of the congregation intone, "Grace of God." This, for me, is the most affecting and unexpected ending of any film I know—one that (again almost wordlessly) reaffirms the dual themes of reconciliation and generational connection. Are the former sheriff—the children's father—and the young man who inadvertently killed him ghosts, or somehow miraculously resurrected, or only symbolically reunited in a kind of timelessly transcendent cinematic moment? We do not know. But there they are, sitting companionably together—the sheriff with his family, their adversaries and friends—partaking of the emblems of the Lord's atonement.

Other films

Other examples of films that in noteworthy ways highlight this theme of generational connection include the following:

- *Sansho Deiu* (*Sansho the Bailiff*), 1954 (Japanese), directed by Kenji Mizoguchi: After his father's and sister's violent deaths during a devastating medieval civil war, a Samurai's son finds his mother, who was blinded and made a concubine, and vows to follow his father's noble example. The camera's final pan of landscape, water, and sky suggests the family's reunion beyond this life.
- *Ordet* (*The Word*), 1955 (Danish), directed by Carl Dreyer: During a wake, encouraged by her seemingly demented uncle who preaches the resurrection as though he were Christ, a young girl's faith miraculously brings her mother, who has died giving birth, back to life, in turn uniting their family in a shared religious commitment.
- *Secrets and Lies*, 1996 (British), directed by Mike Leigh: A black professional woman in London seeks out her birth mother, a lower-class white woman who, while still a young girl, had given birth and had the child taken from her

without ever seeing it. They and the woman's family are eventually reconciled.

- *Children of Men*, 2006 (British), directed by Alfonso Cuarón: Amid horrific civil strife, the human race has remained sterile for twenty or so years until a young black woman gives birth. Others give their lives to assist her and her child to safety.
- *Riding Alone for Thousands of Miles*, 2007 (Mandarin Chinese), directed by Zhang Yimou: Attempting to be reconciled with his dying son—a filmmaker—an elderly Japanese father travels to China on his son's behalf to film a Peking opera star, now imprisoned. Although he and the opera star share no common language, he locates and befriends the singer's young son. Though he returns, too late, to his now deceased son's bedside, we sense that the old man's wordless encounter with a little Chinese boy—an unforeseen bonding between surrogate father and son—will, despite their future physical separation, unforgettably continue.

Exceptional Soviet writers

During the latter part of my teaching career, Gary Browning, my close colleague and department chair, urged me to make another stab at a lengthy critical investigation of Russian literature. The result was my last scholarly monograph, *Myth and Symbol in Soviet Fiction*, focusing on major works by ten Soviet authors.

Rereading this study nineteen years after its first publication, I marvel again at these authors' honesty, courage, and genius. Boris Pilnyak—who before the formation of the Soviet Writers' Union had, like Yevgeny Zamyatin in St. Petersburg, headed the (at that time) less state-dominated Moscow association of writers—was eventually sent to Stalin's camps, where he subsequently perished. Only two, Zamyatin and Andrey Tarkovsky, managed to emigrate. Most of the rest were utterly suppressed until after Stalin's death. Unlike the others, Tarkovsky was a filmmaker, but an auteur, the author of his own scripts. Before his emigration, his post-Stalin era films were issued in the USSR, but he was only allowed to make them after long constraining intervals, and his films were never widely distributed.

Though little known outside Russia (with the exception of Pasternak's *Dr. Zhivago*), the work of each of these authors was a sensation when it first appeared in the Soviet Union. Although written under unprecedented external constraints, they offer as impressive a body of writing as anything that emerged during the same period in the West. As it turns out (though I was less aware of it at the time), they also abundantly convey the same thematic concern: the sacred and lasting tie between "children" and their "fathers."[3] To my mind at least, these two quite disparate sources—particular films from post-World War II international cinema and selected works by Soviet writers—thematically converge in a truly profound manner.

Jungian archetypes

In my scholarly investigation of these Soviet authors, I was prompted to apply as an interpretive tool the psychologist Carl Jung's theory of archetypes.[4] Briefly put, the psyche in each of us is, according to Jung, composed of opposed urges. One possible manifestation is the inferences of our dreams, which pose predicaments analogous to the challenges that confront the adventurous heroes of legend. In Jung's scheme, a nearly universal threat and obstacle for both mythic hero and individual psyche is the so-called Terrible, Great, or Earth Mother. Personifying both procreative and destructive natural forces, this matronly figure has engendered the mythical hero and nurtured him as a child but would keep him forever confined and dependent. In an effort to achieve his own personal individuation, The Hero—or his equivalent in our individual psyche—is thus pitted in a life-and-death contest with the Mother's smothering, engulfing force. (I emphasize that the Terrible Mother is a purely symbolic conception and not a real person. Certainly not *my* mother, and I hope not yours.)

Another female figure, the *Anima*, becomes the hero's supportive sister, affectionate paramour, and inspiring muse. As in normal human life, union with the *Anima* makes possible the Hero's biological extension of himself into the future in the form of a child. The works I consider often feature the portentous appearance if not loss or absence of such a child. This surviving—or just as often, absent or destroyed—child serves, in my view, as a reliable barometer to the ultimate optimism or pessimism of an author's outlook in the context of Soviet Russian life's often grim reality. My investigation pays special attention to the Savior Hero (my own term), Great Mother, *Anima*, and Child archetypes. The Savior Hero, generally a work's male protagonist, becomes the bearer of traditional but lost values—what is most sublime and needful in human life.

Superb studies dealing with individual Soviet authors, particularly dissertations mostly written during the fifteen years preceding my investigation, had already identified a number of such archetypes, further elucidating and enhancing our appreciation of the works in question. My own special contribution was to trace these archetypes' remarkably recurring and largely unconscious pattern from one author to the next over some seven decades in Soviet letters. In my view, this close fit strongly substantiates Jung's archetypal theory.

Failed family connections and the yearning for family ties—Olesha, Platonov, Pilnyak, Rasputin, Aytmatov, Bulgakov, and Pasternak

In these works by Soviet authors, blizzards, water, fire, moonlight, and wolves are frequent primordial motifs—suggesting both the threatening, destructive menace of elemental forces generally equated with the Terrible Mother and also the lustful, rapacious, anarchic component of everyone's *id*. Burrows, deserts, and excavations also figure as significant Earth Mother emblems. Haunting images of life-threatening burial, often ambivalently associated with public works and the ideology of large-scale social progress, recur in the writing of Yury Olesha and especially Andrey Platonov, himself an experienced land renovation engineer as well as writer (like Zamyatin, a naval architect, who supervised the building of Russia's first icebreaker). In Platonov's novel *Chevengur*, a young boy actually yearns to return to his mother's womb. In his acclaimed last novel, *Kotlovan* (meaning a "foundation pit"), the central image is an excavation that—like the dams in Pilnyak's *The Volga Falls to the Caspian Sea* and in Valentin Rasputin's *Farewell to Matyora* (the name of an island: note the root for *mother—mat'*—in that title)—is perhaps the ultimate violation of Mother Earth herself. *Kotlovan*'s excavation sinks ever deeper without coming to fruition.

With their incomplete or devastated womblike architectural constructs, Platonov's novels reflect the failed search for a social utopia, in lieu of which physical hardship, sterility, and parental neglect prevail. Social control opposes spontaneous, authentic fellow feeling, such that in the works of both Platonov and Rasputin characters even seek an elusive peace in the grave or through drowning. In works by Pilnyak, as still later in those of Chingiz Aytmatov, sterility becomes a major theme. In Pilnyak's repertoire, various young persons or those still in their prime either succumb to venereal disease or die violently, precluding their chance for either a full life or offspring. A key family name in Pilnyak's oeuvre is *Bezdetov*, "childless"—as also *Bezdomny*, "homeless," in Mikhail Bulgakov's *The Master and Margarita*.

In other works, female figures, particularly maternal ones, become a source of spiritual, even supernatural, virtue and wisdom. Their fate and that of children, often orphans, reinforces their authors' greater sense of helplessness and more despairing view of the future. Filial ties and nostalgia for a departed father are also poignantly depicted, while in writing that appears after Stalin's collectivization of agriculture and successive industrial Five-Year Plans, Mother Nature becomes far less a threat, or no threat at all, by contrast with the brutal oppression and regimentation on the part of zealous, ideologically driven communist leaders.

Platonov, for example—regarded by some as one of Russia's greatest and most Dostoevskian twentieth-century prose writers—grieves at the suffering and death of children, concluding that this alone negates the prospects for any utopian social order. Despite his avowed atheism, Platonov nonetheless yearns for connections with ancestors. The dire circumstances of Platonov's fictions uncannily foreshadow the tragic loss of his own son—who, in an officially instigated reprisal against his father, was arrested at the age of fifteen as a counterrevolutionary and sent to the forced labor camps. There the boy contracted the tuberculosis that led to his early death and infected his father, leading to Platonov's own untimely demise. Orphanhood is also prevalent in works by Pilnyak, Pasternak, Aytmatov, and Tarkovsky.

Despite the hardships that Soviet life created for families, which still largely persist in present-day Russia, the sacred and universal human yearning for lasting ties between parents and children is nevertheless reflected in a number of the characters in these stories and novels. As my study concludes, "Such writers . . . tend to share a common concern about the loss of heritage and the consequences of its disruption, effacement, and failure to be remembered."[5]

Tarkovsky

In a class all his own, the filmmaker Tarkovsky draws on childhood memory, sacred Christian lore, and science fiction. Several of his films arrestingly depict the crucial role of children who, as their elders pass from the scene, play a hopeful, even catalytic role—responding to their fathers' legacy and bringing forward what is vital for succeeding generations.

In his 1966 film *Andrey Rublyov*, Tarkovsky hypothetically reenacts the fourteenth-century career of Russia's and perhaps the world's greatest icon painter. In this movie, during Russia's oppressive Mongol occupation, a young boy, the son of a deceased bellmaker, pretends to know the secret his progenitor took with him to the grave. Exercising both bravado and pure faith, he helps rediscover his father's lost art, affording renewed hope for Russia's future emancipation by successfully casting a new bell for the cathedral of Russia's besieged capitol, Vladimir-Suzdal. His efforts inspire the iconographer monk Rublyov both to assume the role of surrogate father and to once more pick up his brush and begin painting the icons for which the historical Rublyov is world-renowned. The film thus demonstrates the continuity of influence and inspiration from a deceased bellmaker to his impetuous son, and from his son to one of history's supreme artists—and centuries later to Tarkovsky himself.

Then there is Tarkovsky's 1980 movie *Stalker*, whose protagonist despairs at others' unwillingness to follow him to a remote place called the Zone and a room there that is sacred to him. This mysterious person, referred to as "the Stalker," returns home and laments his lack of success to his wife (played, significantly, by Tarkovsky's own wife). He goes to bed, and she then speaks directly to the camera, conceding the hardships they have experienced but explaining that life has meant more to her because she joined him, a misunderstood idealist and dreamer. (Is she really speaking about a character in a film, or Tarkovsky himself?) Viewing these scenes, I'm reminded of the frequent rejection Mormon missionaries experience and the sorrow they feel at the world's general indifference to their message. The aura of the hallowed Zone and room, so dear to the Stalker, in turn uncannily recalls the reverence for an LDS temple felt by its attendees. How did Tarkovsky, who like all Russians his age was subjected to monolithic atheistic indoctrination, come by such insight, such feelings? Toward the end of the movie, we discover that the Stalker's crippled young daughter, who in an earlier close-up appeared to be walking normally but as the camera pulls back is clearly seen to be transported on her father's shoulders, has inherited her father's telekinetic gift and clairvoyant—or *spiritual*—sensibility. Like the bellmaker's son in *Andrey Rublyov*, she exemplifies the promise of generational continuity.

Tarkovsky's culminating 1986 masterpiece *Sacrifice* is, in my view, when its symbolic import is sufficiently fathomed, the most sublime religious film ever made. In this movie—filmed in Sweden in a language Tarkovsky did not know, using the admiring Ingmar Bergman's camera man, crew, and actors—a character named Alexander, a former actor and professor, falls to his knees and vows to renounce all his possessions and, like those in certain monastic orders, become mute if God will only spare his family and, with them, humankind from a third world war and nuclear holocaust. What Alexander so fears may be only a bad dream (we can't be sure), but it *is* averted. Dutifully and to his family's chagrin, he then burns down their home and refuses to speak. An ambulance is summoned, and—not unlike the protagonist at the end of Dostoevsky's profound novel, *The Idiot*—Alexander is led off to an asylum. As the ambulance passes by, we see his young son, called Little Man—who due to an operation on his throat has so far throughout the film not spoken—watering a dead tree that, according to his father, will yet come alive if nurtured with sufficient faith. (The tree of life?) Then Little Man finally (miraculously) speaks: "In the beginning was the Word? What is that, Papa?" And we recall Alexander's earlier words to Little Man, written by a dying filmmaker: "There is no such thing as death. Only the fear of death."

As in Mizoguchi's film, the camera now scans both water and sky, suggesting an eternal connection, then comes to rest on the dead tree.

In our wishful thinking we are tempted to imagine green buds bursting from its withered branches. Finally, across the tree's image we read the film's dedication to Tarkovsky's own son Aleksey, long detained in the USSR after his father's defection, but who, because of his father's illness and just before Tarkovsky's death, managed to receive for him the jury's Special Prize at the 1986 Cannes film festival—a marvelous instance where art and life converge.

Conclusion

Reconciliation across the generations is a theme with profound resonance for Latter-day Saints. Since the appearance of Elijah to Joseph Smith and Oliver Cowdery in 1836 in the Kirtland Temple (see D&C 110:13–16), we believe that the "spirit of Elijah" has been poured out over all the Earth, tying together through priesthood ordinances and bonds of sympathy all the generations of humankind. The prominence of this same theme in the creations of both certain modern filmmakers and writers from a Soviet culture that had severely undermined traditional concepts of family and religion is indeed a testimony to the universality and endurance of these sacred impulses within the human spirit.

Notes

1. Thomas F. Rogers, *Myth and Symbol in Soviet Fiction: Images of the Savior Hero, Great Mother*, Anima, *and Child in Selected Novels and Films* (San Francisco: Mellen Research University Press, 1992).

2. *Pather Panchali* (1955), *Aparajito* (1956), and *Apur Sansar* (1959), based on the Bengali novels *Pather Panchali* (1929) and *Aparajito* (1932), written by Bibhutibhushan Bandyopadhyay.

3. Particularly noteworthy in this respect are Chingiz Aytmatov, *The Day Lasts More Than a Hundred Years, The Execution Place*, and "The White Steamship"; Mikhail Bulgakov, *The Master and Margarita*; Yury Olesha, *Envy*; Boris Pasternak, *Doctor Zhivago*; Boris Pilnyak, "Damp Mother Earth," *Ivan Moscow, Machines and Wolves, Mahogany, The Naked Year*, and *The Volga Falls to the Caspian Sea*; Andrey Platonov, *Chevengur, Dzhan*, "The Epifan Locks," and *Kotlovan*; Valentin Rasputin, *Farewell to Matyora* and *Live and Remember*; and Yevgeny Zamyatin, *We*. Note that

because conditions at the time of writing did not always allow formal publication, many works by such independent-minded Soviet authors were circulated informally. These works are therefore listed by title, but without a year of publication or other publication information.

4. Carl G. Jung, *The Archetypes and the Collective Unconscious*, Bollingen Series 20 (New York: Pantheon, 1959).

5. Rogers, *Myth and Symbol in Soviet Fiction*, 331.